History Of The People Of The Netherlands

A HISTORY OF THE PEOPLE OF THE NETHERLANDS

By PETRUS JOHANNES BLOK, Ph.D.

PROFESSOR OF DUTCH HISTORY IN THE UNIVERSITY OF LEYDEN

TO BE COMPLETED IN FIVE PARTS. 8°

G. P. PUTNAM'S SONS

NEW YORK & LONDON

HISTORY OF
THE PEOPLE OF THE
NETHERLANDS

99677

BY

PETRUS JOHANNES BLOK

Professor of Dutch History in the University of Leyden

PART III.

THE WAR WITH SPAIN

The Prologue, 1559–1568.   The Revolt, 1568–1609.
The Truce, 1609–1621

TRANSLATED BY RUTH PUTNAM

WITH MAPS

G. P. PUTNAM'S SONS
NEW YORK & LONDON
The Knickerbocker Press
1900

The Knickerbocker Press, New York

TRANSLATOR'S NOTE

PROCEEDING with his story of *The People of the Netherlands*, Professor Blok has devoted two volumes (III. and IV.) to the period of the Eighty Years' War. His narrative runs from the beginning of the revolt against Spanish authority, 1568, to the Treaty of Munster, 1648. The years 1559–1568 he treats as forming the prologue to the struggle for independence. He suggested that this material might be put into one volume of the English version, in which the greater weight is given to the social and economic conditions than to the political affairs of the people. But in this epoch of change and transition many more details were necessary to gain a knowledge of these conditions than in the earlier periods of Netherland history. Part III. comprises, therefore, Vol. III. and half of Vol. IV. of the original, from 1559 to the end of the Truce, 1621. The bibliography for the period is indicated in the article on the historical sources in the Appendix.

R. P.

New York, Sept., 1900.

PREFACE

THE period of the Eighty Years' War takes a peculiarly interesting place in the history of the Netherland people; not only because, under the influence of the difficult circumstances in which the population of the Netherland provinces were then placed, the foundations were laid for a new state destined to appear on the world's stage as the equal of the great European powers, but also because, during the period of transition, the dominant traits of the Netherland national character became clear.

It will appear in the following pages how good and evil alternated in the war, how, under the direction of the three great Orange princes, well aided by distinguished generals — their own kinsmen and Netherlanders — and by skilful statesmen, among whom John of Oldenbarnevelt is preëminent, independence was first won from Spain; how in the midst of great dangers the political condition of Europe again and again lamed the power of the doughty foe; how, when the Truce was concluded, the enemy took the decisive steps on the path which necessarily led to the complete freedom of the Seven Provinces; how commerce and manufacture, not only in spite of, but actually because of, the war, developed vigorously; how the theological opinions of the majority took a definite direction; how political institutions were crystallised into form; how art and science enjoyed a period of bloom at the close of hostilities, when security and prosperity crèated favourable conditions. Thus the period of

the war is an important period for our history, not only
from a military, a theological, and political standpoint, but
also from a general social point of view.   This period has
been the favourite of the historians.   A full discussion [1]
of the manner in which it has been treated by earlier and
later writers, from partisan and from non-partisan points
of view, is given in the appendix.   As will be seen, the
material is very rich, and the later literature, both narrative and critical, very extensive.   General interest was
aroused by Schiller's enthusiastic pæan on the Netherland struggle for freedom, still more by Motley's fascin-
ating painting of so many beautiful pictures from the
" trial between oppression and freedom."   But the
works of these great word artists entrance the reader
rather than convince him of the justice of their representations.   Sound criticism based upon comprehensive
knowledge of the sources did not come into being until
the middle of the nineteenth century with Bakhuizen van
den Brink.   His *Studien en Schetsen*, and, still more,
Fruin's *Tien Jaren*, show, in a masterly fashion, how
keen judgment, broad conception, and good form can be
combined.   In the second half of this century, many followed the example given by these two scholars,—Arend,
Van Rees, Brill, Van Vloten, Wijnne, and P. L. Muller;
from the Catholic side, Kervijn de Lettenhove, Nuyens,
and a number of others throw light upon greater or lesser
portions of the period in articles and works more or less
exhaustive.   Up to the second half of this century,
treatises from the Protestant standpoint were in the majority.   Then followed those based upon Catholic principles.   A bitter dispute was waged anew between the
advocates of the two great theological parties,—a contest
by which historical truth was purified.   Fruin's masterly
articles in *De Gids*, the *Bijdragen*, and in other publications set a standard of scientific valuation of various

[1] See p. 500.

kinds of opinions and information. Thus the literature upon the Eighty Years' War waxed to a mighty mass.

Whoever is desirous of treating the epoch cannot complain, as in regard to earlier times in the Netherlands, of lack of sources or of lack of predecessors. On the contrary, the difficulty is to find the way through the wilderness of documents and studies. An attempt is made in this book to overcome this, and to put together a narrative which, though based upon independent source studies, is at the same time, so far as possible, drawn from existing literature on the period.

Where various conceptions of persons or affairs render the final judgment uncertain, the aim of this work is to attain the impartiality whereof our Fruin has given us the example, and which chiefly consists in trying to free oneself from all prejudice both in politics and theology. The writer does not deny that he finds it difficult to exercise impartiality in this fashion, but he thinks he has conscientiously tried to reach the high standard which he deemed necessary in the discussion of a period that, more than any other, quickens the heart-beat with the thought of the heroic struggle waged by our forefathers for the dearest property of mankind, for what they deemed right and freedom. He has refrained entirely from polemics, both in order to avoid marring the coherence of the narrative, and because the critical discussion of the numerous facts necessary to be treated would have increased the size of the work beyond bounds.

The compass of the portion treating of the Eighty Years' War is already greater than was planned. In writing, the author became convinced that it was impossible for an understanding of the whole development of our existence as a people to abbreviate the narration of the events, to condense the sketch of the conditions in times so fruitful in change. The sieges of Haarlem, Alkmaar, Leyden, and Antwerp, the campaigns of Prince

William and Prince Maurice, are not only of interest in military history; they are closely interwoven with the entire social history. The involved course of the political and theological changes needs to be outlined to show how a free republic was formed from the Burgundian monarchy. It was also impossible to touch briefly the manner in which, at the time of the war in the north, the foundations were laid for the bloom of the commerce and manufacture developed in the seventeenth century.

The days of Prince William, of Maurice and Olden-barnevelt, are rich in remarkable, in striking events. To the author, the work of embodying these events in a narrative has been a two-years' task of indescribable pleasure. May he have succeeded in making his readers share in the feelings which animated him during his labour!

P. J. BLOK.

LEYDEN, June 18, 1896.

After four years I have nothing to add to this Preface. I saw through the whole of this English version of my book pen in hand, and am fully satisfied by the admirable manner in which the translator has achieved her difficult task.

P. J. B.

NOORDWIJK ON THE SEA, NEAR LEYDEN,
         Sept., 1900.

CONTENTS

HISTORY OF THE DUTCH PEOPLE

THE PROLOGUE

ON August 7, 1559, the States-General met at Ghent.
It proved a notable occasion, for it was the last
time that a prince of the house of Burgundy ever took
part in an assembly of the deputies from the seventeen
provinces of the Low Countries.

Four years had elapsed since Charles V. had abdicated
his sovereignty as king, duke, count, and lord, in favour
of his son. Now Philip was about to leave the northern
provinces which he had received so solemnly on October
25, 1555, and return to Spain. He had assembled the
States to take farewell of them and formally to commit
the administration into the hands of his chosen regent,
his half-sister Margaret, duchess of Parma. Anthony
Perrenot, bishop of Arras, spoke in the king's behalf,
asking the States and all public officials to lend the royal
representative their support in the maintenance of the
Catholic religion and in the execution of the placards
issued to check the new sects. At the same time he asked
for an extra tribute or *bede* of three million guilders.

The demand gave the States their opportunity. They
declared themselves ready to make the desired grant, but
in doing so claimed a right to make their own conditions.
They demanded the dismissal of all Spanish troops
stationed upon Netherland soil, and pointed out the

desirability that the Netherland government should be administered by the regent in consultation with the native nobles whose influence at that moment threatened to be overpowered by that of Granvelle, the bishop of Arras, or, still worse, by that of Philip's Spanish advisers. Philip was indignant at the demands and, in his answer to the States, declared that they were ill-informed, that he had intrusted the government to his sister, born and educated in the provinces, and to faithful servants. In respect to the Spanish soldiers, he thought they were indispensable to protect the frontiers against France, but still he consented to send them away within three or four months, as the States made a point of it.

A few days later, Philip sailed from Flushing to bury himself for the remainder of his life in Spain, busied with his attempts to rule his widespread dominions in every detail, with a complete misconception of them. He had arranged the government, but many points were left unsettled, among them the question regarding the new taxes, of which the latest tribute was the heaviest. The debts were heavy, and the government had to depend upon the States. In their turn they wished to stipulate that the so-called *aide-novennale*, the *bede* of 1558, should only be levied by them. This implied frequent sessions during the nine years and a consequent opportunity for the deputies to discuss public affairs, a state of things greatly feared by the government.

Philip was gone, and the weak administration of the duke of Savoy, late governor of the Netherlands, was replaced by the stronger hand of Margaret of Parma,—stronger inasmuch as she was a member of the king's family and devoted to his service and to the execution of his will. The young nobles — the prince of Orange, the count of Egmont, the marquis of Bergen, the count of Hoogstraaten, and others — had all gradually assumed

a somewhat arrogant tone under Savoy. They now expected to be the actual administration and to have Margaret as a figure-head to their action. On the contrary,
they found speedily that they were ignored. Margaret
accepted advice, it is true, but it was exclusively the advice of Anthony Perrenot, bishop of Arras, now elevated
to a cardinalship under the name of Granvelle. The
president of the privy council and of the council of
state, the Frisian, Wigele or Viglius van Zwychem van
Aytta, and the count of Berlaymont, one of the heads
of the financial administration, composed the regent's
real council. This *consulta*,[1] or after-council as it was
called, discussed and decided every item of administration, and nothing was broached in the council of state,
privy council, or council of finance, which had not been
fully decided beforehand.

Among the young nobles, William of Orange, count of
Nassau, was not the first, but he was undeniably one of
the first. Members of the house of Nassau had played
an important part in the Burgundian court for several
generations. William, offspring of the Protestant German branch of the house, had inherited, at the age of
eleven, the rich possessions of his cousin René of Orange
Nassau. This succession had been allowed on condition
that the young Protestant heir should be educated under
the direct supervision of the emperor's sister, Mary of
Hungary, the then regent of the Netherlands. In October, 1544, the young prince came to Brussels and thence-
forth was a member of the household of Charles whenever
the emperor was on Netherland soil. The prince's marriage with Anna of Egmont, countess of Buren, the
heiress of the famous imperial general, Maximilian van
Buren, had increased his wealth so that he was one of
the richest nobles in the Netherlands. Moreover, he

---

[1] See Fruin, *Voorspel van den 80 jarigen oorlog.* Collected works, p. 287
(The Hague, 1900).

possessed marked talents, so that from an early age
Charles V. regarded his opinions as valuable, and consulted him beyond the warrant of his years.   At twenty-
two the prince was a member of the council of state.
He also took an important part in the negotiations which
led to the peace of Cateau-Cambresis, and accompanied
the duke of Alva to Paris to serve as hostage for the fulfilment of the conditions of the treaty.

In 1559, he was member of the council of state and
stadtholder of the important provinces of Holland, Zealand, Utrecht, and Burgundy, offices which assured him
an influence in the government.   As one of the Order of
the Golden Fleece he was ranked among the first counsellors of the Burgundian rulers.   He was, at the time of
Philip's departure, a brilliant nobleman well known for
the gorgeousness of his palaces and the luxury of his
entertainments, for the perfection of his cuisine, as well
as for his courtly manner, his eloquence, and his states-
manlike talents in general.   Everything seemed to point
to his playing a great rôle in the Netherland government.

Besides him there were others, the talented marquis of
Bergen, John of Glimes, a clever man forced into a narrow sphere by his appointment as stadtholder of Valenciennes.   It was well known that he was opposed to
persecution of the heresy prevalent in his government
from the influx of Calvinist preachers from France, and
Granvelle complained of his slack coöperation in the
execution of the placards.

A less clever man, but rather dangerous on account of
his popularity, was the conqueror at Gravelines, Lamoral,
count of Egmont, prince of Gaure, stadtholder of Flanders.   He, too, was prominent on account of his wealth
and as a finished courtier and valiant soldier, but otherwise he was a man of little significance, vain and without
any political penetration.   In addition to these three,
there were an increasing number of less distinguished

nobles: the counts of Hoorn, Mansfeld, Megen, and Hoogstraaten, the seigneur of Montigny, and others.

Now, as has been said, these nobles, especially Orange and Egmont, had expected to play an active part in Margaret's government, but scarcely weeks had elapsed after Philip's departure when it became clear to them that they had no hand in the administration, that all was done in the *consulta*, and that of the three members of that body—Granvelle, Viglius, and Berlaymont,—it was the first who exerted a paramount influence over the regent. In his youth Orange had been on good terms with Granvelle. Gradually they became alienated. In 1559, the death of Anna of Buren left Orange a widower and free to form a new matrimonial alliance which might add lustre to his position. In his negotiations he felt that Granvelle secretly thwarted him, and when he married (1561) Anne, daughter of Maurice of Saxony, the famous opponent of Charles V., he was fully aware that Granvelle had used his influence to prevent the king's giving his consent.

Granvelle's position, too, changed by 1560. Philip had obtained the pope's consent to a rearrangement of episcopal authority in the Netherland provinces and to a creation of new archbishoprics and sees.[1] Among the new princes of the church was Granvelle, who was made archbishop of Mechlin at the same time that he received a cardinal's hat.

Thus by 1561, Granvelle and Orange had both advanced in dignity and in pretensions, the former by his new honours in the ecclesiastical realm, the latter by his alliance with German ruling princes, which placed him in a new sphere.

The discontent of the nobles had been growing for two years. In 1561, when the prince returned from the celebration of his wedding at Leipsic, this discontent flamed

[1] See Part II., pp. 322–323.

out into open protest.   They saw that they were being
bent to a policy which sacrificed the Netherland interests;
they saw that Philip's dream was to make a monarchy in
which the will of the king should be as supreme as in
Castile.   They had no desire to see the interests of the
Netherlands subordinated to those of the Catholic religion, which was indeed their religion, but in which they
were far less zealous than the king.   With anxiety they
watched the government employ a policy towards England and Denmark which ignored the interests of Netherland commerce, a vital question for the provinces, to
pursue the ends of a Catholic dynastic policy in the
Baltic, or towards the great island across the North Sea.

With apprehension they noticed that the government
stood on the point of supporting the Guises on account
of these Catholic dynastic interests in France.   With
sorrow they saw how the ties with the German empire
became looser,—the ties with that empire of which they
were in part vassals, to a certain degree subjects.   In
short, the Netherland nobles demanded a government
adapted to Netherland interests, not to those of the
Catholics or Spanish-Hapsburgs.   They did not intend
to have the Netherlands sacrificed to the king's religious
and political theories which were not theirs.

Orange and Egmont opened the conflict.   In the summer of 1561, they wrote to Philip to complain of Granvelle's unendurable absolutism.   This was the beginning
of a correspondence which dragged on for three years.
The king answered the nobles pleasantly but ambigu-
ously.   " Tell me all about it and everything shall be
made right," he wrote while he was, meanwhile, direct-
ing the regent not to discuss matters of importance with
the council of state.   He did not know that one of his
secretaries, Erasso, was in constant correspondence with
the Netherland nobles, so that his smooth words were
little reassuring to them in the light of his secret phrases

to their opponents. The cardinal became more and more unpopular. Pasquinades were levelled against him with increasing impudence, and the government did not protect him. In 1562, a league of the great nobles sprang into existence. Margaret, too, felt that her minister had lost his usefulness, and complained, too, that he made her his tool. The nobles refused to go to the hollow meetings of the council of state, resumed their attendance on Philip's assurance that matters should be improved, and again abstained when no change was forthcoming.

Meantime another incident occurred.

In the spring of 1562, civil war broke out in France, and the king ordered that a portion of the bands of ordnance —which were, after the departure of the Spanish troops, the only standing army in the Netherlands — should be sent to help the Catholics. This request aroused bitter opposition. At the demands of Orange and his adherents, the council of state summoned a number of prominent Netherlanders to discuss the matter. All the provincial stadtholders and the knights of the Fleece were asked to appear at Brussels (August, 1562). Under direction of Orange and Egmont they declared that they were opposed to the plan, and only reluctantly consented to aid the French pecuniarily. This was the utmost that Granvelle — who was not greatly in favour of the king's scheme — could obtain.

Philip was furious at the opposition. Still higher rose his wrath when he heard that Orange and Egmont had taken advantage of the repeated discussions with the stadtholders and others at Brussels to form a league, an alliance against the cardinal. Orange was the soul of the league, whose purpose was to force Granvelle's removal and thereby to strengthen the influence of the great nobles in the government. Nearly all the stadtholders and a few others took part in this. Berlaymont and Aerschot alone refused adherence thereto, the former from fear of prejudicing the interests of his family, the latter from dislike to Orange and Egmont.   The allies availed themselves of the services of a very clever man, the diplomate Simon Renard, a close friend of Egmont and a bitter foe of Granvelle, who had insulted him, in his opinion, and was probably the writer of more than one of the bitterest pasquinades directed against the cardinal —the first political writings of this nature in the Netherlands.   In 1562, it was decided to send Montigny — a member of the council of state — to Madrid to inform Philip by word of mouth of the serious state of affairs in the Netherlands.   This helped little or nothing.   By the following year the bitterness against Granvelle had greatly increased.   The league spread to the petty nobles.

In March, 1563,[1] Orange, Egmont, and Hoorn united, as members of the council of state, in a letter to Philip, violent in tone, filled with complaints of Granvelle, and demanding his immediate removal.   Philip hesitated, according to his habit, and wrote[2] to " *mes cousins* " to send one of their number, preferably Egmont, to Spain to tell him all about it.   Granvelle had long since indicated him as the most manageable of the three.   There was much discussion among the allied nobles and their friends as to their best method of procedure.   The final decision was that another letter should be sent by the three leaders, as Egmont was loath to undertake the journey.

The letter was more urgent than its predecessors.[3] The writers demanded, moreover, the convocation of the States-General to put an end to the existing confusion, and declared that they could not appear again in the council as " the shadow we have been during four years."

The regent, too, now urged the cardinal's dismissal, and he himself, informed of the king's state of mind by

[1] *Corresp. de Guillaume le Taciturne*, ii., p. 35.
[2] *Ibid.*, p. 41.   [3] *Ibid.*, p. 42.

spies, declared his willingness to leave his post if it would
serve his prince, although he would regret the defeat of
the king's authority and consideration.

Philip consulted his Spanish advisers. The duke of
Alva strongly urged that the king should retain Granvelle
in office and punish the leaders of the league as severely
as possible, at any rate enforce their return to the council of state. When the king finally decided to sacrifice
Granvelle, Alva urged that he should not do so openly.
This last advice Philip adopted, but delayed in his customary fashion, so that it was January, 1564, before it
was finally decided. Philip then sent a private letter to
the cardinal telling him to leave the Netherlands, while
the three gentlemen, after waiting six months, received
a brief and dry answer advising them to return to the
council, and adding " my intention is to consider further
what action will be best." Armenteros, Margaret's secretary, carried the first letter with him, but the last was
despatched so as to reach the nobles after the cardinal's
departure. Thus the matter seemed cleverly planned,
the wish of the Netherlanders fulfilled, and the reputation
of the king maintained.

The cardinal's position had grown very precarious
during the six months, but, in spite of being the butt of
ridicule and the object of dislike, he was greatly surprised
and disappointed at the king's final command. He wrote
to Philip in a dignified manner warning him again that the
nobles were dangerous, and against the convocation of
the States-General. On March 13, 1564, he departed
from Brussels, nominally to visit his family in the
Franche Comté. As a matter of fact, he never saw the
Netherlands again.

The very uncertainty which attended Granvelle's departure and the chance of his return marred the good
impression which might have been made. The objectionable figure in the administration was gone, yet the king's

tone in his letter to the nobles showed that he was not inclined to adopt their plans. Meanwhile the league against the cardinal remained in existence. How numerous the discontented noblemen were is shown by the history of the livery. Two thousand coats, with ornaments which suggested either a cardinal's hat or a fool's cap, were already for sale in the Brussels shops when, at the regent's request, Egmont, in order to remove the appearance of personal dislike for the cardinal, persuaded the nobles to adopt a new emblem for their sleeves, the bundle of arrows of the Spanish real, the token of unity later so famous in the history of the republic.[1]

The nobles again took their seats in the council-chamber, but they found it very difficult to operate the government machine as set in motion by Granvelle. He had ruled alone while excluding the majority of the three administrative councils—Councils of State and of Finance and Privy Council; but now that he was gone these three were left without cohesion. The nobles thought of changing the council of state (it was at this date on a par with the other councils and specially charged with the direction of civil and military matters) into an executive body of government, composed of a greater number of members of the upper nobility, with extensive privileges and practically independent of the national government, as the privy council had to do with jurisdiction and the council of finance with the domain.

This was a scheme with which Philip had no sympathy whatsoever. Viglius and his fellow-jurists were terrified at the thought of an influx of untrained nobles into the administration. From the time of the rise of Burgundian power jurists had played an important rôle, and were now quite unwilling to be displaced. Thus the administration was divided against itself. There was a pressure of the

[1] Fruin, *Voorspel.*

lesser nobles to come in and a pressure from the jurists to keep them out.

The first effect of the nobles' influence was not encouraging. Soon nothing could be done without their mediation or that of their servants. Financial judgments, pardons, were bought; old suits of the nobles against the royal domain were revived and brought to trial; justice was for sale. The middle point of avarice was the regent's favourite secretary, soon notorious as Argenteros from his greed and avarice.

This confusion gave great pleasure to the cardinal and his friends. And still sharper were their comments when the nobles urged the king to convene the States-General. Philip would not hear of such a step, and began to repent the departure of the cardinal, especially when the council of state demurred at enforcing in the Netherlands the decrees of the just-ended council of Trent.

Among the many problems with which the nobles had to struggle, after the departure of Granvelle, the persecution of heresy on the basis of the placards was one of the most important. Calvinism had entered the province from France in spite of preventive measures taken by the government.

The disposition of the Catholic population itself was just then favourable to the spread of heretical ideas. Many Catholics who adhered to the form of their faith were alienated by the behaviour of many of their priests, who were unchaste, worldly, luxurious, and neglectful of clerical duties. How much more earnestly did the Calvinist and Lutheran preachers pursue their task! Just at this epoch the number of Calvinists increased in many a village and city where the Catholic priests had lost caste from their behaviour, and Catholicism lingered half a century longer in places where the priests lived up to their vows.

Among the nobles a plan was conceived of attempting

a reform within the Church.   The council of Trent was slow to arrive at a decision, and by 1564 little was hoped for from its deliberations.   The soul of this scheme was Louis of Nassau, Orange's right hand, whose Lutheran family and ties with France seemed to make him the person to bring about a reformation in the Catholic Church in the Netherlands and neighbouring regions which should unite the moderate Catholics with those of similar tendency among the Lutherans and even among the Calvinists.   It was thought that an agreement might be attained between Condé on the one side, Landgrave William of Hesse and other Lutheran princes on the other, possibly on the basis of the so-called Wittenberg Concord-Book.   Guy de Bray, an influential Calvinist preacher, interested himself in these plans and promised his coöperation, and the moderate spirit manifest among the authorities and population of the Netherlands seemed favourable to such plans, although up to this period similar schemes had failed in France and Germany.

The nobles found a theologian ready to coöperate with them in François Baudouin, a native Netherlander and disciple of the famous Cassander.[1]   Baudouin had already made attempts of this kind in France, but had always met with disappointment.   His appointment as professor at Douay (September, 1563) gave him opportunity to return to his native land, whence he had been banished as heretic.   He was promised a seat in the privy council if he succeeded, and Orange had a conference with him in the summer of 1564 to draw up the outlines of the ambitious plan of theological unity.   But the time for such compromise was past.   It was only the nobles, lax as they were in religious matters, who could conceive it possible.   Neither king nor reformers were willing to yield one iota of the beliefs which were their life.   The king was determined to crush out heresy, the Calvinists

[1] See Part II., 386.

and Lutherans would not return to a church which they thought had sprung from the Evil One. Attempts of one kind and another dragged on through 1564, but came to nothing. Baudouin returned to France. Neither Calvinist nor Lutheran showed any disposition to yield, and the council of Trent, having finished its deliberations, laid down a definite law of orthodox Catholic opinion without the least concession to Calvinist or Lutheran doctrines. There was no choice between acceptance and separation.

At the end of 1564, three points were the main topics of discussion in the council of state—reformation in the national government, improvement of financial conditions, measures regarding religion.[1] The discussions lasted throughout the winter 1564–65. It was finally decided to ask the king to grant greater power to the council of state, to convene the States-General, and to moderate the placards against heresy. It was further decided to send Egmont to Spain to lay these matters before Philip. Viglius drew up the instruction. In the meeting held to approve the instructions Orange gave a long address, sketching the programme for the future. The contents were as follows[2]:

We deceive both ourselves and others if we try to disguise illness and remedy with smooth words. We must tell the king plainly how the matter lies; it cannot be postponed longer. Above all, we must make him understand that religion has received a severe shock in the adjacent countries, and has also suffered in the Netherlands so that it cannot be maintained — considering the shameful life of the priests—by the severity of the placards or by the erection of new bishoprics. The people will not longer endure the fury of the inquisition, the judges

[1] Hopperus, *Recueil et memorial des Troubles du Pays-Bas*, ed. Hoynck v. Papendrecht, p. 36.
[2] See Van der Haer, *De Initiis Tumultuum Belgicorum*, p. 185.

are so notorious from their quarrels that they lack the power to force men to their duty. It thus follows that the government cannot be properly wielded except by the institution of a governmental council; confusion had ensued from the division among various councils. Further, in this government council certain distinguished men must be included who are respected by the people. Finally the king must be shown that the resolutions of the council of Trent could not be adopted; the provinces border on Germany, whose princes, both Protestant and Catholic, will refuse the council from serious grounds; the king must be shown that the regent must postpone the execution of these resolutions. The king must be persuaded to relax his strictness about heresy. " I am Catholic and will not deviate from religion, but I cannot approve the custom of kings to confine men's creed and religion within arbitrary limits."

The prince's words rang throughout the assembly room, where such language had never been heard hitherto. The speech made such an impression on Viglius that he was attacked by apoplexy in the following night. The instruction was brought by Hopperus to the form desired by Orange.

From this moment it was plain that either the king or Orange must yield. Two principles were irreconcilably opposed to each other in the Netherlands—the principle of Catholicism with its unlimited royal autocracy as Spain recognised it, in opposition to toleration in the realm of religion with a national government according to ancient principles based on ancient privileges. The future conflict was, for a great part, foreshadowed in this speech.

In January, 1565, Egmont set off for Spain. There were certain rumours afloat that Granvelle had advised the king to sacrifice a few heads to assure quiet in his northern dominions, and certain members of the league pledged themselves, as they bade the count farewell, to

avenge any ill that might befall him. No apparent ill
did befall him; he was delightfully entertained and returned safely in the spring, hardly conscious until he was
again in the Netherlands that Philip had promised nothing
in answer to the earnest representations of his Netherland
nobles. The king's reply embraced little more than a
protestation of adherence to the Catholic faith wherein
no change was to be permitted, besides a plan of calling
a convention of theologians so as to consult with the
council of state regarding means of bringing erring
spirits to better opinions. Not a word of the demanded
reform, just a few vague promises about the king's
coming to the Netherlands; not one word on the moderation of the persecutions, not one about the assembly of
the States-General! And soon came rumours of a conference at Bayonne in France between the duke of Alva
and Catherine de Médicis, on a possible coöperation between the Catholic powers for the maintenance of the
ancient faith. This conference did not actually come to
pass, but it caused many meetings among the Protestants.

Meanwhile the theologians met and advised a proclamation of the resolutions of the council of Trent, at
the same time advising some leniency in the execution of
the placards.[1] Philip's answer did not come for months.
It was dated Segovia, October 17, 1565, and approved
the decision of the theologians about doctrine, etc., and
entirely disapproved any suggestion of amelioration in
the execution of the placards, adding that the slightest
gentleness towards heretics made them more shameless.
At the same time the king refused to allow any change
in the form of government, and nominated the duke of
Aerschot, Orange's foe, as member of the council of
state. Just freed from fear of an inroad of the Turks in
the south, Philip took heart to show his hand in the
north. It was a declaration of war against the nobles.

[1] Hopperus, *Recueil*, p. 48.

The delay in the arrival of Philip's despatches had caused an appearance of calm in the Netherlands. This letter from Segovia, with its plain expression of his relentless intention of persecution, was like oil to a quiet fire. The agitation had spread quietly during the interval. The lesser nobles had grown stronger in their union. Louis of Nassau at their head formed a link with the greater. Among these young nobles were a few Calvinists, notably Philip and John of Marnix, Floris of Culemborg, and Nicholas de Hames. They were in close relations with the Calvinist preachers and consistories, which now existed in the most important cities.

The Calvinists had been encouraged by the attitude of the nobles and officials towards the persecutions, even though the placards had been strenuously executed in some cases, Ruard Tapper, a native of Enkhuizen in Holland, appointed inquisitor in 1537, being notorious for his severity. The stake had become a painfully ordinary sight in Netherland cities; many suffered punishment for their creed, while many more fled to England and Germany. At the same time the lukewarm coöperation shown by most of the stadtholders,[1] by the nobles in the country, and the magistrates in the cities, led the reformed to protest in a way to threaten a serious popular rising. There were too many conferences between the Calvinist preachers and congregations with the lesser nobles during the summer of 1565 while the king's decision was still in abeyance.

But that decisive answer put an end to all hope of leniency. The privy council begged Margaret to publish the king's orders in a modified and softened form, while making one more effort to convince him of the danger of his policy.[2] Orange and Egmont, however, urged an immediate publication, even though they knew

[1] Hopperus, *Recueil*, p. 62.
[2] *Ibid.*, p. 58.

that a great revolt might ensue, and their advice was adopted.

The mandate sent to the prelates, universities, and cities accordingly made a deep impression everywhere. The Brabanters were very indignant, claiming that no inquisition had ever existed on their soil, and that their privileges were infringed by its establishment.

Flanders, Namur, and other provinces protested too. Incendiary documents appeared pasted upon the churches and town halls in many a city, yes, even upon the walls of the palaces of the regent and the Brussels nobles, all testifying to the disappointment of the people. This ire was more and more excited, too, by widely circulated and eagerly read pamphlets. There was a universal cry that the Spanish inquisition was coming, and tales of its martyrs ran around like wildfire.

At the time of the arrival of Philip's despatches it chanced that the Netherland nobility were gathered in Brussels in large numbers to take part in the marriage festivities of Alexander Farnese, prince of Parma, the regent's son. They, too, were very indignant at Philip's arbitrary command. Their presence in the capital gave an opportunity for open expression of their indignation. Towards the end of November, about twenty of the young nobles, under the leadership of Thoulouse and De Hames, entered into a secret compact. This was the famous Compromise or alliance of the nobles. Copies of the original document were immediately made and circulated among the petty nobles in the country, with the result that in a couple of months the number of the signatures had reached three hundred.

The contents of the articles, written in the court tongue, French, was somewhat as follows [1]:

The nobles stated that a handful of strangers, for their own profit, had persuaded the king not only to refuse to

[1] *Archives de la Maison d'Orange-Nassau*, ii., p. 2.

ameliorate the placards against heresy, but to render them more severe, and even to introduce the Spanish inquisition, " which is not only unjust and contrary to all laws divine and human, surpassing the greatest barbarity that was ever practised by tyrants, but is to God's great dishonour and to that of the whole Catholic faith which they pretend to maintain," and would militate to the ruin of the Netherlands.   The nobles declared that it was their duty to prevent the introduction of the inquisition in any form, at the same time asserting that they would maintain the king's authority and prevent any disturbance of the peace.   They promised to stand by each other like brothers and faithful comrades against anyone who tried to punish or persecute one of the allies either on account of the inquisition or of the placards, because of the compact or under any pretence whatsoever.   It was expressly declared that the compact sprang only " from a holy zeal and laudable desire to maintain the glory of God, the majesty of the king, public peace, and the security of our persons and property."   In case of doubt the signers were to submit to the joint resolution of all or of those who were appointed thereto.   The document ended with a solemn appeal to God's protection for their confederation and alliance.

The great nobles—Orange, Egmont, and the others— were not involved in this for the time being.   Probably in the beginning they did not even know of it, but they acted in a spirit similar to the spirit expressed in the formal document by refusing to execute the king's commands, and by declaring that, if the placards were not ameliorated, they must resign from their positions in the government.   Even the regent, although not inclined to follow their example wholly, urged the king to compliance.   Orange and Hoorn again absented themselves from the council of state.   Egmont followed their lead hesitatingly, telling the adherents of the government that he could not endure the daily protests of his friends, and deciding that his honour was at stake.[1]

The allied nobles now conceived far-reaching plans. If the king refused to yield, they determined to seek alliances abroad, in Protestant England and Germany, among the Huguenots in France.   It was not until the end of February, 1566, that Orange openly acknowledged the compromise, either then first hearing of it, or — what was more probable — considering that the time was but just ripe, while he had been cognisant of it from its inception. He now endeavoured to persuade the other nobles to join the movement.   Bergen, Montigny, Hoorn, and Hoogstraaten agreed, but Egmont, Megen, and Mansfeld refused, while the last two ranged themselves decidedly on the side of the government.   Egmont, loyal and devoted to the government, was very anxious to avoid any appearance of opposition and of anti-Catholic sentiment.

The loss of Egmont's support was a serious blow for the plans of the confederated nobles.   No armed resistance was possible without him.   The advice of the prince to the confederates was, taking this fact into consideration, to make one more appeal to the regent before taking decisive steps.   The confederates adopted the suggestion, a petition was drawn up, and on April 3d the petty nobles flocked into Brussels from all quarters, from Friesland, as well as from Artois and Luxemburg, to the total number of about four hundred instead of the thirty-five thousand soldiers the regent had been warned to expect with them.   The text of the petition had been carefully prepared by Louis of Nassau,[2] probably not without the coöperation of Orange, Brederode, and others.   On April 5th, towards midday, Brederode and Louis of Nassau, arm in arm, led the procession to the

---

[1] Hopperus, *Recueil*, p. 68.

[2] *Apologie* of Louis of Nassau ; *Bijdragen en Med. van het Hist. Gen. te Utrecht*, p. 216, 1885.

palace, where the regent, surrounded by the knights of
the Golden Fleece, gave them audience and received the
document from Brederode's hands.

The petition began with a protestation of loyalty to
the king.[1]   The confederates then proceeded to declare
that it was their duty to give warning of the dangerous
condition of public sentiment.   There would be no safety
in the country if the placards were executed.   They
therefore implored the regent to send an envoy to Philip to
demand the amelioration of his orders against the heretics.
For the time being, pending the king's answer, the petitioners demanded suspension of the inquisition and of
execution of the said placards, and finally they declared
that they were unwilling to incur the responsibility of a
revolt by concealing the true state of affairs, and deemed
that they had acted as good and loyal and faithful vassals.

A story is current that Margaret was filled with anxiety
and foreboding about the petitioners and that, just before
they arrived, Berlaymont whispered to her encouragingly,
" How, Madame, afraid of these beggars!"[2]   On the receipt of the petition, however, she preserved an appearance of calm and answered with dignity the short but
vigorous speech with which Brederode delivered the
document.   She reserved a fuller reply until the morrow.
Then she informed the confederates that before the offering of the petition she had decided, on the advice of the
stadtholders, of the knights of the Golden Fleece, of the
council of state, and of the privy council, to publish a
moderation of the placards.   A suspension was beyond
her power, but she hoped that they would be content
with this step for the present and would support her in
the maintenance of the ancient religion.[3]

Two days later the confederates presented a second

[1] *Archives*, ii., p. 80.
[2] See Gachard, *Études et notices historiques*, i., p. 130.
[3] *Archives*, ii., p. 84.

document, expressing their disappointment at the restricted jurisdiction of the regent, and asking permission to have their petition printed to prevent the circulation of false reports as to its tenor. Margaret agreed to this, only begging that there should be no secret meetings, and that no new members should be received into the compromise. This dissatisfied the confederates, and some bitter words were exchanged. A couple of days of feasting followed, and then the nobles separated, leaving the interests of the Compromise in the hands of Brederode, Louis of. Nassau, Culemborg, and Van den Bergh.

The course events had taken left the regent displeased and the nobles not satisfied. Orange, too, was disappointed at the result and talked of going to Germany, an idea that perhaps had some connection with the current rumour that Philip considered him the cause of all ill, and thought that he was plotting to restore the shaken royal authority by force of arms. There was mutual distrust, and the distrust was not without reason.

It was at this time that the name of Beggars, or Gueux, as applied to the confederates, came into vogue at one of the feasts in the house of Culemborg. Brederode, possibly in reference to Berlaymont's contemptuous term, proposed the adoption of the name. Soon the Beggar (Gueux), as denoting the nobleman of the Compromise, could be recognised from a simple grey garment. This was somewhat similar to the livery of the days of Granvelle, but now there was a beggar's wallet as decoration. Moreover, on the breast was worn a silver or golden medal, on one side of which was a portrait of the king, on the other, two clasped hands and the inscription *fidèles au roy jusques à la besace*.

1566. Up to this date, the people proper of the Netherlands, the burghers and the lower classes, had taken little part in the movement against the government. Only a few had ever heard the truth of the action

of the great nobles in relation to Granvelle.   The cardinal had, however, been considered the very personification of the Spanish system of government, and hated
accordingly.   The numerous pamphlets and pasquinades
against him had had a wide vogue among the burgher
population at Antwerp, Ghent, and Brussels.   Nor had
it been a secret that Orange and Egmont were the leaders
in the opposition to the cardinal, and their popularity
throughout the provinces had increased accordingly.
They were regarded by the people at large as zealous for
the maintenance of national liberty, for a government by
natives, for diminished severity in the observance of the
placards—the blood placards to which so many sacrifices
had fallen in the past years.   Not that Calvinism or the
doctrine of the Baptists, or Mennonites, found many
adherents among the well-to-do citizens.   On the contrary, although heresy was spreading to all classes of
the population, it was in the main—just as in the time of
the Baptists—the lowest classes who were chiefly affected
by its spirit.   In proportion to the whole population, the
number of Calvinists was small, and chiefly to be found
in Artois, Flanders, Brabant, Hainaut, Holland, and
Zealand.   Even Increased by those of Mennonite opinions
in the Frisian and Holland country districts, by the
Lutherans of foreign birth in great commercial cities like
Antwerp and Amsterdam, the whole number was far inferior to those who were somewhat indifferent to Catholicism and yet were averse to persecution.   Only a very
few zealous Catholics shared the king's opinions and
thought that heresy must be rooted out by unyielding
severity, and even, if need were, with Spanish help.

Thus the desire for amelioration of the placards was a
universal popular wish, and the movement among the
nobles, especially their appearance at Brussels in April,
was watched with the greatest interest during the spring
of 1566.   The cry of *Vivent les Gueux !* was soon heard in

burghers' circles, and the Beggar's medal was seen in many places.

The Calvinists especially had watched the course of events with the closest attention. They fixed their hopes on the action of the nobles, and expected instant amelioration, if not abolition, of the placards. The petition, translated into German and Dutch, together with the regent's answer and the nobles' reply, was read with the keenest interest by the Calvinists.

The king's letter from Segovia, in November, 1565, had brought bitter disappointment. By the following spring the situation was strained. The widely scattered pamphlets nursed excitement. The preachers lost no opportunity of encouraging their congregations by pointing out the sympathy of the nobles. Religious freedom seemed in the near future, and a longing to see it in actual existence began to be manifest among the poor persecuted people. There was constant talk of the triumph of heresy, of the fall of the old church, and of vengeance upon the persecutors. They gloried in the Psalms of Israel, and were full of expectation of what was to come, of the kingdom of liberty that was about to dawn in the name of God and of Christ. There were all sorts of rumours abroad in the spring of 1566, and the moment of redemption seemed nearer and nearer. All the heretics saw more in the action of the nobles and the answer of the regent than really existed.

Neither the great nor the lesser nobles, as we know from their letters, really were moved by the motives attributed to them by the heretical portion of the population. Amelioration of the placards, convention of the States-General, they wished, and nothing more. They had not the slightest wish to see the ancient church overthrown, or any sovereignty of heretical opinions. At the end of 1565, Hoorn was actually terrified when he heard of the expectations and dreams of the multitude.

The Compromise expressly stipulated the maintenance of the Catholic doctrines, and although the petition did not do the same in so many words, that it breathed the same spirit was not to be doubted, so that many upright Catholics found no difficulty in taking part in the movement, and many a " Romish Beggar " set his signature to the document " as well as another." Neither Brederode nor Nassau — to mention these alone — thought at that time of joining Calvinism, which they considered deviated too much from Romish doctrines and bore a dangerous democratic character.

But the Calvinists, who watched certain of their own people come to the fore in the movement, counted all the confederated nobles as sympathisers, to the profound annoyance of the good Catholics among them who, in consequence, soon began to hesitate and to draw back.

The regent's answer to the petition, with its phrase " amelioration of the placards," was also rated by the populace as favourable to them—beyond the truth.

In May the sermons began to be given in a more open manner. Great multitudes assembled, first in the fields, later before the city gates, to hear the preaching. A synod of the Calvinist congregations met at Antwerp and, making use of the favourable opportunity, organised a general movement among the Calvinists throughout the Netherlands for the purpose of showing the government their strength and the significance of their demands. Many exiles returned, first secretly, then openly; the placards were considered practically suspended! Antwerp was the centre of all this. Sometimes as many as twenty or thirty thousand people, says an eye-witness,[1] flocked to hear the open-air sermons outside that city, protected by watchers employed in the name of the consistories.

Meanwhile the fulfilment of the promise made to the

[1] Burgon, *Life and Times of Thomas Gresham*, ii., p. 134.

confederates was discussed earnestly by the regent with the council of state. As early as April 10th, Bergen and Montigny were appointed envoys to Spain to urge Philip against the introduction of the Spanish inquisition, and to beg him to come to the Netherlands and to convene the States-General. Granvelle wrote from Rome in the same spirit. Viglius and Berlaymont drew up a placard moderating the persecution temporarily, which was given to the provincial Estates before the end of the month. It was deemed so little to the purpose that it was soon termed a " murderation " instead of a " moderation."

The regent was placed in a very critical position. Private despatches from the king commanding stringency, concessions, which meant nothing, sent openly to the council of state, increased the uncertainty, while the Antwerp synod, under the secret leadership of Aldegonde, proceeded to organise Calvinist preaching. The ministers Guy de Bray, Peregrine de la Grange, Jean Taffin, François du Jon, Petrus Dathenus, Caspar van der Heyden, Hermannus Moded, and others, both from French and Netherland congregations, aroused their people with earnest harangues.[1]

A steadily increasing movement made itself felt throughout the whole land, especially in Flanders, in Artois, in Holland. In Holland, though, affairs took on a somewhat different character from that evident in the other provinces. The many Lutherans at Amsterdam affected the theology, and a certain disposition was evinced to adopt the Augsburg confession as the basis of a creed. A commission from the Calvinist congregations at Antwerp tried to persuade them to accept the

[1] Very important documents regarding the activity of the consistories in 1566 and 1567 can be found in the Records of the Blood Council, compare Bakhuizen van den Brink, *Het Huwelijk*, etc., p. 113, and the appendices to the work of Langeraad (Guido de Bray), Zierikzee, 1884.

Netherland-Calvinist confession of 1559, but Holland people declined to consider the propositions.[1]

The regent was at her wits' end. The council of state could give her little consolation. Aerschot, Aremberg, and Berlaymont were as helpless as she. Orange, Egmont, and Hoorn continued to urge the convention of the States-General and the abolition of the placards as the only effective measures to allay the disturbance. The regent sent messenger after messenger to Philip, but no letter came to her. For three months the Brussels government was left in a helpless condition without one word from Spain, where the king deliberated, as of old, with his council and the two envoys from the Netherlands. The increasing numbers of open-air congregations, and the fact that the members carried arms as they listened to the expounding of their faith, put the regent in constant fear of some sudden revolutionary outbreak. In her dilemma she finally appealed to the confederated nobles for aid, and implored them to use their influence to check these dangerous assemblies. In accordance with her request, which was indeed almost a supplication, Brederode, Louis of Nassau, Culemborg, and Van den Bergh met at Lier, July 2d, to discuss the situation. They also invited certain ministers, deputies of the Antwerp synod, to confer with them. In reply to the demand that the public sermons should be relinquished for a time, the preachers said that matters had gone too far, that the people could no longer be restrained, and that if the sermons were abandoned a serious uproar would ensue. Threats that the nobles would use force if the meetings did not cease, affected the synod little under the circumstances.

It was decided to hold an assembly of the confederates at St. Trond, on territory under the jurisdiction of

[1] See Fruin, *De voorbereiding in de ballingschap van de gereformeerde Kerk van Holland, Archief von Kerkgesch.*, v., p. 7.

the bishop of Liege, as they thought that ecclesiastic was too weak to resent an intrusion on his domain. The regent was greatly disturbed at this new assembly, and called on Orange and Egmont to help her check it. At this moment the former was in Antwerp trying to preserve the peace, and the latter was busied with the affairs of his stadtholdership of Flanders. They consented to act in the name of the government, and held a notable conference at Duffel with Brederode and Culemborg. The two great nobles would hear nothing of Calvinism, and had no sympathy with the popular disturbance. They were willing, if need were, to ally themselves with the lesser nobles, but in no case could they permit the preachers or the common people to have voice in the affair. Such was their opinion.

Deputies of the Antwerp synod took part in the meeting at St. Trond. Attempts, made not without the prince's cognisance, to erect one church body from the Calvinists and Lutherans had failed, but the Calvinists had greatly increased in strength and were becoming a force that could not be ignored. The deputies earnestly implored the nobles at St. Trond to protect them in the exercise of their religion. The meeting finally closed with an assurance to the people that they should suffer no violence for their religion until otherwise ordered by the States-General. It was also decided that a deputation of twelve nobles should present to the regent an answer to the demands of Orange and Egmont, a second petition of which the contents were arranged. Then the assembly adjourned.

The new document complained bitterly that persecution had not ceased, that the delay in Philip's answer had prevented the promised amelioration of the placards, that certain Romish prelates were assuming a menacing tone. It stated that all action of the nobles had been in the interest of peace, that they had had no secret negotiations with France or other power. They did not deny that, out of fear of the Spanish troops whose coming was rumoured, they had consulted with a few friends about help in case of such an event. The petitioners begged the regent to place Orange, Egmont, and Hoorn at their head to advise and protect them. Further,. the document made a statement concerning the negotiations with the consistories at St. Trond and of their inclination to co-operate with the nobles under certain conditions. There was some parleying to and fro, and finally, after a fort-night's deliberation, the regent summoned the knights of the Golden Fleece to meet at Brussels on August 18th, and promised to give the confederates her answer on the 20th.

While events passed thus with unexpected rapidity in the Netherlands, in Spain Philip and his advisers con-tinued to deliberate on what had better be done. Finally it was resolved at Segovia that the king must go to the Netherlands, that the episcopal inquisition should be substituted for the papal, that the placards should be moderated and a universal pardon granted for what had already been done. In return the great nobles must promise their coöperation in preserving peace; leagues and confederations must cease, as well as all sermons and secret assemblies. If the rebels took up arms, then the regent was to defend herself with the help of the bands of ordnance and the garrisons. The king apparently ap-proved the resolution, at least he wrote in that spirit to the regent.

The spirit of revolt, meanwhile, gathered strength in the Netherlands. The populace began to take matters into their own hands and to express in riotous acts their hatred for the priesthood and the Romish ceremonials. Towards the end of August an armed mob fell on isolated churches in Ypres and Courtrai, threw down the images, ill-treated the priests, and plundered the rich buildings

and the well-stocked treasuries. This iconoclasm spread
from village to village, from city to city. In West
Flanders soon not one church was untouched. At Antwerp, Orange succeeded for a time in holding the mob in
check, but during his absence in Brussels on August 19th,
at the regent's command, the rabble fell on the churches,
and in the space of four hours the beautiful cathedral of
Notre Dame was reduced to a ruin of its former self.
Gresham, the English agent, writes[1]: " and coming into
Oure Lady Church, yt looked like hell where were above
1,000 torches brannyng and syche a noise! as yf heven
and erth had gone together, with fallyng of images and
fallyng down of costly works." These same turbulent
scenes were enacted in Holland, Zealand, and other
regions in the north. Everywhere fanaticism and avarice
went hand in hand; church ornaments, products of mediæval ecclesiastical art, fell as booty to thieves and plun-
derers when they escaped destruction by iconoclastic
Calvinists in a zeal which they counted as holy. The
authorities almost everywhere lacked energy and strength
to oppose the onslaughts. Bruges, Mons, Courtrai,
Douay, and Arras were almost the only towns where the
riots were successfully met by the courageous attitude of
the armed citizens.

Unspeakable was the injury inflicted on the treasures
of mediæval art. This rage of iconoclasm lasted more
than a month, while the government at Brussels watched
its mad course in impotent indignation.[2]

On August 12th, the regent received her brother's letter.
One came to the prince of Orange at the same time, ex-
pressing full confidence in him, with friendly expressions.
It was not known that the hypocritical king had taken

[1] Burgon, *Life and Times of Gresham*, ii., p. 139.
[2] Marnix of St. Aldegonde, one of the few educated nobles, himself a
firm Calvinist, wrote a *Vraye narration et apologie des choses passées au
Pays-bas touchant le fait de la religion en l'an 1566.*

the precaution to declare all concessions illegal before a
notary! But even had he been sincere it was plain even
to him that these unwilling and inadequate concessions
could not stem the current of the revolt. No one of the
three chief nobles thought that the concessions were
sufficient under the circumstances. They wished more
now, and refused to use force against the riots unless the
regent would meet the wishes of the nobles as expressed
at St. Trond.

So the anxious duchess was forced to yield, at least in
the chief points. On August 23d, she concluded an
agreement with a deputation of the confederates, wherein
she granted, in return for promises of immediate help,
permission for preaching where sermons had already been
given, provided the congregation carried no arms. No
rioting was to be allowed and Catholic services were not
to be disturbed. Further, she promised immunity for the
signers of the Compromise and of the petition. This
agreement was published and for a moment the storm of
iconoclasm held up.

The nobles made a great mistake in permitting the
dissolution of the confederation at this juncture.[1] They
should not have trusted a promise forced from a hard-
pressed and reluctant government. They actually threw
their best weapon away, voluntarily. They thought that
all was won, at least the majority thought so, and thus
they separated, rejoicing over the success finally obtained.
Orange returned to Antwerp to restore order and to end
the insecurity which had almost caused the cessation of
commerce, while he sent Brederode as his representative
to Holland. Egmont went to Flanders for the same
purpose, Hoorn to Tournay.

Action, however, was difficult until it was known how
the king took what had been done. Prince William
cherished no illusions on the subject. He knew that

[1] *Archives*, ii., p. 240.

Philip would insist on complete restoration of the ancient religion in all its rights, and that force must be met with force. Orange and his brother began to take measures of precaution, and opened secret negotiations with German colonels about the levy of mercenary companies in Germany, so as not to be defenceless when the "bear dance should begin." Louis privately, but with his brother's knowledge, entered into relations with the Huguenots and an English agent.

The king was indeed wroth when he learned what had passed, and determined to avenge the insults offered to his church and to his authority. His first intent was to go in person to the Netherlands in February, at the head of an army, and punish all who had worked against him; so at least he wrote privately to the regent, so run the despatches of Montigny and others from Spain, while his letters to the council of state were somewhat calmer. Montigny and Bergen, detained by the king in Spain, gave a clear warning of what was to come.

What was the action of the nobles to be ? Submission or opposition ? Aremberg and Megen had deserted the popular cause, Mansfeld followed their example, Montigny advised yielding, Egmont hesitated. Orange and Hoorn believed in opposition, but the prince was unwilling to risk formal steps without Egmont. He tried to assure himself of support in Germany and left no stone unturned to win over Egmont to the party of opposition. In early October Hoorn, Hoogstraaten, Orange, and Egmont had a conference at Dendermonde. It was hoped that the latter could be persuaded to a combined step, allied with a convention of the States-General, to force the king to act as they wished, but Egmont, attached as he was to royal authority, refused to enter on this road.

Meantime, as the autumn went on, the government felt itself stronger. Philip sent large sums of money which enabled the regent to levy troops. Noircarmes was sent

to Valenciennes to quiet the city by force of arms, during
the absence of the stadtholder, Bergen.   The lord of
Hierges, Berlaymont's son, and other stout loyalists were
placed at the head of troops elsewhere, and it was evident
that the administration was fully determined to assert
itself with or without troops from Spain, and to avenge
itself for its recent humiliation.

And what were the Beggars doing ?   A feeling of insecurity had again affected the Calvinist congregations
and the petty nobles.   There was an attempt to revive
the Compromise so as to demand the maintenance of the
accord of August 23d, but this failed.   Troops to the
number of eight thousand were actually collected during
the summer and retained by means of *wachtgeld*, or
pledge money, for the Beggars' service, but the expense
borne by the congregations was so heavy that the mercenaries were dismissed in November, and the majority
passed directly into the service of the government.
Another scheme was on foot—the minister Dathenus ap-
pears to have been the sponsor thereof — to raise three
million guilders and offer them to the king for the grant
of religious freedom.[1]   It is possible, however, that this
somewhat naïve suggestion was only a cloak for collecting
a war fund.   There were many attempts, moreover, to
secure coöperative action, but the majority of the city
government were afraid to commit themselves, and these
failed, just as did an effort to convene the States-General,
although the latter emanated from Egmont himself.

It was more and more evident that no leader was forthcoming for the discontented.   Orange and Egmont both
kept in the background [2]; the prince was unwilling to venture action without Egmont.

---

[1] Compare the documents given by Langeraad (Guido de Bray), Appendix on p. lii.

[2] The prince's attitude in these days is shown clearly from the letters in
the *Archives*, ii., *passim*.

In these circumstances the Calvinists resolved finally to help themselves, — the more moderate Lutherans also drawing back,—and an assembly was held in December. It was decided to use the sums already collected, not to bribe the king, but to collect troops through their fellow-Calvinist, the elector palatine. The military command was to be offered to Orange, who must promise to maintain the reformed religion. If he refused, Hoorn and Brederode were the next choice, one or both together. The leader was to have a council of six nobles, members of the Compromise appointed by the consistories, six merchants, and a few other members.

The two first-mentioned nobles declined the dangerous honour at once. Brederode thus became the chosen leader of the Calvinists, a man full of zeal for the Calvinist cause, but ill fitted for the difficult post.

Thus the "wonder year" came to an end, and the government was triumphantly recovering from the rude shocks received during 1566.

While the Beggars (a name now generally used for the Calvinists and their protectors) were thus hesitating, the regent proceeded to use vigorous measures to recover her lost balance. Noircarmes's harsh steps in Valenciennes aroused great bitterness. The two preachers and popular leaders, Guy de Bray and Peregrine de la Grange, appealed to the knights of the Fleece and the confederates to aid the city, held in actual siege by Noircarmes's troops. Dathenus succeeded in assembling a somewhat disorderly little force, which was scattered near Waterloo and Lannoy by the well-trained government troops. Noircarmes took immediate possession of Tournay and Lille, and put an end to all revolt in the district. Attempts to arouse further opposition in Flanders were suppressed by Egmont himself. Dathenus, Gilles le Clercq, and other Calvinist leaders fled to Holland, and the government's real intentions were soon revealed by the suppression of

public sermons, in spite of the accord of August 23d. The
regent had lost her fear of the nobles, great and small.

The prince spent the autumn of 1566 in Utrecht and
Amsterdam, where he attempted to bring the accord into
vogue. He was not much surprised at the defeat of the
Beggars. In answer to their request to be their leader,
he urged them to accept the Augsburg confession and
thereby obtain the alliance of the Lutheran Germans.
On the refusal of the Calvinist consistories to consider
this, he held back in spite of his brother's constant
efforts. In the beginning of February, 1567, Orange returned to Antwerp, waiting to see what time might bring
forth, but wholly unwilling to assume the command of a
Calvinistic popular revolt.

In Amsterdam, the great Beggar, Brederode, entered
into negotiations with the Huguenots and with friends in
England, and succeeded in collecting a small military
force. He drew up, moreover, in the name of the confederated nobles, a new petition urging the maintenance
of the accord of August 23d and permission to hold
public sermons. The regent answered that she knew
nothing of any " confederated nobles," that she had
never intended to allow public sermons, and that she
advised the nobles then gathered together to disperse
and to obey their king,—an advice that was not followed.
Now Orange had allowed all Brederode's actions to take
place before his very eyes in spite of the regent's protests. He was still waiting. Egmont meanwhile ranged
himself on the side of the government, returned all correspondence to Orange and his friends, and formally
severed his relations with them.

The prince's waiting attitude exasperated the Calvinists, who made repeated attempts to win him over to an
open espousal of their cause, but he persevered in his
position, with his eye fixed on Germany. Brederode
continued his activity, on the other hand, and his army

near Antwerp increased. The Beggars made an attempt to take Walcheren by force, but failed. Bombergen was more successful in an attack on Bois-le-duc, but Megen, the royalist stadtholder of Gelderland, also succeeded in gaining mastery of Harderwijk and Utrecht, while he seriously menaced the safety of Amsterdam and Vianen. Brederode hastened to Holland to protect his cities, and on March 13th an actual battle took place, in his absence, between the Beggars' troops under the inexperienced Thoulouse and a force of three thousand trained soldiers under the lord of Beauvoir. The Beggars had only numbers in their favour, and they were cut to pieces. Orange was blamed for this defeat, as he had, with the Lutherans' aid, held the Calvinists in check within Antwerp, when they were ready to burst out to help their brethren.[1] Eleven days later Valenciennes opened its door to Noircarmes.

With this step the revolt was practically suppressed. Brederode's own city of Vianen was held by German mercenaries under Eric of Brunswick, and the great Beggar took refuge at Emden. Several less fortunate nobles were captured as they attempted to reach Germany, delivered over to the Frisian stadtholder Aremberg, and confined at Vilvoorden.

By that time the prince too had forsaken the land. Louis had warned him not to count on German help. The Calvinists at Antwerp were furious at him and threatened his life. The regent showed no disposition to be kindly towards him. "As far as we can see, it looks as though it were up with this land," he wrote on April 9th to the landgrave of Hesse. He had one last meeting with Egmont at Willebroek, whereof legend preserves the memory in the laconic farewell words: " Adieu, landless prince "; " Adieu, headless count."

[1] Burgon, *Gresham*, ii., p. 206, " for the Martinists and the Papists grew all in one company together against the Calvinists."

Orange, after offering his resignation, left Antwerp on April 11th, first for Breda.   On the approach of Noir-carmes's troops he proceeded to Germany and took refuge in the Nassau castle at Dillenburg, pursued by the invectives of those who sympathised with the government and by the loud complaints of the Calvinists, who imputed their defeat, and not wholly unjustly, to his hesitating attitude.   To Egmont and Hoorn he wrote two very remarkable Latin letters of farewell,[1] to the latter at the castle of Weert, where he had withdrawn in November, refusing to be involved in further action. The prince considered that his rôle in the Netherlands had been played to the end.   He distrusted the Spanish king too much to witness the victory of the principles which he had contested.

Opposition was at an end.   Many cities accepted government garrisons, while preachers and religious leaders, both Calvinist and Lutheran, abandoned the country. The regent was unwilling to accord any liberty even to the Lutherans, although the German princes made special efforts in their behalf.   Such nobles as had not chosen voluntary exile sued for pardon.   Among those who fled was De Hames, who entered the imperial service in a campaign against the Turks.   Many of the magistrates who felt they had compromised themselves followed the nobles' example and left the country.

Now that tranquillity had been restored, the regent did not wish the exercise of over-severity towards the culprits. Granvelle and Pius IV. also wrote to Philip advising moderation at this crisis, advice in which Hopper, Viglius, and other counsellors of the duchess concurred.   Noir-carmes was, on the other hand, pitiless, and had many hundreds at Valenciennes put to death, among whom were De Bray and De la Grange, the courageous preachers.

Time showed speedily that Philip had no intention of

[1] *Archives*, iii., 68 *et seq.*

following the counsel of moderation, even though it came from pope, bishop, and jurist.

A placard published on May 24th[1] contained no signs of gentle methods. On the basis of placards published in July and August against preachers and iconoclasts several stipulations were repeated anew. Preachers were to be punished with the gallows, and so were those who harboured them or offered their dwellings or property for assemblies of the reformed, in so far as they were obstinate heretics. Participants in such meetings could be punished arbitrarily, whether they were only present from curiosity or as heretics, armed or unarmed. Parents, guardians, patrons, and lords were responsible for their children and wards. Any informer would be free of penalty. Iconoclasts were to be punished with all severity. All those who celebrated baptism, marriage, communion, psalm-singing, or burial, except with the rites approved by the Romish Church, should be punished with halter or sword. All pastors must keep baptismal records, with names of parents and guardians. Midwives must swear to inform the pastor if a child were not baptised within twenty-four hours. Careful supervision must be exercised by the spiritual " scholastic " and two magistrates over the schoolmasters. Any teaching of false doctrine was to be punished by loss of life and with confiscation of property. In the same way, in accordance with the placard on the press, printers, sellers, and buyers of forbidden books were all to be punished alike. Members of the consistories and the " authors " of the riots were to suffer death and the confiscation of property. Severe punishments were imposed on those who collected money without royal command. Participants in seditious assemblies were threatened with capital punishment and confiscation of property. Exiles, apostates, renegade monks, etc., " those who had come hither

[1] Bor, *Historie der Nederlantsche oorlogen*, i., p. 170. Amsterdam, 1679.

under pretext of religion," must leave the cities within twenty-four hours on pain of corporal punishment. Whoever moved from one place to another must give a paper giving the cause of the change signed by the pastor and authorities. Anyone who insulted a priest with word or deed was subject to corporal punishment and confiscation of goods. An instruction for the judges directed rigour towards the heretics, especially against the chief authors of the evil that had happened.

In the course of the summer, thousands and thousands left the land as a result of this terrible placard. East Friesland, Westphalia, the Rhinelands, the English ports, soon harboured an untold number of Netherlanders, men women, and children. The number of emigrants within thirty or forty years is reckoned at about four hundred thousand.[1] Many Calvinists from the south settled in the palatinate at Heidelberg and Frankenthal, and many more on Cleves territory.

The king was determined to have nothing more to do with any " amelioration " of placards. The time had come to show a strong hand. He let it be understood that he was coming himself to reform the Netherlands into a kingdom like Castile, wholly subordinate to royal authority. Nor did Philip intend to leave a woman longer at the helm. His spies in the provinces, Alonzo del Canto, the controller of finances at Antwerp, and the Augustinian monk, Lorenzo de Villavicencio, at Bruges had cast suspicion upon Margaret. Philip was advised to draw the sword from the scabbard, and to drench it in heretics' blood. He was urged to avenge the insult to the Church. At the end of 1566, the regent was informed that the chosen instrument of vengeance was to be the duke of Alva, who was to come as captain-general, to do what she refused or hesitated to execute.

Margaret protested vehemently against this measure

[1] Leyden University Library *Pamphlets*, No. 127.

and threatened to resign, but did not succeed in moving
the king.   The plan for his own coming was abandoned
on the score of his health, while preparations were pushed
on for Alva's expedition.   The duke journeyed north by
way of Italy, and gathered from the Spanish garrisons of
Naples and Milan and from a newly levied Italian regiment a force of eight thousand infantry and two thousand
cavalry under the command of the skilled officers, Alfonso
de Ulloa, Sancho de Londoño, Julian Romero, Gonsalvo
de Braccamonte for the infantry, Ferdinand of Toledo and
Chiappino Vitelli for the cavalry, while further Sancho
d'Avila, Christopher de Mondragon, Basta, Avalos, and
other distinguished colonels accompanied the duke.

In June, this well-equipped army of the "Black Beards,"
one of the most brilliant of the century, left Italy and
reached Luxemburg by August.   On the 22d of the
same month, Alva entered Brussels in state, fully conscious of the import of his mission.

Then in truth the tragedy was to begin whose approach
the prince of Orange had pictured when the letters arrived
from Segovia.

CHAPTER I

A N oppressive atmosphere hung over the Netherlands in the summer of 1567.

The nobles had receded from their first attitude of independence. Many, and there were some Catholics among them, had followed the example of the prince of Orange and withdrawn to Germany to avoid the vengeance of the government.

The majority, however, of the Catholic members of the Compromise had turned to the rising sun. They exerted themselves to win the regent's favour, while she showed a certain humility in her bearing towards the doughty duke. The high clergy, suddenly spurred to action, longed to avenge the insults offered to their church and to root out heresy. The new bishops considered that the moment was come to reform the existing abuses upon the basis of the decrees of Trent.

The burgher class felt a sense of insecurity. Commerce and industry had been affected by the riots and by emigration. In the summer of 1566, business had practically been at a standstill. Market and bourse were disturbed. By the spring many more or less compromised merchants, even magistrates,—Lutherans and Calvinists,—had taken refuge in England, in Emden, Wesel, Cologne, and in more remote spots. The English merchants considered transferring the staple to Hamburg as a safer place.

Among the workpeople, too, there had been much emigration. The severity of Noircarmes at Valenciennes had a speedy effect. Many renounced their homes and betook themselves to Norwich, Sandwich, Colchester, Maidstone, Southampton, and other English towns where the cloth industry made great advances. Fishermen and others too followed this example. Some joined the so-called " forest Beggars,"—the remnants of the Calvinist troops chased out by Noircarmes and Beauvoir, increased by the country people and others. These outlaws lurked in inaccessible places in forests and morasses of Flanders, and made raids now and then upon lonely convents and farms.

What was to be done ? Alva's presence spread alarm in France among the Huguenots as well as in the Netherlands. A juncture of Spanish and French forces to suppress all heresy was feared. On his first arrival, however, the duke seemed inclined to accept the regent's representations that leniency would now be the safest policy. He received both Egmont and Hoorn in a pleasant fashion and took pains to be agreeable to the prince's son, the count of Buren, then a student at Louvain. The prince was encouraged by this unexpected graciousness and wrote a letter of welcome to the duke.[1]

But the graciousness was short-lived. On September 20th, the first session of a new court of justice was held, which destroyed all hopes of leniency. Alva established a so-called " Council of Troubles," consisting of the Spaniard, Juan de Vargas, the Spanish Netherlander Louis del Rio, Noircarmes, Berlaymont, and five well-known Netherland jurists. The purpose was to deal in a summary manner with all cases of rebellion against Philip's established government in the Netherlands, to punish the heretics and the iconoclasts of 1566.

Before the first meeting of this council extraordinary,

[1] Kervyn de Lettenhove, *Documents inédits sur le 16ᵐᵉ siecle*, p. 45.

some arrests extraordinary had taken place.   On September 9th, the counts of Egmont and of Hoorn had been summarily made prisoners of state at a banquet given by Ferdinand of Toledo, Alva's illegitimate son, on the charge of treason.   On the same day, the burgomaster of Antwerp, Van Straalen, a devoted adherent of the prince of Orange, and the secretaries of the two suspected counts were also arrested.   From that day Alva discarded his outward show of friendliness and proceeded to handle affairs without gloves.

The regent was ignored in the matters of the arrests and of the disposition of the two noble prisoners in the citadel of Ghent.   There was but one authority in the land.   In the beginning of October, this autocracy was confirmed by Alva's formal appointment as Philip's deputy, and in December by the departure of Margaret from Brussels.   The ex-regent again warned her successor of the danger of his policy, but her words fell on empty ears.   Philip's directions were to be carried out to the letter by his new lieutenant.

The Council of Troubles went directly to work.   An investigation was instituted into the details of the events of the past two years.   Suits were begun against the absent Orange, Louis of Nassau, the counts of Hoogstraaten, Culemborg, Van den Bergh, and Brederode, as well as against the prisoners in hand.   There were daily new arrests of iconoclasts, preachers, members of consistories, suspects in general.   By March 3, 1568, the number of accused persons reached five hundred.   Sentences were pronounced rapidly.   In January, eighty-four inhabitants of Valenciennes were condemned to death and their property confiscated.   Others were sentenced in groups of thirty, forty, fifty at a time.   The court was popularly termed the " Council of Blood," and deserved its name.   All its members, however, did not manifest the same zeal.   Vargas and Del Rio alone fulfilled Alva's expectations; the others rebelled, occasionally, at the methods enforced by the new regent.

Terror spread over the land. No one was safe from the accusations of personal enemies and of venal informers. Yet no one ventured to raise a voice of protest, no one dared to assert that the ancient privileges of the land were infringed. The new council paid no heed to the *jus de non evocando* which provided for trial on the native soil of the accused. Hollander and Fleming alike were summoned to Brussels, and the cherished charters were ignored.

In January the prince and a number of other gentlemen were solemnly cited to appear before this court. The fact that knights of the Fleece must be tried by their peers was regarded as little in their cases as in those of Egmont and Hoorn. Then followed a series of sentences of perpetual banishment and confiscation of goods pronounced against Marnix, Brederode, and the petty nobles. The young count of Buren was actually shipped off to Spain, university privileges being ignored like those of the provinces. "*Non curamus privilegios vestros*," Vargas was wont to declare in barbarous Latin.

From Dillenburg the prince issued, on March 4, 1568, an eloquent protest against the kidnapping of his son and against his own indictment. But his and similar protests [1] were as air to Alva. The leaders of the disaffection must be punished. Such was the demand of both king and lieutenant, although the latter seems to have hesitated a little concerning Egmont, whom he held in high esteem as a distinguished warrior, as conqueror of Gravelines.

The prince of Orange now finally took a decisive step and assumed arms, reckoning on aid at home and abroad.

The prevailing discontent in the Netherlands, the growing hatred against Alva, the bitterness of those still

[1] These are printed by Bor with those of the prince and other documents of the day at the end of the first part of his *Oorsprongh*, etc.

secretly adhering to Calvinism, the personal popularity of both Egmont and of the prince seemed to be gages of his success in obtaining the support of the population to resist the hangmen who were administering the king's government. Was he not sovereign prince of Orange, and thus justified in taking arms against a fellow sovereign, be it even the king of Spain ? He counted on the support of the Lutheran princes, of the Huguenot leaders, of Queen Elizabeth of England, and on the coöperation of the Netherland exiles. Some of the last were in Condé's camps; some were gaining an unenviable reputation as sea Beggars, leading a piratical existence at the cost of friend and foe; others again — Brederode [1] and Hoogstraaten among them — waited at Emden, Wesel, Cologne, and elsewhere for the least sign from the prince to make a strike at Alva. In the early spring many of the noble fugitives took a written pledge of an alliance to " free the fatherland, liberate the prisoners from the claws of the ill-wishers who were bringing Netherlanders to frightful punishments, their property to confiscation, their children to beggary." [2] Subscription lists were added to the manifest, which Brederode and his friends headed with large contributions.

In the early part of 1568, the refugees in England and the forest Beggars in Brabant made some demonstration. No concerted effort, however, could be made without money, and that was difficult to obtain as the exiles were cut off from the enjoyment of their own revenues. Finally, sums were collected with great difficulty and the opening of a campaign was planned for the early summer. Louis of Nassau was to cross the Ems and make his way to Holland by way of Groningen and Friesland. In Gelderland the count of Hoogstraaten was to lay siege to Roermond and prepare a way over the

---

[1] In February he died suddenly in a castle at Recklinghausen.
[2] Te Water *Het Verbond der Edelen*, ii., p. 109.

Meuse for the prince himself, who was then to press into Brabant. The sea Beggars were to coöperate with Louis at the mouth of the Ems,[1] a body of Huguenots under De Cocqueville were to attack Artois, while assistance on the coast was expected from the Netherland refugees in England.

Sancho d'Avila easily repulsed the Roermond enterprise. Hoogstraaten's troops, under De Villiers, were defeated at Daelhem on April 25th. Villiers was captured and forced to give information regarding the prince's plans.

Louis of Nassau met better success. At the end of April he pressed into Groningen, his little force augmented to about eight thousand men by accessions of Germans, Walloons, and emigrants. On May 23d, a pitched battle occurred at Heiligerlee, which resulted in the defeat of the royalist troops and the death of Count Aremberg, Alva's stadtholder. On the other side, Adolph of Nassau, the prince's third brother, perished.

The way appeared open to Louis. Armed peasants, encouraged by his victory, flocked to his standard, which bore the legends *Nunc aut nunquam*, " Now or never," and *Recuperare aut mori*, " Win or die." The prince begged his brother not to delay before Groningen, but to press on to Holland. Louis disregarded this advice, and by laying siege to the well-defended city gave Alva opportunity to take measures to recover from the defeat.

Before setting out to vindicate Philip's honour and authority in the north, the lieutenant-governor wished to leave matters secure in the capital. He feared sympathy for his illustrious prisoners. Informed of the prince's plans of campaign, by De Villiers's confession, he determined to take measures which should effectually prevent an uprising in Brabant and probable rescue of Egmont

---

[1] See Blok's *Lodewijk van Nassau*, p. 60 *et seq.*

and Hoorn.   Therefore, he hurried through their trials, or rather he conducted farces under the name of trials. The conclusion was foregone.   On June 5th, the sentence of capital punishment for treason against their sovereign was executed upon the two counts.   Their heads fell on the scaffold in the great square at Brussels.   The populace, barely grasping what had taken place, showed their sympathy for the martyrs by thronging up to the scaffold to dip their handkerchiefs in the blood and to press kisses upon the coffins.   Egmont did not relinquish hopes that mediation might come from the knights of the Fleece, or pardon from the king, until the very last moment.   His trust was vain, for the king had repeatedly urged Alva to end his hesitation and inflict the long-prepared death sentence upon the prisoners.

Universal was the alarm, widespread the terror.   The popular songs were full of it.   Numerous pamphlets in French and German, scattered over Europe, published the details of the execution of the sentence, and awakened pity for the fate of the victims.   Even Alva told the king that " it had hurt him in his soul."[1]   Vargas alone said coolly that it was " a useful thing " and a " good example."   The last did not admit of doubt.   The population of the Netherlands was undoubtedly paralysed with terror, and thus rendered inactive.

This was precisely the result Alva hoped to effect. He proceeded to declare Orange condemned by default, his property confiscated.   He was then free to hasten to the north.   Among other confiscations was that of the estates of Montigny, the luckless envoy to Spain.   He lingered on two years in captivity and was then murdered.   His fellow envoy, De Berghes, died of disease before this date.

On Alva's approach at the head of a strong disciplined force, Louis of Nassau raised the siege of Groningen and

[1] Reiffenberg, *Cor. de Marg. de Parma*, p. 253.

retreated towards the Ems.   Alva pursued him, and upon
the borders of that river was fought the battle of Jemmingen, disastrous indeed for the Nassaus.   The lieutenant-governor succeeded in cutting the little force to
pieces.   Louis escaped to Germany with a few followers.

The undertaking of the Huguenots in Artois had failed
too, and no troops were left to the patriots but the force
under the prince of Orange.   After the success of Heiligerlee there had been manifestations of sympathy
throughout the Netherlands very encouraging to the
active rebels.   Now all hope of coöperation was killed.

Meanwhile the prince had issued manifestoes and appeals, in French and in Dutch, urging the Netherlanders
to defend their own.   He declared he was loyal to the
king, that it was Alva's tyranny alone which he proposed
to resist.   *Pro lege, rege, grege*, " For the law, the king,
the people," was the legend upon his standard.

On October 7th, the prince's force actually crossed the
Meuse near Stockhem, a feat which excited Alva's surprise.   " Is the prince's army a flock of wild geese ? " he
exclaimed when he heard the tidings.   The passage was,
according to some authorities, accomplished by placing
a heavy mass of cavalry in the stream to break the force
of the current, so that some protection was given to the
foot soldiers.   It was the one brilliant incident of the
campaign, which otherwise proved a wild-goose chase.

Alva's tactics were to refuse battle while constantly
worrying the enemy, and thus to gain time until the
coming of winter and lack of money rendered it impossible for the force to hold together.   He was successful.
No Brabant city offered shelter to their invading friends,
the prince's money came to an end, and the hard winter
of 1568–69 proved a faithful ally to Philip's lieutenant-
governor.[1]   The bishop of Liege refused to allow the
prince to recross the river near his capital.   As he marched

[1] *Archives*, iii., p. 211.

through Hainaut, Alva pursued him, and a sanguinary skirmish took place near Quesnoy. It was a disorganised force that finally succeeded in reaching French soil to make a junction with their Huguenot friends. Discouragement met them. The king of France protested against their presence in his realm, while the German mercenaries cried for their pay and disbandment. The prince led the Germans down to Strasburg, where he melted his last plate to satisfy in some measure his clamorous men, and let them go.

Then, with only twelve hundred horse, Orange, accompanied by his two brothers, Louis and Henry, turned southward, and marched straight through France to join the Huguenots, who were barely holding their own in Gascony against their opponents.

In the spring of 1569, this brilliant campaign with the army of the duke of Deux Ponts, who had the command, somewhat retrieved the prince's military reputation, but did not advance his own prospects. The future looked dark. Alva could well consider himself lord and master in the Netherland provinces. Philip counted himself perfectly assured in his position and able to ignore all protests, imperial and otherwise, against his infringement of privileges. The emperor retreated from his feeble attempts to assert the rights of members of the empire, when he was tempted by a new family alliance with the Spanish monarch. The death of Philip's heir, Don Carlos, in July, 1568, and of Philip's wife in the autumn, opened new dynastic possibilities, and the emperor, although personally interested in the affair of the Netherlanders, was unwilling to offend Philip by further efforts in their behalf.

Nor could aid be expected from France or from England. The defeat of the Huguenots at Jarnac in March and again at Moncontour in October, were heavy blows. In October, too, Orange took refuge in Dillenburg, and the Spaniards felt relieved that he was no longer a present element in the French situation.

Elizabeth of England, too, who had coquetted with the Huguenots and the prince, now began to evince a friendliness for Spain, and even offered Philip the king her good wishes in his contest with his rebels. To be sure, this friendliness was soon marred by the revival of old-time quarrels about commercial questions and piracy, but Alva did not anticipate open war as a result of these disagreements.

The prince and his confidants at Aachen, in Jülich, Cologne, Nassau, and East Friesland under protection of the Protestant or semi-Protestant princes, in England, in the Huguenot armies, all alike found themselves forced to await the outcome of the future. Meantime pamphlets setting forth the justice of their cause were scattered broadcast over Europe. One Jacob van Wesenbeke, ex-pensionary of Antwerp, refugee in Germany, did good service with his pen. His famous brochure, "*La description de l'estat, succès et occurrences advenues au Pais-Bas au faict de la religion*,"[1] speedily translated into Dutch, gave a detailed account of the events of 1566. It declared that the prince and his friends had not lost heart, that Orange was true to the promises of the *Wilhelmuslied*. This song, generally ascribed, though without sufficient ground, to Marnix, and set to an old French melody, in these years assured the "poor sheep who are in sorry need that their shepherd will not sleep although ye are scattered."

Another remarkable treatise written at this period is a sharp attack on the Catholic Church by Marnix in his *Beehive of the Holy Roman Church*, wherein the talented author unsparingly laid bare the failings of the ancient faith according to the views of an ultra-Calvinist of that time.

---

[1] See Bakhuizen van den Brink, *Studien en Schetsen*, i., pp. 255–281.

Meanwhile the Beggars of the sea, caring little for the prince's admonitions, though many had received commissions from him, made the North Sea insecure, and occasionally raided the seaside villages, churches, and cloisters, and sold their booty in England or East Friesland, Hamburg or Bremen.   Protests by the government at Brussels to German princes and cities which offered shelter to the Netherland refugees availed little.   Both English ports and coasts and the above-named princes and cities reaped too much profit from the presence of the Netherlanders and the sale of the booty to drive them away from their soil.

There were theological differences among the exiles. The " orthodox " of Emden were mainly from Holland, Friesland, and Groningen, and were not averse to the Augsburg confession.   Those who had fled to the Palatinate came, as a rule, from the southern Netherlands, and, with Dathenus as their leader, would not hear of any accord with the Lutherans, and distrusted the prince of Orange upon this point.[1]

The duke of Alva enjoyed the fruits of his victories. He made a triumphal entry into Brussels after the prince's unsuccessful campaign.   He then proceeded to have a statue made from the cannon captured at Jemmingen, representing himself as conqueror with his foot upon a two-headed monster—nobles and people of the Netherlands.   The monument bore an inscription in elegant Latin, vaunting the suppression of the revolt by himself, " faithful servant of the best of kings."   But he did not rest content with this glorification.   He determined to make a substantial harvest.   The moment seemed favourable for the imposition of new financial burdens upon the Netherlanders.   The nine-year tribute pledged to the king in 1558 had expired, and it was again time to assure a full treasury for a series of years.   According to custom,

---

[1] Compare Fruin, *De voorbereiding in de ballingschap*, etc., p. 17.

this could only be done by a convention of the States-General, a step which the strong government now did not need to dread. Alva resolved to convene them accordingly.

Meanwhile the good understanding between the duke and the court at Madrid had been more or less shaken. In Spain, Alva's old opponent Ruy Gomez; in the Netherlands, Hopper and Viglius; in Rome, the pope and Granvelle, all united in protesting against the severity of his proceedings.[1] Philip was not unmoved by the representations made to him. In February, 1569, he let Alva understand that he was ready for a general amnesty now that all revolt was crushed in the provinces. It was, however, not until the following July that Alva published the king's proclamation, which was accompanied by a papal bull promising forgiveness to all who returned to the bosom of the church. Meantime the Council of Troubles continued their hangman's work,— at least the Spanish members did. Finally it was forced to publish the amnesty. The difficulties encountered by Alva in pushing through his financial schemes, too, undoubtedly affected the delay in the measure for mercy.

He wished to introduce direct taxation in order to avoid in future the convention of the States-General customary under the Burgundian princes.

In Castile a similar system of fixed taxation had existed since the middle of the fourteenth century under the name of *alcabala*.[2] By the end of the fifteenth century this had changed from a percentage on sales to a direct imposition. The assessment upon the population of the districts was left to the district officials. Such an arrangement of taxation between government and subjects was termed *encabezamiento*, or capitalisation. Under Charles

[1] See *Documentos inéditos para la historia de España*, v., 35, 36.
[2] Häbler, *Die wirtschaftliche Blüte Spaniens im 16 Jahrh.* Berlin, 1888.

V. the government had at first imposed the taxes.   This
encabezamiento was adopted at the instance of the Castilian
Cortes and, by the end of Charles's administration, this
capitalisation was the ordinary form in which the alcabala was paid.   Philip introduced the alcabala into the
colonies first with a low percentage, two per cent., which
was repeatedly increased even in Castile.

Alva now urged upon Philip the introduction of a
similar system in the Netherlands.   In the last years
money had actually been sent from Spain for Netherland
use instead of the provinces furnishing supplies to the
royal treasure.   He proposed an imposition of ten per
cent. on all transfers of commodities, five per cent. on
transfers of real estate.

This " tenth penny " was not a wholly new institution
in the Netherlands.   It had been imposed in 1543, 1552,
1562, and 1565, but always as an imposition extraordinary, and one acknowledged as difficult to raise.   On
March 26, Alva convened the States-General and expounded his proposition.   In addition to the above-mentioned imposts he also asked for the direct imposition
of a hundredth penny on all property, real and personal.

The governor's manner of treating the States-General
was arbitrary and arrogant.   He would permit none of
the discussion between the deputies of separate provinces
as a whole or individually, which had been customary
under Charles V.   In a tone unheard by the States since
the days of Charles the Bold, Alva ordered the deputies
to submit to the king's will without reservation.   Nevertheless various of the provinces ventured to hesitate; in
some this hesitation was confined to the " third estate,"
the burghers, while nobles and clergy showed a greater
willingness to yield.

Alva now began to treat with the provinces individually.
He threatened reluctant cities with loss of privileges or
with garrisons.   These arguments proved effective in

part, and the duke finally consented to a certain compromise. The hundredth penny was promised for six
years, while the imposition of the tenth penny was
bought off with a cash sum of two million guilders paid
in the form of the capitalisation customary in Castile.
But the matter was not settled with these promises.
Many and various difficulties arose in regard to the payments. Some provinces recommended less oppressive
forms of taxation; in others the nobles and cities disagreed; others said that they were rated too high in the
assessment of their share of the whole contribution;
others made their consent dependent on that of Flanders.
Finally the duke, weary of the discussion, recurred to his
proposition of the imposition of two million annually.
He now restricted this to two years, terminating with
August, 1571. Again there was opposition, met by the
duke with threats, which in Flanders was alternated with
various concessions.

The history of the long-drawn-out negotiations showed
that there was little hope of adjustment without radical
change in the financial arrangements of the provinces.
Alva determined to put an end to all traditional usages
and to regulate the financial relations of sovereign and
states definitely according to his own theories.

It is not surprising that Philip and Alva cherished this
desire. A good financial administration is absolutely
necessary for a strong monarchical government. And it
is even less surprising that the provincial Estates opposed
the measure in every possible way. The existing arrangement, bad as it was, still left the purse-strings in the hands
of the assemblies. The new plan would deprive them for
good of any check upon the national government. Moreover, it could not be denied that the tenth penny would
seriously hamper commerce, especially petty commerce.
The bitterest opposition to this tax was in the great trade
centres of Flanders, Brabant, and Holland. It was, in

general, in the " third estate " in the cities, while nobles
and clergy cared less. The merchants protested that
their credit would be ruined by the ordinary imposition
of the tenth penny. Still the manner in which a compromise was finally made really justified Alva's opinion
that the actual right of the sovereign to the tenth penny
was not denied, but rather confirmed.[1] He determined
to return to it after the expiration of two years.

There was another scheme that the duke had greatly
at heart. He wished to unite the provinces into that
one indissoluble kingdom dreamed of by former Burgundian princes. The moment seemed favourable for the
prosecution of this scheme.

Before Philip's departure in 1559 this had been discussed. One kingdom, one capital, one church, one
army, one national law; municipal spirit and individual-
ism curbed in every particular, and one nation, general
submission to one will, had been the scheme.

Now the plan was more comprehensive.[2] Not only
the Burgundian Netherland provinces but the neighbouring portions of the German empire were to come under
Spanish influence. East Friesland, Jülich, Munster,
Cologne, Aachen, Treves, trembled before the Spaniard
and saw their independence assailed. The Spanish regent
repeatedly demanded the banishment of the Netherland
refugees, the total suppression of heresy, etc. Even in
Dillenburg and the Palatinate there was some anxiety,
which was echoed in Hesse and Saxony.

By 1570, many steps had been taken towards the desired
unity. The bishops were effecting improvement in
ecclesiastical conditions and thereby strengthening the
influence of the church; plans for citadels in the cities
were under way; the state arsenal was in force at

---

[1] See Bakhuizen van den Brink, *Cartons*, p. 119.

[2] *Archives*, Supplement, p. 73*. A plan, probably that of Hopper, is
given in full.

Mechlin; the duke had demanded written copies of existing privileges and usages of the various provinces, and had
a draft drawn up by his jurists, which was the basis of the
famous Criminal Ordinance of July, 1570, designed to be
the criminal statute-book of the new kingdom; the universal pardon, the amnesty of 1570, also came into being;
various nobles received commanderies; in the interest
of Netherland commerce relations with England were
brought on a better footing in 1570, although mutual
distrust still remained.

Before the plan was realised in its entirety, however, it
was destined to be pushed into the background by new
complications.

The measures for unification aroused the greatest opposition. Ancient privileges in all legal, military, and
ecclesiastical details were dear possessions. The Netherlanders were afraid of citadels bristling over the land.[1]
The activity of the Council of Troubles, the repeated
efforts to impose the hated tenth penny, cast suspicion
upon the intentions of the government. The demand for
copies of their precious privileges aroused fear of their
revocation. The prohibition to seek other universities
than Louvain, Douay, or Rome; the punishment inflicted
on the poor wives of the exiles who maintained correspondence with their husbands, the renewed search for
culprits, drove many more into exile. The renewed
publication of the " blood placards " boded little good.

The impression made by the penalties and the unfortunate campaigns of 1568 began to weaken as the dissatisfaction increased. The relations here and there secretly
maintained with the prince of Orange and other exiles
fed the fire of discontent.

In 1570, the refugees in Germany, who had hitherto
preserved silence, presented a petition at the diet of

---

[1] At Amsterdam the scheme was bought off for 200,000 florins. At
Groningen Robles began to build. Pachieco made the plans for Flushing.

Spiers, in the name of their native provinces, begging emperor and empire to free them from the unbearable yoke of persecution.   But the words fell flat on imperial ears.   Philip II. had just married the daughter of the emperor, who could not venture to espouse the cause of his son-in-law's enemies.

The vaunted amnesty made slight impression upon the land.   In May, 1570, four pastors were burned in The Hague, and soon the fagot blazed everywhere again. The so-called pardon was greeted by the populace with the doggerel lines:

> "Oh, your pardon we don't heed,
>   It is vain deception.
> Ours will come from God himself," etc.[1]

In addition to the ills inflicted by man, the Netherland population in these darkest times suffered frightfully from inundations which swept over the land as the result of a severe storm.   Friesland was the chief sufferer, twenty thousand being the estimate of the people lost there and in Groningen, but the ports in Flanders and the adjacent country, as far as Ghent and Bruges, were also seriously affected.   In Zealand more than three thousand persons were drowned.   In Holland, especially along the Meuse, many perished from the bursting of the dykes, one hundred and twenty-eight homes being swept away at Scheveningen alone.[2]

The prince of Orange, after his misfortunes of 1568, was considered by the government as wholly innocuous and no longer an element to be feared.   Nevertheless he was busily employed throughout this period of apparent inaction in making plans for the future.   His secret agents were everywhere in the Netherlands, urging the people not to lose heart, and collecting from congregations and scattered sympathisers money for a new

[1] Van Vloten, *Geschiedzangen*, i., p. 378.   [2] Bor, p. 330.

campaign. An extensive secret correspondence was maintained between these agents and the prince. Discovery was guarded against by a use of classic names to designate cities, of pseudonyms for individuals, and of the signs of the Zodiac for months. This system was perhaps designed by John Basius, the prince's secretary, who was very zealous in the matter. Other valuable auxiliaries still remaining in the Netherlands, were the Holland nobleman Adriaan van Swieten and Paul Buys, pensionary of Leyden.

The leader in the relations with Holland and the Sticht was the Walloon nobleman Diedrich Sonoy, to whom the prince gave a new commission on February 8, 1570, empowering him to raise funds. This he did mainly through the Calvinist preachers who managed to keep their congregations together secretly. Jacob van Wesenbeke was another valuable coadjutor who maintained communication in the various cities, collecting money and planning for the surprise of certain places with coöperation from across the borders.

The prince, too, kept constantly in touch with the Beggars of the sea. But they were an unruly set, and many of their piratical operations reflected little credit on the commission they bore. Neither their admirals, Dolhain and Lumbres, nor their captains, Lancelot, bastard of Brederode, or William de Lumey from the famous house of La Mark, were able to maintain order. The Beggars plundered freely, and found market for their stolen goods in England and at La Rochelle, the famous Huguenot port in France.

The hope constantly cherished by the prince's followers was that Deventer, Utrecht, or Nimwegen could be surprised and a centre for operations obtained. Orange then proposed to coöperate with Germany, assume his ancient stadtholderships in the king's name, and lead an organised revolt against Alva at the head of the

Calvinists, a step he had hesitated to take in 1566 and
1568.

That hesitation of former years was, however, one of
the reasons why the Calvinists feared to trust him in
1570.   They were entirely unwilling to adopt the Augsburg confession, and they dreaded Lutheran influence.
In the winter 1570–71, however, their confidence in the
prince was increased by the fact that he took the zealous Calvinist, Philip Marnix, into his personal service.
In 1571 a synod held at Emden adopted, after some
difficulties, Guy de Bray's confession of faith, which was
also accepted by the Hollanders on the basis of church
doctrine.   This was an important decision which affected
the later Calvinist movement.   It was a victory of the
so-called " precisians," although many others continued
to hold more liberal opinions.   This step satisfied one
party, but it alienated, in a measure, the Lutheran German princes.   Action did not seem any nearer, for money
came in very slowly.   Merchants were not inclined to
make ventures on such uncertain returns.   To be sure,
on December 9, 1570, the stronghold of Loevestein was
surprised and taken by the prince's agent, Herman de
Ruyter.   But he was not reinforced and was unable to
keep his prize, so that his feat, brilliant as it was, counted
for nothing.   To escape capture he himself set fire to
the powder in the castle and perished with friends and
foes in the explosion.

The prince's position, hopeless as it was, was rendered
more difficult by the conduct of his wife, Anne of
Saxony.   After being so far unfaithful to her husband's
cause as to offer her own submission to Alva repeatedly,
she proved also unfaithful as a wife,[1] and in March, 1571,
was secluded a prisoner in Dillenburg.   The prince, too,
was in constant danger of assassination at the hands of

[1] With the father of the artist Rubens. See Bakhuizen van den Brink,
Het huwelijk van Willem van Oranje.

Alva's hirelings; but in spite of all he preserved his courage and continued his correspondence with his friends.

From the side of France the prospect at last began to brighten. In the peace of St. Germain, August, 1570, civil war was ended in France. Louis of Nassau, himself a declared Calvinist, an intimate friend of the noble Huguenot Coligny, and a great favourite among the Huguenots, came into prominence through this peace. One of the articles moreover stipulated the restoration of the principality of Orange to the prince, who in latter years had enjoyed little more of his French possessions than his princely title.

Great hopes were entertained of persuading the young French king, Charles IX., to assume arms against Spain. His mother, Catherine de Médicis, seemed not averse to the project. In the summer of 1571, Louis of Nassau and his friends were very active in working out a plan of coöperation between sympathisers in the Netherlands, in Germany, in England, where Elizabeth showed some friendliness. The betrothal of Margaret of Valois, sister of Charles IX., to the Huguenot, Henry of Navarre, apparently sealed these hopes with the signet of certainty. Again the prince planned to cross the Meuse with a new force maintained by German and French money. The sea Beggars were ready to descend upon Holland and gain a city for the prince's headquarters. In the summer of 1572, attacks were to be made from every vantage point.

Alva was ill prepared for all this. The difficulties of his position had greatly increased. Pursued by personal hatred everywhere in the Netherlands, by dislike which found utterance occasionally in bitter pasquils, his enemies had gained Philip's ear in Spain, and he received very cold support from his king, who also refused to recall him from his charge. He had antagonised Netherland officials like Viglius and Hopper by persisting in the persecutions, and his only supporters were

Spaniards like Vargas and Roda. It was under these circumstances that in August, 1571, he reverted to his scheme, postponed in 1569, of increasing royal revenues by the imposition of the tenth penny.

The term of postponement for which so much had been paid was at an end, and now a large sum—the figure of fifty million is mentioned—was required. On July 31st, Alva issued a placard announcing the imposition and declaring that the consent of the States had been implied two years previously. The provincial Estates immediately assembled and protested. The deputies urged measures less injurious to commerce. A new convention of the States-General was demanded, but Alva was determined not to permit that. He insisted peremptorily that his will should be obeyed. But in the intervening two years the effect of his voice had weakened. It was known that he was in some disfavour with Philip; rumours began to come from France of the proposed action against Spain, and the opponents to Philip's will did not lose heart. Appeal after appeal, statement after statement, and deputation after deputation were despatched to Spain to point out to the king the deleterious effect of this method of taxation upon a commercial nation. Much was hoped from the hostility between Ruy Gomez, the king's near adviser, and Alva, his distant lieutenant. In Brussels, in the spring of 1572, the guilds began to venture on hostile demonstrations against the Spanish garrisons, the shops were shut by hundreds as a protest against the tenth penny, and the lower classes of the population began to suffer seriously from the cessation of manufacture. Vague rumours were current of a design to make a sudden attack on everything Spanish, of a Netherland vesper, which tended to increase the general uneasiness.

The raids of the sea Beggars meanwhile were unceasing. The islands of the north, Ameland, Terschelling,

Texel, Wieringen, suffered repeatedly; Monnikendam, Workum, the Frisian convents along the coast, Petten, and other villages on the coast were attacked and plundered. All the dwellers near the sea suffered and no one dared offer resistance; nay, more than that, the Beggars were actually sheltered by the peasants from measures taken against them by the Spanish governors, by Robles in Friesland and Groningen, by Bossu in Holland. Piratical operations received no check until Bossu's admiral, Boshuizen, succeeded in capturing eight ships and a hundred freebooters. But the thinned ranks of the Beggars were soon reinforced from England, and the piracies and raids began anew.

In February Philip's final orders arrived in respect to the financial measures. The taxes were to be raised according to the scheme proposed. Alva published the despatch triumphantly.

The agitation increased throughout the land. Protests and appeals were showered anew upon Philip. Noteworthy among these documents was a statement by the three bishops of Flanders, wherein it was urged that the tax of the tenth penny fell mainly on the lower class and would be exceedingly detrimental to commerce. Even Alva was not strong enough to withstand the storm of indignation. On February 26, 1572, a placard was published which gave a slight alleviation to the situation. All raw materials and all cloths and silks sold at wholesale were declared exempt. A slight tax only was imposed on goods for foreign markets. On account of the bad harvest of 1571 all imposts on grain and other victuals were deferred for one year. In spite of concessions, however, the tenth penny remained oppressive, especially to petty traders. Statistics for Brussels and Louvain show that all meats were taxed three times as high as formerly. So the bitterness increased and found voice in such rhymes as:

> "Oh, Netherland, thou art in straits,
> Death and life are at thy gates.
>   Serve Spanish tyrants if you will,
> Or follow, you and all your mates,
>   The prince of Orange still !
> Help him to be your guide and stay
> Or aid the wolf to gain his prey,
>   But quit your neutralising ;
> Abjure the despot's cruel sway
>   With all its tyrannising ! "

The time was ripe.   So felt the adherents of the prince; so he felt himself.   " If we only had money, we might hope with God's help to achieve something." [1] This crisis was also perceived by some of the advocates of the king's authority.   Granvelle exclaimed grimly: " Happy are those who died without having witnessed the ills which are before the door and which we may expect at any moment." [2]

The critical moment had indeed arrived.   Suddenly, like a thunderclap, came the tidings that Briel was in the hands of the Beggars.   This was as unexpected to the prince's party, to himself in Germany, and to his brother in Paris, as it was to Alva.

What had really happened ?   As already said, the Beggars of the sea had found shelter in their piratical raids for themselves and their booty not only in the sequestered nooks of Friesland but in the English and German harbours.   Dover and Emden were open to them.   Alva's complaints to queen, emperor, and imperial princes resulted in occasional warnings by these several sovereigns to the freebooters to keep out of their ports.

In the spring of 1572, in consequence of an intimation from Elizabeth that his presence was undesirable, Lumey left the English coasts with about fifty vessels of various

---

[1] Bor, i., p. 362.   [2] *Archives*, Supplement, p. 112.*

kinds which had collected together in connection with certain plans of Count Louis.[1]

Lumey was accompanied by his vice-admiral the Groningen noble, Barthold Entens of Mentheda, besides William of Blois-Treslong, Jacob Cabeliau, Nicholas Ruichaver, Roobol, Oom Hedding, Marinus Brand, and other more or less famous pirates of the time. On April 1st, the wind drove them into the mouth of the Meuse. They learned that Briel was without a garrison, approached it with a couple of hundred men, set fire to the gates, and pressed into the startled city.

The raiders began at once to carry off their plunder to their ships with the intention of sailing away again, when Lumey, at Treslong's instance, who had many friends in Voorne, where his father had been bailiff, determined to maintain the position he had gained and to stay in Briel for the purpose of holding the city for the prince, his patron.

Neither Louis nor the prince was pleased at this step, which was considered premature. They, however, awaited further developments and hastened preparations to strike a blow from their side.

In Holland the impression made by the capture of Briel was deep. The prince's adherents began to show signs of life everywhere, thinking that this action had been taken at his behest. Alva, not grasping the significance of the event, at once sent troops to Flushing to protect the island of Walcheren, but the city, the prince's ancient possession, refused to accept the royal garrison, while it opened their doors to the Beggars. The refugees flocked thither, too, under the prince's trusty equerry, Jerome T'Seraerts. Other troops, English and French companies among them, soon ventured to show themselves in Zealand and Flanders.

[1] *Hist. Man. Comm.*, 13th Rapp., App., iv., p. 3, etc. See further, *Athenæum*, 1895, No. 3545, and *Calendar of State Papers*, Foreign and Domestic Series, and Spanish papers of this time.

Events now moved quickly. Bossu, the prince's successor as royal stadtholder of Holland, Zealand, and
Utrecht, at once took measures to drive away the Beggars
with his trained soldiers.   He soon found that this was
no light task.   The Beggars not only held their own but
gained ground, and soon Voorne and a great portion of
Walcheren were in their hands.   Some secret aid was
given by England; from France came Huguenot volun-
teers, while sympathisers within the provinces were still
timid in declaring themselves.

Meanwhile Louis of Nassau hastened his preparations,
left Paris quietly in mid-May, and on the 24th actually
succeeded in surprising Mons, the capital of Hainaut.
Alva was also ready by that time and sent his son, Don
Frederick, into the field.   He promptly mastered Valenciennes, and then laid siege to Mons (June 3d) with
twenty thousand men, to oppose Louis's little force.

On June 7th, the prince of Orange with twenty thousand men crossed the Rhine at Duisburg.   A few days
later the French noble, Genlis, appeared in Hainaut with
a little force of Huguenots.   The defeat of these allies was
the first disappointment.   On June 19th, Genlis's troops
were entirely routed, and he himself was taken.   From
his papers and his confessions Alva obtained, as he had
from Villiers in 1568, the plan of the prince and his allies.
Thus enlightened, he straightway prepared to counter-
vent his adversaries.

Very deliberately had the prince undertaken his second
expedition over the Meuse.   His advance seemed un-
bearably slow to those who were watching events in the
Netherlands.   Lack of money again hampered his movements.   His appeals for aid were constant in the early
summer of 1572.

"Do not be so devoted to your money that you rate it
higher than the lives of yourselves, your wives, your children,

your descendants, to your great shame and eternal disgrace in a moment in which we with one thought, which springs from the heart, strain every nerve to help you and to free you. Think of God's wrath and of the contempt of foreign peoples and princes. Think of the hateful yoke which you let rest upon you and your children, if you refuse the money that we need to come to you with our army." [1]

Thus he appealed to the Holland cities, an appeal which incidentally reveals their lack of generosity. Many proclamations were issued. Famous is the one drawn up by Wesenbeke and issued without the prince's cognisance,[2]—a thundering attack on " the tyrant hated by God and by mankind," who pressed the Netherlanders under his iron hand.[3]

The Beggars' song, too, rang through the land:

> " Haste, seventeen provinces,
> Now rise to your feet,
> Meet the Prince's arrival
> With friendly feelings ;
> Rise with your banners
> Each as a faithful man,
> Aiding to banish
> Duke Alva, the tyrant."

The *Wilhelmuslied* was heard clearly from the trumpets when the prince took Roermond on July 23d, a capture which was, in spite of the prince's efforts, stained by murder, by sack, and by attacks on priests and monks, children and cloisters. Orange remained for more than a month in the camp of Hellenrade, expecting word from Coligny, who had promised to bring a considerable force to aid him in the south, and had advised the prince to await his coming.[4]

[1] Kluit, *Hist. der Holl. Staatsregeering*, i., p. 377.
[2] Kervyn, *Documents inédits*, p. 166.
[3] Bor, *Authentyke Stukken*, i., p. 131.
[4] *Archives*, iii., p. 490.

This delay afforded Alva opportunity to work out his plans and exposed Louis to great danger. On August 27th the prince penetrated farther into Brabant. Thienen and Diest opened their gates, but the more important cities of Louvain and Brussels refused him admission, to his bitter disappointment. He had attributed the defeat of 1568 to the lukewarmness of the Netherlanders — now again no hand in Brabant or Flanders was stretched out to him.

Bitterer disappointment, too, was in store. On September 5th, sure news of the frightful massacre of St. Bartholomew reached him. Coligny himself had fallen. Nothing more was to be hoped for from France. No wonder that the prince "found himself marvellously astonished and in extreme disappointment,"[1] as the French ambassador wrote to his master.

The prince succeeded in taking Mechlin, and later Termonde and Oudenarde in Flanders. Meantime Alva adopted the same tactics which had been so successful in 1568. He refused open battle, knowing that distress and poverty would be effective weapons in dissipating the rebel force. As Orange lay in camp, on his way to aid Louis in Mons, Julian Romero made a midnight attack. His followers wore white shirts outside their clothes to prevent mistakes in the dark. The prince escaped with his life, thanks to a little dog which roused him in time, but his force was too greatly weakened for him to proceed in his plans. He retreated to Brabant, and Louis, deprived of his last hope, capitulated six days later. His defence had been very valiant, and even his Spanish foes expressed admiration for him.

The enterprise had failed in every point. Disheartened, the prince returned to Mechlin. On the last of September he again retreated with unpaid, plundering, and mutinous troops, whom he disbanded at Roermond.

[1] *Archives*, iv., p. ciii.

Holland was the only place where armed resistance was still on foot. Thither the prince made his way. On October 20th, he crossed over the Zuyder Zee at Enkhuizen. He was, trusting in God, determined *d'illec attendre ce qu'il Luy plaira de faire.*[1]

In Holland, however, affairs were far from hopeless. At the end of May, Enkhuizen declared for the prince; Sonoy, now governor of this region in the prince's name, at once proceeded thither with a force levied in Bremen, Hamburg, and East Friesland at Briel. He opened communication with Lumey, now commissioned governor of Holland by the prince, and with T'Seraerts, who was holding out at Flushing and Veere against the Spanish garrisons of Middelburg and Arnemuiden. In June, the little towns of Medemblik, Hoorn, Alkmaar, Edam, Monnikendan, and Purmerend followed Enkhuizen's example, and admitted garrisons in the prince's name. One city after another followed suit or was taken by the Beggars, until Amsterdam was almost the only strong town left in Spanish hands. Naturally this did not come to pass, however, without bloodshed and lawless acts on the part of the Beggars. Priests and monks were harassed and ill-treated, churches and convents sacked. Especially notorious is the shameful mistreatment, crowned with murder, committed by Lumey and his men upon the persons of the luckless Gorcum martyrs, whose death on June 9th at Briel, whither they had fled, horrified all pious Catholics and shocked intelligent Protestants.

These events in Holland found a speedy echo elsewhere. In Friesland many towns, spurred to action by Frisian sea Beggars, like Duco van Martena and others, refused Spanish garrisons. Count Joost van Schaumburg, appointed governor by the prince, established a provincial governor at Franeker in opposition to the royalist headquarters at Leeuwarden. In Zealand there

---

[1] *Archives*, iii., p. 512.

was a bitter struggle between the Beggars and Mon-dragon's Walloons, a struggle which has been recounted by Roger Williams, the English volunteer, whose *Memoirs* give a reliable picture of these events.[1]   In Guelders the Count van den Bergh, Orange's brother-in-law, appeared with some German troops, then pressed on to Overyssel, plundering and murdering as they went.

Nearly everywhere it was the citizens themselves, in-dignant at the tenth penny, who admitted the Beggars into the towns at the instance, generally, of the prince's agents.   The magistrates were, as a rule, forced to con-sent to this step or flee to other cities still held by the Spaniards — to Amsterdam, Utrecht, Nimwegen, Arn-hem, Bergen-op-Zoom, and Antwerp.   The number of officials and priests who fled out of Holland in 1572 in fear of the dreaded Beggars was reckoned at about four thousand, among whom were the members of the court of Holland; of these only two were left at The Hague. The then advocate of Holland, Van den Eynde, was under arrest at Brussels, as Alva distrusted him.   The whole administration of Holland was disorganised.[2]   An assembly of the Estates was desirable, but there was no one to convene them.   The pensionary of Dordrecht was the functionary on whom the duty would devolve in absence of advocate and stadtholder.   He had fled. Dordrecht itself could perform the act as the oldest city of Holland, but the corporation feared to take the com-promising step.   Finally, however, they did so, not in virtue of the pensionary or of Dordrecht's seniority, but simply as member of the Estates.   Thus an assembly of the nobles and cities of Holland was called into being.

This remarkable assembly met on June 19th.   Its legality was less than questionable, like the whole revolt,

[1] *Memoirs of Roger Williams*, p. 159.
[2] Bakhuizen van den Brink, *Eerste vergadering der Staten van Holland* in *Het Nederl. Rijksarchief*, i., p. 9, etc.

as it undoubtedly bore a revolutionary character. It included the seigneur of Wyngaarden, the only member of the nobility, Arend, seigneur of Duivenvoorde as Lumey's representative, and several deputies from the cities Dordrecht, Haarlem, Leyden, Gouda, Gorkum, Alkmaar, Oudewater, Hoorn, Enkhuizen, Medemblik, Edam, and Monnikendam.[1] Orange sent Philip of Marnix, seigneur of St. Aldegonde, to represent him personally at the Estates thus convened. Marnix read as his credentials a letter from the prince, thanking the Estates for their recognition of his government and promising his support of them in return. To maintain his troops he asked for supplies which should begin at once with one hundred thousand crowns a month.

The Estates decided to secure the necessary sum from an appropriation of the taxes and of current tributes, from a forced loan levied upon the rich citizens, from treasure in churches and convents, and from the sale of silver and gold vessels as had " more ornament than use." On the following day the assembly formally acknowledged the prince of Orange as governor-general and lieutenant of the king over Holland, Zealand, West Friesland, and the territory of Utrecht, and adding, for a show of legality, " as his Excellency was previously under commission of his royal Majesty," without infringement of the nation's customs and privileges.[2] This step could hardly be defended, considering the prince's resignation from his posts, his flight, and his armed rebellion, considering the nomination of Bossu as his successor, and the legal sentence pronounced against him in 1568.[3]

The Estates went farther on their illegal way by acknowledging the prince as " chief member of the

---

[1] *Ibid.*, p. 32. Amsterdam, Rotterdam, Schiedam, Delft, Woerden, and Schoonhoven were still in Spanish hands.

[2] *Ibid.*, p. 38.

[3] *Ibid.*, p. 23.

States-General of the Netherlands,'' and as one having therefore the right to protect the same Netherlands from invasion and foreign oppression and as the protector and head of the land in the absence of his royal Majesty. Both this and the land and sea were under his administration, and on the latter Lumey was his lieutenant. Finally it was promised that Estates and prince should stand by each other, and Marnix declared that the prince's intention was that religious freedom should be maintained both for the Reformed and for the Catholic faiths, and the clergy should not be disturbed as long as they were not hostile or until the States-General decided otherwise. This the Estates fully acknowledged.

The session lasted only a few days. Then the deputies returned home, leaving a few representatives to conduct negotiations in the troublous times of the transition of Rotterdam, of Delft, and of Schiedam. The court was reinstated in the interests of justice. Paul Buys acted as advocate of Holland and later received a definite appointment as such. At the prince's instance new members of the treasury were appointed by the Estates, besides stewards, receivers, and three commissioners for the war. Finally a list of new candidates for the court was drawn up for the prince to select the officers.

Thus the government of Holland was rearranged, and it only remained to reduce Amsterdam, Woerden, and Schoonhoven. This was an easy matter with the two small places. Amsterdam was more difficult, and when the prince arrived, Lumey was engaged in laying formal siege to it, aided by Sonoy; and the revolted Hollanders were chafing under the temporary rule of the lawless Lumey and longing for the prince's coming.

Meanwhile the duke of Medina Celi arrived, July 11, 1572, at Sluis in Flanders, to replace Alva with a gentler government, but he did not wish to take the reins till the stronger hand had restored order. So Alva lost no time.   His son Frederick was soon in the field with fifteen thousand Spaniards and Italians.   First he punished Mechlin severely for having opened its doors to Orange, and then he turned north.

The troops did not meet with all the success expected though they inflicted much damage.   Zutphen was taken by storm on November 16th, and its inhabitants were slaughtered almost to a man.   The same thing happened at Naarden, which was almost wiped from the face of the earth.   Then Frederick marched on to Haarlem, where, on December 11th, he opened a siege destined to prove famous from the obstinate resistance made by the burghers.

The prince made two attempts to succour the valiant city.   Both failed.   During the progress of the siege the king's governor, irrespective of the royal will, was making superhuman efforts to conquer the difficulties—financial, political, military, and religious—which confronted him. It was no slight matter to meet the daily expense of eight thousand guilders, a sum hard to raise from a population impoverished by the cessation of commerce and the prevalence of piracy.   Courts had been reconstructed, but still justice was almost at a standstill, and the depredations of the lawless soldiery could not be checked. Moreover, there were constant controversies between Calvinists and Catholics, which the prince tried his best to settle.   His lack of skilled leaders, too, was a serious drawback in the face of the Spanish veterans.

In the beginning of July, Orange succeeded in collecting about five thousand men in the vicinity of Leyden, but his hope for reinforcement from Louis—now restored to health — was disappointed.   Money had failed, and German troops were not forthcoming.

On July 12, 1573, the starved burghers were forced to capitulate, and the long siege of Haarlem came to an end. The people were spared to some degree the scenes of

horror enacted in the other cities.   Frederick allowed the
citizens to buy off the plundering usually permitted to
the besieging troops, but the defenders themselves were
cut down without mercy, three hundred being bound back
to back and drowned in the Haarlem lake.   Ripperda,
Lancelot of Brederode, and other officers were beheaded.

Deep was the impression made by Haarlem's fall.
The prince did his utmost to counteract the sinister and
depressing influence by travelling around from city to
city to offer words of personal encouragement to the
despondent citizens.   He was urged by his adherents in
the Waterland on the Y and Zuyder Zee to seek the protection of some powerful potentate, and answered: " We
have made a treaty with the Supreme Potentate of potentates, and are wholly assured that we and all those who
trust to Him shall be relieved by His powerful and
mighty hand." [1]

Nevertheless Orange, as an intelligent statesman, did
not neglect to try any way to obtain deliverance for the
Netherlands.

During 1572–73 there were many attempts on the part
of German princes to effect a reconciliation between
Philip II. and his former stadtholder.   The king of
France, too, repenting his sanction of the massacre of
St. Bartholomew, exerted himself to make new relations
with the Protestant princes.   Orange repeatedly said that
he did not cherish the slightest illusion in regard to an
accommodation with his nominal sovereign.   He had no
intention of yielding a single one of his demands as to
religious toleration, home rule, etc., and he knew perfectly well that Philip would be equally uncompromising,
but he never refused an opportunity of a conference that
might lead to an alliance.   He watched every political
friction in western Europe from which might result a
spark of hope for the Netherlands.

[1] *Archives*, iv., p. 177.

His own anticipation was fixed upon an understanding with France, an illusion which haunted him until his death. He built little trust on Elizabeth's fickle promises or upon the German prince's. It was France, the hereditary foe of the house of Burgundy, whose interests, he thought, would be furthered by aiding Philip's enemies. Thanks to the prince's encouragement, thanks, too, to a few successes obtained in Zealand, the Hollanders took heart to resume the unequal strife without any foreign ally proper. They promptly rejected the offers proclaimed by Alva in the king's name (July 16, 1573), in which the latter, like " a hen calling her chickens," promised pardon to all those who would return to the comfortable shelter of that monarch's motherly wings.

The patriots were also encouraged by a mutiny that had occurred in the victorious army before Haarlem. It was evident that the conquests had been dearly bought, and the Hollanders hoped to reap some benefit from the exhausted condition of the Spaniards. Medina Celi warned Alva repeatedly that they were seriously weakened, but the latter refused to give heed to his colleague's remonstrances, and determined to repeat the lesson which Haarlem had learned. On July 16th, his troops appeared before Alkmaar and laid siege to that city.

Sonoy came to the rescue of the small band of valiant defenders, and called in the sea to aid him. The latter proved an efficient ally. It rushed in through the opened sluices. The pierced dykes forced the besiegers to yield their ground before their new foe. This summary action met great opposition from the peasants, who saw their crops ruined before their eyes, but it proved successful in routing the enemy. Alkmaar was relieved (October 8th), and prospects at once brightened. Three days later the Spanish ships under Bossu were put to flight by the Beggars under Cornelis Dirksz., burgomaster of Monnikendam. The Spanish admiral was captured, while

other plans of attack on Groningen and places in the
north seemed to promise well.

At the same time these reverses aroused the spirits of
the enemy. Speedily Delft, Schiedam, and Rotterdam lay
like islands in the midst of a troubled sea of Spanish rule,
while by October 30th Leyden found the foe at her gates.

The prince's faithful right hand, Marnix, too, was at
this time a prisoner and owed the safety of his person solely to the fact that Bossu was in the Beggars'
power. To add to the dangers of siege and battle a pest
began to rage in the land.

A change now ensued in the political aspect of affairs
from Alva's departure and the arrival of a successor less
energetic in character and method. The duke was quite
content to be relieved from his task. Indeed he had repeatedly implored his sovereign to recall him. Medina
Celi had come to replace him, but shrank before the
difficulties of the post. In 1572 deputies from the provinces that had not seceded — Hainaut, Brabant, and
Flanders — journeyed to Spain to protest against the
tenth penny. Received coldly at Alva's instance, they
remained until Philip, uneasy at the strength of the revolt, actually consented to a suspension of the tax, in
consideration of a new promise of two millions a year,
while he gave a general assurance that the tenth penny
should be abolished. This was a victory for the Netherlanders against the duke. " God and men are against
me," Philip's faithful servant is said to have exclaimed
at this time with a pathos worthy of a better cause.
Even Medina Celi undermined him secretly, and he
trusted no one. Alva had intended to serve both king
and church as well as possible. Now no one appreciated
his activity. He longed to go, and on October 29, 1573,
he was granted permission to depart.

Medina Celi was no longer considered. He had
indeed already returned to Spain, and the new appointee

was Don Luis de Requesens y Zuniga, governor of Milan, known as Requesens. He was as unwilling to accept the post as Medina Celi, but finally yielded to Philip's insistence, and arrived at Brussels in November. On December 18th Alva shook Netherland dust off his feet, and, accompanied by Vargas, made his way to Spain by way of Milan.

It was a pitiful condition of affairs that he left behind in the land where he had been supreme for five years. Antwerp had never regained her commercial position lost in 1566. What the troubles of that year had left undone, the raids of the sea Beggars had completed. Brabant had suffered under the campaigns of both parties. In Holland, Zealand, and Friesland reigned hopeless confusion. Here, too, the depredations of the sea Beggars had gone hand in hand with other events to ruin commercial enterprise.

The discontent aroused by Alva's administration, when, according to Requesens,[1] six thousand Netherlanders of all ranks and conditions had been executed, by the financial burdens, was directed against him as a personification of their ills. The duke departed under the curses of the Netherlanders, Catholic and non-Catholic. A " new song " rang after the late governor, jeering at the " old man called Alva, who sails off without paying anyone."

Meanwhile the prince held his ground at the head of his fishermen and peasants, his " petty folk," with whom he had allied himself by a closer tie by partaking of communion according to Calvinist rites.[2] This action, greeted with jubilation by the Calvinists, united his cause with that of the zealous believers whose courage and fidelity he had learned to rate as the strongest support of the revolt.

[1] The eighteen thousand boasted by Alva is far too high. Gachard, *Études* ii., p. 366.

[2] Hessels, *Archivum*, ii., p. 469. Compare Fruin, *De voorbereiding*, etc., p. 15.

There were many Laodiceans among those who had given their early coöperation in the contest against Spain. By 1573 many middle-class citizens were inclined to submission rather than to endure the state of unrest necessitated by military opposition, a state deeply antagonistic to their innately peaceful burgher nature. They hated Alva's tyranny, they hated the tenth penny, but, on the other hand, they thought that destruction to all material prosperity stared them in the face. The prince used all his powers of persuasion to encourage this class. He found that he could reckon more surely on those who had actually suffered banishment and confiscation, or had even been exposed to death at the enemy's hand. The returned exiles, preachers, and zealous Calvinists proved the stanchest adherents to the cause. With these the prince was to conquer or perish, and with them alone. Neither Lutheran friends and relatives nor the Anglican princess in England were willing to furnish him adequate support. This explains why, in October, 1573, he openly joined the church which had already won his sympathies in the days when he had fought in the midst of the Huguenots, and had lost his early aversion to Calvinism under the impression of the living belief of his fellow warriors. The die was cast which was to decide his further fate.

The fate of the Netherlands, too, was decided at the same time. Without him opposition might have melted away. In the eyes of Spain, the prince was regarded as the virtual soul of the rebellion. Many schemes to assassinate him were constantly on foot. With him disposed of, it was thought all opposition would dissipate. But in 1573 matters were not so far advanced. He seemed but an impoverished nobleman, at the head of a handful of armed peasants and fishermen, contending against the sovereign of the richest realm in the world lying on both sides the sea. His destruction could only be a question of time; such was the general opinion.

But general opinion did not yet recognise the prudence of the man, the power of despair, the peculiar geographical characteristic of the provinces where water might be converted into a powerful weapon of defence, the hostile attitudes of the French and English governments against Spain, not to mention the ambiguous position of the emperor himself, the significance of Protestant sympathy in the adjacent countries, and, finally, the increasing debility of Spain herself.   All these causes coöperated to disappoint the hopes of the Spanish government that the rebellion would be speedily suppressed.

The year 1560 may be taken as the date when the Spanish prosperity which had dawned under Ferdinand and Isabella reached its zenith.[1]   From that year many causes contributed to its decline.   One of the chief was the Spanish aversion to labour, especially to manual work. " Not gold and silver," writes an anonymous author in a memoir to King Charles II. of Spain, " but sweat is the most precious metal, a coin always current and never depreciated."   But that coin, too, was scarce in Spain.

Rich as was the soil of the peninsula, its fertility had almost vanished with the Moors.   Manufacture, too, had lost ground.   Charles V. made vigorous efforts to revive work both in field and factory, but his efforts were rewarded with scanty success.   It was deemed better to be a nobleman, poor even to beggary, than to demean oneself with work of any kind.   Poverty was no disgrace : labour was; and the whole nation showed the effects of the theory.

Public finances were in as bad condition as private. The state indeed seemed on the verge of national bankruptcy in spite of the rich treasures that had come from across the sea.   Another fact, that was less known, was

[1] Compare Häbler, *Die wirtschaftliche Blüte Spaniens.*

that the population of Spain was at this date (1573) at a complete standstill. Just before, the increase had been very rapid. The change shows plainly that Spain was much less vigorous than it seemed to a superficial observer. No; the conflict with the Netherlands was no strife between an earthen and an iron pot, but rather— posterity has learned to comprehend what was a miracle to the contemporaneous world — a struggle between a colossus on crutches and an opponent tiny but still full of activity and strength.

CHAPTER II

THE new governor was received by the loyal portion of the Netherlanders with coolness, and with distrust by the party of opposition. A prince of the blood would have been more welcome than this Spanish grandee who could not even speak French.

Requesens himself, diplomate rather than warrior, was animated with a desire to pacify the Netherlands with gentle methods. He counted much on an amnesty issued in 1574, from which only about three hundred persons were excluded, while papal forgiveness was offered for heresy. Orange and his adherents were, naturally, among the exceptions. This failed, however, to inspire confidence. The new *Pardona* was dubbed Pandora, Catholic lack of faith towards Protestants was called to mind by the Calvinists, and Requesens' friendship for the Jesuits was looked at askance.

A certain inclination to consider the propositions was evident in the prince's camp towards the end of 1573. The imprisonment of Marnix gave opportunity for a friendly correspondence between Romero and the prince. The latter made it clear that the king would have to promise freedom of conscience and the maintenance of ancient privileges. Further negotiations, however, showed the impossibility of finding a meeting-ground.

Every attempt failed. Neither offers of pecuniary

indemnification to the prince himself, on condition of his leaving the Netherlands, nor propositions to the Estates of Holland could shake either the one or the other in their resolution to continue the struggle so long as no trustworthy peace was made.

In the autumn of 1573, the prince sent Lumey to Paris to reopen relations with the French court. There was even some talk of a revival of the invasion as planned by the French before St. Bartholomew's night, but the disturbance among the Huguenots, the election of Anjou as king of Poland, and the long illness of Charles IX. which ended in his death (May, 1574), prevented the realisation of these projects.

The position was undoubtedly very precarious, although something was gained by the naval victory of the Beggars under Louis de Boisot, in Zealand near Roemerswaal, over the great Spanish fleet (January 29, 1574). The admiral Mondragon held the fortress of Middelburg until February, and was then obliged to yield.

By that time the prince was already in Zealand and at once proceeded to reorganise the government. As the majority of the nobles were Spanish sympathisers, their representation was restricted to the first noble, then the imprisoned count of Buren, the prince's eldest son, in his capacity of lord of St. Martensdyk. Orange appointed Arend van Dorp, governor of Zierikzee, to represent him in turn. The bishop of Middelburg, representative of the Zealand clergy, was ignored. The prince gave the little cities of Veere and Flushing representation in the body of the cities side by side with Middelburg and Zierikzee. A little later he himself bought the marquisate of Flushing, and thus gained great influence. A council composed of the commanders and deputies of the cities beside the admiral and a deputy from Holland, was empowered to administer ordinary business and to conduct military affairs. All officials were the trusted friends of the prince and adherents of Calvinism.   Measures were set on foot to obtain possession of the islands of South Beveland and Tholen, still held by the Spaniards.

In Holland, the prospect was less favourable.   The Beggars were driven from Friesland by Robles, Sonoy had suffered defeat in Waterland, Leyden was hard pressed by a Spanish force under Francesco de Valdez. The Spaniards had learned the best methods of fighting on Netherland soil.   They changed their tactics and abandoned their ancient methods of storming a city.[1] Instead, they cut off supplies or occasionally surprised their foe on dark winter nights, and this policy proved advantageous.

In the early spring of 1574, when Leyden was actually beleaguered, Count Louis finally appeared at the borders with his army.   On February 19th, he arrived in the neighbourhood of Maestricht with about ten thousand men, accompanied by his brother Henry and Duke Christopher of the Palatinate.   His force was, however, composed of unreliable and discordant elements and characterised by the old failings of mercenaries, lack of discipline and valour.   The poor population of the Meuse were subjected for the third time to forced levies and plundering — the churches and cloisters suffering especially.   The Spaniards, surprised only for a moment by the incursion, at once collected all their mobile troops on the Meuse.   Sancho d' Avila, with Mondragon, the valiant foe of the Zealand Beggars, made Maestricht his headquarters and from thence inflicted fairly important defeats upon the Nassau army.   Despairing of crossing the Meuse at that point, Louis then hastened northwards to try to make his passage near Roermond.   That city, too, had received a Spanish garrison at the eleventh hour. Louis hastened still farther north in the hopes of making

[1] Compare Fruin *Het beleg en ontzet van Leiden in 1574* ('s Gravenhage, 1874), p. 11 *et seq.*

his way into the Betuwe over the Waal near Nimwegen and of joining the troops collected by the prince near Bommel. At Mook he found that the enemy had hurried ahead of him on the left bank of the Meuse, had crossed and were ready to oppose him. On April 14th, Avila opened battle and won a complete victory although his force was smaller; better discipline and training gave him the advantage. The valiant Nassau commander, his brother Henry, and Christopher of the Palatine all fell on the field, while the whole army of patriots was dispersed.[1]

Deep was the disappointment of the prince and bitter his plaint over the misfortune that seemed to pursue him. Nevertheless this dire disaster was not sufficient to shake his confidence in his cause. In a letter to his single remaining brother, Count John, in which he describes exhaustively the chances of the war and the forces still at his disposal, he expresses the strongest faith in divine aid.[2] He points out that Holland had held her own against Spain for two years according to his prediction. But these two years were on the point of expiration and help must be obtained from France, England, or Germany. If help failed, " the poor inhabitants, forsaken by all, will nevertheless hold on as they have done hitherto and as I hope can continue to do, and if God does not punish us and destroy us utterly, then it shall "—so he declares—" cost the Spaniards half Spain in money and in men before they subdue us." Rightfully the prince boasts : " We shall always have the honour of having done what no other nation before us has accomplished." He had at his command 71 companies of infantry in Holland, 14 in Zealand, 20 in Waterland, in all 15,000–16,000 men and 100 large and small ships of war, distributed in the same proportion over the three regions. They would maintain their position with this equipment as long as they

[1] See Blok, *Slag op de Mookerheide.* Groningen, 1891.
[2] *Archives*, iv., p. 386 *et seq.*

could.   That the prince meant what he said was shown
by the rejection of the secret offers of the Spanish government made to him at this time through Leoninus, professor at Louvain.   The former continued to regard him
as one who was seeking his own interests and hoped to
separate him from the cause of the rebels by satisfying
personal ambition.   But his persistent answer that there
could be no peace in Holland and Zealand without removal of the Spanish troops, religious freedom, and
maintenance of privileges showed plainly that nothing
was to be obtained by that method.

There was some question, however, as to whether the
Hollanders and Zealanders were quite as stanch as their
leader, whether discouragement might not gain ground,
and whether the new pardon of Requesens would cause
the defection of many.   Immediately after the battle of
Mook, therefore, Orange returned to Holland in order to
cheer up his adherents — a needful step, since the siege
of Leyden, abandoned at Louis's approach, had been
renewed on May 25th.   No preparation had been made
for this, and the burghers were ill supplied with all
necessaries.

Thus began one of the most remarkable sieges in the
struggle against Spain.   It was noteworthy, not from
deeds of arms, but from the steadfastness of such men as
Dirk van Bronkhorst and Jan van der Does, undaunted
city officials; as Pieter Adriaanszoon van der Werff, the
well-known burgomaster; and Jan van Hout, the secretary.
The burghers, too, were full of courage at the beginning,
but the prospect of starvation was so imminent that the
mass of people lost heart and only held out because the
leaders would not succumb.   On June 1st, the prince convened the Estates at Rotterdam to gain their consent to
the one plan he deemed promising for the relief of the
beleaguered town.   The Beggars had never met with
success in any land encounter with the Spaniards.   Now,

far inland as Leyden was, the prince proposed to bring in
the sea as their ally. When he laid the scheme before
the Estates, the opposition was immediate. They
thought that the only sure outcome would be utter ruin
to the country. But the prince's arguments finally prevailed. The sluices were opened and the water flowed in
to within a short distance of Leyden, as far as the dikes
held by Valdez. The city and her immediate environs
remained high and dry. The roads to Haarlem, Utrecht,
and The Hague were open to the enemy. The waters
finally ceased flowing, and at the same time the leader's
direction and encouragement were lacking. The prince,
wearied out with his anxieties and exertions, had succumbed to a fever and lay at Rotterdam so seriously ill
that his physicians had warned him to prepare for death.
It chanced just at the moment of the crisis in his illness
that the steward of Holland, Cornelis van Mierop, came
to his bedside unannounced, accompanied by a couple
of messengers from Leyden, who wished to see " his
Excellency." The tidings that Leyden was still holding out put new heart into the invalid, " and from that
hour he began to improve," says Bor.

In the city, Bronkhorst, Van der Does, and Van Hout
were using all their energies to keep the half-hearted from
yielding. Certain royalists called " glippers," who had
taken refuge in the Spanish camp, urged their fellow
townsmen to capitulation. In early September, discouragement began to gain the upper hand, and it was with
the greatest difficulty that the faithful officials postponed
negotiations. Anxious days of hope and fear followed:
of hope at the sound of the cannon roar that seemed to
approach over the flooded land; of fear for the increasing
misery.

In mid-September came the report that the prince had
recovered and that relief was being pushed forward. A
letter from Orange himself worked like an electric shock

upon the fainting hearts.   But the water was still low.
A fortnight more passed without action.   Suddenly, on
September 20th, a northwesterly storm broke.   The water
rose higher and higher and the fleet sailed on, though
under difficulties.   The Spaniards on the dikes tried in
vain to repel these newcomers.   Finally, on October 2d,
the beleaguering force, fearing the rising water, stealthily
retreated.   It was just in time.   Leyden could not have
held out one day longer, but would have been forced to
capitulate in the very face of relief.

The fleet's approach had been watched from the city
with the keenest anxiety.   Flags were displayed on
towers and mills to show that the burghers were still
holding ground.   In the early morning of October 3d,
the amazed Leydeners saw that the enemy had abandoned their positions.   Soon a couple of Boisot's ships
sailed up to the city walls.   Leyden was saved!

The liberators, whose boats were laden with herring
and bread and all kinds of edibles, were received with
jubilation, and, after the first hunger was appeased, the
churches were filled with the grateful population, who
thanked God for their rescue from the dire need, bearing
witness to the strength of " the right hand of the Lord,
strong to work miracles as in ancient times."   On the
following day, the prince came from Delft and stayed
ten days in Leyden.   He reduced the town corporation
from forty to sixteen members, and appointed new government and judges.   The untrustworthy were removed
as far as possible.   But the change was not so comprehensive that the prince did not find cause for complaint in
the lack of coöperation of the municipal government.
As a " recompense and reward for the piety and unheard-
of constancy," also " in alleviation of the hunger, anxiety,
and misery " endured in the siege, the city received a
university—" her best pearl."

The relief of Leyden was a turning-point in the history

of the revolt.   Had Leyden fallen, Holland would have
been practically lost.   The pluck of the city made a deep
impression upon the population as well as upon the
Spaniards.   It was expected that Amsterdam would now
declare for the prince.   This did not happen, but a
serious mutiny against Valdez, among the troops which
had been stationed before Leyden, wrought the enemy
infinite injury.   Under a self-chosen leader, an *eletto*, the
soldiers placed their commander and other officers under
arrest, abandoned the entrenchments still held, and forced
the then stadtholder of Utrecht, lord of Hierges, to let
them enter this province.   Thus suddenly Holland between the Meuse and Haarlem was freed from the enemy.

Meanwhile neither Estates nor prince had conquered
their serious difficulties.   The expenses of the war were
heavy and there were no regular supplies to meet them.
In November, the prince declared that he would withdraw
to Germany unless proper provision were made and his
own authority more firmly established.   Accordingly,
on November 12th, the Estates begged him to assume the
" superintendence, authority, and direction under the
name of Governor or Regent at the voluntary *collatie* of
the Estates, vassals, inhabitants, and heirs of the countship of Holland," bestowing on him " absolute might,
authority, and sovereign control " for the direction of all
common affairs of the land.[1]

In regard to supplies they were less generous, and tried
to retain complete control of the purse-strings.   It was
only on the prince's refusal to take any further steps
without a fixed allowance that they voted the forty-five
thousand guilders a month which he deemed requisite.

The prince showed his talents as a statesman in this
negotiation.   He became virtual sovereign of Holland
and Zealand, although he was still entitled " governor in

[1] From the *Remonstrantie* as appendix to Bisschop, *Woelingen der
Leicestersche partij in Leiden*.   Leyden, 1867.

behalf of the king,'' and although he asked the endorse-
ment of the Estates for all important transactions and
intentionally left many a sovereign act in their hands, as
for instance the peace negotiations opened by Requesens
in 1574, which hung on for some time, and exercised his
authority in the municipal governments, through his
chief adherents in Holland, the North, Bommel, and
Buren which was included by a special provision in
1574.[1]

Requesens was in great embarrassment. He, too,
lacked support in men and money.   The council of state,
the privy council, and the council of finance had all lost
their best members; Viglius old and weak, the incapable
Aerschot, the insignificant Berlaymont, and the senile
Assonleville bore almost the whole burden of government.   More efficient officials were difficult to find, as
Philip had no thoughts of reformation to the mind
even of his loyal Netherland nobles.   The Council of
Troubles was the only college of administration still
effective.   Meanwhile financial difficulties became alarming.   Philip's total revenues were 10,000,000 crowns,
while army and navy alone cost 8,500,000.   Nothing
came in from the Netherlands, which amounted to a loss
of 2,000,000 crowns for the treasury, and when Alva departed 6,000,000 crowns back pay was due the soldiers.
After that matters went from bad to worse.   The natural
result was a mutiny, and that ensued.

Before the battle of Mook, mutineers, also under an
eletto, had seized the town hall at Antwerp and ter-
rorised corporation and governor into acceding to their
demands.   Similar scenes were enacted at Bruges, Ghent,
and elsewhere, and there were serious manifestations of

[1] Van Wijn, *Bijvoegsels en Aanmerkingen op Wagenaar*, vii., p. 23 ;
Muller's claim (*De Staat der Vereenigde Nederlanden*, p. 127), that a ratification of the alliance by the town councils was needful, does not seem
proved.

insubordination in Gelderland, Overyssel, Utrecht and
Brabant, and even in Requesens' own body-guard. Discontented soldiers plundered whole districts, and the
governor could not stay them.   His treasury was empty,
and all his efforts to obtain supplies failed.

The Estates of the loyal provinces complained loudly,
but refused pecuniary aid unless the governor withdrew
the troops into the fortresses and fulfilled certain other
conditions.   The Estates thought that he was completely
in their power and must yield to their demands.   But
they were playing a dangerous game.   They did not see
that the governor's stress must necessarily drive his un-
satisfied hirelings to extremities to the inevitable injury of
the loyal provinces, which were laid waste by the desperate soldiery.   Peasants, too, were driven to beggary, and in their turn made raids in Brabant, Flanders,
Hainaut and Artois, plundering isolated farmhouses and
cloisters.

On May 1, 1574, Requesens convened the States-
General at Brussels.   He encountered bitter opposition
at the outset.   The deputies refused to furnish any supplies unless their own stipulations were granted—abolition
of the tenth penny and of the Council of Troubles, the
king's presence, return to the conditions under Charles
V., pacification of Holland and Zealand, dismissal of
foreign troops, etc.   The governor's appeals to the individual provinces were more effective; at least Hainaut,
Artois, and Namur yielded, but these concessions availed
little in the face of the opposition of Brabant and Flanders.   Finally Requesens saw no other way to turn than
to renew negotiations with the prince of Orange.   Attempts to treat individually with them failed.   In the
spring of 1575, a peace conference was formally opened
at Breda.   Rasseghem, Leoninus, Sasbout, and Suys
represented Philip's lieutenant, while Marnix, Paulus
Buys, William van Zuylen van Nyevelt, and others

appeared for Orange and his people, and the emperor sent the count of Schwartzburg, the prince's brother-in-law, as his personal deputy.

It was a long parley, and some points of discussion were referred to Spain.   Philip entirely refused to consent to any real concessions to Protestants, and it soon became evident that no compromise was possible between king and prince.

Orange made use of the negotiations on his side to point out the increasing weakness of the national government to the loyal provinces and to urge them to make common cause with the rebels.   At the same time he strengthened the alliance between the rebel states and put the government on a better footing.   Until this date, the prince had carried on the government of Holland with three " Councils next to His Excellency," as they were called, which had been established in 1573 to replace the disorganised colleges.   In addition to these councils of state, of finance, and of the admiralty, to which the prince appointed members at the nomination of the Estates, there was the council provincial, reorganised in 1572 for the administration of justice.   In Zealand, after the conquest of Middelburg, the prince reorganised the administration in simpler fashion.   In the north, Sonoy and the " Deputed Council of the North Quarter " had control.   The council were deputed by the municipal governments.   In Buren the prince exercised control as representative of his son.   In Bommel there was municipal government.   It was very necessary for the sake of regular government, especially for the effectiveness of military operations, that there should be more unity in the administration of the provinces.

Deputies from the cities in revolt, both great and small, assembled, together with the Holland nobles, to discuss the peace conference.   The prince took advantage of this convention to endeavour to obtain a better administration and closer union. Difficulties arose at once.[1] The Zealanders and North Hollanders, on an independent footing as they were, and afraid of the supremacy of the great south Holland cities, were little inclined for a plan of union like that proposed by the prince through Paul Buys. The relation of the people and the government to the prince, too, gave rise to all kinds of differences. On one side they wished to make him sovereign, and exhausted themselves in expressions of thankfulness for his paternal attitude towards the provinces. On the other side the great influence upon affairs exercised by the Estates, which he himself had inaugurated, pleased them, and they feared to lose their influence. This inclination came out very clearly whenever financial questions arose. Moreover, the regulation of religious affairs was no easy matter to settle, as the prince desired to give the Catholics greater freedom than the dominant Calvinists deemed right. Finally, the majority of regents were opposed to greater burgher influence in the government, which the prince, personally popular among the burghers, considered an excellent balance to the measures of aristocratic governments like those of the Zealand and Holland cities. After the rupture of the peace negotiations, these points were discussed unceasingly in the revolted regions. Interesting in regard to these deliberations is a letter of the prince, May 25, 1573.[2]

" His Excellency would consider it advisable that all governmental orders relating to war, policy, and national council should be approved not only by the magistrates and archers' guild of the cities, but also by the communities, in order to secure better obedience and to the end that they could not complain that the ordinances enacted by their consent (this

---

[1] Muller, *De Wording van den staat der Vereenigde Nederlanden*, p. 127. Haarlem, 1878.
[2] Kluit, *Historie der holl. staatsregeering*, i., p. 133. Amsterdam, 1802.

is about a year past)[1] should now be changed without their knowledge."

After much wrangling over these points, a union between Holland and Zealand was discussed in June. An ordinance was adopted concerning the " Common Means" which they were to obtain from imposts on wine, beer, corn, sheep, horses, cattle, sowed land, turf, coal, and weighed goods. Zierikzee opposed committing the government to the prince, whereon Holland went her own way, and on July 11th begged him to act " as sovereign for the sake of the unity which cannot exist among many, differing in character." They chose him as " Head and Supreme Authority," and committed to his charge the government of the territories and cities of Holland with the stipulation " that so long as war exists " he should have full authority to do everything needful for their conservation and protection. If need were he might change the municipal governments. The Estates and, further, the officers, magistrates, *Schutterijen* (armed burghers), guilds, and communities in all cities and villages, were to swear an oath of fidelity to the prince. A council was to support him. The captains of the burghers and deacons of the guilds counted as representatives of the communities, as was the ancient usage in such cases. At Gorkum and Schoonhoven alone did the magistrates refuse to convene these officials, declaring that it was unusual. They would not hear of a convention of " all communes," although the prince had desired it.[2] The *Landraad*, or national council, was established in August, not wholly to the prince's liking, but its power was limited, as the Estates wished to retain influence in affairs. In the following autumn this council was

---

[1] As the *Res. van Holland* for 1574 is lacking, it is not quite plain what this means. Compare Note 2, p. 146.

[2] Kluit, i., p. 133.

abolished, and the difference in opinion between the prince and the Estates prevented a definite regulation. Then Orange with a few deputies held control for the time being.

Meanwhile, the war, interrupted for a time after the siege of Leyden by the peace negotiations, was resumed in the spring of 1575. In April, the lord of Hierges appeared in Kennemerland to drive Sonoy out of the north. Sonoy held out valiantly, but, embittered by the opposition of the West Friesland Catholic peasants to his measures and by a rumoured conspiracy among them, was guilty of shameful cruelty towards the unfortunates. A court extraordinary imposed upon the accused tortures and punishments which equalled the worst stories of the cruelty of the inquisition, and they did not cease until the prince interfered on the appeal of the victims. But Sonoy, displeased at the mediation, goaded on his subordinates repeatedly to a continuation of the torture.[1] Thus the population of the West Frisian country, especially in the region of Hoorn, whose schout was one of the most relentless persecutors, were punished in a frightful manner for alleged misdemeanours which excited the suspicion of Sonoy and his followers. Sonoy's " blood council," almost as cruel as that of Alva, yes, surpassing it in many respects, has never been forgotten in that region. Hierges soon withdrew from the north, took Buren by storm and Schoonhoven by siege in August. Woerden saved itself by inundations, and the enemy failed in attempts to reach Dordrecht, but that city was in imminent danger until the spring of 1576. There was some loss in Zealand. By means of a brilliant night attack and a long wading expedition at low tide, Mondragon succeeded in reaching the island of Schouwen and laid siege to Zierikzee. This occupation divided

[1] Bor, i., p. 624 *et seq.*

Zealand from South Holland, as it had been separated from the north by the fall of Haarlem.

Under these circumstances Requesens —usually called the Great Commander from his dignities in Spain— should have pushed on military operations. But he lacked the sinews of war. The revolt of the Netherlands had now cost Philip more than 42,000,000 of ducats. By this date he had exhausted all resources of loans and mortgages. Nothing was left to him but to declare state bankruptcy.[1]

The condition of Spanish finances had become absolutely rotten; all forms of taxation had been carried to their bitter end. Foreign bankers made increasing demands. The interest of the national debt of 34,000,000 ducats amounted to 2,000,000, a third of the state revenues. So the king considered that the time had come to take a radical step which he hoped would help him temporarily. It was the second time that Philip had resorted to this measure. In 1557, at the time of the French war, he had gone through the process.

On September 1, 1575, a decree suspended all payment to national creditors. A serious financial crisis was the necessary result of this, and the credit of the Spanish king fell so low that it was impossible to get Spanish exchange accepted in the Netherlands, let alone to send cash from Spain to the provinces. Even the single banking house on which the king could reckon to some degree—the Fuggers, of Augsburg—refused for a long time to negotiate loans for the Spanish government.

Requesens, despairing of help from Spain, convened an extraordinary assembly of the council of state, of stadtholders, and of knights of the Fleece to obtain their advice on what financial measures could be taken to assure regular pay to the soldiers, and thus avoid mutinies.

[1] Häbler, *Die Wirtschaftliche Blüte Spaniens*, Berlin, 1888, p. 113.

He then demanded a loan from the provinces of 1,200,-
000 guilders.   There was much discontent at this demand, but finally one province after another agreed from
fear of the more dangerous discontent of the unpaid
troops if they acted in concert.

Thus with the troops pacified, danger increased for
Holland and Zealand.   The prince felt that the time
had come when they must have foreign help.   His marriage with Charlotte of Bourbon-Montpensier had brought
him into connection with the French royal family, but
the princess, a fugitive abbess and convert to Calvinism,
was virtually abandoned by the royal family, and Henry
III., successor to Charles IX., the culprit of St. Bartholomew, seemed little inclined to help, the more so because
civil war had just been renewed in France, with the Duke
d'Alençon at the head of the " Politiques," the mid
party between Huguenots and Catholics.   The prince
therefore turned his hopes to England.

Elizabeth, afraid of a French sovereignty in Holland
and Zealand, sent one ambassador to the prince and one
to Requesens at the time of the Breda peace conference.
Orange made use of this opening, and sent, December,
1575, an embassy to London which was followed by
another from Requesens.   Elizabeth coquetted with both
parties in an equivocal manner.   Both embassies were
still in England when the news came that Requesens
had succumbed to a short illness on March 4th.

CHAPTER III

PACIFICATION AND UNION

THE condition of the Netherlands after the unexpected death of the regent was far from satisfactory.

Apart from the revolt in Holland and Zealand, there was widespread dissatisfaction over the manner in which the ordinary administration was conducted. Alva had been sufficiently all-powerful to suppress murmurs while pursuing his own way. The same abuses continued under Requesens, and the discontent found voice. Especially in Brabant and Flanders, where commerce and manufacture were at a forced standstill, and the foreign merchants ceased to come because the entry to the Scheldt was unsafe owing to the depredations of the sea Beggars, complaints were many and loud. Ghent, Brussels, Louvain, and other cities protested vigorously as well as Antwerp, the chief sufferer, and the commercial interests of the formally beleaguered Amsterdam, too, were greatly hampered by the rebels. In addition to the loss of commerce the raiding of the troops was a constant affliction.

Even Granvelle,[1] at a distance though he was, saw the situation plainly, and wrote urgently to Philip II., advising a radical change of policy. Hopper, who could be considered the special representative of the Netherlands in the king's council, warned his royal master that there

[1] *Corresp. de Granv.*, vi., p. 33.

was danger that all the provinces would accept foreign suzerainty unless their own sovereign gave them proof of his " fatherly love." A memoir drawn up by the lord of Rasseghem, now member of the Brussels council of state, was in the same spirit as Hopper's remonstrance.[1] This urged the appointment of a prince or princess of the blood, regular payment of the troops, confirmation of the privileges, native nobles in the council of state, Netherland instead of foreign soldiery, and finally a comprehensive amnesty with restoration of confiscated goods and renewal of the negotiations of Breda.

Immediately after the death of Requesens the council of state assumed control, disregarding the nomination of Berlaymont and Mansfeld made by the dying governor with his last breath. The king confirmed the council for the time being. This executive body was composed of Viglius, Berlaymont, Aerschot, Assouleville, and the Spanish Netherlander Roda. Sasbout, too, had a seat; Rasseghem and Mansfeld were present at the sessions. It was a very inefficient machine of action, not only because of the incapacity of Berlaymont and Aerschot, and the infirmity of Viglius, but also because the Netherland members disagreed among themselves and with the overbearing Roda.

The oft-suggested methods of restoring peace were urged anew upon Philip. It was even hoped that he would take counsel with the pope and yield on the religious question.[2] But the king was deaf to representations, accompanied though they were by friendly messages from the English queen, and to intimations from his rebellious provinces that they would welcome peace. As usual, the delays in the answers from Spain were excessive. " If Death had to come from Spain we would be certain of a long life," once said a Spanish official of high rank

---

[1] *Corresp. de Philippe II.*, iii., p. 461.
[2] Kervijn de Lettenhove, *Huguenots at Gueux*, iv., p. 27.

in Italy. In April, Philip appointed his bastard brother, Don John, as new lieutenant-governor of the Netherlands, but it was three months before the council of state were informed of the fact. In June, Philip wrote to them that he must reflect until August or September before answering their representations of March. He continued eternally *négociant*. Meanwhile events did not wait his pleasure.

The people in Brabant and Flanders, driven to desperation by the lawlessness of the Spanish troops, finally took arms against them. Mondragon's force in Schouwen revolted against their officers, took Mondragon himself prisoner, abandoned the island, and made their way to Brussels, plundering as they went. They seized Aalst and established their headquarters under their *eletto*. Thither flocked the troops. Holland, Zealand, Gelderland, and Utrecht were almost emptied of the hated foreign soldiery.

The council were in despair. The stream of revolt was rising, and they did not know how to stay it. The Spanish generals were indignant at the evident distrust entertained by the council towards them, and had their own complaints to prefer at the levy of German and Walloon troops. Confusion increased in Brabant and Flanders. Aalst and the citadel at Antwerp — also in Spanish hands—were watched anxiously.

The prince of Orange was not the man to let such a chance slip by. On April 25, 1576,[1] Holland and Zealand had been united into a closer union under the prince, who was at the same time endowed with sovereign rights for the time of the war. He, however, was firmly convinced that these two provinces alone could not maintain the unequal struggle long. Thus when the union was formed it was also determined at his instance " to proceed to a change of lords and to open negotiations with

[1] Muller, *De Wording*, etc., p. 147.

the king of France, his brother, or any other foreign potentate who would receive these lands of Holland and Zealand under his rule and protection."

In May, 1576, accordingly, they tended to Francis, duke of Alençon, only brother of the French king, the sovereignty of Holland and Zealand under restricted conditions; which were to be sworn to by the duke and by the Estates in accordance with the ancient usage when the dukes of Brabant made their *joyeuse entrée* into Brabant.

This plan fell through. France was afraid of Spanish strength. The prince's hope of French aid, founded on the ancient enmity between France and Burgundy, vanished in smoke, like so many expectations of this kind in the early years of the revolt.

But something better soon offered itself. The council of state at Brussels were so hard pressed by the Spaniards that it seemed as though the other provinces might be induced to join the new union and present a united front to Spain. The prince, now established at Middelburg, appealed to the provincial Estates of Gelderland, Brabant, Flanders, Artois, and Hainaut, to a mass of nobles and to other individuals in the south, urging, in eloquent letters, the need of coöperation in the face of the pressing danger.[1] The Estates of Holland sent similar appeals to Amsterdam and to the citizens of Utrecht. The prince's agents were busied everywhere. Meanwhile, by August the council of state at Brussels were virtually prisoners in the hands of the citizens.

There had always been many sympathisers of the prince at Brussels and Antwerp. These were chiefly to be found among the lower classes and merchants with whom Orange had been popular in his brilliant youth. Now they considered him as Egmont's friend, as Spain's foe, upon whose head now rested a laurel wreath won by four years

[1] Bor, i., p. 694.

of heroic struggle.   His opposition to Spanish influence
dated, they remembered, from the days of Granvelle.
The proclamation of general pardon had brought many
Calvinist exiles back to Flanders and Brabant.   These
naturally wished nothing better than adherence to the
prince and expulsion of the Spaniards.   Among the
clergy, too, the prince had at least two friends of great
influence.   But his chief hope was based on the young
Baron de Hèze, his own godchild, the most popular man
in Brussels, and upon the popular leaders in general whom
he tried to influence through his Brussels agent, the
French noble Jean Theron, a faithful follower and clever
diplomat.[1]

In the Brabantine capital affairs took, meanwhile,
another turn.   The Spanish generals, with Roda and
others of their countrymen, fled before popular dislike
to Antwerp.   De Hèze was appointed first colonel of the
German and Walloon mercenaries engaged by the Estates,
and soon after governor of Brussels.   He at once used
his new position to urge negotiations with the prince.
At the same time he entered into relations with Hendrik
de Bloyère, the advocate Liesfelt, De Backere — influential citizens and adherents of the prince.   On September
4th, these confederates, with De Hèze's own lieutenant,
Glimes, as their leader, arrested the whole council of
state, with the exception of Roda who escaped to Antwerp.   It was a remarkable drama played that day at
Brussels.   Mansfeld and Berlaymont, Assonleville and
Sasbout with Del Rio, were incarcerated in the *Broodhuis*,
before which Egmont and Hoorn had lost their heads.
Aerschot was soon liberated on account of alleged illness;
Viglius, actually ill, had to remain in his house.   It was
no secret that the prince was the heart and soul of this

---

[1] See the studies of Ritter on *Wilhelm von Oranien* and the *Genter
Pacification*, 1576, in Quidde's *Zeitschrift für Geschichtswissenschaft*,
p. 28, 1890.

movement.[1]   He now proceeded to open communication
with Jan van Hembyze, schepen of Ghent, Philip of
Egmont, eldest son of the count, the count of Roeulx,
stadtholder of Flanders, the Lalaings, and other distinguished nobles of Brabant, Flanders, and Hainaut.   He
tried to come to some agreement with his old rival, the
duke of Aerschot, with his brother, the marquis of
Havré, and to overcome the distrust of the family of
Croy by the assurance that he did not wish a part in the
government nor any change in religion.   He seemed to
succeed with Havré at least.

Meanwhile Orange stayed at Middelburg, fearing the
effect of hastening south too soon.   Some of the Ghent
citizens turned to him for aid against the raids of the
Spanish mutineers from Aalst, who seemed to have some
understanding with the garrison of the Ghent citadel.
The prince at once accepted their request, and sent eight
companies under Colonel van den Tympel to Ghent.
Ryhove, lord van der Kéthulle, and his brother the lord
of Assche, opened the gates amidst the jubilation of the
populace.   The disturbances increased in Brabant and
Flanders.   There was much dissatisfaction at the treatment inflicted on the council of state, the legitimate
national government.   The Estates of Flanders and
Hainaut protested against the revolutionary acts of Hèze,
Hembyze, and the rest, afraid of the king's vengeance.
Roda declared from Antwerp that the king's authority
was now vested exclusively in him, the single free member of the council, during the imprisonment of his *con-
frères*.   Finally, old Viglius and Sasbout were set free,
but Berlaymont and Mansfeld, Spain's most faithful
adherents, remained in prison, while Del Rio was treated
even more severely.   A nominal legal government was
now restored in the persons of Aerschot, Viglius, and Sasbout, who chose their colleagues.   It was evident that

[1] De Jonge, *Unie van Brussel*, p. 187.   *Archives*, p. 412 ; Ritter, p. 34.

this council of state would not succeed in enforcing their authority unless they yielded to the public demand for a convention of the States-General, and such convention was wholly in accord with the prince's plan.

At the time of the arrest of the council of state, in default of any legitimate government the Estates of Brabant had invited the other provinces to send deputies to Brussels. Flanders and Hainaut alone ventured to respond to this invitation. Later, a certain show of legality was obtained for this proposed assembly by the approval of the revived council of state, and the States-General was convened on September 22nd. The council declared that royal authority was vested not in Roda at Antwerp, but in their members, and that they were forced by circumstances to yield to public opinion. Three days later the deputies of Brabant, Hainaut, and Flanders appeared at Brussels and assumed at once the functions of the States-General, although the other provinces failed to coöperate with them for a long time. The conduct of military affairs was intrusted to Aerschot, together with the Hainaut noble, count of Lalaing, as lieutenant. The prince's influence upon the assembly was very apparent. It was determined to send embassies to Queen Elizabeth, Henry III., Emperor Maximilian,[1] and the pope, to state their position. A letter was written to Philip on October 17th—with the complete approval of Orange—wherein the States defended the action of September 4th, declaring that the people could only have been held in check by this act of sovereign authority. They complained of Roda's arrogance, and asserted their own fidelity to the king and the Catholic faith, while assuring the king that there could be no tranquillity in the land until the Spanish troops were withdrawn.[2]

[1] On October 12th, Maximilian was succeeded by Rudolph II.
[2] De Jonge, *Resolutions des États-Généraux des Pays-Bas*, i., p. 244.

On September 27th, the States-General wrote to the prince asking for peace negotiations with him and Holland and Zealand.   He acceded immediately, but substituted Ghent for Brussels as the seat of the proposed parleys.   The States hesitated to accept this choice, as Ghent was notoriously prone to revolts and uproars. But the tidings that Don John was already on his way to the Netherlands ended their indecision.   The prince, who had promised to withdraw his troops from Ghent in case of its selection as a place of treaty, changed his intent on a request from Ghent itself.[1]

The negotiations were opened with mutual distrust. The leaders of the States feared lest the prince might encourage popular revolts at Brussels or Ghent, while he dreaded lest on the arrival of Don John, Aerschot and his friends would be alienated from the national cause by Spanish promises.   But time pressed, and the negotiations proceeded.

On October 19th, the abbot of St. Geertrui, Leoninus and seven deputies, appeared to represent the provinces taking part in the States-General; Buys and Marnix and an equivalent number came on the part of the Estates of Holland and Zealand and of the prince.   There was complete unity in regard to the dismissal of the Spaniards, maintenance of ancient privileges, etc., but the question of Don John's recognition and of religion gave rise to difficulties.   Leoninus and his friends insisted on receiving the king's lieutenant provided that he ratified the peace they were about to make.   In regard to religion, Holland and Zealand refused to consider complete freedom for the Catholics in their territory as decidedly as the other provinces declined to accept anything which implied violation of the orthodox religion.   It was finally resolved to leave this point—as far as Holland and Zealand were concerned—to the decision of a States-General

[1] *Archives*, v., p. 467.

convened after the peace. On October 28th, the deliberations were closed, and the treaty was accepted subject to
the confirmation of the States-General—that of Holland
and Zealand was assured. Delay ensued. Orange began
to suspect secret negotiations between Aerschot and his
friends with the king, " who does not treat with us with
Flemish, but with Italian and Spanish methods." He
urged further that the treaty when confirmed should be
sealed in all cities by magistrates, guilds, and " schut-
ters." Finally a decision was reached, urged by the
evident desire for peace. Before that peace was in being
the matter was hastened by an unforeseen event.

As early as October 20th, a couple of companies of
Spanish troops under Montesdoca had gained control of
Maestricht, and recompensed themselves for the long delay in their pay by atrocious plundering and deeds of lawlessness. Many men, women, and children perished,
while the German garrison was almost annihilated.

This seemed a signal for a general onslaught of the
Spaniards. At Antwerp, Champagney was governor.
His German mercenaries, under the count of Eberstein,
had been won over in part by the Spaniards and offered little resistance to the strong Spanish garrison of the citadel
under officers like the commander of the fortress, Sancho
d'Avila, Romero, Valdez, Verdugo, and other well-known
leaders.[1] Troops sent by the States were dispersed by
Romero near Mechlin, but another Walloon detachment
under Havré and the young count of Egmont was admitted within the walls of Antwerp by the Germans, to
the annoyance of their leaders, who retreated to the
citadel. In all, the States had about eight thousand
men within the city, to which the Spaniards could oppose
only about half that number. Preparations were made

[1] Important for the attack on Antwerp is Roda's letter to the king,
November 6th, with Champagney's comments. *Corresp. de Phil. II.*, v.,
p. 11, and the latter's letter to Don John, *ibid.*, p. 33.

to beleaguer the fortress while Sancho d'Avila turned his cannon upon the city.

It was Sunday, November 4th, when the roar of artillery announced to the surrounding region that the struggle between the troops within and without the citadel had begun.   The Spaniards in Aalst heard and came to join the fray, crowned with oak garlands in token of victory. There was a fierce battle on the streets of Antwerp, re-sulting in the defeat of the States' troops.   Egmont and others were taken prisoner, while Champagney and Havré escaped to the prince's ships on the Scheldt, and Eber-stein was drowned in an attempt to cross the river.   Ant-werp became the scene of a frightful massacre.   The desperate soldiers, ill paid and ill fed, regarded the rich commercial city as their lawful prey.   Robbery and murder, enforced levies and plundering, continued for three days long.   Neither churches nor convents, women nor children, were spared.   The number of slain is put at from six to seven thousand.   The value of the booty could not be estimated.   The city hall,—lately rebuilt, —with all the registers of exchequer bills, contracts, and agreements with foreign merchants, was burnt down with a mass of other buildings — yes, whole streets.   The Spanish fury destroyed a great portion of what remained of Antwerp's ancient commercial prosperity.   More and more did foreign merchants avoid the insecure city on the Scheldt, and for years after the events the results were evident in the distrust which prejudiced the credit of the trading citizens.

The Spanish fury aroused dire dismay throughout the land.   It was felt that the Spanish troops must be re-moved at any price if other cities were not to be exposed to Antwerp's fate.   Popular revolts took place at Brussels and at Ghent animated by bitter hatred for the Spaniard. Under the impression of these popular movements and of the danger menacing from the Spanish troops, the States-

General and the council of state — a mere tool of the States — yielded to the urgent demands to approve the Pacification framed at Ghent *pour prévenir et éviter de plus grands inconvénients*. The news that Don John was at Luxemburg hurried the final resolution. On November 8th, the Pacification was signed.

The articles asserted that the Estates of Brabant, Flanders, Artois, Hainaut, etc., together with the prince, the Estates of Holland, Zealand, and their allies, made peace and mutually pledged each other to force the departure of the Spanish soldiers. Immediately after this an assembly of the seventeen provinces should be convened in the " form and manner " of that when the emperor had abdicated in favour of Philip.[1] This assembly should regulate national affairs in general and the matters of religion in Holland, Zealand, Bommel, and Buren. No hindrance was to be imposed on the intercourse between the provinces. All edicts against heresy and Alva's criminal ordinances were to be suspended " until the States-General ordered otherwise," and the prince was to remain admiral and stadtholder for his Majesty in Holland and Zealand until the decision of the States. All prisoners, especially the count of Bossu, were to be freed. All confiscated property was to be returned to the prince and to others condemned by Alva's sentences, and the sentences reversed. Alva's trophies were to be destroyed. All ecclesiastical property was returned to the courts, even in Holland and Zealand, and special stipulations, too, were made about the possessions of exiled monks, nuns, and priests. The coinage, changed in Holland and Zealand at the time of the war, was to be made uniform again with that in the provinces. The States-General should consider the payment of the prince's debts resulting from the campaigns of 1568 and

---

[1] Ritter, p. 42.

1572. The twenty-fifth and last article provided that provinces not yet admitted should be received on the same conditions as those party to the transaction.

This important state document was of the greatest weight for the history of the Netherland provinces. It united all in the revolt against Spanish tyranny, against foreign troops, forces upon which Spanish sovereignty was obliged to depend. Apparently the prince had attained his aim. His ideal, the government of the Netherlands with the supervision of the States-General deputed by the provinces, and this representation of the whole people under the king's constitutionally limited nominal sovereignty, seemed to have been attained.

It was by no means true that Orange was the universally acknowledged head of the revolt. The negotiations at Ghent had shown plainly that the nobles of Brabant and Hainaut were quite disinclined to accept his leadership. This mutual distrust boded ill for later coöperation between the prince who relied upon the people and the nobles who resented all popular interference in state matters.

And there was more. The dominant Calvinists in Holland and Zealand would not consent to an exclusive mastery of Catholicism even in territories beyond their borders, where their fellow believers — few though they were in number, still exiles or half in hiding—looked to Holland and Zealand for aid. The obedience to the king, which virtually did not exist in the revolted provinces, was, on the other hand, for the majority of the population elsewhere a stipulation almost as important as that of the maintenance of Catholicism. What might be called, to a growing extent, a vague theory, a pretext, a fiction, for Holland and Zealand, was, in the eyes of the majority of the people of the other provinces, still the basis of all social and political order.

It is hardly necessary to say that Philip II. was highly dissatisfied with the course events had taken after the death of Requesens. Every step was hateful to him, but he sought, as of old, protection through his favourite system of delay and procrastination. Not until he received the news of the *coup d'état* of September did he resolve to send Don John. And then this new lieutenant set out without direction as to policy, because the king could not decide upon his course. His instructions were dated October 30th, and were in the main the embodiment of the ideas of Hopper and Viglius which Philip had at last adopted.

The document began with an order for a universal prayer to implore God to extend His divine goodness over the Netherlands. A declaration of the king's desire to restore peace, with the maintenance of the Catholic religion, followed. Don John was further exhorted to follow in the footsteps of previous regents of royal blood. Restoration of every desirable ancient custom and form of government was promised, pardon to everyone except to the prince, as "the inventor, author, and promulgator of all evil," convening of the States-General, etc. ; all that had been asked for was granted, only allied with complete maintenance of the ancient faith. Holland and Zealand were to be forgiven if they repented their evil ways. If they did not, the obedient provinces must help coerce them. Moreover, the chapter of the Golden Fleece was to meet.[1] A second note followed this first instruction, ordering Don John to yield the last point and dismiss the Spanish troops.

In all this the king forgot two things. Times had changed. What would have satisfied the Netherlands ten years previous was no longer adequate. In the second place, the Netherlanders would not receive from him, the Spaniard, what they would have taken from Charles V.

[1] *Corresp. de Phil. II.*, iv., p. 453, *et seq.*

Moreover, between September and November circumstances had altered so greatly that his concessions made no impression.

Don John reached Luxemburg on November 3rd. Disguised as a servant he had made a rapid journey through France. Letters from Roda about the occurrences at Antwerp reached him at the same time with the news of the Pacification of Ghent and the greeting in the name of the States-General and the council of state. The latter sent one of its own members, the Utrecht provost, Jan Fonck, to Luxemburg to reconcile the governor with the new state of affairs. Another emissary of the States-General was charged to discover the governor's plan and to advise him to go to Brussels alone and unarmed.

The young passionate Don John was not the man to conduct affairs successfully in the Netherlands under these difficult conditions. Having won his military reputation as a youth of twenty-four, when he conquered the Turks in the battle of Lepanto (1571), he considered himself the heir of the traditions of Charles V. Large of stature, attractive in person, valiant and courteous, pious Catholic and man of the world at the same time, he resembled his famous father far more than did his royal brother, although, passionate and capricious as he was, he lacked his father's political talents. His mother, Barbara Blomberg, was a washerwoman of Ratisbon with whom Charles V. had had a brief alliance. He was brought up in Spain with great secrecy until after the emperor's death, when Philip informed him of his parentage. He believed that he was destined to play a great rôle in the world's history. He hoped to be acknowledged as infant of Spain and then to become champion of Catholic Christendom, unfurling the banner of the Church on one side against the Turks, on the other against the heretics. What attracted him to the Netherlands was the reputation to be won in the struggle against Orange, and the chance that might offer, after the establishment of peace, of freeing Mary Stuart from the imprisonment in which she had been held for years by the heretic Elizabeth. This romantic task, well befitting a knight, attracted the young prince. When he received the news of his appointment in April he hastened to Spain from Naples in order to discuss with his secretary and friend, Antonio Perez, the basis of the policy to be pursued in the north.[1]

Bitter was his disappointment to find his hands bound by the Pacification. He counted that document " *un régime aussi contraire au service de Dieu qu'à l'obeissance due au roi.*"[2] " Everything is confusion and uproar," he wrote to her who had taken the place of mother to him. " They conspire in the king's name and levy troops to drive out the Spaniards." He waited at Luxemburg, and the rumour that Orange was having his palace at Brussels put in order added to his annoyance. At first he concealed his feelings and declared that he wished for peace, to Roda's deep disappointment, who had expected him to place himself at once at the head of the Spanish troops and to maintain the king's authority. Counting all the Spanish garrisons together, Don John could reckon on at least ten thousand men. But to carry out his English plans peace was necessary in the Netherlands. So Don John went as far as his instructions allowed him and declared his willingness to agree to the departure of the Spanish troops.

But the States-General demanded more. They wished him to confirm the Pacification. Don John demanded in his turn, disarmament, dismissal of all the troops hired by the States, cessation of negotiations with the prince— whom he did not intend to pardon, let alone enjoy such a position as the Pacification gave—and with the duke of

---

[1] See Stirling Maxwell, *Don John of Austria*, 2 vols., London, 1883.
[2] Kervijn, *Les Huguenots et les Gueux*, iv., p. 170.

Anjou. He knew perfectly that the States had been negotiating with both since his arrival.

Negotiations with the former could hardly seem strange after late events, and many of the nobles had also lent ear to Anjou's agents. The continued uncertainty in the Netherlands during the autumn made many in the south as well as the north think that a French prince would be their best protector, but Henry III. showed no readiness to furnish aid. He was afraid of embroiling himself with Spain.

The prince, always thinking of the continual struggle between France and Burgundy, never put aside the thought of French aid. It was undoubtedly owing to him that the States-General, distrusting Don John's real intentions, decided in mid-November to send a deputation to Anjou. The prince went farther, and even urged taking possession of Don John's person, while he was supported in his plans by Hèze and his friends, who desired nothing better than to offer Anjou a protectorate. It did not, however, come so far, owing to England's opposition, to the hesitation of Henry III., and to the negotiations with Don John.

The new governor finally consented to come to an understanding with the States-General in which the loyalist party gradually gained the ascendency. The bishop of Ypres and other faithful clergy assured Don John that they did not consider the Pacification antagonistic to ecclesiastical interests. It was apparently agreed that both Spanish troops and the mercenaries in the service of the States should be dismissed. Negotiations about the Pacification were continued at Namur, and by mid-December Don John set out on his further journey, though still disinclined to accept the document. He distrusted the leaders of the Netherland government as the

---

[1] So the duke of Alençon was called after the peace of Monsieur in 1576.

tools of Orange, " whom they regarded almost as their father." [1]

The prince had no faith whatsover in Don John, no matter what promises might be wrung from him.   Anti-Spanish documents, with extracts from Roda's inter-cepted letter and pamphlets, prepared at the prince's instance, were scattered broadcast.   These were not without effect in delaying the negotiations, but the majority of the States-General were unwilling to yield. Aerschot urged that body and the council of state to re-move to Namur, where it was thought that they would be freer from the influence of the prince of Orange, of Hèze, and of the popular party, which included the Brussels populace, where sympathy with Orange was manifest. Meantime a nominal assembly of the States continued in existence at Brussels.   It was augmented by the de-puties of Holland and Zealand and the representatives of Groningen and the Ommelands, and this body rejected Don John's propositions.   At Namur, too, no progress was made.   Don John lost all patience and yet did not dare risk a formal rupture, comprehending that, lacking money and troops as he did, he was in no position to subdue the whole Netherland people, when his prede-cessors had not succeeded in quelling the revolts of Hol-land and Zealand.' [2]   Still greater was his annoyance when, on Jan. 9, 1577, the portion of the States at Brussels and the council of state pledged themselves formally to the maintenance of the Pacification.   This so-called union of Brussels was indeed of great weight.' [3]

In December, 1576, the seventeen provinces, except Luxemburg, which held to Don John, were at last repre-sented in the States-General.   Friesland, Groningen, and the Ommelands had not been gained over without violent

[1] *Corresp. de Phil. II.*, v., p. 45.
[2] *Ibid.*, p. 45.
[3] De Jonge, *Onuitg. stukken*, ii., p. 161.

disturbances, and special efforts of a deputy of the States-General, François Martini Stella, who had incited the populace of Groningen to rebel against Robles, the Spanish governor, and depose him. Friesland, too, was won with similar methods, and George de Lalaing, count of Renneburg, appointed governor in behalf of the States.

How changed was the position of the prince! A twelve-month back ruin had stared him in the face. Now everything seemed to point to his speedy victory. Zierikzee and Oudewater had been garrisoned by the prince's troops immediately after the Spaniards' departure. Muiden, Weesp, Haarlem, and Schoonhoven came over to him one after the other on condition of the Catholic religion being permitted. Goes and Tholen followed suit. Amsterdam alone in Holland remained on the Spanish side.

When the Spanish garrison of Utrecht capitulated in February, 1577, serious questions arose in regard to the stadtholdership there. The prince, as stadtholder of Holland and Zealand, claimed it in virtue of the ancient union between Holland and Utrecht in 1534. The clergy preferred Bossu or Hierges, who had declared for the States-General, but they were unwilling to be rivals to the prince,[1] and, in March, his party finally won the day, but the States-General and council of state did not confirm him until October. The fortress was demolished by the jubilant population, as were those at Antwerp, Ghent, Lille, Valenciennes, and elsewhere during the course of the year.

Popular as the prince was at this date, it was not surprising that he succeeded in persuading the deputies at Brussels to make a formal declaration in favour of the Pacification. The union of Brussels lent new force to the Pacification after the negotiation with Don John,

[1] Compare Bondam, *Onuitgegeven stukken*, ii., pp. 158–165.

which might have cast doubt on its maintenance.¹ The
members of the council of state signed it.   Popular
demonstrations in many cities forced the acceptance of
the union ; and popular demonstrations, too, demanded
the definite termination of the uncertain relations with
their accredited governor.

To this last demand the States-General yielded.   They
fixed January 23d as the date when Don John must accept
the Pacification or be himself refused.   Only four days
intervened between this ultimatum and the appointed
day.   The would-be governor yielded to the representation of Aerschot and his royalist friends and declared
that he would recognise the Pacification.

This was an unexpected change in Don John's policy,
which put the prince in a critical position and necessitated great caution in his political negotiations.

Aerschot and his party were jubilant.   The prince
remained firm in his attitude of refusal and advised the
States to beware of Don John's compliance, which was,
in his opinion, hypocritical.   He suggested the importance of many more conditions, he urged probable aid
from France and Germany, he warned them, before they
accepted a treaty with Don John, to beware of " Spanish
cunning." ² But his words booted nothing.   On February
7th, the States ratified the eternal edict discussed at Huy,
giving notice thereof to the prince " so as to preserve
good relations."   Five days later, Don John signed this
document at Marche, where he happened to be at the
time.

This " peace of the duke of Aerschot," as it was called,
confirmed the Pacification, as the clergy and the council of

---

¹ Bussemaker, in his *Afscheiding der Waalsche gewesten van de Generale
Unie* (Haarlem, 1897–98), sees here an attempt on the part of the States to
force Don John to renounce his opposition on one side, and on the other to
keep Orange as friend.

² Kervijn, iv., p. 309.

state had declared that it was not antagonistic to religion or to royal authority. The States-General promised six hundred thousand guilders immediately towards the wages of the Spanish and Italian soldiery, and more later towards those of the Germans. The Spaniards were to depart within twenty days. The Catholic religion was to be maintained everywhere (thus also in Holland and Zealand). This last stipulation was flagrantly at odds with the Pacification, wherein the matter of religion was left to the decision of a future States-General. But the States ignored that consideration and set their seal to the document. To Anjou, they wrote a polite note declining his offers with courteous expressions of gratitude. To the prince they said they had awaited his answer in vain and finally had proceeded to the signature in the interest of peace and prosperity of *nostre pauvre commune patrie*, and from fear of letting slip the good chance of peace.[1]

The prince and the Estates of Holland wrote at once pointing out the weak places in the treaty, but saying that, prejudicial as it was to them, they would still sign, provided that a written promise were given that all relations with Don John should cease if the troops were not withdrawn at the specified date.[2] The States-General were forced to be content with the fact that Holland and Zealand had not given a decided refusal.

In the spring of 1577, the chief provisions of the edict were actually carried out. The Spanish troops evacuated the citadels at the end of March, and, at the end of April, set off for Spain overland. They would have gone earlier had the States not been somewhat behindhand in furnishing the stipulated sums. Don John remained meanwhile at Louvain, as the States had yielded to the prince's demand that they should delay receiving the governor in Brussels until the troops were off. It was

---

[1] *Corresp. de Guillaume le Taciturne*, iii., p. 215.　　[2] *Ibid.*, p. 225.

not until May 1st that he was free to enter the capital of
the Netherlands. He brought with him the king's ratification of the perpetual edict, which he delivered to the
States with a word about the unusual celerity with which
the king had approved the treaty, a proof, he said, *com-
bien le roi vous aime et désire votre bien.*[1]

In fact, as is shown by the correspondence between
Don John and the king, they were anxious to secure
peace and had decided to be content with the treaty,
which differed in one important particular from the Pacification. Don John counselled his brother thus to regain
the shaken confidence of the people.[2]

With this restoration of customs and privileges, Don
John did not consider himself the proper governor for
the Netherlands. He advised Philip to appoint Margaret
of Parma, Christine of Lorraine, or some other woman
of royal blood. It was evident from his letters that he
thought the task of subduing the provinces effectually
should be postponed, not relinquished. At this crisis it
was a great loss for the Netherland provinces that Hopper, the only man in the king's council who understood
the Netherlands, had died in December, 1576.

Don John was now the officially recognised governor
of the Netherlands. Nothing could have been more
brilliant than his formal entry into Brussels on May 1st.
But the young prince did not feel at ease. He trusted
none of the nobles who surrounded him — not the weak
Aerschot, "the lamp lighted by Champagney after dinner," nor his insignificant brother Havré, nor the untrustworthy Champagney himself. He was perfectly
conscious that they were afraid of the prince and jealous
of his influence in the south. At the same time he knew
that they regarded Orange as an aid against Spain and

. [1] Kervijn, iv., p. 341.
  [2] See *Corresp. de Phil. II.*, v., pp. 155–163, 198 ; compare *Archives*, vi.,
p. 83.

were unwilling to shove him wholly aside.[1] The king
had finally allowed his brother to have his secretary,
Juan d' Escovedo, with him, which was some relief to
his loneliness, but the young prince saw plainly that his
dreams were never to be realised. He was never to
receive the hand of either the imprisoned Mary Queen of
Scots or that of Elizabeth of England. He was not to
be the Catholic champion of all Europe. He considered
himself out of place, and " as a ball in a tennis court,"
tossed from hand to hand.[2] To prevaricate cleverly was
no work for this fiery champion.

But his sovereign refused to recall him, and Don John
finally made a virtue of necessity and opened negotiations with the man whose influence he felt at every turn
—" the arch rebel, the pilot who steers this boat."[3] A
formal conference was accordingly opened at Geertruidenberg for negotiations between the king's governor and
the prince. The history of the days of Requesens
repeated itself, and the clever diplomate Leoninus
tried to lure the prince to an arrangement, but it was
soon clear that no agreement could be reached. There
were mutual complaints of infringement of the Pacification. The prince demanded Amsterdam, Utrecht,
and his own home of Breda, the liberation of his son,
still prisoner in Spain, restoration of his property in
Burgundy and Luxemburg, and, above all, guarantees
for the fulfilment of the king's promises, and freedom
of conscience in the Netherlands. *Calvus et Calvinista*
(bald and Calvinistic), as he called himself in a somewhat
exaggerated way as to the last characteristic, he would
not for a moment accept the stipulation in the eternal
edict that Catholicism should be the exclusive religion
even in Holland and Zealand. To the great discomfit-
ure of the governor, both his own envoys and other

[1] *Corresp. de Phil. II.*, v., p. 225.
[2] *Ibid.*, p. 247; compare Bor, i., p. 887.   [3] *Ibid.*, p. 245.

prominent nobles showed, however, no aversion to liberty of conscience. He wrote: " Bad and good, all alike want liberty of conscience, and they will never be diverted from this idea by kindness, only by energetic measures." [1]

Don John was indignant at the demands made, he was alarmed at the rumours current in regard to his own personal safety, about rumours of English and French intrigues, etc. He felt himself utterly at sea and powerless. By June he no longer felt safe at Brussels. On the 11th, he retreated to Mechlin, while he sent Escovedo to Spain to represent the serious state of affairs to the king.

It was perfectly true that Orange was trying to undermine him everywhere. The prince had no faith in any pretence of peace with Spain, and left no means untried to impress its hollowness upon the people. Not many weeks passed before Don John changed his tactics. The queen of Navarre passed through Namur on her way to take the waters at Spa. Thither went the governor to greet her and give her " godspeed " on her journey. No sooner had he bidden her farewell on June 24th, as she sailed off from Namur on her barge, than he started off on a hunting party with his body-guard. The game hunted was, however, the citadel. He seized it suddenly and established himself securely there, declaring that it was a measure of personal safety. From this stronghold he wrote to the States-General and to the provincial Estates and stadtholders and other dignitaries, promising to respect the Pacification, but demanding the following items: a personal guard; an oath of fealty from the stadtholders and colonels of the army, offered to him personally; right of nomination to all vacant posts, removal of suspected persons, like Marnix and others from the States, and, finally, common war against

[1] *Corresp. de Phil. II.*, v., p. 350.

the prince in case he refused to treat.[1] His attempts to
seize Antwerp and other citadels failed.[2]

At Brussels, this behaviour of Don John made a deep
impression. The States-General considered it a proof of
the treachery which Orange had feared. They now followed the prince's advice and appealed to the emperor
for mediation, to Elizabeth for aid, while the prince
again turned to Henry III. Even Berlaymont's sons
and Aerschot seemed to be forward in these attempts.

Orange reaped all the advantage he could from this
event.[3] He actually succeeded in persuading the Estates
of Gelderland to consent to make common cause with
Holland and Zealand for the sake of freedom.   In
Utrecht the excitement produced an invitation to the
prince to visit the city, and a pressure by the people upon
the Estates to acknowledge the prince as provincial
stadtholder.

The Brussels population, too, were roused, and not
without the prince's previous knowledge. The " true
patriots,"[4] as they had called themselves since the events
of 1576, made themselves heard. It was chiefly the
guilds, the small citizens, who, egged on by Marnix and
Théron and Hèze, clamoured that the prince of Orange
was the only man to withstand the Spaniards.[5] A college of eighteen people, composed of two from every
nation of the guilds, was led by the jurist Van der
Straeten. This college, together with eight representatives of magistrates and citizens, assumed the defence of
the city and the administration of municipal government,
and armed the citizens. These were not Calvinists in
the main. Indeed there were not more than seven or
eight hundred in the whole city.[6] The majority were
Catholics. The movement in Brussels bore a distinctly

[1] Kervijn, iv., p. 439.
[2] *Archives*, vi., p. 113.
[3] *Ibid.*, p. 134.
[4] Renon de France.
[5] Kervijn, iv., p. 467 *et seq*.
[6] Van Meteren, p. 142.

Orange character.   He was regarded as the one man to bring order into affairs, and the Catholics did not count it dangerous that he himself was a heretic and exercised a considerable influence upon the government through his heretical friends and allies.   But, though the Calvinists were in the minority, they made up in zeal what they lacked in numbers.   The English queen, too, lent a hand to rouse popular revolt in Brussels, and she thought that her best defence against Don John.   The States sent her an embassy to insure coöperation.

Owing to the pressure of the armed citizens in Brussels, the States-General yielded to their wish, and, on September 6th, a resolution was taken by the majority to invite the prince to come to Brussels and assume the leadership, to defend the country from Spanish tyranny, and for the restoration of peace.   Champagney, Leoninus, the abbots of Maroilles, Villers, and St. Geertrui, and the advocate Liesvelt, were the bearers of the message.   The prince answered that he would come after consulting the Estates of Holland and Zealand, thankful for the confidence reposed in him, and glad that they had decided to unite in an effort to preserve the land.[1]   On September 18th, he went to Antwerp, joyously welcomed by the people.

One point only delayed his proceeding to the capital of Brabant.   The States-General asked him to permit the exercise of the Catholic religion in Holland and Zealand.   His reply, that he could do nothing without consulting the Estates, aroused suspicion among some members of the States-General, who, moreover, had not quite relinquished hope of patching up a peace with Don John.   There was accordingly more backing and filling, and Don John did not know what to do.   The Spanish troops he had asked for did not come.   Philip, angry at his brother's lack of success, had resolved to recall him,

[1] *Archives*, vi., p. 157.

but left him meanwhile without instructions for three months, while he let him feel that the renewal of hostilities was very undesirable.[1] In despair Don John promised to yield to all the demands of the States and to withdraw to Luxemburg. On September 23rd, the treaty with Don John was approved in the assembly, although Holland and Zealand endeavoured to persuade the States to defer action. On the same day the prince entered Brussels.

The very same crowd which had received Don John with every show of homage and manifestations of joy now welcomed the " Restorer and Defender of the Fatherland's Liberty " with equal demonstrations. Escorted by three hundred armed Antwerpers, Orange reached the gates of the capital at about four o'clock, where the citizens in arms, twenty-six companies, four thousand strong, awaited him. Aerschot, Egmont, Hèze, and many more nobles took part in the procession which passed through gaily decorated streets. Shouts of joy rang through the illuminated city until late in the evening, and all Brussels made festival at the coming of the man who had fled as an exile ten years previous and now was received as a sovereign.

In Holland and Zealand there was great anxiety for the prince's personal safety, which showed how much affection he had won. The arrival of his brother John from Germany, on October 7th, restored to some extent a sense of confidence in Holland.

A thrill of triumph must have passed through the prince when he entered the gates of Brussels. He seemed to have attained what he had awaited for ten years. On that day the Netherlands seemed united for good against the Spanish regent, who, forsaken and in despair, was forced to declare himself ready for anything at Namur.

There was some more parleying, and then the States,

[1] Burman, *Analecta*, i., p. 76 ; Bondam, *Onuitg. stukken*, iii., p. 163.

on October 8th, informed Don John in insulting terms that they no longer acknowledged him as governor, but wished one of royal blood as was their due, threatening even to beg aid from all sovereigns and peoples against him. The regent replied in terms equally sharp. He had heard that troops were on their way to him. War was as good as begun.

Before the arrival of the new Spanish troops, however, much had changed in the opposition party. Certain of the Brabant nobles, notably Egmont, had been carrying on secret negotiations with the emperor's twenty-year-old brother Matthias.[1] They wished to have this prince of the blood to hold in check the Calvinist populace and the prince, whom they feared while they found him indispensable. Matthias did not wait for urging. He fled secretly the night between October 2nd and 3rd, possibly not without his imperial brother's knowledge, from Vienna, and travelled post-haste to the Netherlands. A few days after his flight, the nobles who had invited him informed the States-General of their action, and urged his immediate recognition as governor. The prince, who had kept out of the affair, although not wholly without cognisance of the plan, opposed any formal recognition, and succeeded in persuading the States to receive him only as a prince of the blood for the time being, so as to avoid alienating France and England.

Before the young archduke's arrival, the prince had spoiled his opponents' game by a clever counter-play. The populace in Brussels, still with the Eighteen at their head, had become steadily more and more at odds with the States-General. Now the prince received the Eighteen repeatedly at his own table and interchanged with them promises of mutual devotion, he " their trust and refuge."[2] By the help of the citizens, to whom he com-

---

[1] *Bul. de la com. d'hist.*, 3rd series, p. 283.
[2] See Bussemaker, *De Afscheiding*, i., p. 195.

plained of the machinations of the nobles, he obtained a post which he had desired in the days of Granvelle, that of Ruward of the province. Popular opinion forced the Estates of Brabant to accede to this. Similar pressure was exerted in the States-General, the opposition of the nobles who had called in Matthias was overweighted, and the nomination was confirmed.

The prince appeared to hesitate, and to accept the new title only out of respect to the fiery wish of the populace. When this was accomplished, the new ruward of Brabant went to Antwerp in order better to watch affairs in Ghent.

Aerschot, made stadtholder of Flanders in September, was then in Ghent trying to persuade the provincial Estates to refuse their confirmation to the elevation of Orange. He succeeded in obtaining a resolution to that effect, and at the same time in pushing through the recognition of Matthias.

The answer to this thrust at Orange was a popular revolt. Finally Aerschot, Sweveghem, Rasseghem, Hessels, the old councillor from the Council of Troubles, the bishops of Bruges and Ypres, and several others were all imprisoned in the house of Ryhove, one of the leaders of the movement. Here, as at Brussels, the government was reorganised under the influence of the guilds in a democratic fashion, while the ancient privileges existing previous to 1540 were restored. Jan Van Hembyze was the head of the Eighteen, the majority of whom were Calvinists, while Ryhove was made commander of the burgher guard and great bailiff of Ghent.

The States-General were very indignant, and imputed, in spite of the protestations of Marnix, the responsibility of this event to the prince of Orange. Aerschot was released at the instance of the States, but the unfavourable impression of the incident could not be effaced. Distrust of Orange was strengthened.

Egmont, Lalaing, Hèze, and others began to be alienated from him from fear of the Calvinistic democracy with which he seemed allied ; and there were others in whom the nobles found ready allies. The clergy were in terror at the increase of Calvinism through the return of the exiles of 1566 and drew back from relations with Orange and his followers. The patricians in the cities, too, feared that the increase of the democratic agitation boded the destruction of their sovereignty. Such were the elements of a vigorous opposition to the prince which began to be manifest in the States-General as well as throughout the various provinces.[1]

Meanwhile Matthias had arrived in the Netherlands on October 30th. The States-General delayed three weeks before responding to his announcement of his arrival. The prince, however, having quickly decided that all could be saved by means of the archduke, urged his acceptance, and drew up a plan whereby the new governor would be wholly subordinated to the States-General and to a council of state nominated by that body.[2] Anjou meanwhile resumed his offers of aid, and the fear of French intrigues entertained by Aerschot and others really induced the recognition of Matthias by the States. They declared Don John a public foe, and, on December 8th, requested the archduke to take the governorship for the present, on the condition of the king's approval, with the union of Brussels as a basis. At the prince's request this was formally renewed in a way to show that Romish and non-Romish were allied in the struggle for privileges.[3]

Matthias accepted. At the instance of Brabant the new council of state was appointed by the provincial Estates individually. In addition to Havré and Sasbout, there were Marnix—at the prince's suggestion—Leoninus,

---

[1] P. L. Muller in Fruin's *Bijdr.*, vii., p. 254.

[2] Kervijn, v., p. 511.

[3] De Jonge, *Onuitgegeven Stukken*, ii., p. 163 *et seq.*

the abbot of Maroilles, and the advocate Liesvelt, while all the governors had seats *ex-officio*. These appointments were made, though not without vigorous opposition, under the influence of the Brussels College of Eighteen. They had protested vigorously against the first nominations, which were, they asserted, wholly in the interest of Brabant, not for the common weal of the land. The composition of the council showed plainly how great was the power of the Brussels democracy.

After Christmas, the prince visited Ghent, where he was received with festivals and demonstrations which showed that he was as popular there as elsewhere. There was much indignation in the States-General that he did not use the power given him by this popularity to free the members of the corporation who were still in prison. What he did do was to renew the close union between Brabant and Flanders which had existed in the days of the Arteveldes, and confirmed, amid the applause of his followers, the democratic form of government. In Brussels he could obtain anything he desired from the citizen government in order to subordinate Matthias to his influence. It was the Brussels commonalty who forced the States-General to make the prince lieutenant-general to Matthias. The honour, also suggested by Elizabeth, was bestowed, after some show of opposition on the prince's part,[1] in response to a request from Matthias on the ground of Orange's *expérience des affaires d'état tant de guerre que de paix*.

On January 18, 1578, Matthias made his formal entry into Brussels with a brilliant escort of the nobles, besides the imperial emissary, the count of Schwartzburg, and the prince himself. There was another carnival of symbolic representations and illuminations.

For the time being, the nobles who were jealous of Orange's authority were thus defeated. The prince was

[1] *Archives*, vi., p. 279; compare Bussemaker, i., p. 216.

the virtual head of the government, with the young, unskilled archduke as his clerk. The union of Brussels had confirmed the coöperation between Catholics and Protestants, promising protection to both, wholly according to Orange's idea of toleration. But the manner in which he had carried affairs so far, although proving his brilliancy as a statesman, also revealed the difficulties which were in store for him. It was a question whether he could continue to hold the nobles in check, keep the confidence of the populace,— his somewhat dangerous ally, — and succeed in making Calvinists and Catholics work together.

In respect to this last relation the union of Brussels was still defective. The times were not yet ripe for the prince's ideas of universal religious freedom.[1] In the municipalities where Calvinism was in the ascendant, neither preachers nor congregations were willing to allow free exercise of religious rites to followers of the papacy, which they regarded as the pool of unrighteousness. There was political as well as theological antagonism. In Holland and Zealand, too, the Catholics were suspected of secret sympathy; if not secret coöperation, with the Spaniards. In spite of the active part many faithful Catholics had taken in the opposition to Alva, there was some ground for the suspicion of double-dealing on the part of others. On the other hand, upright Catholics cannot be blamed for opposing freedom to the heresy which they honestly believed the work of the devil. They might dislike persecution, but they could not accord the heretic equal rights with the faithful.

These sincere convictions were diametrically opposed to each other—two worlds separated by a steadily deeper groove. The idea of a " Christianity above differences in creeds," conceived by Orange and a few others, was

[1] Compare Fruin, *De weder opluiking van het Catholicisme*. De Gids, 1894, No. 1.

simply incomprehensible to the great majority on both sides. Yet more than that, it seemed against God's commands. Thus Calvinism and Catholicism stood opposed to each other.

And the prince, whose best support against Spain was the Calvinists, was forced, where he and his had the power, to permit Calvinist propaganda even while he tried to protect the Catholics as far as possible — a difficult task, which won him little more than ingratitude and distrust from both sides. For the Catholics considered him the arch-Calvinist, and did not understand the necessity he felt, as Čalvinist leader, to spare his turbulent allies.' Often the Calvinists, too, who felt little for his political convictions towards their beloved faith, were restrained from revolting against him simply by faith in his leadership, tried through years, and by the instinct that they would be lost without him.

In the course of 1577, Calvinism had increased greatly in the Netherlands. Wherever the prince's soldiers had penetrated and the prince's influence reached, the exiles had returned, as they had to Holland in 1572, and those who had remained at home ventured to discard their outward signs of Catholicism. Under the *régime* of Hembyze and Ryhove, the rapid spread of Calvinism at Ghent soon made that influence dominant. At Amsterdam, the government could withstand with difficulty the pressure of the Calvinist burghers, whose numbers increased almost in proportion to the need of the hard-pressed city. In Friesland, Groningen, and the Ommelands, Calvinism spread, although the city of Groningen remained Catholic. In the spring of 1578, the town governments were forcibly changed in many Frisian cities by Renneberg. In Utrecht, the prince had established the reformed doctrine in February, 1577, while the archbishop's rights were respected. It was remarkable, how-

[1] *Apology of the Prince*, p. 112.

ever, that in Artois, South Flanders, and Valenciennes, where Calvinism had once been so strong, there was now virtually no sympathy for the reformed church. The reason lay in the radical uprooting of the new doctrine by Egmont, Noircarmes, and Alva, and the vigorous reorganisation of the Catholic Church in these regions.[1] This very spread of Calvinism added to Orange's difficulties. The Catholics feared their domination, and in spite of pacification and union this question of religion was the great hindrance to active coöperation against the common foe.

In the spring, the prince thought the time had come to realise his plan of a general religious peace,[2] and finally under his influence a scheme was drawn up by the council for all the provinces, providing that wherever a hundred people desired to exercise one of the two faiths, it should be allowed.

When this project was presented, in June, to the States-General, it aroused vehement protests from the Catholics, who declared, not without justice, that it was in conflict with the Pacification, which had expressly excluded Calvinism from all provinces except Holland and Zealand. It was urged, in reply, that circumstances had changed, and that now the Calvinists had rights in other provinces. The decision of the majority was that the archduke should send the articles to the several provincial Estates to ascertain their opinion. The scheme met violent opposition or postponement of decision. In Antwerp alone the religious peace was proclaimed. The actual result of this attempt was that theological differences were more sharply defined. The prince appreciated the significance of the situation, and felt that the moment was coming when the Pacification, on whose construction

[1] P. L. Muller, *Bijdragen tot de Geschiedenis der Scheiding van Noord-en Zuid Nederland;* Fruin's *Bijdr.*, 3rd series, vii., p. 8.
[2] *Archives*, vi., p. 386.

so much pains had been expended, would fall apart from
the force of religious difference.   And just in those early
days of 1578 there was the greatest need of coöperation.

After the Pacification, Holland and Zealand had implored the prince to free them from the burden of the
troops employed against Alva, but he succeeded in convincing them that they must be slow in disbanding their
forces, and retained forty-five companies of foot-soldiers
and thirty ships, so little faith did he place in the endur-
ance of peace.   The States-General had in their service
about fifty companies of German and Walloon foot and
fifteen hundred cavalry under Bossu, Egmont, and other
nobles—an incoherent mass, camped on the Meuse in
the neighbourhood of Namur, ill paid, insufficiently fed,
and consequently untrustworthy.[1]

Ill paid !   The ancient evil of Netherland finances had
not improved during the disturbances.   The central government was weak, and each province felt that it must
look out for itself.   The burdens were heavy.   The
" state of war " of 1578 shows the sums needed.[2]   So
little was contributed that often Holland and Zealand
were the only provinces to fulfil their duty towards the
generality, and they acted under the prince's personal
influence.   According to the ancient division,[3] Holland's
share in the common taxes was 11 per cent., Zealand's, 3
per cent. ; Flanders, rated for 33 per cent., Brabant, for 25
per cent., complained of the high taxation.   So, too, did
Artois and Hainaut, both rated for about 5½ per cent. ;
and even the Sticht, which of old did not have more than
1 per cent. to pay.   It was thus comprehensible that the
soldiers often received wages for only one month of the
twelve, and equally comprehensible that they tried to compensate themselves for their lack of pay by plundering.

Appeals to Elizabeth for aid resulted in a treaty
(January 7, 1578), wherein she promised to act as mediator

[1] *Archives*, vi., p. 249.   [2] Van Meteren, p. 152.   [3] Part II., p. 264.

between the States and Don John. If that failed, she was to aid the States on condition of receiving Flushing, Middelburg, Bruges, and Gravelines as pledges. It was long before the promised five thousand foot or one thousand horse or the ton of gold were seen. But finally four thousand Scots and a few hundred German horse, strengthened by a number of Huguenots, arrived. Elizabeth had appointed Duke John Casimir of the Palatine as her commander.

Don John, meanwhile, prepared for the contest with a smaller but better organised force than that of the States. By this time Philip had consented to recall his unwilling governor and to reappoint as regent Margaret of Parma. Her son, Alexander Farnese, prince of Parma, had already joined Don John. The attack was opened by the royalist troops, the army of the States was repulsed, and on January 31st, Don John won the battle of Gembloux. It was a bitter defeat for the Netherlanders, and plainly displayed the weakness of their leaders. Had Don John then had money and the king's confidence he could have reinstated Philip's authority in the south, but he was without either.

There was, meanwhile, virtual anarchy in several of the Brabant and Flemish cities. All Flanders was prey to a Calvinistic terrorism which made the Catholics long for Don John's sovereignty. The States-General seemed utterly incapable of preserving social order. Orange, on his side, was only partially successful in his attempt to smooth the disorders.[1] Catholics had lost faith in him. He strained himself to the utmost. Troops were collected from all sides; corn was stored in the cities; stadtholders were sent to their provinces. German troops were levied under Martin Schenck and other well-known mercenary captains. Bossu was charged with the care of Brussels, where chaos reigned and democracy had degenerated into

[1] Bussemaker, i., p. 238.

anarchy. There seemed urgent need of foreign suzerainty, and negotiations were renewed with Elizabeth and with Anjou. The young duke was burning with impatience to distinguish himself. His royal brother was sufficiently alive to the danger of England in the Netherlands to further his plans. Anjou collected troops in the north of France, and on July 12th appeared at Mons in Hainaut, where he was received by Lalaing with open arms. His fifteen thousand men followed speedily, and he actually succeeded in wresting a couple of little fortresses from the Spaniards. In addition to other contingencies, the States-General were afraid that Hainaut might ally herself to France,[1] and they hastened to make a treaty with the new-comer, so as not to alienate him. This was signed August 13th, and stipulated the terms on which this *Defenseur de la liberté des Pays-Bas* would be received. There was to be an effort to create an alliance between Elizabeth, the Huguenots, John Casimir, and others. Anjou was specifically excluded from the government for the time being.[2] John Casimir also appeared with a small Protestant army paid by English money, and advanced first to Zutphen and then on to Brabant, doing much damage, and received with great jubilation by the Flemish Calvinists. To the forty thousand men at the disposition of the States-General, Don John could oppose less than twenty thousand. After suffering a defeat in August near Rymenam, he withdrew to the vicinity of Namur and pitched camp at the junction of the Meuse and the Sambre.

Six months had elapsed since his success at Gembloux, but nothing further had been accomplished. Philip now ignored him, and sent a messenger directly to the States. He was left without orders as to his further proceedings

[1] Bussemaker, i., pp. 223–243.
[2] Muller and Diegerick, *Documents concernant les relations entre le duc d'Anjou et les Pays-Bas*, i., p. 408.

and without funds.   He protested to the French court
against Anjou's intrigues, but received no satisfaction.
His health began to suffer from the mental and physical
strain of his uncomfortable position.   Philip finally wrote
one kind letter, but sent no word as to his policy.   Despairing letters from Don John in his last days are still
preserved, with the king's autograph note, " There is no
need to answer." [1]   Finally a camp fever threw the unfortunate commander on a sick-bed, and on October 1st
the emperor's youngest offspring, bitterly disappointed
in every one of his ardent expectations, expired in the
midst of his sorrowing army.

Prince Alexander of Parma was charged with the command by the dying regent, who had not yet been replaced
by the duchess according to their distant brother's
promises.

Parma speedily had the opportunity to show that he
possessed marked knowledge of statecraft as well as
extraordinary military talent.

A regular guerrilla warfare ensued in Flanders between
the regular and irregular troops collected on her soil.
Those under Montigny, Lalaing's younger brother, began
to mutiny. [2]   The state of affairs became very critical;
neither the States-General nor the prince seemed able
to avert the dangers of a religious war such as these
skirmishes had become. [3]

Spanish sympathisers rejoiced at these evidences of
civil war.   The situation became more critical when
Anjou's army dispersed and a portion of the troops
joined the " Malcontents," as Montigny's Walloons were
called.   La Motte, too, commander at Gravelines, who

[1] Kervijn, vi., p. 254.
[2] Bussemaker, i., p. 390.
[3] See Muller in Fruin's *Bijdragen*, vii., pp. 247, 349; and Bussemaker,
Afscheiding, i., p. 255.

had played a double part for some time and been in secret treaty with Don John,[1] opened negotiations with him and furnished him with ammunition.

Montigny was just the man to attract the discontented people at this crisis. His personal relations with the Catholic nobles, his position as member of the Estates of Hainaut, as belonging to the family of Lalaing, his popularity among the Walloon soldiers, made him a personality of weight. Then, too, there were many Walloons —nobles and clergy—who were still faithful to Don John and willing to excite disaffection to Orange in any possible way, in the hopes of attaining reconciliation with the king. Among them were the Baron de Licques, the seigneur of Havroult and Rossignol, and clergy like the prior of Renty, and Jean de Sarazin, the newly appointed abbot of St. Vaast. Attempts to seize such places as St. Omer, Douay, and Bouchain failed, but gave evidence of Walloon hostility towards the prince's party.

Anjou's attitude, as a Valois, was very uncertain and shifty. He actually proposed to Lalaing to make him the head of a Walloon Catholic confederation of Hainaut, Artois, Namur, and South Flanders, and he himself sent troops to Montigny.[2]

In Artois, party spirit ran high. In Flanders the evil was still worse. The violent Calvinist, John Casimir, was exasperated at the slight support furnished him by the States, and began to fish in the troubled waters to see what he could find for his fellow-believers, whom he considered betrayed even by Orange himself. Hembyze and his crowds jeered openly at the authority of the archduke, the prince, and the States. Thus Flanders began to be virtually alienated from the States-General equally with Hainaut and Artois. The prince only succeeded in maintaining a show of peace, for no real harmony was possible among the discordant elements.

[1] Bussemaker, i., pp. 284, 324 *et seq.*   [2] *Ibid.*, i., p. 420.

Finally, at the end of the year 1578, Anjou, having failed in an attempt to seize Mons, returned to France. John Casimir, too, left his discontented army and went to England, where Elizabeth received him with great coolness. Two elements of strife were thus removed, but the intrigues of La Motte, Montigny, and the Spanish sympathisers finally bore tangible fruit. Parma had assured them that he was quite ready to adopt, according to the king's behest, conciliatory and gentle measures, but " force must also be exercised,"[1] he wrote significantly. In December, Montigny, La Motte, and others decided to submit to the king openly. On January 6, 1579, the long-desired alliance was made at Arras between Hainaut, Artois, Lille, Douay, and Orchies. These provinces and cities declared that they would be forced to resort to the king for the maintenance of the Pacification in the midst of the increasing confusion, on account of the undermining of the Catholic belief and the violation of the privileges, unless the States-General would coöperate with them within a month for the maintenance of the Pacification and for a peace with the governor on the basis of that treaty.

This union of Arras was not a reconciliation with the king,[2] but evidently it would soon lead to that result. Everything tended thither. The Walloons were filled with wrath at the Flemish Calvinists, at the prince, at the States-General, and it was too deeply rooted to be eradicated. The course of affairs in Hainaut and Artois had undoubtedly been affected by the turn of events in the north of the Netherlands.

With his far-reaching political insight, the prince had appreciated the danger threatening the alliance of the provinces from the attitude of the nobles and the antagonism between Catholics and Protestants. He had therefore conceived the idea of making a closer union in

[1] Kervijn, v., p. 294.   [2] See P. L. Muller, p. 432.

the north as a counterpoise to these evidences of dissolution.[1] The kernel of this alliance was the confederation of Holland and Zealand, which had been under his leadership from the autumn of 1577, and strengthened by the addition of Utrecht, according to the terms of the ancient union existing in the time of Charles V. It seemed safe to count on Friesland, Groningen, Drenthe, and Overyssel, and on the aid of the stadtholder of the north, the count of Renneberg. Deventer was in opposition. In Gelderland the election of John of Nassau (March, 1578), as against Bossu and Hierges, showed the prince's influence.[2] Count John was in full sympathy with his brother, except in the point of asking French aid. The zealous Calvinist could not forget St. Bartholomew.

There were many difficulties to be overcome before this projected union was accepted by the northern provinces. The fears entertained by the Catholics of the Protestants were justified by what happened wherever the Calvinists gained the dominance. John of Nassau himself was not wholly free from blame. Then, too, the supremacy of Holland and Zealand was always dreaded by their lesser friends, and the old nobles were afraid of being ruled by Calvinist burghers.

John of Nassau did not lose hope. In the Estates of Holland the majority voted for a union on the proposed basis (August 29th). The Estates of Gelderland were convened in special session in September, and there appeared five deputies of Holland, among others the pensionary John of Oldenbarnevelt.[3] Nothing was effected, however, either by their pleading or by the presence of

[1] This was suggested as early as 1576. Bondam, *Onuitg. stukken*, i., pp. 39, 51, 217, 271 ; ii., p. 71 ; iii., pp. 97, 199, 260. See also P. L. Muller, *Geschiedenis der reg. in de Nader Geunieerde Provincien* (Leyden, 1867), and his union of Utrecht. Utrecht, 1878.

[2] *Archives*, vi., p. 289. The prince himself would have been preferred as stadtholder.

[3] Nijhoff, in the *Bijdragen*, i., pp. 104–144.

troops under John Arnhem, who attempted to intimidate
the Estates.   Violent altercations occurred in the assembly between the Catholics and the zealous Calvinist
count of Culemborg.   The general opposition throughout
the provinces only began to be diminished when the
magistrates were changed for those of other opinion.[1]
The other provinces showed equal reluctance to accept
the scheme.

In November, on the return of Count John from a
journey to Germany, and when, too, it was evident that
affairs in Hainaut and Artois would speedily result in a
reconciliation with Spain, discussions of the plan of union
were renewed at the prince's instance.   A notable conference of deputies from the various provinces was held
at Utrecht at the end of the month.   On December 6th,
the union was provisionally signed by the representatives
of Holland, Zealand, and Friesland, with the Estates
of Utrecht.   The deputies then adjourned until January
10th, when a definite and final resolution was to be
taken.   In Gelderland the opposition was the strongest,
but a majority of votes prevailed, and her deputies were
present when the conference opened on January 10, 1579.
Difficulties of all kinds were presented, but Count John
succeeded in pushing the scheme through.   On January
23rd, the union of Utrecht was formally signed by the
count himself as stadtholder of Gelderland in behalf of
the province, and by the deputies of Holland, Zealand,
and the Ommelands.

The treaty made the provinces " to become one whole
as if they were one province."   At the same time it was
expressly stated that this new bond was not in any way
to the prejudice of the Pacification of Ghent.   The con-
tracting parties promised to stand by each other with
body and property and blood as against all force and
power.   To this end the union was to strengthen the

[1] Van Reyd, p. 17.

cities and build new fortifications. In conjunction with the provincial stadtholders, this central body was to garrison the cities at their pay, while the soldiers were to take an oath to union to city and to province. Further, all inhabitants between eighteen and sixty were to be registered so as to be ready for a draft for national defence. The expenses were to be met from the domains, from the regular taxes imposed for the purpose, and farmed for three-month terms, or raised by collection. In matters of treaty or peace, impost and contribution, unanimity was obligatory: in other cases a majority of votes was sufficient for a decision. If unanimity could not be obtained, then a provisional decision, valid for the time being, was permitted to the stadtholders of the United Provinces. This was also to hold good in any case of disagreement among the provinces. No province was free to form a confederation or alliance with any neighbours or lands without consent of the others. The admission of others into the alliance must depend on the unanimous approval of all. In regard to mintage, ordinances binding on all were to be made later. In regard to religion, " those in Holland and Zealand " should do as it seemed best to them, while the others could act in accordance with the religious peace, or take any measures which seemed best to preserve quiet and prosperity, maintenance of law and justice on the ancient footing. It was expressly stated that there could be no inequality in the taxation imposed upon inhabitants and strangers, no introduction of unjust imposts or ship-money, without " common consent." Articles 19 and 20 provided for an assembly of deputies at Utrecht, where matters should be decided unanimously or by majority of votes, and those not represented should be equally bound by the resolutions. Obscurity or ambiguity in interpretation should be decided by common consent of the allies, or, if they failed to agree, by the stadtholders.

Nothing could be altered in the union without unanimous approval. The stadtholders, magistrates, and chief officials of provinces or cities, all archers and guilds, were obliged to take an oath to the union, and, according to the final Article (number 26,) the stadtholders and chief members and cities were to set their seal and signature thereon.

Thus, instead of the Pacification and universal union, two separate unions arose in the Netherlands, the germs of two separate political bodies. The one, claiming to rest upon the Pacification, continued the opposition to Spain, and declared plainly that its aim was common defence. The other, claiming equal adherence to the Pacification, urged the maintenance of Catholicism, and showed unmistakable inclination to reconciliation with the king.

In the spring of 1579, these opposing principles were developed. The States-General and the prince tried hard to prevent the imminent separation, by negotiations with Montigny and the Estates of the dissenting nine provinces, and by efforts to hold the Flemish Calvinists in check. All failed. In April, Montigny signed the declaration that all troops and fortresses under his control should return to the king's authority.

On May 17, 1579, the Estates of Hainaut and Artois and the representatives of Lille, Douay, and Orchies signed the formal treaty of " reconciliation " in the abbey of St. Vaast at Arras. It was therein stipulated that, with the preservation of Catholicism and the royal authority, the privileges should be maintained, the Pacification, union of Brussels, and eternal edict confirmed. Foreign troops were to be replaced by a national army, citadels and fortresses were to be committed to the charge of native Netherlanders. In six months a prince of the blood should be appointed governor. In the course of the year Mechlin and Nivelles in Brabant, Aalst,

Geertsbergen, Bourburg, and Bailleul in Flanders all followed this lead.   They all threw themselves into the king's arms, chiefly from aversion to the " gulf of disorder " which had opened in Flanders, from fear of the " wolves ready to ravish us," as the Mechlin people declared.[1]   Thus the separation of these regions and cities from the remaining Netherlands was complete.

By the date of this last event the adherents to the union had increased.   The deputies of Gelderland returned home to consult their principals.   Count John changed the corporation at Arnhem, and in that manner compelled the division of the Veluwe to accept on March 9th.   The Betuwe signed on March 5th, Venloo on April 11th.   The various portions of Friesland signified their acceptance in the spring.   Overyssel finally declared that they could not sign the union, but that they considered themselves eternally allied with them and the States-General.   Drenthe signed in April, 1580.   Groningen hesitated, but the union exercised authority there.   Moreover, in the course of 1579 and 1580, Antwerp, Lier, and Breda in Brabant, Ghent, Ypres, Bruges, and the Freedom of Bruges signed too.

A long time elapsed, however, before Orange and Renneberg gave their consent.   The latter waited for the prince's action.   Orange hesitated.   The union of Utrecht, although it unquestionably emanated from him, did not wholly please him.   It did not escape his notice that the Catholics, especially the Walloons, would inevitably disapprove it, especially because of the scenes of iconoclasm for which its founder, Count John, was evidently responsible, and also because of the unmistakable inclination of its advocates to decide religious questions in favour of Calvinism.   Again, in April, the prince endeavoured to effect a general union on the basis of

[1] Kervijn de Volkaersbeke and Diegerick, *Documents inédits*, i., p. 423.

the religious peace,[1] but was forced to relinquish the plan for lack of support. In the spring of 1579, while the negotiations with the Walloons were still in progress, the prince feared to vitiate them by entering the union. Not until the futility of the first scheme was evident, until the reconciliation of the Walloon provinces was certain, did he decide to sign. On May 3rd, he did so. Renneburg followed his example a month later. Both specified that the archduke's rights were not to be restricted.

The die was cast. The union of Utrecht now allied the provinces; under the prince of Orange the struggle was renewed against Spanish authority, which, under Parma and with the support of the Walloon provinces, had no intention of yielding.[2]

[1] Van de Spiegel, *Onuitgev. stukken*, ii., p. 23.
[2] See, for his position, *Archives*, vi., pp. 536, 613.

CHAPTER IV

THE STRUGGLE BETWEEN ORANGE AND PARMA

AGAIN the decision was left to the test of war. Spain's outlook was far from unfavourable in spite of the fact that not only Holland and Zealand but the whole north stood opposed to royal authority. But this apparent union was vitiated by the differences between Romanists and Calvinists, which enabled Parma to reckon on many sympathisers, although the rebels were temporarily dominant.

The new regent was admirably adapted to his task. Possessing, as he did, extraordinary talent both as general and statesman, he was exactly the man to wrest one advantage after another from Orange, to press him back foot by foot, employing political skill on the one hand and accomplished military science on the other. Of average height, he had a well-formed oval face, with a high, narrow forehead, an aquiline nose, and great dark, piercing eyes,—a " fell countenance," as his contemporaries said. He combined the deliberate cleverness of the Spaniard with the diplomatic skill of the Italian. Trained in the art of war and in statecraft as it then existed, he was not filled with chivalrous ideals and fantastic dreams of fame like his predecessor. He was of practical mind, with no conscientious scruples about using any serviceable expedients to destroy his foes, coolly reckoning on his chances, free from all passion,—

the most dangerous opponent whom Prince William had encountered. Had the king given him a free hand, Orange would speedily have been forced to yield. But —luckily for Netherland liberty—from the very beginning, Philip II. hampered the plans of his lieutenant in more than one particular.

In the last days of Don John's administration, Spain had consented to take part in a conference intended to effect an accommodation between Philip and his rebel-, lious subjects. Emperor Rudolph, at the instance of the German princes, had urged this step, as his predecessor had done before. Maximilian's efforts had been met coldly; Rudolph's were accepted owing to the reverses of Spanish arms and the loss of Spanish authority. Deputies were duly selected by pope, emperor, king, and States-General, and the conference was appointed to meet at Cologne. But before the session opened in the early summer of 1579, Spanish affairs under Parma had so far revived that the Spanish point of view changed, and the conference was entirely ineffective. After six months of discussion the envoys adjourned. It was again plain that war was the only solution.[1]

Parma was already at work. He was sure of the greater part of the south; Luxemburg, Namur, Hainaut, Artois, southern Flanders, and southern Brabant were wholly in his power. Liege[2] had declared neutrality. The early spring of 1579 was devoted to making preparations and to advancing upon Maestricht, highly important from its command of the Meuse region. A three-months' siege ended in a violent assault on June 29th, when the city was forced to yield. More than half the inhabitants

[1] Important for these negotiations are the documents in the collections of the *Nuntiaturberichte aus Deutschland*, 3rd division, 2nd part, on the basis of which Hansen gives a study entitled, "*Der Niederl. Pacificationsdag zu Köln, 1579.*" *Westd. Zeitschrift*, xiii., p. 3.

[2] Thomasson, *Krijgsbedrijven van Alexander Farnese in Limburg, 1578-79.* Maestricht, 1890.

fell victims to the pest during the siege or to the sword afterwards. The prosperity—commercial and industrial —of the place was destroyed. The male inhabitants in the villages were reduced from one thousand to thirty or forty, churches were laid low, tilled land devastated. This was an important gain for the Spaniards, and other circumstances, too, furthered their interests at this time. The Catholics were embittered by a savage attack upon an Ascension-Day (1579) procession at Antwerp. Matthias, Havré, and several other distinguished nobles were present and greatly incensed at the insults to their religion. The archduke threatened to leave the province. Certain nobles publicly deserted the patriots' cause. Egmont forgot his father's wrongs and went over to the king, taking Nivelles, Geertsbergen, Ninove, with him. Aerschot, disappointed at the result of the Cologne conference, followed his example, as did Schetz and others, while, as a matter of fact, Renneberg, the prince's stadtholder, was already in correspondence with Alva through his secretary, Bailly.[1]

The Calvinist riots at Ghent were to a great degree the occasion of the nobles' revulsion of feeling. Well might the prince say : " *Ces émeutes de la Flandre gâtent entièrement nos affaires.*" [2]   Scarcely had he left the city when the fanatic Ghent Calvinists, led by Hembyze and Dathenus, egged on by John Casimir, gained the ascendency. Neither Catholics nor moderate Protestants, like La Noue, were safe. Orange was distrusted because of his parleys with France, and the recall of John Casimir was urged. With the help of Ryhove, who remained true to him, Orange succeeded in undermining the influence of Hembyze and Dathenus. They became his open enemies and attacked him bitterly. On August 18th, the Prince reappeared in Ghent, where his personal influence was

[1] Trosée, p. xlviii.
[2] *Corresp. de Guillaume le Taciturne*, iv., p. 142 ; see, too, Bor, ii., p. 75.

still strong. The two demagogues found that they could not hold their own against him, and fled to the Palatinate to seek protection from John Casimir.

It was necessary to put a final stop to the possibility of such scenes. The prince determined to make himself official head of the government in Flanders. After filling the municipal government at Ghent with his adherents, he restored order at Bruges in the same manner. But, although the Estates of Holland gave him permission to wield the stadtholdership in Flanders, he did not carry out his more comprehensive plan at the time, probably on account of his negotiations with Anjou. Meanwhile, La Noue, his Huguenot ally, succeeded in repulsing the enemy's advances in southern Flanders.

In the face of Parma's menacing attitude, the need of a strong foreign ally was very pressing, and the duke of Anjou seemed the desirable personification of that alliance, as he had obtained his brother's forgiveness for his independent expedition into the Netherlands and as his prospective marriage with Elizabeth was again under discussion. Under these circumstances, it was not wonderful that Orange renewed negotiations with him in June, 1579, since the moment seemed favourable for securing French aid by taking the duke as lord of the land.[1]

There were many difficulties to be overcome. In January, 1580, the States-General urged the prince to draw up a draft of the conditions on which the duke might be accepted as sovereign lord.[2] The actual author of this resolution is plain enough. By January 13th, the draft was ready. It was approved, and sent with a memorial from the prince to the provinces for discussion. In mid-

---

[1] *Documents*, ed. Muller et Diegerick, iii., p. 193.
[2] Compare Muller, *De verkiezing van Anjou*, Fruin's *Bijdr.*, 3rd series, viii., p. 339.

February, the deputies were to return and arrive at a decision.

The draft was in the same spirit as the treaty made by the duke in 1576 with Holland and Zealand.[1] Independence in respect to France, maintenance of privileges and of the religious peace in the other provinces, of the *status quo* in Holland and Zealand, recognition of the unions, restriction of sovereign right in financial and military realms, freedom of assembly for the States - General, which was to be convened once a year,— such were the principal stipulations. Probably Anjou thought that, when once sovereign, he could find means to do away with the restrictions, and was much pleased with the draft. The Netherland provinces, in spite of the prince's warnings and explanations, were less inclined to accept it. Flanders alone, now wholly under the prince's influence, approved the scheme. But the others delayed or refused assent outright.

In Utrecht, Gelderland, Overyssel, and the north in general the fact was prejudicial to the plan that Count John did not evince the least sympathy for it, and remained fixed in his aversion to the French prince. He wrote that he counted the French and Spanish alike.[2]

Thus opposition was rife, but the prince did not despair. Summer came, and the matter was still hanging fire. The Netherland state machinery was a complicated engine with numerous wheels which had to be put into operation one by one. In the midst of these negotiations, the patriots' cause suffered new and serious injury.

Renneberg,[3] the prince's stadtholder in Groningen, yielded to his sister's persuasion and to Parma's flattering offers and went over to the royalists. Catholic though he was, Orange had trusted him implicitly, and hastened from the south to try to hold him back, but it was too

---

[1] See p. 98.   [2] *Archives*, vii., p. 48.
[3] Compare Trosée, p. cxxviii. *et seq.*

late. Renneberg refused to see him, and the defection became a fact.

This event was full of calamity to the authority of the States in the north, as it was well known that there were many zealous Catholics in Friesland, Drenthe, and Overyssel, as well as in Groningen. The step had been foreseen long enough in advance for the States' sympathisers to assure themselves of Leeuwarden and Harlingen. For a time Renneberg was restricted to Groningen alone. But soon luck turned. Royalists, weary of the raids of the States' troops, rose in revolt in Zwolle, Deventer, Twente, and Salland. More and more territory came under Parma's lieutenants. A bitter guerrilla warfare began, which harassed this region for fourteen years.

The College of the Nearer Union was the proper power under the circumstances to maintain order in the north and to conduct the defences. It was a very difficult part for the college, which was only half recognised and scantily obeyed.

After the conclusion of the union, Count John of Nassau could have been made " Director," but was reluctant to ally himself with so weak a cause. There were other reasons of a personal nature, too, why he declined to be head of the alliance. But during the prince's absence in the south he had finally consented to assume the conduct of the union temporarily. Buys, the skilled advocate of Holland, and others were conjoined with him as council, and an organisation in financial and military affairs was initiated by the appointment of a receiver and treasurer-general, and of a commission for drafting instructions for the officials, raising funds, levying troops for the union, etc. After March, 1579, Count John left the further directions largely to appointed deputies of the united provinces, and confined himself to the duties of his stadtholdership and the military affairs of the union. In this he was very successful. Amersfoort, for instance, was reduced in a couple of days.[1] The difficulties he encountered at every turn were great, the chief points still being the arrogance of the Calvinists and their disregard of the stipulations of the religious peace, in spite even of the warnings of the " pope of Geneva," Beza, the head of the Calvinist theologians.[2]

By the end of 1579, thanks to the exertions of Count John, a certain order was instituted. Reinier Cant (of Amsterdam), Buys, Karl Roorda from Friesland, Floris Thin of Utrecht were, with Count John, the most influential members of this college that wielded authority east of the Meuse. They were all old, proved friends of Orange whom he could trust to render Renneberg's defection as little injurious to the cause as possible. The college was established first at Campen, and later at Amsterdam, where it was more convenient to act than at Utrecht, the seat of general government, according to the stipulations of the Union.

In August, 1580, Count John resigned his offices in order to return to his German estates. This was a serious blow to the prince. The count's position in Gelderland was, however, far from pleasant. Indeed, he often literally lacked bread and fire in his house, while he was exposed to treachery on all sides, and had begun to suspect the good faith of his brother-in-law, William van den Bergh, who was, indeed, in correspondence with Parma,[3] whom he joined a little later. The count thought the situation hopeless. At home his private affairs needed attention owing to the death of his wife and to the youth of his children. At last, after long hesitation,[4] he relinquished his stadtholdership to Leoninus and to the

[1] P. L. Muller, *Geschiedenis der regeering in de Nader Geunieerde Provincien*, p. 42.

[2] *Archives*, vii., p. 248.

[3] *Ibid.*, p. 138.

[4] See his letter of the summer of 1579, *Archives*, vii., pp. 108–120 *et al.*

council of Gelderland, and departed for Nassau, uncertain of return.

His son, William Louis, remained behind in Friesland, valiantly fighting at the head of his regiment, devoted to the Netherlands and to his uncle.   Well might the prince exclaim at that period :

> " Donec eris felix multos numerabis amicos,
> Tempora cum erunt nubila, nullus erit." [1]

In the south, too, military operations were turning out ill for the prince's party.   La Noue, his valiant Huguenot ally, called the " Iron Arm," after several marked successes, was taken prisoner.   Parma kept him in close captivity for a long time.   He used the leisure afforded him by his five years' imprisonment in the isolated castle of Limburg to write his famous *Discours politique et militaire.* [2]

In the face of these disasters the need of securing an ally became more and more patent.   Orange accordingly pushed on the negotiations with Anjou, and succeeded in persuading the States to send a formal deputation to the duke, who was waiting impatiently in the castle of Plessis-les-Tours.

The embassy, which set sail on August 24th from Flushing and landed on the following day at Dieppe, consisted of Marnix, the two Flemings, Provyn and Noël de Caron; two Brabanters, the lord of Ohayn, and the clerk of the Estates, Hessels; further, of the pensionary of Ghent, and Caspar of Vosbergen, bailiff of Veere; thus two deputies only from the north, while Flanders and Brabant were well represented.   This was wholly in accord with the actual position of affairs.   Flanders had agreed; so had Brabant, with some restrictions; but it could hardly be said that there had been any evidence

---

[1] *Archives*, vii., p. 231.
[2] Compare Hauser, *François de la Noue.* Paris, 1892.

of sympathy in the north, as the provinces had refused
their consent or sent in declarations of little significance.
Accordingly, Brabant and Flanders alone—so the prince
planned—were to be immediately ruled by Anjou.   In
the north, the prince was to govern the other provinces
by means of the college of the nearer union, and the
sovereignty of Anjou should be only nominal.[1]

After much friction and many difficulties, the famous
treaty of Plessis-les-Tours[2] was adopted (September 19th)
wherein the duke of Anjou was made " prince and
seigneur " of the Netherlanders as his predecessors of the
house of Burgundy had been.   The Twenty-seven Articles
accorded him only a restricted power, an authority dependent on the coöperation of the States in the most
important points.   At his death, one of his legitimate
male heirs was to be elected by the States, who would
rule during a minority.   The religious peace was to be
maintained, except in Holland and Zealand, where everything was to be *in statu quo*.   The duke promised to reside
within the provinces, and gave all due guarantees as to
the convention of the States, raising of money, etc.   He
also pledged himself to gain the help of France, while the
Netherlands were always to be independent of the French
crown.   He was also to make treaties with England,
Denmark, Portugal, Scotland, Navarre, the Hanse towns,
and the German princes.   The provinces were to furnish
2,400,000 guilders annually.   They protected themselves
from French aggression by the provisions that the commander of the French auxiliaries could only be appointed
in conjunction with the States; no French garrison
could be placed, nor French troops wintered in any place
without its consent, etc.   An oath was to be taken to the
duke in every province.   Any infringement of the new
treaty on the part of the new sovereign released the

[1] Muller, *De verkiezing van Anjou.*
[2] Muller and Diegerick, *Documents*, iii., p. 469.

provinces from all obligations.   Matthias was to receive *raisonable satisfaction et contentement*.   Certain other details were left to further negotiations.   In this manner Orange considered that the goal of his policy—French aid for an independent Netherland state—was attained.   In connection with the stipulations regarding Holland and Zealand, according to secret promises given in August by Des Pruneaux in the duke's name, Anjou gave a secret declaration wherein he assured to the prince compensation for the outlays of the campaigns of 1568 and 1572, and recognised Orange and his lineal successors as sovereigns of Holland, Zealand, and Utrecht.[1]   On January 23, 1581, this declaration was repeated in another form, but still secretly, at the same time with one wherein Anjou formally announced to the States his speedy arrival in the Netherlands to assume the sovereignty.[2]

On the formal choice of a new sovereign, the formal abjuration of the present nominal overlord was a necessary rite to give the new government the basis of legality. In one only of the Netherland patents of freedom, namely in the *Joyeuse Entrée* of Brabant,[3] was there the formal expression of the right of renouncing a prince who had failed to keep the oath he had once sworn; but the right was indicated as one of passive opposition, not of actual resistance.   Charles V. considered this article dangerous and tried to have it erased from the *Joyeuse Entrée* when his son swore to it in 1549.   The article was, however, left unchanged after a declaration of the Estates of Brabant as to its true signification.   But a doubt remained even in the Brussels circles as to the exercise of this right.

[1] Kervijn, v., p. 600.   Compare, regarding the much-discussed point, Muller et Diegerick, *Documents*, iii., p. 663.

[2] Kervijn, v., p. 608.

[3] Poullet, *Mémoire sur l'ancienne constitution brabançonne*, p. 372.

Considering the fact that the king declared his willingness to maintain the privileges, it was difficult to base an abjuration on the Brabantine charter.   An argument was therefore drawn from the natural relation between sovereign and people.   It was urged that the king's powers emanated from the will of his subjects.   That a tyrant forfeited allegiance was expressed, under the influence of the revival of the Greco-Roman traditions, in many a writing of western Europe, especially in France among the Huguenots.[1]   This idea was strongly urged in Hotoman's *Francogallia*, and in the famous book, *Vindiciæ contra Tyrannos*, where Jewish, Greek, and Roman history were cited to prove the formal right of opposition to, and of withdrawal from, abused authority.

In his first defence in 1568, the prince of Orange had presented this theory.   The right of rebellion, as based on the *Joyeuse Entrée*—acknowledged by him as early as 1560—and the theory of original popular right, are repeatedly referred to in his writings and elaborated by his adherents, especially by Marnix and other writers of his party.   " You represent the entirety of the people whose freedom and prosperity you have to care for, and in this capacity you receive the king's oath on your privileges," he declared to the States-General in 1576, and in this spirit were all his utterances respecting the relation between sovereign and people.   Orange can therefore be regarded as the champion of these ideas in the Netherlands; he, the great statesman, whose word was law for many and whose peer was not found in the royal camp.

The people did not rest content with the idea of " right."   In many eyes opposition to a tyrant became rather a duty, something bidden by God's commands, a conscientious demand, especially when not only civil but religious liberty was at stake.   The Calvinists, indeed,

[1] Ritter, *Deutsche Geschichte*, i., p. 489.   See also his study in Quidde's *Zeitschrift für Geschichtswissenschaft*, i., p. 44, 1890.

deemed obedience to the king an absolute crime as soon
as it was plain that he would not suffer Protestantism in
his lands.   And this sentiment was clear as the sun in the
peace negotiations at Cologne.

These ideas were what animated the members of the
States-General when they considered the abjuration of
Philip II. in conjunction with the election of Anjou.
The discussions were begun at Antwerp, but the place
proved peculiarly exposed to the disturbances of the
Calvinists and to the intrigues of the royalists, so that
the continuance of the central government in the city on
the Scheldt became insecure.   It chanced, too, that the
prince's presence was very necessary in the north after
his long absence, and it was decided to remove the seat of
the central government to Holland.   In October, 1580,
the States-General took a resolution to this effect, which
was carried into execution before the winter.   Matthias,
too, followed the States to Holland, making a strange
appearance in the midst of the negotiations with the new
overlord.

After Marnix returned from France with Anjou's definite declaration and with the signed compacts, the matter was pushed on more vigorously, and the resolution
to depose Philip II. was taken on July 22, 1581.   Four
days later, the deposition was solemnly pronounced in
an assembly of the States-General at The Hague.   An
exhaustive document, setting forth the reasons of the
deposition, was immediately printed and scattered over
all Europe.   It began with the statement, " Because it
is known to all men that a Prince of the land is appointed
by God head of his subjects .   .   .   as a shepherd for
guarding his sheep; and that the subjects are not made
by God for the sake of the Prince," but enjoy the natural right to free themselves from a tyrant, etc.

The document further proceeds to give an historic review of the causes of the revolt, and concludes with a

vigorous assertion " to make known " that the States-General " has declared and does herewith declare the King of Spain *ipso jure* deposed from his sovereignty, while the major part of the land " — so it was prudently stated—had accepted the duke of Anjou as sovereign in his place. Until his arrival, the States-General—to whom Matthias was said to have resigned the authority—was charged with the administration for the time being, while waiting for the nomination of a " Head and National Council " of all the provinces except Holland and Zealand. These two were to be ruled by Orange and by the provincial Estates as before. A new oath was imposed on all officials, wherein fidelity was promised to the national council and supremacy appointed by the States.

In the days of the Cologne negotiation great changes had taken place in Spain. Cardinal Granvelle, after fifteen years of half-exile in Rome, had been summoned to Spain to aid the king with his counsel on Netherland affairs.[1] " The quicker you come, the better satisfied I shall be," wrote Philip.

The policy of the Spanish government towards France was one of the first problems encountered by Granvelle, who was thoroughly at home in all the traditions of the relations between the Burgundian territories and France. In connection with the relation to France, Granvelle proposed the following policy for the Netherlands: negotiations with all rebels who were inclined thereto in order to sow dissension and to win over the nobles; compensation for all who were ready to submit; vigorous continuation of the war against the prince and his irreconcilable allies. The cardinal thought that everything could be replaced on the footing it had been before the introduction

[1] Philippson, *Ein Ministerium unter Philipp II.*, p. 63, Berlin, 1895. Philip was much occupied at this time with Portuguese affairs. The cortes acknowledged him as king (January, 1580), but his accession was disputed by other heirs for some years.

of Alva's ruinous system.[1] He approved Parma's energetic military measures, and suggested that Margaret
should be reinstated in the civil government, while the
conduct of the army should be left to her son. In June,
1580, the duchess appeared on Netherland soil, but neither she nor Parma was pleased with the project of
joint rule, and she had already retreated to Italy before
Philip's formal consent (1581) to her withdrawal. She
died in 1586.

Granvelle, however, did not really trust the efficiency
of either war or negotiation, as long as the prince of
Orange was there in person to animate opposition. Plans
of putting him out of the way had been discussed more
than once. Now the cardinal suggested substituting a
ban of outlawry for plans of secret assassination. In
November, 1579, he demonstrated the feasibility of this
project,[2] and suggested thirty or forty thousand crowns
as a price to attract some French or Italian bandit to risk
his life in taking that of Orange. He urged that this was
a usual method in Italy, and that the timid prince—so
did this otherwise clever statesman misjudge his antagonist — would probably die of fright before the deed was
accomplished.

And the king allowed himself to be persuaded without
much difficulty. Parma's chief objection was that the
proposed ban of outlawry might arouse new sympathy
for the prince. He finally gave his formal consent. But
when the document reached him in May he hesitated
again for three months before he had it printed and distributed. This "Ban and Edict in Form of Proscription,"[3]
issued against the prince as " chief disturber of all

---

[1] *Corresp. de Granvelle*, vii., p. 403.

[2] *Ibid.*, vii., p. 496 ; compare 503.

[3] Reprinted with other important documents in the collection *De Moord
van 1584*, issued by J. G. Frederiks, 's Gravenhage, 1884. Compare Fruin,
De oude verhalen van het moord van Prins Willem I. De Gids, 1884.

Christendom and especially of these Netherlands," calling on everyone to help this pest out of the world. Whoever succeeded in accomplishing this good work was promised forgiveness for all sins, a patent of nobility, and twenty-five thousand gold crowns. The document, which further comprised an exhaustive review of the reason for the ban, bore the date, " Maestricht, March 15, 1580."

In December the prince answered with his masterly Apology or Defence.[1] It was an eloquent attack on the king and his policy, a clear exposition of all that had passed, a brilliant defence of his own life and of the task he had set himself, an historical document of high value, although the contents are not always above criticism. Still who could expect strict impartiality in an apologetic writing of this nature, in a vindication presented to the world in the midst of such a contest ?

The document was dedicated to the States-General, " whom alone in this world we acknowledge as our over-lords." After a rapid survey of events from his arrival in the Netherlands as heir to René of Nassau, the de-fence proceeds step by step to a vindication of the prince's every deed in the revolt of the people against the " Spanish domination " from Granvelle to Parma. Nor does the author shrink from personal attacks on the king's character. He attacks Granvelle with weapons of sarcasm and withering irony in answer to the insulting accusations made against him in the prologue of the ban. The con-clusion of the long treatise is a forcible appeal to the States-General to accomplish " what you wished to ex-press by the token of a bundle of arrows engraved on your seal." If he were no longer trusted he was ready to go, even if it were " to the end of the earth." But if

---

[1] First published at Leyden, 1581, and repeatedly reprinted. The Apology was probably composed by the prince's chaplain and confidant, Pierre de Villiers, but the prince's own part therein is evident. See also Motley, *Rise*, iii., p. 371, note.

they would remain under his direction he would continue the struggle and maintain the resolutions of the States with all fidelity in accordance with the design on his coat-of-arms, *Je maintiendrai Nassau*, which is printed at the beginning and end of the defence.   The document was translated and sent with an explanatory letter to all the monarchs and princes of Europe, and also scattered in great numbers throughout the neighbouring lands.

Both ban and apology made a deep impression everywhere, and especially in Holland and Zealand.   The States-General gave the prince a vote of confidence, and promises of effectual assistance and of a body-guard.

Meanwhile arrangements for receiving Anjou had been pushed on in Holland and Zealand.[1]   In June, 1581, Matthias, a fifth wheel in the government coach, received his dismissal, and returned to his native land in October without formal leave-taking.   The promise of an annual pension of fifty thousand guilders remained nothing more than a promise.   The attempt to retain the Netherlands by the introduction of the younger branch of the house of Hapsburg had failed entirely.

The prince, invited to share control of the administration with the States-General, made a show of hesitation, and then consented.   Nominally the States exercised authority.   Orange was to fulfil his function with continuous reference to the *landraad*, which was, in point of fact, a new council of state.

In Holland and Zealand the relations between the provincial Estates and the prince were very ambiguous. On the one hand, the prince possessed the " high sovereignty " conferred on him at the beginning of the war ; on the other, he had gradually conferred upon the Estates a large share of the administration, which had increased

---

[1] The council east of the Meuse had gradually assumed conduct of affairs instead of the college of the nearer union.

during his absence in the south. Now that the king was deposed, however, a change here, too, was necessary. The prince could not exercise " high supremacy " in virtue of his stadtholdership, for he no longer represented anyone. In both these provinces there was aversion to a recognition of Anjou as actual sovereign.

The Holland cities were exceedingly desirous of making the prince count, in accordance with the secret agreements,[1] and offered him the dignity, which he refused, evidently from fear of displeasing Anjou, who, as sovereign of the Netherlands, should necessarily be count of Holland and Zealand in name. At the prince's request, immediately after the abjuration of the king, June, 1580, the " high supremacy " was conferred upon him for the period of the war, as in 1576, but with this difference, that now the stadtholdership would disappear and he would become virtually, though temporarily, sovereign. He and the Estates of Holland drew up (March, 1581) a new set of government instructions, which really changed former conditions very little.[2] The administration was considered in being only for the time of war with the prince as sovereign of Holland and Zealand, in conjunction with the council of Holland and under conditions of the maintenance of national and municipal privileges, while the Estates, composed of the representatives of the nobles and fourteen cities,[3] were recognised in a mass of important points; in questions of contribution, of peace, war, or of change of government the little cities, too, were to be convened. No persons not members of senate or town councils (*raad-* or *vrœdschappen*) could represent the cities in the Estates,—hence-

---

[1] Compare Bor, ii., p. 181.

[2] *Res. Holl.*, 1581, p. 64 *et seq.*

[3] Dordrecht, Haarlem, Delft, Leyden, Amsterdam, Gouda, Rotterdam, Gorkum, Schiedam, Schoonhoven, Briel, Alkmaar, Hoorn, and Enkhuizen. Later Medemblik, Edam, Monnikendam, and Purmerend were admitted.

forth to convene in The Hague.   The majority were
to decide in all cases, except in regard to contributions
or subsidies, in which no city could be involved against
its individual will.   In matters of peace, war, or governmental change, in case of failure to agree, the decision
rested with the sovereign and some members of his
council or that of the province.   Three colleges of deputed councillors and his Excellency were to assist the
ruler in the government,—one for general government,
one for finance, and one for marine affairs.   The influence
of the guilds and militia in state affairs was destroyed
by an express prohibition to consult them regarding
national affairs,[1] " except with approval of the Estates,"
restrictions which secured the government in Holland to
the patrician families.

In Zealand, the government remained on the same
footing as before, owing to the opposition of Middelburg.
Orange remained in possession of the functions of *First
Noble*.[2]   The cities—six in number — formed the college
of the Estates, together with the First Noble.   Here,
too, a college of deputed councillors was instituted for
the actual administration, at whose head was—after May,
1578—a councillor pensionary, who directed affairs and
was consulted in all important points.

A college of the same nature (deputies of the Estates)
was instituted in Utrecht at the time of the disturbances
in 1576, and was definitely regulated in July, 1581.   Each
of the three orders represented in the Estates appointed
three members to transact petty business, while larger
matters were settled by the Estates.[3]

---

[1] Kluit, *Historie*, i., p. 218 ; *Res. Holl.*, 1581, p. 111.

[2] In 1581 he bought the marquisate of Flushing and Veere and became
First Noble in his own right instead of in behalf of his son, whom he had
represented as lord of St: Martensdyk.

[3] S. Muller, " De oprichting van het college van Gedeputeerde Staten
van Utrecht " in *Bijdr. en med. Hist. Gen.*, 1887, p. 337.

...... the lay power of the chapters
...... This was due to the Cal-
...press the Catholics in every pos-
... adjustment did not take place until
..... did not regain any political in-
.... privileges. The old archbishop,
...... at Toutenburg, who had stayed at
... ..., did not long survive the fall of his
..gust, 1582, he died almost unnoticed.
... Orange, to whose government Utrecht
..... itself, remained as undefined as before.

...... in Gelderland was not less strange.
... .eparture of John of Nassau, chancellor and
... had been charged with the administration.
... .came evident that the count did not intend
....., Orange was offered the stadtholdership. Again
..... araid of offending Anjou, and refused. It was
.... given to Count William van den Bergh in oppo-
..... to the ultra-Calvinist, count of Nuenar. Den
..... fidelity ' to the national cause was somewhat
..... suspicion, but he was supported by the chancellor
' ......

In Overyssel, Drenthe, and the Ommelands little was
changed. Overyssel wished Orange for stadtholder.

In Friesland ' the Estates were comparatively independent, as elsewhere in 1576. On the discovery of
Rennberg's treachery the administration was conducted
by the deputed Estates. The prince became stadtholder,
with Merode as his acting representative. In March,
1581, Orange was, however, forced by the growing difficulties between the Friesland Estates and his lieutenant
to go thither himself. He assured greater power to the

' compare Part II., p. 175.
' Van Reid, p. 88.
Schotanus. De wording van het College der Gedeputeerde Staten in
Friesland, ... 'Gids, 1888, p. 107.

former without, however, being able definitely to fix the relations for the future.

Thus on the abjuration of Philip in 1581, and awaiting the arrival of the new sovereign in the provinces of the north, the government was *de facto* in the hands of Orange as stadtholder and of the Estates.   The general national government was in his hands and those of the national councils and the States-General; the provincial governments in that of the stadtholders and of the provincial Estates.   In the state colleges the most influential members were the representatives of the town councils, close corporations since the fifteenth century, whose members were chosen from the few patrician families. In Gelderland, Overyssel, and Utrecht, and in Friesland to a lesser degree, the representatives of the landed nobles were very influential.   Thus the way was paved for an aristocratic governmental form, which took little heed of the rights of the " community," which contributed nothing to the control of national, provincial, or municipal affairs in Holland and Zealand,— in the other provinces very little.   And, what was perhaps still more important for the future, everywhere the opinion gained credence that the origin of sovereignty was not vested in the lord of the land, but in the Estates as representing the subjects.   They could bestow the " high sovereignty" on whom they wished—on Orange, on Anjou, on Elizabeth.   And, so long as one of these did not wield the sway, the sovereignty was vested in the States themselves —a theory whose results were to be evident at a future day.   This theory was, as said before, to a great degree supported by the prince of Orange, partially because he had gained force thereby for the revolt against Spain, partially because his personal influence in most of the provinces was strong enough to overcome the difficulties for the national government inherent in such a theory. For the time being, governor in behalf of the States-

General, ruward of Brabant, stadtholder of Utrecht,
Friesland, and perhaps Flanders, sovereign chief of
Holland and Zealand, influential in Gelderland, Overyssel,
and the Ommelands — Orange's authority was great
enough to overshadow that of the States.   The gratitude
due him from Anjou, the dependence in which the new
sovereign would be placed in respect to the strongest
man in the land, seemed to offer him the opportunity to
continue under Anjou the rôle he had played with Matthias, in order to make the new sovereign virtually his
tool.

Little was effected by military operations during the
year 1581.   In the north, Renneberg was forced to renounce the siege of Steenwijk and turn north to defend
Groningen from the troops of Sonoy, of William Louis
of Nassau, and of William Norris.   Shortly afterwards
(June, 1581) he succumbed to an illness and died.   He
had gained neither honour nor profit from his desertion of
the patriot cause, and was mourned by few and cursed
by many as the cause of the resumption of the unholy
war in the north.   Francesco de Verdugo succeeded him
in command of the royalists, and waged a continuous
guerrilla warfare with the troops of the States.   Both
forces were prevented from venturing a pitched battle by
lack of money and men.

In the south fighting went on around Cambrai and
Tournay.   Anjou had some success, but he was unable
to pursue it owing to the same deficiency in funds.   The
little army of the States under the prince of Epinoy,
almost the only one of the south Netherland nobles still
in their service, could only inactively watch Parma's advances.   The surprise of Breda by the enemy opened the
conquest of all Brabant to Parma, while the loss of Tournay gave him opportunity to press far into Flanders.

The new protector of the provinces, Anjou, had hoped
to obtain the hand of Elizabeth at the same time with

the sovereignty of the Netherlands. His negotiations with the English queen, which hung fire for months, finally ended in smoke. There were many cross-currents. Catherine de Médicis was the soul of the numerous intrigues in which the marriage plans were involved. She was determined to secure the possession of the Netherlands to her youngest son, either by an English alliance with the support of arms, or by a Spanish marriage with these as a dowry.[1]

In October, the duke went to England, was brilliantly received, actually exchanged rings with his promised bride, who was in correspondence with Parma at the very time she heaped terms of endearment on her "beloved frog," who had very little to recommend him.

The Netherlanders grew weary of the delays, and finally (January, 1582) sent Marnix to England to tell their sovereign-elect that they would be obliged to choose another protector unless he came in person to fulfil his promises. The duke bade farewell to his bride with protestations on both sides as affectionate as they were hollow, and landed at Flushing with a brilliant escort, which included Elizabeth's favourite, the Earl of Leicester, and young Philip Sydney, afterwards so famous in the Netherland wars. He was received with all honours by Orange and the prince of Epinoy. A few days later the duke made his formal entry into Antwerp, where he received homage as the duke of Brabant and established his temporary residence. In early March, the States-General, convened at Antwerp, gave formal greeting to the new sovereign.

No appropriate fair expression was wanting on these occasions, but nevertheless confidence was by no means established between the new ruler and his subjects.[2] Scarce a fortnight had passed when Anjou began to

---

[1] Compare Kervijn, *Les Huguenots et les Gueux*, vi., p. 110.
[2] *Archives*, viii., p. 73.

complain of the difficulties raised by the Calvinists in regard to the exercise of Catholic rites by his followers. There was constant friction, too, between his frivolous French nobles and the stiff-necked Flemings, and distrust of the presence of his troops in Flanders. They had to withdraw to Dixmuiden. It was a thorn in the eyes of the Antwerp Calvinists that at the duke's pressure more and more freedom was accorded to the Catholics, who had been restricted to the exercise of the rites of baptism and marriage by a decree of 1580.

Then came another wave of profound distrust which threatened to sweep the French from Antwerp. On March 18th, Anjou's birthday, the prince of Orange, whose popularity was still in the ascendant, was dangerously wounded by a would-be assassin, Jean Jaureguy. The first thought of the people was to suspect treason on the part of the French. They recalled St. Bartholomew's night, and it was only with difficulty that the alarmed populace were persuaded that this attack upon the prince was the work of a miserable Spanish bankrupt, d'Anastro, and his fanatic Basque clerk, who, persuaded by his employer, had made the attack, and was slain by the prince's halberdiers immediately after the commission of his crime. On his sick-bed, the prince himself took measures to allay the distrust of Anjou. At the same time, he wrote to Marnix,—in behalf of the murderer's accomplices, —a touching letter which shows his noble character and lofty spirit. He begs that " they shall not be made to suffer torment,"[1] but that the people shall be contented with a speedy death if it be found deserved. How many would have thought and written so at that time and under those circumstances ?

Slow, very slow, was the recovery from the dangerous wound. The prince's sister, the countess of Schwartzburg, and his wife Charlotte were faithful nurses, day

[1] *Archives*, viii., p. 80.

and night. The princess was sacrificed to her devotion. She fell a victim to her overexertion, and died on May 5th, a few days after the prince was strong enough to go to church for the first time. His unexpected recovery was a tremendous disappointment to the opposition party, who had already disseminated the news of his death, and rejoiced thereover. As late as September, Granvelle would not believe that the prince was still living. Indeed he had already devoted his offices to his son still detained in Spain. These were dangerous, sombre days for the Netherlands. Marnix, the prince's confidant, sent to the new sovereign as the personal representative of Orange, had great difficulty in keeping Anjou in the right path. The duke was very anxious to receive homage in Flanders, and to have Brussels as his capital, while the proverbial tendency of the French courtiers to prodigality came constantly in conflict with the low state of the finances in the new government.

The pecuniary difficulties were enormous, arising from the hereditary faulty institution of the Netherland finances and the old jealousy among the provinces, each afraid to pay for its neighbour. The prince of Orange, confirmed by Anjou in the dignity of lieutenant-general in the Netherlands, and thus assured of maintaining the position he had held under Matthias, took infinite pains to arrange everything, to organise the army, the court, the government. The national councils—those for the whole land as well as for the territory east of the Meuse —were effective allies, so that the defence of the east against Verdugo and the south against Parma could be satisfactorily pursued, although Lier in Brabant fell into the hands of the enemy, followed by Oudenarde in Flanders. So precarious became the situation that Ypres, too, was regarded as insecure. It was not until August that Anjou received homage at Ghent, where the Calvinists received the Catholic French sovereign with

great coolness.   Suspicions of a new conspiracy against
the lives of Anjou and the prince seemed to strengthen
the bond of common danger and common contest between them.

The French duke, who had arrived at the wished-for
sovereignty of the Netherlands, did not feel at home in
the midst of the people he was to govern.   Neither the
language nor the ways of the Netherlanders were calcu-
lated to gain his sympathies.   The first gave him and his
great difficulties; the latter were little in accordance with
the wanton usages of the immoral French court where
the duke and his courtiers had been educated.   The insignificant appearance of the " little Italian," the "frog,"
as Elizabeth had called him, his little thin figure with his
great head, his irregular features, did not, in spite of his
unmistakable elegance, inexhaustible flow of words, and
great liveliness, correspond to the ideal of their ruler
as cherished by the Netherland people.   The evident aversion to his French suite, the ineradicable distrust of the
Calvinists for the brother of the man of the St. Bartholomew's night, embittered Anjou and his followers.   They
complained of the limitation of monarchical power,
strange to a prince brought up in an atmosphere where
the king's word was law.   In France the absolute monarchical power was a rich source of profit for the courtiers.
Here they were entirely excluded by the restrictions of
the solemnly sworn treaty.   In place of the fame and
honour and profit they had dreamed of, they found little
more than distrust, confusion, uncertainty.   It was the
courtiers who urged Anjou to attempt to increase his
power and to free himself from the dependence upon the
States-General and the prince of Orange.

Nor were the Netherlanders better satisfied.   There
was no word of French alliance or even of substantial aid.
The small force which had accompanied Anjou was weakened by illness and cowardice.   Plundering, they ravaged

the open country of Flanders, excluded from the cities and opposed by armed peasants.   Some measures taken in the course of 1582 were insufficient to restore confidence between the French troops and Flemish population.   Nothing more was to be expected from England now that the nuptials of Elizabeth and Anjou were indefinitely postponed, and the Spaniards made steady advances.

Under these circumstances Anjou did not turn a deaf ear to his mother, who urged him to take a bold step, assert his authority, and make himself master of a city. He made his preparations, and at the end of 1582 ten thousand men were assembled on the Netherland border under Marshal Biron, a consummate intriguant, who then proceeded alone to Antwerp to perfect his plan in concert with Anjou.

Orange, although still weak from his wound, spent the whole autumn at Antwerp busied with the organisation of the new government and in preparations for an offensive attack upon Parma, which he intended to make with the aid of the expected French force and of newly levied Swiss, English, and German troops.   At the same time he was considering the further regulation of the government in Holland and Zealand, where they desired to make him count, and were unwilling to accept the prince's proposition that he should still be " Sovereign Chief " while Anjou bore the count's title.   On August 14, 1582, Orange finally allowed himself to be persuaded to accept [1] the countship, although all was to be done in secret, so as to avoid arousing Anjou's suspicion.   The prince was fully aware of the discontent of the duke and his friends, but he relied on his own personal influence to keep his French ally in check.[2]   His confidence made it possible for Anjou to push on his plans of seizing

[1] Kluit, *Historie*, i., p. 293 ; Bor, ii., p. 200.
[2] *Archives*, viii., p. 143.

Antwerp, although the increase of the number of French in the city had awakened some suspicion, and the municipal government ordered the watch to be doubled on the night of January 16th–17th, and lights to be kept in all windows.

In the early morning of January 17th, Anjou asked Orange to review the troops gathered before the city, but both the prince, who was ill, and Norris declined to consider the invitation. At about midday, when the burghers were at dinner, Anjou left Antwerp to hold the review, but scarcely was he outside of the Kipdorper gate when he gave his favourite, Rochefort, a prearranged signal and hastened back into the city at the head of his men, who cried: "*Ville gagnée! Tue! Tue!*" ("City gained! Kill! Kill!"). The French, three thousand strong, rushed to the Bourse and began to plunder. A violent street battle began. Orange at once assumed the leadership, and, unwilling to embitter the French, tried to restore tranquillity with as little loss of life as possible. Marnix, who had been very zealous for the French, lost heart at once and sought refuge in Zealand. Thus the French Fury, a counterpart of the Spanish five years previously, ended without serious results. A plan to seize Bruges was no more successful than that to gain Antwerp. Dixmuiden, Dunkirk, and Dendermonde were, however, left in the control of the French, and Anjou took refuge in the last place.

Indignation at the treachery was widespread, not only in the Netherlands where the French were ill-treated in many places, but in England, Germany, and among the Huguenots, who had never trusted Anjou. The prince, however, succeeded in persuading the States-General to send a moderate answer to Anjou's demand for his papers and to reopen negotiations in spite of the opposition of his friends. Finally a provisional accord was made with Anjou, who promised to dismiss his troops

and pay an indemnity to Antwerp.   This did not, however, restore belief in his good faith very effectually, and
he returned to France under pretext of consulting his
mother and brother.   He was thoroughly disappointed
and embittered.

The prince of Orange had risked his own popularity in
his attempts to preserve the French alliance.   Less than
a month after Anjou's return to France, he, too, left
Antwerp (July 22, 1583), where his person was scarcely
safe, and went back to Holland for good.

At this date a new possibility of foreign aid appeared.
Gebhard Truchsess, archbishop of Cologne, had declared
himself (1582) a Protestant, and married Agnes Mansfeld,
a former nun.   It was hoped that he could carry his see
with him, become the centre of a powerful Protestant
coalition, and a valuable ally to his Netherland neighbours for whom he had shown sympathy since 1574.   But
the orthodox chapter of the cathedral promptly declared
him deposed, and elected Ernest of Bavaria in his stead.
There was some fighting, but Gebhard's cause was soon
lost, and he became a dependent upon the bounty of the
States, instead of an ally to them.   He took refuge at
Delft, where he lived at their expense.

The prince of Orange, although watching these events
with the closest attention, was by their outcome strengthened in his old conviction that effectual aid could be
expected from France alone.   His marriage, in April,
1581, with Louise de Coligny, the admiral's daughter,
widow of Teligny, who met his death at the same time
with his father-in-law, had made his relations to the
Huguenots closer and shown plainly the course he intended to pursue.   Even after Anjou's treason, he
wished to maintain good understanding with France at
all hazards.

This conviction on his part caused discontent in Antwerp and throughout Flanders.   The Ghent Calvinists,

too, were aroused anew, cursing French unfaithfulness and renewing their opposition to the prince's policy. Orange's friend, Ryhove, lost ground daily in Ghent; Hembyze, the prince's fell opponent, was, on the other hand, recalled from the Palatinate (August, 1583) under stress of the imminent danger which threatened Flanders from the south, where Parma had within a short time overpowered Dunkirk, Nieupoort, Veurne, and Dixmuiden. At Ghent there was talk of submission to the king, of negotiations with Parma, in a way that disquieted the prince.[1] In the spring of 1584, Hembyze, too, entered into communication with Parma.

The gradual alienation to the cause of revolt was the chief reason why, after Anjou's departure, Orange transferred the seat of government. It often happened that the deputies of the north failed to be present at the States-General because of the expense involved in going to Antwerp, while the council for the east Meuse region was composed more and more exclusively of members from the north.[2] These facts made the transference very desirable.

The executive control of affairs had again fallen into the hands of the States-General, for after Anjou's treason the national council designed to assist him was dissolved. The council for the east Meuse region was really only a commission of this last body. Strange and confused was the condition of the government, now that this council of the east Meuse was left in existence on a par with the States-General. Still stranger became the constitution of the government in April, 1583, when, on the basis of the stipulations of the union, deputies of the northern provinces met at Utrecht, and a separate representation of the Nearer Union of the Provinces of the North began

---

[1] *Archives*, viii., pp. 294, 300, 391.
[2] See Muller, *De Wording van den Staat der vereenigde Nederlanden*, p. 289.

to be made, which coöperated with the national council of
the east Meuse, but had little to do with the States-
General.   This new gathering discussed plans for the
better regulation of the defence of the north, which
plainly lay nearer their hearts than the interests of
Flanders and Brabant.

The two southern provinces complained of this new
secession of the northern, but the latter took little notice
of their complaints, although the danger for the territory
still under the States in the south, became more and more
serious.   Finally, only Ghent, Bruges, Ypres, Ostend,
and Sluis in Flanders, Brussels, Mechlin, Dendermonde,
and Antwerp in Brabant held out against Parma's army.
Treason, too, was busy everywhere; everywhere Parma's
agents appeared, and Parma's letters and promises had
their effect among the discouraged adherents of the
States in the south.

And in very truth there was reason for the discouragement.   Verdugo was making many reconquests in the
north, and the national council had little power of resistance.   The harassed populations of Overyssel, Gelderland, and Drenthe were ground under the burden of the
guerrilla warfare which had harried the land for three
years ; the Ommelands and Friesland were not much
better off, suffering from both parties and from hostilities
between the cities.   No wonder that fair promises found
hearers more or less ready.

It was lucky for the north that Parma was hampered
by lack of money.   He had indeed a force of sixty thousand men, but half had to be employed for garrisons, and
the other half were as ill paid as the States' troops.
Even the nine hundred thousand guilders per month
which the king expended for the army was too heavy a
burden for the exhausted treasury, and the silver and
gold, precious spices, and other wares imported from
America and India were far from sufficient to meet the

expenses increasing year by year.   Often Parma complained in his letters to the government at Madrid that
at favourable epochs he had been compelled to await
events '' with folded arms.'' [1]

Very serious for the cause of the rebellion was the
treason of William van den Bergh, stadtholder of Gelderland and brother-in-law of Orange.   In November, 1583,
a suspicious correspondence between him and Parma was
discovered, to the great annoyance of Leoninus and other
officials of the States.   The count, his wife, the prince's
sister, their three sons, and several of their friends were
taken to Holland under arrest.   The count lay in prison
at Delfshaven for a year.   His place was filled by Adolph,
count of Nuenar, who, deeply interested in the Cologne
affairs, was chosen for this post with reference to plans of
coöperation with the archbishopric.

The prince was deeply wounded by this deplorable
family event.   Still he did not lose heart.   He did what
he could to keep things smooth among the various allies
and to further the negotiations in spite of all that had
happened, in order not to cut France wholly loose from
the cause of the Netherlands.   He implored the States
'' to dismiss all passion,'' to give no heed to the '' Span-
ishised who only try to make your friends enemies.'' [2]
He did not deny that faults had been committed on both
sides, but he begged them to remember that Philip the
Good and Bruges had again become good friends after
the most bitter quarrels, and that they, too, could forgive
and forget, and accept Anjou as their sovereign.   On
the other side he tried to restrain the duke from opening
negotiations with Parma.   He urged the Ghenters not to
break loose from the other provinces.   He even opened
correspondence with his personal foe, Hembyze.   He induced Holland and Zealand to do more for the general
cause and to diminish the financial stress of the national

[1] Van Meteren, p. 193.   [2] *Archives*, viii., p. 251.

council — chief cause of the ill turn of affairs in the east and south—by effective financial support.

How critical was the situation in the spring of 1584 is apparent from many a contemporaneous document, not the least from a letter of February from Orange to Count John wherein he outlines the position of affairs.[1] He could proudly say that he was not discouraged (*aulcune-ment intimidé*) and without self-praise he could also say that if his advice had been taken the ills would have been avoided.   Still he had to acknowledge that if help did not come from some source, ruin was close at hand.   If Count John could furnish no aid from Germany, if Queen Elizabeth persisted in neutrality, — and both cases were true, — France was the only power which could bring relief.   The prince elaborated this idea in two more important letters of March, 1584,[2] letters which may be regarded as his political testament.

" They tell me that I ought to distrust France.   The dangers which are imminent from that quarter are not unknown to me, better known to me, perhaps, than to those who speak and touch me nearer than anyone else."   To whom could he give more trust ?   The princes of Germany have often been solicited and no aid has been received by them.   If help did come from that quarter, Netherland Calvinism would suffer sorely from the hostile Lutherans.   Unaided, the Netherlanders, even if united, could not maintain the resistance to Spain, in his opinion.   Therefore France, Spain's ancient foe, was his only hope.

" Your theologians and others say that this is contrary to the will of God, but mark well—the minority only is Protestant in the Netherlands, and with the minority the greater part, although strong in their zeal against Anjou and the Catholics, are, when it comes to action, weak and uncertain, as has been

[1] *Archives*, viii., p. 313 *et seq.*   [2] *Ibid.*, p. 339.

repeatedly proven.   Moreover, there is no evangel to prevent
obedience to a prince of a different creed, or to an alliance
with one.   The histories of the patriarchs, of David and of
Solomon, of the Swiss and Poles, of the German princes in the
days of Maurice of Saxony, were all proofs of this.   Freedom
of religious service could always be guaranteed.   And still you
write me that there are those who are presumptuous enough to
accuse my conscience and my honour, which I would find very
strange if I did not recognise the ingratitude inherent in men
and the unbridled desire to speak ill.''

" Who in this world is sufficiently courageous to touch another's conscience ?   And as regards honour — I can say to a
brother without hesitation, is there anyone who has worked
more, suffered more, lost more in order to establish, aid, and
maintain the church than I ?   Let them who criticise me do
more and better than I.   I will serve them and, so far as I can,
honour them.   Continue, brother, to aid me with your advice
for the defence of the good cause wherein, God giving me
grace, I am determined to end my days and never to come to
an accommodation with Spain, knowing that with such would
come the ruin of the churches, of the country, and of many
people, a general tyranny over all inhabitants of this land and
particularly ''—an argument that never missed its effect upon
Count John—'' the destruction of our whole house.''

The Spanish power was not invincible, as had been
repeatedly shown in this war.   The king was, of course,
strong in comparison with the prince, but '' God will aid
in the defence of the cause of freedom and conscience
and of the life of so many brave fellows over whom
Spanish vengeance would burst like a deluge if the Spaniards should regain their ancient power.''   Therefore he
intended to hold his ground and consider no ills for himself and his friends, or incur the guilt of a '' miserable
desertion.''   To those who advised reconciliation with
Spain, the same argument can be offered which they employ against Spain: Is it allowed to submit to the pope's

favourite son and not to the " dubious " Catholic who rules France ?   No ; the Frenchman is always better than the Spaniard.   Again :

> " I do not wish to deny that there are dangers from both quarters, but if we must cross by one of two planks, I think anyone would choose the widest and firmest.   And the king of Spain is much stronger than the king of France, thus more to be feared as a sovereign."

Orange declared he would go to the utmost for the defence of the territory, of religion, and of freedom, " hoping that God by some means will not abandon me in a quarrel so just and so necessary, for which I implore him from the bottom of my heart."

Thus spoke the prince in the crisis of the spring of 1584.   At the same time the government of Ghent had begun to negotiate openly with Parma, a negotiation in which Hembyze played the chief rôle.[1]   The overthrow of Hembyze's government by the opposition just prevented the fall of Ghent.   Hembyze and his friends, Roland Yorke and Seaton, were seized as they were about to deliver the city to Parma, and imprisoned with Champagney.   The fall of Ypres in April, soon followed by that of Bruges, was a fresh misfortune suffered by Flanders.   A few days later Hembyze was reinstated at Ghent, and went on with his game of treason.

Anjou now fell seriously ill of consumption.   Still his negotiations with Orange and the States proceeded, and seemed, owing to the prince's indefatigable efforts, to promise to secure his reacknowledgment as sovereign. All conditions were virtually agreed upon, when the French prince, then in his thirtieth year, passed away on June 10th at Château Thierry.

This death was a serious blow to the prince's policy. There was no other mediator between Catholics and

---

[1] *Corresp. de Granvelle*, xi., p. 481.

Huguenots, between court and people of France. No one was left who could assume the sovereignty but Henry III.; for the head of the French Huguenots, Henry of Navarre, his heir-apparent, needed help himself. The States-General, therefore, authorised their envoys to offer the French king the sovereignty on the same terms as had been promised to his brother.[1] But the jealousy of England toward the French in the Netherlands, the immediate war with Spain which would ensue on the assumption of sovereignty, the dangers which would arise within his kingdom if he made common cause with the prince and his Calvinist friends to the distaste of the Catholic French —all this kept the French king from accepting the offer.

At the same time with the negotiations with Anjou, those regarding the elevation of Orange to the countship of Holland and Zealand were also in progress.

The two provinces desired to maintain independence of Anjou and of the other provinces, and never lost sight of this idea. From the beginning of the revolt, they had taken a peculiar position, which was confirmed by the course of events. The Pacification of Ghent and the union of Brussels had expressly left them their independence. The union of Utrecht was recognised by them because it gave the opportunity to use the other provinces as a bulwark, although, as a matter of fact, little advantage was derived from this bulwark when · there was any question of financial support, to the vexation of the college of the nearer union, and to its successor, the national council for the east Meuse. They troubled themselves little about the States-General. The institution of a high council for Holland and Zealand in 1582 as a court of appeal for the two provinces also rendered them independent in judicial matters, while the other provinces still acknowledged, in a measure, the great council of Mechlin in that capacity. For

[1] Kervijn, vi., p. 533.

this very reason, immediately after the abjuration. of Philip, they were anxious to make the prince their separate sovereign.   The prince cared little for the honour, partially because he was afraid of wounding Anjou in his sovereign rights, partially because he could not approve this separate position of the two provinces in the Netherland state which he projected.   Thus the matter hung fire after the spring of 1582.   Under the impression of the French Fury, the negotiations concerning this change were pushed forward more vigorously, but it was not until April 5th that the nobles and representatives of the big and little cities of Holland set their seals to the official act.   After that, they proceeded to consider the conditions under which the prince of Orange should receive homage as count.

All kinds of difficulties—not alone those which had of old hampered the treatment of affairs in the many-headed body of the States — beset the renewed negotiations.[1] Holland would not enter on the matter without Zealand, and in the latter province Middelburg made innumerable difficulties in the desire to secure her rights against Veere and Flushing.   In Holland, Amsterdam, Gouda, and Briel fought shy of taking any steps for fear of jeopardising their privileges and exciting discontent among the burghers.   It was hoped that Utrecht would enter the combination.   The suspicion entertained of the remaining provinces and of Anjou had to be met with the greatest care, while other plans for strengthening the general national government absorbed attention for the moment. Moreover, the fixing of the conditions involved difficulties.   The regents were anxious to retain as large a portion as possible of the power they had enjoyed during the past year.

On December 30, 1583, the conditions were finally drafted and were accepted by the prince and the Estates

[1] Kluit, *Historie*, i., p. 299.

of Holland.   Before homage was given, the matter was to be referred again to the town councils and special efforts made to convince the hesitating members to approve the measure.

The chief leaders of the Estates, among whom were the advocate Buys and the pensionary of Rotterdam, John of Oldenbarnevelt, aided in composing the articles. The new sovereign was to be absolute, inasmuch as no superior was acknowledged, and all former ties with the empire were considered sundered.   The " true reformed religion " was to be maintained exclusively, but no one was to be harassed on account of his belief.   Careful conditions were made, some taken from the old charters and some from the treaty with Anjou.   Any infringement of these, on the count's part, dissolved all obligations.   It is a very remarkable document, and suggestive of the ancient ideals of all the Netherland provinces in political matters.   Yet the *Joyeuse Entrée* went farther than this in the limitation of sovereign power by the constitutional authority of the Estates—which was, at this time, primarily the authority of the municipal regents.

In the course of the spring of 1584, the articles were discussed in the municipal councils.   By June the matter was so far advanced that thirteen cities had signed, while a few others stated their readiness so to do.   On July 6th, Gouda declared that they would agree if Zealand did.   Amsterdam hesitated, owing to the influence of the burgomaster, Cornelis Pieterszoon Hooft.   All opposition would have speedily vanished in Utrecht as well as in Holland and Zealand.   We possess a memoir, drawn up by the prince in the beginning of July, wherein he urges Holland, for the sake of his own honour and of the general interest of security in the land, to take a resolution in the matter.   The prince made it perfectly clear that the plan emanated not from him but from the Estates, and indicates several points which should be kept in view at the time of the formal homage.[1]

Just then happened what the prince's friends had long feared. After Jaureguy's failure, various other murderers had cherished similar dreams, but also failed in their purpose. A fanatic from the Franche Comté, Balthasar Gérard, succeeded, alas! better.[2]

For years Gérard nursed this plan of ridding his king and his church of a foe. After the publication of the ban, his desire to accomplish the deed, his belief in his own divine mission, had become irresistible. In the spring of 1582, he betook himself to Luxemburg. After Jaureguy's attempt, his own plans took form. A Jesuit at Trier and a monk at Tournay gave him absolution at Easter, as he confessed later under torture, and confirmed him in his undertaking. The councillor Assonleville had spoken to him to the same purpose.[3] In May, 1584, under an assumed name, claiming to be the son of a victim of the Catholic persecution, he obtained access to the prince's chaplain, Villiers, to whom he, showed several blanks signed by Mansfeld, the stadtholder at Luxemburg, and stolen from him. The court preacher, misled by his Calvinist zeal, sent him to Noël de Caron, the ambassador of the States-General in France, who, at his request, charged him with carrying the news of Anjou's death to the prince. Gérard was admitted to the sleeping-room of Orange to give him further particulars of the event, and declared his readiness to carry an answer back to the ambassador. Then, to his chagrin, he was not prepared and not armed.

---

[1] *Archives*, viii., p. 428.

[2] The official account of the prince's assassination was drawn up by Villiers at the direction of the States-General, *Verhaal van den Moort*, Delft, 1584. See also *De oude Verhalen*, etc., in Fruin's collected works now in course of publication, vol. iii.

[3] Compare *De oude Verhalen*, etc.

On July 8th, he went to the prince's house in Delft to examine the exits and the chances offered for escape. Discovered in the act, he explained his presence by saying he had not liked to go into the church opposite the prince's dwelling because of the poverty of his clothing. Orange, being told of this, sent him some money to provide himself better.   With this money he bought pistols and bullets, and returned upon July 10th at midday for his passport, just as the prince's family were going to the dining-room.   The princess was much impressed by the ill appearance of the man, but her husband ordered that he should have his passport, without paying much attention to him.   After dinner, at about two o'clock, the prince, clad in a fine tabbert, passed slowly out of the room, with his family following.   He had had an earnest discussion with the guest of the day, Uylenburgh, upon Frisian affairs, and they continued talking as they crossed a little vestibule towards the stair which led to the second story.   Suddenly the assassin sprang from a little dark bay which led to a narrow passage, and fired.   Two bullets hit the prince.

The wound was fatal.   The prince exclaimed: " *Mon Dieu, ayez pitie de mon âme !   Mon Dieu, ayez pitie de ce pauvre peuple !* " [1] and answered " yes " to the question whether he committed his soul to Christ's hands, and gave up the spirit after a few minutes, his last look fixed on the princess and his sister who stood by him in bitter distress.

Such was the end of the great prince to whom the Netherland nation owes her independence.   His distinguished statesmanship, his indomitable energy, his unbroken courage and firm confidence in the justice of the cause, his broad ideas about the so narrowly understood

[1] In regard to the truth of these words, "a precious legacy which the Netherland people would not allow to be questioned by unjust doubt," see Fruin.

ideas of religion and of conscience, his unstinted zeal for
popular liberty and self-government, give him title to the
admiring homage of posterity, as he received the warm
affection and devoted love of so many who honoured
his life as the father of the fatherland, " the man
his own profit, always seeking the common
giving himself no time for repose.

The dependent love was never more apparent than in
the days of bitter pain which succeeded the murder.
Deep despondency settled on many in the revolted provinces; violent indignation against the assassin who forfeited his life with frightful torture; bitter indignation,
too, against the king whose ban had excited the frightful
murder. And the tears of thousands accompanied the
bier of the great Orange to his last resting-place,—of
thousands, but not of all the inhabitants of the provinces. Many zealous Catholics rejoiced over the fall of
the man who was the personification of the revolt,—the
revolt which finally cost them the liberty to exercise their
own beloved religion.[1]

In the death of the tyrant of the Netherlands in the
cloister of St. Agathe, where the unfortunate pastor
Musius had lived, they saw a retribution for the crime
committed by Lumey against that noble priest and the
Gorkum martyrs, the just punishment of God for all that
the king's authority and their church had suffered at the
hands of the prince, as they thought. And in the assassin
they did not see the treacherous fanatic which he was,
but the martyr for his belief, whose fate they lamented,
whose memory they honoured, whose head they sent to
Cologne as a precious relic, whose reputation they wished
to enhance by a canonisation, a plan that was only relinquished half a century later.[2] Thus contemporaries

[1] Van Reyd, p. 50.
[2] See *Historie Balthazars Gerardt alias Serach* in the above-mentioned
collection ; compare Fruin. [3] Compare Fruin.

misjudged the aims of the great Orange prince, who both from a universal human, as from an especial political point of view, was the champion of freedom of religion and of conscience for all; who, so far as he could, protected the Catholics against the hatred of the zealous Calvinists, and had many a time risked his popularity in so doing.

The future looked dark to the revolted provinces, deprived for ever of the great leader who had shown them the way with so firm a hand.

CHAPTER V

THE prosperity of 1558 was no longer visible in 1584. Flanders had suffered more than the other provinces, and was little more than a desert waste. The storm of iconoclasm, the Beggars' raids, Egmont's troops, and Alva's soldiers all left sad traces. Eight years had elapsed in which the torch of war had not been lighted, but after the death of Requesens mutineering Spaniards had renewed the scenes of devastation. Then came the wild struggle against the malcontents waged by Ryhove's savage troops, and Anjou's expedition, followed by Parma's army.

And the end, as it seemed, approached with rapid strides. One Flemish city after another submitted to Spanish authority until only Ostend, Sluis, and a few places retained the garrisons of the States-General. All the rest of Flanders, shadow of her former self, was under Parma. How forlorn it was is evident from the fact that wolves repeatedly made their way within the city walls. And the end of the trials of war was not come so long as Ostend, Sluis, and the forts upon the Scheldt were still in the hands of the rebels.

Not less wretched were Brabant and Hainaut. Beginning with the prince's campaigns in 1568 and 1572, a succession of armed bodies had passed over the country, living on what they could find. Here, too, city after city had submitted.   Brussels under Hendrik de Bloyere, the burgomaster, persisted bravely in her opposition to Spanish sovereignty, but, blockaded as it was on all sides by Parma, starvation stared the citizens in the face.

Orange's commander, Olivier van den Tympel, began to lend his discouraged ears to Parma's propositions, while the people longed passionately for the cessation of active hostilities.   They held out through the winter, hoping for French aid, but by the spring lost all heart. In March, 1585, Brussels capitulated.   A few months later, Mechlin, too, fell.

Antwerp was at the last gasp.   Blow after blow had been dealt to her commerce by successive events.   In 1580, a consulate was established at London to protect international commerce and the interests of Netherland merchants.   But it proved impossible to transact business safely with the existing state of warfare.   There were not more than ninety thousand inhabitants in Antwerp, far less than in the middle of the century, but still sufficient to assure her influence if her commerce could have been assured.   The French Fury resulted in her further loss, to the gain of Middelburg and of Hamburg, whither English commerce was diverted.[1]   Marnix, appointed by Orange as burgomaster without the walls, saw that the moment was imminent when Parma would lay siege to the city.   On the very day of the prince's death, the fort Liefkenshoek, half built by the States, fell into Parma's hands, and he used it as a base of operations. Antwerp's capitulation, with Zealand still in the control of the Beggars, meant the final blow to her remnant of commerce.

Thus, while Holland and Zealand were making great strides in prosperity, the retrogression of the south was as continuous, as Renon de France complained bitterly. The single territory in the region untouched by war

[1] Van Reyd, p. 42 ; compare Ehrenberg, *Hamburg und England.* Jena, 1895.

was neutral Liege, and it might be involved at any moment.

The lands across the Meuse and Gelderland were in sorry case. Orange's early campaigns, Louis's expedition in 1574, followed by those of Parma in 1578 and 1579, were disastrous for the well-being of the people, who were tired of war in all its phases. Nimwegen, Doesburg, and Arnhem were all " reconciled " to Philip in 1585. In this region were many faithful Catholics who disliked the rule of the States and were more than ready to exchange it for that of Parma. Trading on the Rhine stood still. River piracy had increased to such a degree that the old pathway of commerce was practically closed,[1] to the great detriment of the Gelderland and Overyssel cities as well as to those in Germany.

In the north, guerrilla warfare was unceasing. Through their possession of Steenwijk, the Spaniards had access to the open country of Friesland, while William Louis and Hohenlo were only able to protect the Frisian cities and to repay the raids of Verdugo and Tassis in Friesland in like coin. Famine and pestilence, too, raged. In 1581, thirteen thousand people died of the pest within the walls of Groningen. Naturally commerce had no chance, and the unfortunate peasants were prey now to foe, now to friend; no one thought of their fate.[2]

Such was the condition in the " ruined provinces,"[3] Gelderland, Utrecht, Friesland, and Overyssel. In 1579, they declared that it was out of their power to help wage the common war against Spain. How favourable in comparison was the situation of Holland and Zealand!

They, too, had not escaped the ills of actual warfare. Bor gives a description of an eye-witness of The Hague

---

[1] Kroniek van Phebens, *Werken Hist. Gen.*, No. 7, p. 89.
[2] *Ibid.*, p. 104.
[3] Van Reyd, p. 25.

in 1576.[1] The little town of ten thousand inhabitants, the count's residence from the time of William II., was then deplorable to see. The majority of the inhabitants had taken refuge in fortified Delft. Houses stood empty, displaying burnt windows, doors, and roofs. Troops on both sides had stalled horses in dwellings, and taken for their use, whatever served them, while the trees in the Bosch were, for the larger part, chopped down and sold. Scarce a year later the Estates of Holland[2] complained that time after time the land had been submerged and harvests ruined. The piercing of the dikes to relieve Leyden had been disastrous to the farmer. In general, too, the dikes were weakened by lack of repair, so that several islands, like Duiveland and Schouwen, were threatened with total destruction. In the open country, the people had gone away, died out, or become poverty-stricken. The Estates declared that the population was reduced two-thirds. The country bordering on Utrecht had suffered especially, while Walcheren and south Beveland had been exposed to sanguinary struggles on land and water.

But later these people were better off than their fellows, inasmuch as, after the Pacification and after the regulation of the relations between Holland and Zealand and the other provinces, commerce and industry revived with surprising rapidity. For a time, Amsterdam resisted the authority of the States with so much tenacity that a blockade became necessary, but meantime Enkhuizen, Hoorn, and the other " water cities " on the Zuyder Zee reaped advantage from the circumstance, while Amsterdam retrograded in consequence of the raids of the Beggars and of Bossu's sea fights.[3] As early as 1569, the

[1] Bor, i., p. 676.
[2] Papers of Oldenbarnevelt, *Royal Archives, Documents for 1586,* AA6, No. 1.
[3] Ter Gouw, *Amsterdam,* vi., p. 389.

number of ships sailing to the Baltic was reduced from 250 to 150, and there was a cessation of activity in ship- and house-building.   Many merchants left Amsterdam for Hoorn and Enkhuizen.   Finally the arrival of a grain ship was exceptional.   Want began to be evident.[1]   No wonder that the municipal government finally declared for the States, to avoid seeing their commerce entirely vanish.   Immediately after the *satisfactie* a change was evident, and Amsterdam regained her old briskness, her old business.   In 1585,[2] her territory was increased, and Spieghel mentions "ship rich Amsterdam full of houses close together."

Amsterdam was able again to take her share in the commerce still existing in Holland and Zealand.   Besides reaping advantage from the increase in population, the provinces gained profit from the taxes imposed by them.

The difficulty of raising funds for governmental and military expenses has been referred to repeatedly.   No ordinary revenue sufficed.   Several new imposts were, accordingly, introduced.[3]   *Licenses*, or *permission money* (*verlofgelden*) were the names given to sums paid for franchises allowing exports to the land of the enemy— that is, to Spain and Portugal,— to be sent farther afield by the Spaniards.   In 1572, this species of taxation had been introduced into Zealand by the Beggars, and Holland had adopted it in 1573.   In the first year the yield was 850,000 guilders.   *Convoys*[4] were the taxes paid on all other imports or exports.   There was a distinction between home and foreign convoys, according as they were levied on transactions between provinces or between

---

[1] Ter Gouw, *Amsterdam*, vii., p. 137.

[2] *Ibid.*, p. 416.

[3] Declaration of the Estates of Holland to the States-General in Olden-barnevelt's papers, April 5, 1577.

[4] This name is due to the circumstance that money so derived was expended first on the outfit of ships of war, which acted as consorts to the merchant ships.

other lands. A list drawn up in 1581 shows how much was paid in. Holland found so much profit in these taxes that she urged their adoption by other provinces. So, in May, 1581, the States-General deliberated the question of import and export duties.[1] In the various provinces, toll bureaus were established in the ports and border towns through which transportation passed for home and foreign markets. Toll lists, printed at the expense of the States-General, fixed the rate.

On various sides, meanwhile, the questionable side of this traffic with the enemy became evident. Was not the foe supplied with the wherewithal to prosecute the war ? Champions of this trade urged that they would accomplish nothing by refusing supplies but throwing profitable trade into the hands of Baltic and English merchants.[2] But the opponents, especially the ultra-Calvinist preachers, were vexed at the godless gain, and the army, too, criticised this traffic in the material of war. Thus it came about that as early as February, 1578,[3] and again in May, 1582, shortly after the coming of Anjou, measures were adopted to forbid all commerce with the enemy, a prohibition that was disregarded and speedily rescinded, owing to the pressure of the trade and to the needs of the revenues therefrom accruing.

The advantage resulting to Holland and Zealand from the trade with Spain and Portugal was also a thorn in the eye of the Spanish government. They knew perfectly well that the sums gained from this trade were employed against them. Already Hollanders had been repeatedly harassed in Spanish ports, and then were attracted to those of Portugal — still independent — by special privileges.[4] In 1580 Portugal passed to Spanish rule, and the

---

[1] Placard of the States-General, *Bibl. Thys.* (Leyden), No. 268.
[2] Van Meteren, p. 173.
[3] Placard, pamphlet *Bibl. Thys.*, Leyden.
[4] *Corresp. de Granvelle*, ix., pp. 95, 297.

inclination to injure the Netherland merchants could be pursued with more vigour.   In the Netherlands, under Alva and Requesens, placards were frequently published forbidding all intercourse with the rebels, but these did not have much result.   Spain vainly attempted to persuade France and England to exclude the rebels from their ports; but, as a matter of fact, the latter could count upon more or less open aid from both neighbours. Various plans were formed in Spain for persuading the Scandinavian sovereign to close the Sound to Holland and Zealand ships, or for attacking the latter simultaneously in all Spanish and Portuguese ports.

But the inhabitants of the peninsula could not dispense with the articles, especially the corn, brought by the Hollanders.   Famine would have resulted, though Granvelle thought that corn might be secured from Hamburg and Bremen.[1]

Spain was too poor in marine equipment to put a stop to operations on the sea, however much she might dislike them, and this lack of protection left Spanish and Portuguese traders exposed to Holland and English pirates. Many plans were made to remedy the ill, the most important being a scheme of one Alonzo Guttierez.[2]   But means of realisation were wanting, and all came to naught.

Besides, at the time of the Cologne negotiations, Terranova had suggested a new danger.   He had pointed out that the Hollanders and Zealanders, skilled seamen as they were, might conceive the notion of sailing to India themselves and fetching the products which they were in the habit of buying at Seville and Lisbon from the Spanish and Portuguese fleets.

Thus the Hollanders and Zealanders were practically

[1] See in regard to these plans, *Correspondance de Granvelle*, vols. x. and xi., especially x., pp. 8, 225 ; xi., pp. 178, 341, 349, 356.
[2] *Ibid.*, xi., pp. 139–165.

masters of their own commerce and reaped advantages from the retrogression of the other provinces. Owing to the differences in religious privileges, there was a gradual change among the inhabitants. Catholics begin to flock back to the provinces that returned to Spanish rule, while the Protestants abandoned their homes on royalist soil, and were received with open arms in Holland, Zealand, and the Palatinate, where they were welcomed for the sake of their manufacturing skill. We hear of 136 families who moved in August, 1586, from Antwerp to Middelburg. And the stream of emigration continued to flow.[1] In 1616, the bishop of Antwerp mentions two hundred heads of families who had left the city in the last year, not only Protestants but also Catholics.[2] Thus the marine provinces enjoyed the fruits of Parma's conquests and diplomatic negotiations, although these latter were not without danger to Holland and Zealand.

So imminent, indeed, seemed their fall that the government at Madrid began to consider the best method to assure peace in the Netherlands after their conquest.[3] Granvelle's plan was as follows: Philip William of Nassau, the prince's eldest son, who had been detained so long in Spain, should be appointed his father's successor.[4] Preachers and ringleaders of the opposition, among whom, naturally, Oldenbarnevelt, Buys, Van Hout, Van der Does, Hooft, Maelson, and others were included, must be banished. Care must be taken to provide good books, good schools, good priests, and to take vigorous suppressive measures at the first sign of returning revolt, taught by the example of the first year of the troubles, when Viglius and his followers had made matters much worse by slackness in quelling the movement. Especial attention must be paid, moreover, to the bearing of the clergy, was the opinion of Granvelle, who had, in 1580,

[1] *Kronick Hist. Gen.*, 1885, p. 8.   [3] *Corresp. de Granvelle*, ix., p. 306.
[2] *Belg. Mus.*, iii., p. 115.   [4] *Ibid.*, p. 359.

resigned the dignity of archbishop of Mechlin to Jean
d'Auchin, dean of St. Gudule in Brussels.

In the Catholic church, meanwhile, there had been a
strong revival, and conditions were greatly improved.
Under popes like Pius V. and Gregory XIII., men of
pure and earnest intention, a vigorous activity in clerical
matters was evident.   The Jesuits came forward as the
champions of the Catholic faith, which was again a living
power.   About 1584, this reactionary movement, manifest throughout Europe, became evident in the Netherlands.'   In the north, the bishops had lost their posts,
but in the south they returned with Parma's army and
kept a strong hand on ecclesiastical discipline among
their clergy.   Unchastity, venality, injustice, were suppressed.   It was one man especially from whom reform
emanated.   In 1583, Sasbout Vosmeer, as vicar *de facto*,
undertook the task of the reconquest of the archbishopric of Utrecht for Catholicism, and the result of his
influence was speedily apparent.'   There is no more
talk of ecclesiastics like Nicolaas Nieuwland, bishop of
Haarlem, nicknamed " Drunken Claesgen," of dissol-
ute priests, and scandalous behaviour.   Vosmeer's courage, energy, self-sacrifice, inflexibility, spurred on the
clergy of his diocese to more vigorous activity; a new
spirit reigned in the whole priesthood.   He was aided in
his efforts by the nuncio appointed to Cologne in 1584,
and Catholicism began to regain its hold, but it was still
only a beginning.

On the other hand, Calvinism, too, was an undeniable
force.   It had become the dominant church in five provinces, and from the persecuted had become the perse-
cutor.   In 1571, a national synod had to be held at
Emden, on German soil.   In the middle of 1572, the first

[1] Fruin, *De wederopluiking van het Catholicisme in Noord-Nederland.*
De Gids, 1894.
[2] Compare Van Meteren, p. 136.

private Holland synod was able to assemble at Hoorn. Calvinist congregations sprang up everywhere, so that there was need of more preachers than could be obtained. Support was now provided for them from the property of the ancient church, which was alienated to the state in the spring of 1573. " To create learned and faithful shepherds " was one of the purposes of the foundation of the *Academia* at Leyden after the siege, and the second national synod, held at Dordrecht in 1578, gave evidence of the great advance of Calvinist principles. Almost immediately there was a division between the Walloon and Low Dutch congregations—the former consisting of refugees from the south. There was discussion upon biblical translation and psalm rhyming. For the sake of unity, maintenance of the Confession and the Heidelberg Catechism was prescribed. In Gelderland, John of Nassau reorganised the Calvinist church and held the first synod. In Utrecht, Dathenus began the first Calvinist organisation in opposition to the separate church union under direction of Duifhuis, who hesitated between Protestant and Catholic principles. In Friesland, the two churches contested the supremacy. The Reformed obtained it in 1580 after Renneberg's treason, and also obtained possession of the ancient churches, which they used for the establishment of their congregations and schools. The first provincial synod was held at Sneek in May.[1] Calvinism, too, was organised under William Louis of Nassau. In 1585, a seminary for preachers was established at Franeker. Nevertheless, in spite of this advance, in 1584 Calvinism could not be counted as the universal creed in any one province except perhaps Zealand. Everywhere else the Catholics were very much more numerous, especially in Utrecht and the eastern regions, and to less degree in Holland and Fries-

[1] Compare Reitsma, *Honderd jaren uit de geschiedenis der hervorming in Friesland*. Leeuwarden, 1876.

land. But the Calvinists made up for their numbers by their religious zeal, and the preachers were constantly rousing their congregations, while the Catholics, in spite of certain changes, still, for the most part, regarded the dominance of heresy without resistance. The many indifferent people watched the course of events, ready to agree with the winning side.

Besides this class, there were also to be found, especially in the government circles, a great number of so-called " libertines," men who could be regarded as the heirs of the Erasmians, as the fellow thinkers of the followers of Duifhuis, " pope Hubert," at Utrecht. They had an aversion to the extremes of the preachers as well as to the pressure from the Catholic side, and opposed all attempts to push through ultra-Calvinist principles in church institutions. They were quite willing to grant freedom of religion to the Catholics, and opposed to forcing the Confession as the preachers wished. This school of thinkers found support among the indifferent, with whom they were sometimes confused, and from Prince William himself. With these the Calvinist leaders took decided issue. Violent disputes took place between Dathenus and Moded at Utrecht as opposed to the moderate Duifhuis; between Saravia and Crusius at Leyden as opposed to Coornhert, the philosopher who espoused the principles of toleration and of Christian love in his moral writings, and disliked the exaggeration of the preachers. The contest in Utrecht was especially violent, even after the death of Duifhuis in 1581, when his "congregation of St. James " remained in existence under the protection of the government. To these libertines belonged the Leyden preacher, Coolhaes, who denied the doctrine of predestination, and was removed from his charge by the synod of Haarlem in 1585. Thus Calvinism was already divided into two strong factions. Coexistent with the Calvinists of all opinions, the Mennonites still remained in existence in the country districts of Friesland and Holland. As soon as Spanish pressure was removed they came to the fore. Some of them adopted Calvinism: others never ceased to regard it with antagonism. Such was the state of affairs. A purer and hence stronger Catholicism was on the increase, and with it was Parma's army.

The influence of the war was also felt in the realms of art, letters, and science.

Times were changed in many particulars. There was no longer a desire to adorn churches and chapels, town-halls and private dwellings, with works of art. Calvinism was opposed to such usage in every particular. The storm of iconoclasm which burst in 1566 revived after 1572 in Holland and Zealand, after 1576 in Flanders, Brabant, and in other provinces, put an end to the high tide of ecclesiastical art in some regions for good, in others temporarily, as long as Calvinism was dominant.

The churches, formerly ornamented with works of art, in the midst of which Catholicism was wont to worship, were stripped of every decoration. Nothing was left but bare walls. Scattered everywhere were the old paintings of more or less value, the images of saints, honoured by generation after generation, the marble statues and carved choir-stalls, the pride of many a convent. Carried off and sold or melted were the gold and silver vessels and ornaments used in ecclesiastical solemnities, the chased dishes, the artistic candelabra, the manuscript missals, the wonderful antiphonaries, the evangels decorated with precious stones.

No building of importance was erected during these years. The town-halls and other public edifices destroyed in the war remained in ruins, or were patched up temporarily. The half-ruined convents and churches were, when not used for Calvinist service, neglected or turned into barracks devoted to the uses of the government, or sold for the materials. It was recorded as an exception when an important building was undertaken at Antwerp.[1]

Under these circumstances, the reputation of Netherland art and architecture waned. Only occasionally, when triumphal entries were made into Brussels, Antwerp, and Ghent, by Requesens, Orange, Anjou, Don John, and Parma, did the Netherland artists have an opportunity to display their talents in the way of decoration. Then such men as Lucas de Heere and other artists came to the fore.

. Engraving and wood-carving were exceptions to this general neglect, and were the only arts to flourish. Christopher Plantijn, the prince of Netherland printers and booksellers, the official printer of the States-General, carried on a flourishing business with his clever son-in-law, Johannes Moretus, both true to their motto—*labore et constantia*. The above-mentioned Lucas de Heere, Philippus and Cornelis Galle at Antwerp, Hubert Goltzius at Bruges, and Hendrik Goltzius at Haarlem, illustrated with their fine engravings and drawings the numerous descriptions of remarkable events in the Netherlands, the smaller fugitive writings of ephemeral value, and disseminated, artists and dealers alike, portraits of the prince and other persons prominent in the war, throughout Europe.

Literature and science, too, showed the influence of the times. It was not a period for verses of love and domestic peace, for singing of the beauties of nature and the pleasures of life. The poets of those days found their subject-matter in the disturbances of war and religious contentions, in popular hatred of the Spaniards, in complaints of the burdens of war. Simple popular songs, or rather rhymed descriptions of noteworthy events, songs like *Wilhelmus of Nassau*, satirical songs on the Catholic clergy and faith, answered with bitter

[1] Van Meteren, p. 148.

attacks on Calvinist doctrines — such were the topics touched. Only a few of these refrains, both in the Beggars' song-books and in the collections of the Catholics, rise above mediocre rhyming, more significant signs of the spirit of the times than of artistic feeling. The rhymed psalms of Utenhove and Dathenus are of a somewhat higher grade.[1] These were sung first in the midst of persecution at the open-air conventions, or in some inner room in subdued key. Later they rang out in the newly acquired churches and from the walls of the valiantly defended cities, while on the Catholic side old gentle and devout songs were heard, whose character just at this time was in harmony with the prevailing faint-heartedness in Catholicism.

The same spirit is evident in the prose of the period.[2] The devout books of an earlier epoch emanating from various religious foundations were used occasionally, and a popular volume like *Reynaert de Vos* must certainly have attracted attention in this period of attacks on the Catholic church. Classical influence, so marked in the first half of the century, is sometimes manifest in the rhymed translation of Ovid by the Ghentner Borluut, in Van Ghistele's versions of the *Ars Amandi*, and of Horace, in Coornhert's translation of the *Odyssey*, in Van Mander's version of the *Bucolics*, and in Coornhert's prose translation of Cicero's philosophical writings.

The general statement can be made that the literature of this period is closely connected with the Rhetoricians, whose lack of true artistic feeling begins very slowly to give way to personal enthusiasm and to true talent in art. Jan Baptista Houwaert is one of the best examples of the last of the Rhetorician school.

But a new period began to dawn. Lucas de Heere

---

[1] Kalff, *Gesch. der nederlandsche Letterkunde in de 16de eeuw*, ii., p. 96.
[2] *Ibid.*, p. 152.

wrote his *Hof en Boomgaerd der poesiën*, wherein he criticised the old Flemish style of poetry as rude and unskilled,
taking French and classic forms as his models.   The individual replaces the corporation.[1] Jan van der Noot
showed decided talent.   Karl van Mander was a versatile and learned artist, and Jan van Hout, secretary of
Leyden, and his well-known friend, Jan van der Does, also
deserve mention. Marnix stands by himself. Zealous
Calvinist, he showed himself a keen polemicist in the
Bienkorf (*Beehive*), and in many other masterly political pamphlets.   He also made a poetic version of the
Psalms, which is full of genuine feeling and pure taste.
He and Dirk Volkertzoon Coornhert can be called the
founders of modern Netherland prose.   Marnix, the
courtly noble and skilled diplomate, at home at the French
court and German diet, in the council-chamber and synod,
polemical writer and speaker, whose vigorous style is
recognisable in many an anonymous writing, whose
sensitive spirit expressed itself in attacks full of scathing
irony upon political and theological antagonists, and in
his sensitiveness not always firm or *sævis tranquillus in
undis*, still always Calvinist and Netherlander in heart
and soul, true to his motto—*repos ailleurs*. Coornhert,
calmer of nature, a deeper philosopher, a more liberal
scholar, more simply brought up, secretary of Haarlem,
notary, wood-engraver, poet, theologian, above all, independent thinker in the midst of the religious turmoils of
his time, downright Protestant and Netherland burgher,
averse to extremes, and setting independent opinion
above dogma in either Catholic or Protestant, the very
type of a philosopher in a war of disputes, whose motto
was "*Weet of rust.*"

Coornhert and Marnix held high rank in the contemporary world of letters.   The two great centres of learning in the Netherlands Louvain and Leyden,—Douay

[1] Kalff, *Gesch. der nederlandsche Letterkunde in de 16de eeuw*, ii., p. 239.

hardly counted—attracted scholars more and more. The Reformation had decidedly affected the schools in the Netherland cities. Many of their best men had embraced the cause of reform or come under suspicion of Erasmianism. They were persecuted and banished. Many wandered for years in France or Germany. Louvain was the stronghold of orthodoxy, although there was an occasional rebellious spirit. The opposition of Michaël Baius, professor at Louvain, ardent Catholic and royalist, against Jesuitical tenets is a proof of this. At Leyden, Saravia and Holmannus preached Calvinism in its two extremes side by side; Justus Lipsius taught the classics brilliantly at Louvain, at Leyden, and then again at Louvain; Hadrianus Junius, famous as historian and physician when Leyden was first founded, and Janus Dousa, a learned nobleman and curator of the Leyden school, also Maecenas, poet and distinguished scholar, were the best representatives of the versatile learning of the time of the Renaissance; Petrus Forestus refused a professor's chair at Leyden to be the prince's physician, and won the name of the Netherland Hippocrates. In the midst of war and theological strife, Netherland learning remained worthy of its reputation in the very circles of the opposition against Spain.

CHAPTER VI

LEICESTER IN THE NETHERLANDS

THE prince's death made a deep impression north and south.[1] Parma made steady advances, and there was no one to take the place of the fallen leader; no one to oppose, as statesman and commander, the energetic governor, the indefatigable and successful champion for the rights of the king. Maurice, the prince's second son, was, owing to the detention of his brother, Philip William, in Spain, the natural successor to his father's dignities, but could not be placed at the head of affairs, much as Oldenbarnevelt and others wished to make him count.[2] Count John of Nassau, the prince's only surviving brother, was not equal to assuming his office even had he consented to do so. And among the commanders at the head of the States' troops —Hohenlo, Sonoy, William Louis of Nassau, Norris— there was no one sufficiently distinguished to be compared with an adversary like Parma.

Thus at the prince's death the States-General were forced to become executive. The Estates of Holland were the first to understand this. Their leaders, the advocate, Paul Buys; the able pensionary of Rotterdam, Oldenbarnevelt; the energetic Amsterdam regents, Reinier Cant and William Bardes; the president

---

[1] See Joris de Bye in his *Gedenkschrift*, published by Fruin, *Bijdr. en Meded. Hist. Gen.*, 1888, p. 414.
[2] Des Pruneaux to the French king.

of the court, Van der Myle; William van Zuylen van Nyevelt, Jan van der Does, and others, lost no time. As soon as the prince had drawn his last breath, they hastened to the town-house at Delft and took the first measures to convene the cities and nobles of the provinces, in order, by coöperation with the other provinces, " to bear themselves manfully and piously without abatement of zeal on account of the aforesaid misfortune."

The Holland statesmen convened at Delft deserve to the full the praise given them by later historians.[1]   Their courageous example checked the imminent panic.[2]   Acting in the spirit of the dead prince, they wrote at once to the chief commanders of army and navy, to the cities of the provinces, to the Estates of the other united provinces, urging their mutual fidelity and coöperation. And this was all needful, for the party of reconciliation with Spain came forward amid the prevailing uncertainty. The Catholics were most anxious for negotiations, now that their fellows in the south had obtained such favourable conditions from Parma.   The energetic behaviour of the Estates of Holland and similar expressions in the other provinces of the north speedily bore good fruit. Before the end of July, a government council was established for Holland, Zealand, and Utrecht, consisting of the late prince's most trusted advisers, and, although the council did not actually come into function,[3] the statesmen nominated kept their hand on the helm and maintained the union between the three provinces.   A commission of seven deputed councillors, appointed by the States was nominated in October to conduct the government in Holland.   For the region north of the Y the already existing college of the Deputies of the North Quarter continued its activity.

[1] Wagenaar, viii., p. 3 ; Van Wijn, Appendices and notes.
[2] Compare what the contemporary Joris de Bye says.
[3] Muller, *De wording van den Staat*, etc., p. 152.

Under the influence of Holland's example, the States-General, acting with extraordinary rapidity, appointed (August 18th) a provisional council of state as executive body. This body consisted of eighteen persons, with Count Maurice as first councillor.[1] There were four members from Holland, three from Brabant, Zealand, and Friesland, two from the still free portions of Flanders and Utrecht, one from Mechlin. The other provinces were not represented, as the Ommelands were still, for the main part, in the enemy's hands, and Overyssel and Gelderland were backward. It was decided in secret that this council should sit for three months only. In the council of state it was the above-mentioned Holland statesmen who exercised the most influence. But they could not keep Utrecht, jealous of Holland's influence, from choosing her own stadtholder, Josse Zoete, lord of Villiers. The two other provinces elected no one immediately, undecided whether the dignity of countship should be given to Maurice, or whether, what many deemed more desirable, the sovereignty should be offered to the king of France or the queen of England. In such case they intended to make Maurice stadtholder of Holland and Zealand.[2]

Thus the government was regulated for the time being. But how was the war to be conducted ? Evidently aid was necessary. The negotiations in progress at the time of the prince's death led the French king to believe, after the catastrophe, that he could obtain unrestricted authority, not only in Holland and Zealand but in the other provinces, and he was open to offers.[3] There was, indeed, some continuance of the negotiations, but parties

---

[1] Compare Van der Kemp, *Maurits van Nassau*, i., p. 152.

[2] This is evident from the instruction of the ambassadors to France. V. d. Kemp, p. 161.

[3] Van Deventer, *Gedenkstukken van Johan van Oldenbarnevelt en zijn tijd.*, i., p. 59. s'Gravenhage, 1860.

were divided. Some Hollanders thought aid unnecessary,[1] while others were willing to buy aid from France by submission to her king.

The French king, too, proved only half willing to meet their offers. He knew the strength of the Catholic league in his kingdom. He knew, moreover, that it was supported by Spain, and he felt himself too weak to adopt a strong policy in the Netherlands with a dangerous foe at home. He kept up negotiations, however, out of fear for the plans of Queen Elizabeth; while England, too, had a strong party in the Netherlands, especially in Holland, Friesland, and Utrecht.

Elizabeth had coquetted with the Netherlands for long years. Now various reasons induced her to appear publicly as their protector. English sympathisers in the Netherlands were largely found among the Calvinist congregations, who were deeply averse to any association with the faithless French house. Paul Buys, the advocate of Holland, was reckoned as head of the English party. In the prince's time he had always opposed the French plans, though absolutely faithful to the prince. His well-known immorality, his sharp tongue, his avarice, had, however, weakened his influence in spite of his undeniable ability. His many enemies, especially among the congregations, could not pardon his indifference in church matters, and were constantly on the lookout to undermine his authority and cause his fall.

Finally, passing over the Spanish sympathisers, there was, in addition to the English and French parties, still a third party quite determined to retain their own sovereignty. François Francken, the able pensionary of Gouda, was practically the leader of this division in the States. The faction was small—indeed, in the States-General, Gouda stood alone, but it was animated by a principle of great power—the principle of self-confidence.

[1] See Fruin, De Gids, 1862, i., p. 525.

They did not think that the struggle could be ended without foreign aid, but it was help alone they wished from either power, not an exchange of one tyranny for another. They proudly recalled the first years of the revolt, when Alkmaar and Leyden had shown what burgher valour could do. Rather than throw themselves into the arms of the Valois and expose themselves to Italian treachery, " they would await with a quiet conscience the will of the Almighty," so resolved Gouda at the diet of the States.[1] This attitude also made a deep impression on the despondent. Still, on the whole, the authority of the States seemed too meagre to risk their carrying on the contest alone.[2]

At the end of September, these chances were discussed by the Estates of Holland. Count Maurice urged the interests of his house, referring to the circumstances which had prevented the bestowal of the countship on the prince, but did not expressly discountenance the negotiations with a foreign power. The pressure of Brabant and Flanders, who were really at the last stress, weighed down the scale, and Holland resolved to propose in the States-General an embassy to France. There was some delay, but finally the French party obtained the victory, and Paul Buys was forced to resign as advocate of Holland. There was an interim of over a year in the office before (March, 1586) John van Oldenbarnevelt, the able pensionary of Rotterdam, was appointed his successor. He was already one of the leading statesmen of Holland, and had been a faithful servant of Prince William.

In January, a stately deputation set out for Paris, composed of Elbertus Leoninus, Noël de Caron, Arend van Dorp, Cornelis Aerssens, and fourteen statesmen from the other provinces. Long delays ensued. The king hesitated, and finally roundly refused all offers. In March

[1] Bor, ii., p. 489 et seq.   [2] Joris de Bye, p. 417.

the envoys bade him farewell, and returned to the Netherlands with nothing accomplished.

England was now the only hope, and, at the end of 1586, Elizabeth was finally moved by many circumstances to send Davison to the Netherlands to see what inducements they would offer for her protection.

1584? Meanwhile Brussels fell into the hands of the Spaniards (March, 1586). Shortly afterwards Vilvoorden met the same fate, and Antwerp was hard pressed. The fate of this last city aroused universal alarm. Her possession by Spain was an event which England, too, could not regard with indifference, the more that a speedy decision to furnish aid to the Netherlands would place this important city virtually in English hands.

Meanwhile the authority of the States and of the council of state lost ground. The Union seemed in a condition of decay, as no real central government was in existence. The contributions of the provinces came in not at all, or very slowly. Holland and Zealand bore the whole cost of the war, three-quarters of which had already been gradually shoved on their shoulders. The eastern provinces were long since overpowered by the foe, and thus out of condition to aid in the common cause. As a rule, they sent no representatives to The Hague, where Holland, Zealand, Utrecht, and Friesland — sometimes the first two alone—were obliged to make the most important decisions on their own authority. How lawlessness increased is evident from the placards, issued by the States-General and by the council of state, forbidding the export of provisions. Holland, especially Amsterdam, asked that grain be excepted from the prohibition, and when the council of state refused to agree thereto, Holland, or rather the deputed council of the province, simply decided to make the exception on their own responsibility. The States-General and the council of state were very indignant at this resolution, but were

powerless to resist it. The Utrecht citizens, who had again
attained great influence in the administration, took part
in the matter, unasked, and presented a strong remonstrance to the States-General against the Amsterdam
merchants.   The assembly thanked them kindly for their
interest, but Amsterdam and Holland paid little heed,
and went on their way as though the placard respecting
the grain trade did not exist.[1]

All this had an ill effect upon the condition of Antwerp.
Parma wrote letter after letter, urging the city to capitul-
ate.   Marnix, who was in command, held out bravely.
Then Parma began to build a bridge of ships over the
Scheldt, designed to cut off Antwerp from supplies.
Marnix refused for a long time to believe this possible.
In January, 1585, he realised the extent of the danger, and began to take all the preventive measures.   By
February 25th, Antwerp was, however, cut off completely
from the sea.[2] Covered by two strong forts and a fleet of
well armed men-of-war, protected before and behind by
two great drifting floats, the bridge could bid defiance to
any attack from the sea quarter and from the side towards
the beleaguered city.   The bridge, declared Parma, was
to be his grave or his path to Antwerp.   The besieged
did not lose heart, nor did their friends in Zealand.   Forts
sprang up on the city side, while Parma gathered all the
forces at his disposal.   Every nerve was strained on each
side.   It was a contest calling to mind the old stories
about Troy.   Parma and old Mondragon, Count Charles
of Mansfeld and his hoary-haired father, Count Peter
Ernest, the marquis of Richebourg and Caspar de Robles, Italians, Spaniards, Portuguese, and Walloons, on
the Spanish side; Hohenlo and Marnix himself, Justin
of Nassau and the Zealand admiral Haultain, Captain
Heraugière and the English officers, Balfour and Morgan,

[1] Fruin, *De Gids*, 1862, i., p. 542.
[2] Compare Motley's description, *United Netherlands*, i., p. 129.

Hollanders and Zealanders, French and Scots, covered themselves with glory in the skilful attack and the courageous defence.

From the beginning, Marnix had to combat with burghers' dissatisfaction, and when supplies grew scarce the disturbances increased. The suffering at Antwerp could not, to be sure, be compared with that at Leyden, but the population of the Scheldt city was six times that of Leyden, and this mass was very difficult to hold in check. Moreover, the steadfastness of Marnix was not so great as that of Van Hout and Van der Does. Utterly discouraged and despairing of success, he soon gave ear to the offer of negotiations made to him in June. On July 9th, after nearly a month of parleying, Marnix had an interview with the besieging general. Marnix was too utterly discouraged, and too much impressed by Parma's personality, which he admired greatly, to hold his own and to insist on his conditions. On August 9th, the Broad Council of the city agreed to the terms of the capitulation. Eight days later the treaty was signed. Amnesty, return of the royalists to their property, restoration of the priests, of cloisters, and of churches; departure of non-Catholics from the city within two years, which they might have to regulate their affairs; further comprehensive maintenance of the Catholic religion, liberation of the prisoners, payment of four hundred thousand florins' indemnity, departure of the garrison with the honours of war, with their weapons and baggage,—such were the conditions on which Antwerp returned to obedience to the king.

Great was the joy in the Spanish camp and brilliant the honours showered on Parma when he made his triumphal entry into the city. At the head of his guard and escorted by Aerschot, Chimay, the Mansfelds, Aremberg, and other south Netherland nobles welcomed by Antwerpia, the personification of the city, on a chariot of victory, proudly wearing his order of the Golden Fleece, with which the king's gratitude honoured him, the victor passed into Antwerp. He lost no time in beginning to rebuild the citadel.

The bitterness against Marnix was intense. He was even accused of treason, especially when he seemed to consider that a general reconciliation with Spain was inevitable. He actually did not dare return to Holland to try to further these ideas, although he had promised Parma so to do, but betook himself to his property of West Souburg on Walcheren. The defence of his position in a *bref récit de l'estat de la ville d'Anvers* was published to defend his conduct. The document did not convince his foes, and only proved his own complete discouragement, for he himself began to doubt the fundamental right of the revolt. But all those who knew him were convinced that he—although somewhat weak—was clean of hands and of heart,[1] as La Noue said of him. His political rôle was played out for the time, and he lived in a secluded fashion, devoted to theological studies. The English party was especially embittered at the fall of the important city, which they thought would be relieved by English aid. The refugees from Antwerp—for the most part well-to-do merchants and apprentices — accused Marnix of destroying their prosperity and of wrecking their fallen city. The soldiers talked of his cowardice. They insisted that Elizabeth had promised aid which would have come in time. What was to be expected from those promises ? There were many discussions on both sides of the North Sea. Finally the discussions were concluded in Holland. In July, 1585, a considerable deputation of the States-General appeared at the English court to arrange matters with Elizabeth, or at least to obtain aid.[2] The embassy consisted of twelve statesmen

[1] Compare the important note on St. Aldegonde, Motley, p. 251.
[2] The reports of the envoys, Van Deventer, *Gedenkstukken*, i., p. 78.

and officials, among whom were the agent De Gryze, Noël de Caron, Jan van der Does, Joost van Menin, pensionary of Dordrecht; Valke for Zealand, François Maelson, Hessel Aysma for Friesland, John of Olden-barnevelt, and Paul Buys.

The general situation in the Netherlands was so 'critical, besides the especial stress of Antwerp, that the envoys were ready to yield any concessions in order to obtain Elizabeth's aid.

The queen refused roundly to assume the sovereignty. She was urged that it was very desirable to unite the two States in one body, and that the little coherent provinces needed a sovereign lord to protect common interests against the private pretensions of the provinces [1]—a remarkable plea for a monarchical government in the mouth of those who soon were to rank as republicans! They did not wish to go further than to borrow money and troops under condition that certain cities should be given in pledge, so as to insure the payment of the outlays after the end of the war. The bargaining was close. The envoys demanded a minimum of five thousand foot and one thousand horse. The queen was loath to promise more than four thousand foot and four hundred horse. The deputies offered two tons of gold in behalf of Holland, Zealand, Friesland, and Utrecht. The queen demanded more and better surety about the contributions of the other cities. While they were haggling over this came the news of Antwerp's fall. The queen's learned allusion to the fate of Saguntum while they deliberated at Rome became a picture of the truth, contrary to her expectations. This event clinched the negotiations. Elizabeth despatched Davison to Holland and agreed to

[1] Motley, i., p. 306. The narrative of the envoys is to be found in *Kron. Hist. Gen.*, p. 215, 1866, and less fully in Van Deventer, i., p. 78. In regard to Fruin's opinion that Elizabeth's sovereignty was desired in this extremity, it seems evident that this was only under certain conditions.

send five thousand troops at once under " a gentleman of quality," who was to bear the title of governor-general, and to restore tranquillity with the help of the council of state. The other stipulations were maintenance of all privileges and customs. Flushing, Rammekens, and Briel were the pledged, or cautionary, cities. The governor-general, as well as all other officials, was obliged to take an oath to the States and the queen. Most of the envoys returned to the Netherlands after this agreement.

At the end of October, minor points were settled, and the governorship conferred on Robert Dudley, Earl of Leicester, Elizabeth's friend and favourite. According to his secret instructions, he was to be primarily commander of the English troops, but at the same time first councillor of the States in all political affairs, assisted by two English advisers, who were to have seats in the council of state. He was charged, moreover, with the supervision of the mint, with the duty of securing the regular payment of the war taxes by the provinces, and of gaining their coöperation by strengthening the council of state and reforming the unwieldy body of the States-General.

In Holland and Zealand, there was disquiet. In Utrecht, the ultra-Calvinist count of Nuenar had been chosen stadtholder by the aid of Martin Schenck, recently come over to the States. When the news of Leicester's arrival was known, they began to draw a free breath, especially when the English troops under Thomas Cecil and Philip Sydney garrisoned Briel and Flushing.

At the same time, the States learned something of the instructions given to Leicester.[1] It appeared further that Oldenbarnevelt, when in England, had heard rumours of a plan to ask the stadtholdership for Leicester in Holland

[1] Hooft, *Nederl. Hist.*, p. 1039; Bruce, *Correspondence of Robert Dudley*, p. 12, London, 1844.

and Zealand, making use of the right of appointing governors in provinces and cities. The Hollanders did not have sufficient confidence in Elizabeth's aims to permit this, and accordingly hasty measures were taken to invest young Count Maurice with the office. A stadtholder of the house of Nassau [1] was considered as desirable a protection against an English as a French sovereign. Zealand set the example. Holland followed suit, and on November 1st, Count Maurice, under the title of " Excellency " and " born Prince of Orange," was appointed by the States stadtholder, governor, captain-general, and admiral of both the provinces — a dignity which made him the first officer of the States, while his father, as the king's officer, had stood above them. But at the same time the commission and instruction [2] also gave him sovereign rights in the care for the supremacy, equity, privileges, and welfare of the land and people, for law and for justice, affairs of war and state and police. He even had power to change burgomasters, schepens, and laws—in short, such sovereign rights as earlier stadtholders had exercised in the name of the overlord. It was further declared that Utrecht, joined to the two provinces since 1534, had no right to choose an independent stadtholder. The count of Hohenlo was appointed as the young stadtholder's lieutenant-general. It was further stipulated that Maurice should faithfully support the commands and ordinances of the governor-general to be sent by Elizabeth, and of the council of state. In letters to Elizabeth, Maurice and his step-mother declare expressly [3] that they heartily wish the queen's acceptance of the sovereignty, and urge her to protect the interests of the house of Nassau. The States-General also gave

[1] Wagenaar, viii., p. 105 ; Van der Kemp, i., p. 161.

[2] Bor, ii., pp. 664 and 665. Compare, in regard to this instruction, Van der Kemp, i., p. 14.

[3] Motley, *History*, i., p. 323.

Maurice the marquisate of Bergen op Zoom, held by his father. He had enjoyed that of Veere ever since the prince's death.

On the whole, Leicester was little pleased with this course of procedure. If Elizabeth had been sovereign of the Netherlands, he would have had quite another position as governor. Now he was subordinated to the States-General, whom he contemptuously called trades-folk. Elizabeth's extreme economy in all her arrangements was very annoying to the earl, as well as her extreme caution and fear of war with Spain. Wishing that " her Majesty never send general again as I am sent," he declared, " I will do what I can for her and my country."

In December, 1585, he set sail from Harwich with a fleet of fifty ships, accompanied by the envoys who had still remained in England, and by the flower of England's nobility. Sydney wrote him that he was expected like a Messiah. Elizabeth issued a manifesto, which was sent over Europe, declaring that she took this step as a neighbourly deed towards the oppressed Netherlands and as an act of self-protection against the secret and open hostility of Spain.

The English nobleman come to rescue the Netherlands from their precarious condition, had been Elizabeth's favourite for years, and by many was regarded as her future husband. He had been accused of several murders, among others of that of his wife, Amy Robsart. He was impressive in appearance, cultivated in manner, a typical man of the world. His ability was not, however, equal to his outer man. An indifferent statesman, he was quite unfitted for the task devolved upon him. He was not the man to replace Prince William, whose simple exterior during his last years was in sharp contrast to his inner greatness, a greatness that immediately made a deep impression upon everyone whom he met.

Leicester's reception in the various cities was most brilliant. He did not reach The Hague until the end of 1585, and there he was greeted by the whole population as a sovereign.[1] He wrote enthusiastic letters home. He was greatly impressed by the native manufactures, as in England industry was largely in the hands of foreigners,[2] and by the shipping.

At first the relation between Leicester and his suite with the Hollanders was very fairly smooth. Wherever he appeared was heard "God save the Queen!" as though it were Cheapside.[3]

The first matter to be regulated was the relation of Leicester to the States-General. On January 11th, the whole body suddenly appeared before the earl and offered him the "absolute government" as regent of the provinces. Leicester knew perfectly well that this would not be agreeable to his mistress. After some discussion, a decision was reached at the end of January. Leicester was to be governor-general on the same terms on which Queen Mary of Hungary had exercised the government under Charles V., with this provision: that both the States-General and provincial Estates should assemble at their own instance, while all appointments were to be made from a nomination of two or three persons made by the Estates of the province where the vacancy occurred. The existing stadtholders were to be confirmed by him. A new council of state, consisting of the prince's stanch supporters, two Englishmen, and several other members appointed by the provinces, was to aid him in the government.[4] On February 4th, the new government was formally inaugurated, and the new "Excellency" received homage in the richly decorated great hall of the

[1] Leicester, *Corresp.*, p. 30.
[2] Van Meteren, p. 243.
[3] Leicester, *Corresp.*, p. 50.
[4] The instructions, etc., are to be found in Bor, ii., p. 685.

Binnenhof in the presence of Count Maurice and a full representation of the States-General.

Elizabeth was highly indignant at this event, absolutely at variance with her intentions of holding back. When she received the first tidings she burst into a fit of rage, and the little haste made by Davison, Leicester's own messenger, did not improve matters. She at once despatched Lord Heneage to The Hague to bid Leicester renounce his new dignity immediately and become what he was, — commander of her auxiliaries in the Netherlands, and her representative. At the same time she expressed to the States-General her grave displeasure at the pressure exercised upon her servant, speaking of the " manifest insult," of " very little respect " shown her by the States, of the wounding of her honour. There was even some talk of recalling her disobedient commander. Davison succeeded in calming her a little by representing the urgent need of a leader in the Netherlands, considering Maurice's youth and the fact that Hohenlo was always half intoxicated. It was, however, not until April that a letter from Leicester softened her heart. She forgave him, but continued to give him no other title than " lieutenant-general " until July, when she finally addressed him as " governor."

The result of this hesitation was very bad. The old distrust felt in the Netherlands towards Elizabeth's policy was revived. The consideration of the new governor was not increased through the gossip, by the queen's rage, and by the rumours of his humiliation.[1] This uncertainty affected the supplies. The relations between Leicester and the States began to be strained from other causes. They resented his assumption. He disliked the Calvinism and French sympathies of Maurice and of Louise de Coligny. He even fell out with England's ancient friend, Paul Buys, whom he called a traitor, a devil, an atheist,

[1] Leicester, *Corresp.*, p. 214.

and a secret friend of the Romish church.[1]   The merchants, too, in Holland and Zealand, either members of the municipal governments themselves, or kin to members, and accordingly very influential, were disappointed at the initial results of Leicester's embassy.   They had hoped to have the staple of the English cloths established in some Holland city, but the English merchant adventurers persuaded their government that it was more in England's interest to continue the staple at Hamburg, where it had been since the fall of Antwerp.   Nor did the offer of the Dutch manufacturers to use nothing but English wool have any effect upon this opinion.   The English in their turn complained bitterly of the trade plied by the Holland and Zealand merchants with Spain, the southern Netherlands, and Picardy, whence corn and other provisions, they asserted, were carried to the enemy's land. Many thought it possible to starve out the foe, and in general all trade with the enemy was considered illegitimate.[2]   The energetic measures taken by the governor to put a stop to all this traffic in provisions were resented by the merchants.   In April, a very stringent placard was issued repealing injunctions of 1582 and 1584 against this traffic, and measures were taken to prevent smuggling across the frontier.   It was forbidden to sail to France, Scotland, and England along the coast.   Some articles of the placard gave freebooters of English and Dutch origin the right to stop sailors and investigate the cargoes if they came under the Flemish coast.   The merchants were highly indignant at these regulations, whose tendency, in their opinion, would be to throw trade directly into the hands of the rival Hanse towns.[3]

[1] Compare Leicester's *Correspondence* in connection with the extracts from the unpublished letters, British Museum and State Record Office.

[2] The various arguments of the time for and against this trade are to be found in Deventer, *Gedenkstukken*, i., p. 118 ; compare above, p. 306.

[3] Joris de Bye, p. 419.

The northern passage, which it was necessary to take in order to avoid the freebooters, offered many dangers, especially in spring and autumn. And there was more. " If trade with the west stopped entirely, so would trade with the east." The grain trade on the Baltic would go to nothing if free grain export were checked and the fisheries could not obtain salt.[1] There was also opposition to the restriction of the profitable traffic with Spain. The Spanish government had need of their articles of commerce, and had been willing to overlook the evasion of their own commands. Should the Netherlanders now voluntarily destroy this same commerce ?

Commerce and politics were so closely allied that many distinguished Holland statesmen, knowing how much the licenses and convoys brought into the treasury, how all revenues depended on the prosperity of trade, attempted to convince the governor of the ill policy of his article. But Leicester was little affected by their representations. He was supported by the orthodox preachers, who deemed traffic with the foe unholy and dangerous, and retained the disastrous article, which conflicted with the principle proclaimed in Holland since the beginning of the sixteenth century —" By freedom is commerce attracted, by restrictions frightened away." [2]

The prohibitory restrictions to trade with the enemy were strictly observed. In July another placard was issued forbidding exports to Calais, to the cities on the Somme, — London, Oldenburg, Bremen, and Hamburg, — on the ground that goods were shipped thence to the enemy's country.

The indignation aroused among the Netherland merchants, shippers, and cattle dealers was greater, inasmuch as they considered that the hand of English competition was evident in all Leicester's placards, and the whole

[1] See Van Meteren, p. 232.
[2] Fruin, *Tien Jaren*, p. 194 ; Part II., p. 504.

commercial class was alienated from the new governor. As the Estates of the provinces were composed of these same merchants, their friends and relatives, these bodies, too, became the earl's bitter opponents.

Nor was Elizabeth's representative more successful in war than in his commercial legislation. In June, Grave, in July, Venloo fell into Parma's hands. At the suggestion of Schenck, who with Hohenlo was still in Leicester's favour, an important point on the border of Cleves at the juncture of the Rhine and the Waal was protected by a fort called *Schenckenschans*, which later played an important rôle in military history.

The enemy made several other gains, and in the midst of dangers constant quarrels in the English camp weakened the position of the army of the States and their allies. The conquest of Axel by Sydney and Count Maurice was a slight compensation for other misfortunes and losses, but after Tassis's victory near Boxum in January, 1586, the enemy ravaged the Frisian country unceasingly in spite of the efforts of Count William Louis. No intercourse in Friesland was, indeed, possible without passports from Verdugo, the Spanish stadtholder. These were sold at a very high price.

Another very unpopular scheme pushed by Leicester was the institution of a chamber of finance on the advice of a Brabant adventurer, Reingoud,[1] who had obtained great influence over the governor. He was undoubtedly an able man. His past knowledge of the finances, too, gave him weight, and he was appointed treasurer-general of the new chamber. This new body was, in coöperation with the council of state, to put an

[1] This man had been Egmont's secretary, after going through bankruptcy as a merchant, and served Granvelle, Alva, and Requesens as clerk of finance. Later, he had gone over to the States and put on an appearance of piety to cover up his past career. He succeeded in getting a hold over the governor.

end to the numerous infringements of the marine placards, and to bring into the treasury thousands, rather
millions, in fines imposed on the smugglers and others.
Reingoud himself spoke of certain high-placed government officials who had been guilty of such practices, and
demanded that Leicester should permit him and his
officers an examination of the books of all persons in
office who might come under suspicion. Finally the
chamber was to stop all kinds of abuses in financial matters, it being asserted that great sums were wont to
vanish in the affairs of superiors and officials.

Both Reingoud and his accomplice Perret, controller of
the convoys at Antwerp, were personally distasteful to
the other members of the council of state, and this plan
met with disfavour. Paul Buys was very indignant at
the humiliation offered to him in his appointment as
clerk under Reingoud, a former bankrupt. Both he and
the able Amsterdammer, William Bardes, asserted their
unwillingness to act in such capacity. The council further
declared that it was impossible to punish so-called *lor-
rendrayers* or smugglers, without injustice to many
innocent people; that the examination of merchants'
books in the land was something unheard of and reminis-
cent of Alva's times. Credit would be undermined. It
was also questionable to endow certain officials with
powers extraordinary towards the merchants. Violent
discussions ensued in the council of state. But the governor succeeded in carrying his point, and appointed
Reingoud to the post without consulting the States.
Further, the count of Nuenar and the Utrecht lord of
Brakel, were placed nominally at the head of the chamber,
also without any discussion in the States.

Besides Reingoud, Gerard Prouninck, called Deventer,
and the Flemish Daniel de Burchgrave were prominent
figures in the earl's circle. Prouninck was the cleverest
of the three, a native of Bois-le-duc, zealous reformer,

and on that account emigrant to the north after the submission of his town to the king. He was an able and passionate popular leader, who thought he had found in democratic Utrecht a good theatre for his activity. He was no longer unknown in the north and already employed as treasurer-general *pro tem*. At Utrecht, where he usually lived, he had been held in high consideration by the small citizens, who had made great strides in influence during the past years. It was no chance that Leicester's advisers, his extra council (*achterraad*) were south Netherlanders. These exiles set their hopes on him who was to restore them to their homes at the head of his troops. On his side, Leicester found their support convenient against the Holland and Zealand regents and merchants, more interested in their own defence than in that of the south, already lost. These exiles jeered at the " sovereign " lords, Hans Brouwer, Hans Kaaskoper, Hans Meulder, being the instruments of the sovereign pensionaries[1] by whom the Hollanders let themselves be governed; the same, they said, who had worked secretly against the prince of Orange in his last years. They were anxious to see the mastery of the merchants suppressed and the municipal governments remoulded. In nearly all the cities in Holland where the revolt had gained the victory, the administration had remained in the hands of the higher-class burghers, who had practically wielded affairs for almost two centuries without coöperation of the remaining citizens. It was the persons, not the institutions, which had been changed by the revolt. The Catholic regents had had to yield to Protestants; certain families had made room for others; a few rose from the lower ranks, but there was little real participation of the citizens at large in the government, in spite of Prince William's efforts to bring about a change. Similar conditions existed in the other revolted

[1] Bor, iii., p. 205.

provinces.   Other individuals had taken the place of the earlier regents without change in institutions.   About 1550, the citizens at large had exerted a certain influence. This had virtually vanished.   The bestowal of an important share in administration upon the citizens, either through the means of the guilds or through the archers or through the so-called communities in the cities of Gelderland and Overyssel, would have opened the door for disturbances of the fainthearted and Romish or Spanish sympathisers, who would have insisted on negotiations with Parma.   Indeed, this had happened in Nimwegen, Zutphen, and other places.   Nearly everywhere the administration was wielded by a small class determined to carry on the war to the bitter end.[1]   This had been the progress of affairs at Utrecht.   After the prince's death an hereditary council was established, a close town councillors' college, consisting of life members, vacancies being filled by the survivors.   The new aristocratic government at Utrecht would not hear of any participation of the citizens in the government, especially of the burgher captains, the leaders of the archers, important in the days of war, who had acted as police and, hard workers though they were, had assumed a haughty tone toward the magistracy in the days of Requesens and of the Pacification.[2]

This hereditary council had been abolished when Nuenar was made stadtholder, while the influence of the militia had been restored and the government reformed in a strong democratic spirit with recognition of the stadtholder, who found his support with the democracy. This was the system Leicester found in Utrecht, and Gerard Prouninck, or Deventer as he is usually called, was the acknowledged head of the new Utrecht popular government which he meant to use against his opponents.

[1] Compare Fruin, *Tien Jaren*, p. 39 etc.
[2] Joris de Bye, p. 421 ; compare Fruin in De Gids, 1862, i., p. 538.

Leicester was in high favour with the Utrecht preachers and their congregations, whose orthodoxy, as he wrote, increased daily, so that a vigorous effort of his adherents was possible. A plot was made by Deventer, Reingoud, Burchgrave, and other confidants of the governor. At a given moment a kind of *coup d'état* was to be effected for the purpose of confirming Leicester's authority permanently in Utrecht. Then the work was to be carried on by numerous secret adherents who had conspired in the Holland cities.

At the end of June, the burgher guard suddenly presented a request to the council that sovereignty of the province should be offered to Queen Elizabeth. Other little cities of the Sticht followed suit.[1] Against whom all this was directed was plain from the fact that Paul Buys was placed under arrest at Utrecht.

In the same month, Leicester sanctioned the eviction from the province of several more " Ancient Beggars " suspected of an understanding with Spain. Spurred on by the Reingoudists, the earl undoubtedly was sincere in his belief that Buys, Hohenlo, and Maurice were plotting treachery against him.

The Estates of Holland were highly indignant at these proceedings. Protests were showered upon Leicester, who tried to disavow his own share in them, but the presence of Lord North and the English troops in Utrecht showed his cognisance thereof. Holland gave shelter to the Utrecht refugees, in spite of the Reingoudists' efforts to banish them from Netherland soil. Deventer became burgomaster of Utrecht, although provincial privileges were infringed by the election of an alien, and he was refused admission to the States when he presented himself among the Utrecht delegation.[2]

Feeling sure of Utrecht, Leicester tried to lure Oldenbarnevelt thither in order to place this doughty opponent

[1] Bor, ii., p. 723.   [2] Compare Fruin in De Gids, 1862, i., p. 660.

under arrest, but the advocate induced the Estates to forbid his leaving the province.

The relation between the governor and the States went from bad to worse. Leicester characterised the assembly as a monstrous government,[1] composed of merchants interested in nothing but their own gain. On the other hand, Reingoud, Perret, and Leicester's other councillors were universally accused of lack of honour, ability, and of a tendency to excite quarrels.

In West Friesland, too, a matter came up in which Leicester thwarted the Estates of Holland and their stadtholder. West Friesland had enjoyed a partially independent status ever since its incorporation into the territories of the Burgundian dukes. This distinction between Hollanders and West Frieslanders had gradually disappeared under Philip the Good and his successors, but the fall of Haarlem again isolated the north quarter temporarily and offered an opportunity for the revival of this old separation, inasmuch as Sonoy was an independent governor under the prince. He was glad now to obtain recognition as stadtholder to Leicester, thus asserting the independence of the country under his jurisdiction, of Holland, and of Count Maurice. Leicester was more than willing to foster this inclination of the West Frisians to maintain a separate existence, as it broke Holland's strength. He emphasised it at once by appointing governors at Vianen, Gorkum, and other places, on his own authority and without consulting Maurice.

During all these events the governor showed a lack of character and firmness. Although he really had everything in his hand and had approved every measure in secret, he did not venture to come out boldly, and even was pusillanimous enough to declare the Utrecht refugees under his protection. This was also partly due to his fear

---

[1] Leicester, *Corresp.*, p. 367.

of the queen, who liked Buys and deemed Reingoud untrustworthy, while she disliked the alliance of her deputy with the ultra-Calvinists; but she was too much occupied with the problem of Mary Stuart at that moment to heed the States' complaints.

Another unpopular measure was a regulation made by Leicester whereby he fixed the face value of a new issue of rose nobles at a higher rate than their actual value in gold.   The States urged the results of Maximilian's mint practices as a useful example.[1]

On November 11th, the chief grievances against Leicester's administration were presented to him in a remonstrance drawn up by the Estates of Holland, Zealand, and Friesland.   The earl's sharp answer was little adapted to restore peace, and the repeated refusal of the States-General to admit the burgomaster Deventer to their assembly embittered the contest the more, as the Utrecht deputation of the States-General was unfriendly to Leicester.

There were further differences, too, in regard to finance, while in church matters the opinions of the governors were in direct opposition to those of the Estates of Holland.

In order to win popularity, Leicester had espoused strictly Calvinist views, which were not the sentiments of the much less orthodox States.   They steadfastly refused to follow the wishes of the " precisians " and suppress not only the Catholic Church but all Protestants at variance with Calvinism.   Buys, Leoninus, and Oldenbarnevelt all belonged to the moderate school, who objected to the excesses of the ultra-orthodox.

In Utrecht, Leicester had acted wholly to the minds of the zealous Calvinists, and had given his countenance to the abolition of St. James's congregation, or rather to

[1] Compare Part II., p. 340, and Blok's *Het Kaas en Broodvolk*, in *Versl. en Med. der Kon. Akademie*, New Series, x., p. 257.

their enforced amalgamation with the Reformed Church. The consistory of the Reformed had undoubtedly instigated the disturbances, hoping thereby to gain ground.

In Holland, the opportunity was taken by the Reformed to hold a national synod, which was convened June, 1586, under protection of the governor, and empowered to revise church affairs.   This synod attempted to organise the Reformed Church permanently, in accordance with the strict principles which the zealots had demanded from the beginning.

The Holland officials were greatly disturbed at the synod and at the efforts of the church party.   Many thought of Prince William's warnings against extremes, and pointed out the results of similar action in Brabant and Flanders.[1]   They urged, too, that the persecution under Alva had made no distinction between Lutherans, Baptist, and Reformed, but attempted to root up all alike. The moderates and the " precisians " had experienced the same exile.   A new inquisition would be the logical outcome of a fixed adherence to dogma.   The Estates were not willing to do more than approve the resolutions " provisionally," reserving their supervision over church and school, a restriction which rendered the system of church ordinance uncertain, and showed that when the Estates took the resolution — which was not until December—the tables were, in truth, turned.

By that time a marked change had come about.   Leicester was deeply disappointed at his lack of support from England, especially since Wilkes had replaced Killegrew in the council of state.   Only inadequate reinforcements were sent him, and the subsidies were insufficient.   He was forced to draw on his own purse for the outfit and payment of his troops, and it was very difficult to obtain supplies from the Estates of Holland in their antagonism to him.   Had Parma had troops and money at his

[1] Compare Hooft, *Memoriën en Adviezen, Werken Hist. Gen.*, No. 16.

disposal at this epoch, there is no doubt that the States' losses of the last year would have been followed by that of Gelderland and Overyssel.   Fortunate it was for the Netherlands that Parma was seriously blocked in his military operations.

At the time of the siege and fall of Antwerp, Philip was deeply absorbed in another scheme which threw Netherland interests into shadow.   This was the execution of a long-discussed plan of forming a great Armada, a combined armament of sea and land forces, to make an attack on England, the doughty foe of Catholicism and Spain's supremacy.   Plans of this nature had hung fire since 1583.[1]   Old Cardinal Granvelle agreed in thinking it desirable to replace the " modern Jezebel " with the orthodox Queen of Scots,[2] who was constantly plotting, even from her prison, with the Guises, the French Catholics, and the pope.   In the spring of 1585, the plan took another colour.   France was no longer in a position to take part, as had been proposed.

Under these circumstances, Philip decided to undertake an expedition without France, never wholly trusted, without the Guises, but with the support of the pope and the Italian princes, with a Spanish fleet.[3]   Coöperation from the Netherlands was part of the project, but when Antwerp fell,—and Parma refused to act before that event,—it was too late in the year, and besides very heavy drains had been made on the treasury by the siege.

The following spring finally seemed the time for fulfilment of these projects.   Parma entertained some hopes of winning the hand and kingdom of the captive whom he was to rescue, as Don John had once dreamed of doing, while Philip intended to make the conquest in his own name or for his daughter Isabella, who was to marry

---

[1] Duro, *La Armada Invincible*, i., p. 243.   Madrid, 1884.

[2] Philippson, *Ein Ministerium unter Philip II.*, p. 475.

[3] *Ibid.*, p. 515.

an Austrian archduke.   If England fell, Holland's conquest would not be delayed.   The pope, although entertaining some fear lest the curia's authority might wane under a universal Spanish monarchy, as it had in the most prosperous period of Charles V., still allowed himself to be persuaded to give some financial support.   But what a light fell on the comparison between Spain's plans and Spain's powers when the English sea lion, Francis Drake, half pirate, half admiral, went to the Peninsula "to singe the king's beard," in the autumn of 1585, seized the city of Vigo in Galicia, and rendered unsafe, first the Portuguese coast, and then the wide ocean, committing deeds of lawlessness in the very sight of a Spanish fleet, landing, bombarding, wherever he wished.   Truly a Spanish attack on England seemed a mere fantasy of the brain.

These events kept Parma from pursuing operations in the Netherlands vigorously, since the government at Madrid had no thought but for England, and would not risk troops and men in the Netherlands.   On the other hand, they give the key to Elizabeth's unwillingness to send troops out of England.   The result was that Leicester was helpless with his small force.   He succeeded in taking Doesburg, he laid siege to Zutphen, — a siege famous for the death of Sir Philip Sydney, — while he strengthened the position of the city of Deventer by a garrison of twelve hundred wild Irish under the Catholic William Stanley as governor.   Much had been hoped from this campaign, and nothing resulted.

Leicester finally decided to go to England and urge his difficulties.   During the projected absence of the governor in the field, administration of affairs was left not to the States-General but to the council of state, while Count Maurice as chief stadtholder was to give his signature to documents in addition, and Norris was put in command of the English troops.   Under this *régime* the independence of the various governors was very precarious. According to a secret instruction, they could not be removed, while they showed little inclination to obey the commands of the council. Before Leicester's departure he tried to persuade the Estates of Holland and Zealand to send envoys, as Utrecht had done,— and he thought Gelderland, Overyssel, and Friesland might do,— to offer Elizabeth the sovereignty. They declared their willingness to do this, but entirely refused to allow Maurice to go at the head of this embassy, fearing he might be detained in England. So little real confidence was felt in the governor, although the Estates made a show of affection by presenting him with a beautiful gold vase!

On November 25th, Leicester went to Flushing, where he was detained a fortnight by contrary winds before he could set sail for England.

Leicester's departure affected the position of the national government seriously. The States found themselves obliged to act in many matters for the council of state, which could not maintain authority fitly. They were not interested in confirming Leicester's schemes, as he had, indeed, surmised would be the case. Their first step was to disband sixty-five companies to save expense and to enforce discipline among the remaining troops.[1] They virtually suspended the obnoxious navigation laws, released Buys from confinement, and restored him to authority.

The general distrust of English officers like Stanley and Yorke—who had served under the Spaniards — was confirmed by their defection to the enemy. The city of Deventer, too, went over to the Spaniards; the fortress of Wouw near Bergen op Zoom and the city of Gelder were betrayed to Parma. There were ill reports about other

[1] Joris de Bye, p. 423.

places. Wilkes and Norris did their best to retrieve the reputation of their fellow countrymen, but the queen's neglect to pay her troops, added to the lawlessness of the English at this crisis, rendered their efforts futile. Moreover, Leicester's secret instruction to the governors was discovered and aroused bitter indignation against them and against the English in general, an indignation increased by the turmoils of Leicester's adherents in Utrecht, Friesland, and the north quarter of Holland.

Under these circumstances the Estates of Holland decided to give Maurice the title of " prince," in order to enhance his position. Hohenlo was made his lieutenant-general, his military reputation being little affected by his drinking habits and his roughness. Permission was granted the Holland cities to take mercenaries into their service for their own safety. The whole province was placed under the stadtholder,[1] ignoring the council of state. A new oath to the Estates of Holland and of Zealand was imposed upon the soldiers. The governors of the fortresses and Sonoy himself were made subordinate to Maurice in spite of Leicester's orders. Thus a provincial army came into existence. These measures, justified by the danger of the moment, were all in direct conflict with the rights of the council of state and of the States-General. Oldenbarnevelt was the soul of all this.

The States-General were persuaded by Holland's energetic leaders to adopt similar measures. They, as sovereigns, confirmed the national council of state, purified of dangerous elements by the dismissal of Meetkercke and other suspicious persons. A violent letter was sent by Oldenbarnevelt to Leicester in the name of the States-General, criticising his policy and his methods, and reproaching him bitterly for the secret instructions to the governors and for the treason of Stanley and Yorke. An

[1] Joris de Bye, p. 424.

accompanying letter to Elizabeth repeated these re-proaches.[1] The English States councillor, Wilkes, vainly tried to prevent the despatch of these inimical epistles.

On their receipt, Elizabeth was as indignant as Leicester at this tone of the States, *aspre et malcourtois.* She declared that her lieutenant-general should never return where such was all the thanks he received for his valuable services. The States replied proudly that it had always been the custom of their predecessors to present all difficulties freely to " our princes and governors."

The critical situation in England at that minute — it was the days before and after Mary Stuart's execution — made an accommodation seem desirable, and a better humour was attained by the efforts of certain English statesmen, friendly to Holland. Leicester's return, moreover, seemed a matter of moment to the Netherlands, as Sonoy, the Frisian malcontents, and the municipal government of Utrecht, relying upon Leicester, began to oppose the States openly, and refused to acknowledge Maurice's authority. At this juncture Wilkes took a step which threw oil upon the flames. Undoubtedly instructed by Deventer and others regarding the governmental form of the provinces, the English statesman declared that he relied on the sentiment of the people to support Leicester against the States, whose sovereignty he denied. He claimed that, in default of a prince, the people, not the States, inherited the sovereignty. " The sovereignty, in absence of a lawful prince, belongs to the community, and not to you, my lords, who are no more than the servants, members, and deputies of this same community," restricted by instructions and commissions; and " still less do Your Excellencies represent the sovereignty," which was given by the community to Leicester through the means of the States as their

[1] See Motley, ii., p. 195.

servants.[1] Thus ran the remarkable theory in Wilkes's remonstrance (March, 1587) to the States-General and the Estates of Holland, who had invited him to state his ideas.

The States were ready with a counter-argument. In the name of Holland's government, François Francken, pensionary of Gouda, compiled a long and elaborate document, a comprehensive *Justification* or *Deductie*, wherein he ventured the assertion "that the land had been ruled for seven hundred years by counts and countesses upon whom the nobles and cities, as representing the Estates, had lawfully conferred the sovereignty." Further, it was claimed that the municipal town councils were as old as the cities themselves, or so that no memory existed of their origin. " In these colleges," says the document, " is lodged the power to dispose of affairs concerning the state of the city, and what may be decreed in that same college must be accepted by the citizens at large." " Cities and nobles together represent the whole state and the whole body of population." And the deputies who wield the government are not the States themselves, but " represent their principals," and in this wise stand for the populace of the land, " who are averse to all ambition." Whoever, therefore, opposes the States opposes the people, and if " the commons should take a stand against their lawful representatives, the States, then the state would be wrecked of itself." On this ground was asserted a right of opposition to Leicester's measures and to his *achterraad*, which was criticised severely.

This answer was not sent to the English state-councillor immediately, as in the meanwhile Buckhurst, as envoy extraordinary, was making an effort to smooth over affairs. The document itself, the disposition evident therein, the fundamental ideas, belong to the most remarkable phenomena of the time. The *Deductie* is the manifesto of

[1] Kluit, *Holl. Staatsregeering*, ii., p. 281 ; compare Bor, ii., p. 218.

the aristocratic government, — according to the senior Hooft, " our most necessary and surest reasons,"[1] and wholly consistent with the national character, which, in general, demanded no share in the government of the States for the people.[2]

In general, but there were also individuals who shared the democratic theories of Wilkes. Deventer, the majority of the preachers of the Reformed Church, and finally the Leicester sympathisers in Friesland, led by the councillor Aysma, let no opportunity pass to express their democratic opinions against the States and the " counts," as Maurice, William Louis, and Hohenlo together were usually named. In pulpits and private conversations, in pamphlets and letters in the assembly of the States, too, they asserted that the sovereignty was lodged not in the States but in the people, and they egged on the discontent at the States' behaviour towards Leicester, and urged the latter to place himself at the " head of the folk " against the presumptuous regent-aristocracy. Deventer despatched letter after letter to Leicester, urging his return to the Netherlands. His honour, his good name among posterity, the honour of the English nation, were all involved. Envoys were despatched to England—Moded among the rest—to implore Leicester's speedy return from fear of the measures of the States' party against him and his friends. They tried to form new leagues and accomplish an offer of the sovereignty to Elizabeth which would strengthen Leicester. They cast doubt, too, on the authority of the " so-called " States-General as against the council of state, and appealed to the union of Utrecht as asserting the right of the individual provinces as against the general assembly.

Their plans failed, as Holland resisted these measures

---

[1] Hooft, *Memoriën en Adviezen*, p. 23.
[2] See Fruin, *Tien Jaren*, p. 42.

in the States-General and the council of state.   But Holland, too, desired Leicester's return, as it was dangerous to risk losing England's support in a critical time.   Popular disturbances and Parma's advances caused deep anxiety, which increased with the news that Sluis was beleaguered.   At that minute came tidings that Leicester was on the point of returning, and great was the rejoicing.

There was, to be sure, a turn of feeling when the States obtained information of a secret letter from Leicester to his secretary, expressing his wish that his adherents should try to make his authority wholly independent of the States, while he was willing to be assisted by a council composed of Netherlanders.   He also said that if the States refused to accord him the unlimited power he desired, he would try to win it with the aid of the communities and the preachers.   If that failed, he would go home, and the queen would wash her hands of the Netherlands.[1]

The indignation which animated the States when Oldenbarnevelt brought forward these documents showed their opinion plainly.   Oldenbarnevelt declared that he would offer his resignation if he were not vigorously supported in his opposition to the English governor.   There was, indeed (April, 1587), some talk of replacing him by François Francken, but finally the advocate's motion was adopted.

While this feeling was still rife in the States, Leicester arrived at Flushing.   The distrust toward him was evident from the cool reception accorded him by the States and from the way in which his propositions respecting the relief of Sluis were met.   It was too late to prevent disaster there.   The town fell in the beginning of August, to the deep annoyance of the English governor, who accused the States and the States' commanders of neglect of duty and disobedience, nay, more,—but unjustly,—of treason and secret understanding with Parma.   And the people

[1] Van Deventer, *Gedenkstukken*, i., p. 164.

sided with him. The members of the council of state meeting at Flushing and Middelburg, were not sure of their safety in the midst of the raging multitude.[1] Thus the second period of Leicester's administration began ill. The " fire of ancient faction " flamed out. In August, the Estates of Holland published a declaration in which their claims of sovereignty were made clear, and complaints of Leicester's encroachments were preferred in detail. The distrust between the governor and the States increased on the discovery of continuous negotiations existing between Elizabeth and Parma.

From the spring of 1587, the queen had been intent on averting the pressing danger of a Spanish attack on England. She was not wholly pleased at Drake's raids on Cadiz and Lisbon, where he burnt many ships. Leicester conceived the plan of fortifying several ports on the island of Walcheren to offer to Spain at the proper moment as a price for a favourable treaty. In August, Leicester finally announced these negotiations verbally.[2] He soon discovered that he had jeopardised his popularity among the Calvinist congregations, who were his chief support. Opposed to all approach to Spain as to the devil, they were at once alienated from their friend. He then tried to save himself by a disavowal of all peace projects. This, of course, was of little avail in the face of information furnished the States, and it became more and more evident that he would have to treat openly or lose the game entirely.

Immediately after the fall of Sluis, he began to take his measures. His adherents had expected a *coup d'état* at the beginning of September. In a certain sense Leicester had free hands, as Wilkes and Norris had returned to England, and Killegrew, the former's successor, was wholly in his service.[3] But no *coup d'état* came.

---

[1] Joris de Bye, p. 428.   [2] See Muller, *De wording*, etc., p. 452.
[3] Van Deventer, *Gedenkstukken*, i., p. 168.

He was in a hard place.   His hypocritical acknowledgment of peace negotiations after his repeated denials
occasioned a violent popular outbreak.

Then, too, it became clear on the other side, that Parma
was only making a show of wishing peace, while he was
engaged in active preparation for the attack on England.
Leicester hastily informed his government of an equipment of three hundred thousand men which Parma was
setting on foot, and negotiations were broken off.   Leicester felt that the situation was too difficult for him.   He
could not regain his popularity, and he begged to be relieved from his post.   His remonstrances and missives of
this period, directed to the States-General and to the
provincial Estates, showed how incensed he was at the
opposition.   And Holland was not slow in her answer.

Elizabeth insisted that Leicester should play out his
rôle to the end, and he made one desperate attempt to
retrieve himself.   He published a manifesto to the States,
which was printed and scattered through the provinces,
defending his attitude towards Holland and towards the
queen's peace projects.   Then, with the aid of Sonoy,
Deventer, and other adherents, both open and secret, he
tried to obtain possession of Amsterdam, Enkhuizen,
Leyden, and other places; but all these plans miscarried.

In close connection with these undertakings, was a
missive addressed to the Estates of Holland by a number
of Holland preachers, and supported by the government
of Utrecht, where Leicester made his headquarters, and
which was the middle point of the disturbances.   The
document is a remarkable evidence of the compass and
significance of the plans of Leicester's adherents and of
the gradual disappearance of the limits between the
church and politics.[1]

The Estates of Holland decided to hold an extra session
to discuss the strained situation.   Oldenbarnevelt was

[1] Joris de Bye, p. 420 ; Bor, iii., p. 73.

the chief leader of the Estates.   On October 18th, the assembly expressed a disapproval of the interference of the ministers in the affairs of the government.   They further complained bitterly of the efforts to stir up the flame of discontent and " to fish in troubled waters." A special protest was sent to Utrecht, complaining of the presence of Brabant and Flemish refugees, who might easily induce the same submission to Spain which had taken place in those provinces.   Leicester, in his turn, published a defence.[1]   But the most important of all these remonstrances and declarations was the deduction of the right of the Estates to the government of Holland, wherein Wilkes's theories were combated in brief.   This was disseminated widely by the Estates as a testimony to their right of sovereignty, as representing their principles, the nobles and cities of the province.

Leicester was bitterly disappointed at the turn of events.   He stayed at Medemblik for a few days, and then went to Flushing, " to keep an eye on Parma," he said, but really on his way to England.   Killegrew and others tried to reconcile him with the States, but matters had gone too far on both sides.   The earl's rôle was played out, and there was nothing for him but to go home.

The queen wrote indignantly to the States, complaining of their ill-treatment of her representative, of their selfishness, etc.   A not less violent farewell letter from Leicester (December 6th) followed.   He stated all his grievances, and said that he was departing for England, implying that he would never return.   It was not, however, until the following April that official information of his resignation came to the States-General.[2]

This delay had serious results.   Leicester's adherents continued to hope for his return, and the reputation of the States-General and of the Estates of Holland suffered

[1] See Bor, iii., p. 82.   [2] *Kron. Hist. Gen.*, 1866, p. 282.

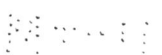

seriously in the spring of 1588 from the prevailing uncertainty, which the English government increased by an ambiguous declaration.   Lord Willoughby, who succeeded Leicester in the command of the English troops, showed little disposition to render obedience to the States.   His brother-in-law, who commanded at Geertruidenberg, declared plainly that he would have nothing to do with them.   Maurice and Hohenlo were openly defied by the other English commanders, and were accused of being secret friends of Spain, while the preachers supported the Leicester party from the pulpit.   The general condition of rebellion and revolt increased. Sonoy and Deventer held their own at Medemblik and at Utrecht in opposition to Maurice and the States. The country districts of Oostergoo and Westergoo in Friesland showed a disposition to make a separate peace with the Spanish stadtholder, Verdugo, and William Louis had difficulty in preventing it.   In many important fortresses the unpaid forces began to mutiny.   The preachers were still applying to England.   In the midst of the unceasing confusion the commission of the council of state expired.

The States' government, Oldenbarnevelt at the head, supported by Maurice and Hohenlo, maintained order with a vigorous hand.   The young Orange prince restored quiet in Walcheren.   Sonoy, supported by England, had Medemblik blockaded.   Maurice regularly besieged the town, and at the end of April, Sonoy succumbed, and his example was followed by the other rebels.   The garrison at Geertruidenberg — English and mercenaries — threatened to sell the town to the enemy, but they, too, were pacified by partial payment.   The Leicester party had lost courage.   Deventer held on a little longer in Utrecht, but the States were the acknowledged sovereign, after Leicester's definite resignation.

The heart of the ex-governor of the Netherlands was

full of bitterness when he returned home. " *Non gregem sed ingratos invitus desero* " was the legend he had engraved on the medal struck on this occasion. A medal was struck in Holland at the same time, which bore the legend, "*Libertas ne ita cara ut simiæ catuli,*" with the representation of an ape who hugged its young ones to death. Thus ended in violent quarrels and with mutual complaints the sovereignty of the defenders of the Netherlands against Parma. Count John of Nassau's prognostication proved true. Leicester was not the man to ally himself with a form of government on the basis of popular sovereignty or coöperation of the subjects in important affairs.

CHAPTER VII

THE ESTABLISHMENT OF THE REPUBLIC OF THE
UNITED NETHERLANDS

THE attempt to establish an " eminent head " with
authority derived from the States, under an English
protectorate, had thus failed completely.   With Leicester's departure, the idea of the sovereignty of the provincial Estates had, however, gained strength.   For it
was their sovereignty which the governor and his party
had opposed, and their sovereignty to which Oldenbarnevelt and his party had appealed as against Leicester.
The defeat of their opponents signified the victory of the
principles of sovereignty vested in the provincial Estates,
a principle that, although politically unjust, had come to
the fore through the force of circumstances.   It was now
a question how far this principle could be applied to the
organisation of the government without making a complete change—a difficult act under the pressing danger
of Parma's advances.   That this was accomplished in
1588 and in the succeeding years — with the good and ill
it carried with it — is due to one statesman, to the energetic John of Oldenbarnevelt.

Born at Amersfoort, probably in September, 1547,
Oldenbarnevelt had studied law at Louvain, Bourges,
and Heidelberg, travelled through Italy and France, and
then settled at The Hague as advocate of the court of
Holland.   He was on the side of the revolt from the

beginning of the troubles. He was one of the three advocates of the court who remained at The Hague in 1572 when the president and council of Holland fled to Utrecht. He speedily became one of the most zealous adherents of the prince of Orange. Exact and industrious, resolute and prudent, the young Oldenbarnevelt was a man of acknowledged importance among the prince's friends; ambitious, naturally inclined to dominance, he was fitted to play an important rôle. At the end of 1576, Rotterdam offered him the office of pensionary, which carried with it the privilege of appearing in the provincial Estates, whither the pensionary of a city accompanied one or more members of the town council. He speedily obtained great influence. Important matters were intrusted to him, and his advice was taken on dangerous complications. In the meetings of the college of the nearer union and of the States-General, where he often represented Holland after 1579, his voice, too, was of great weight. During the last years of the prince's life, he was one of the first members of the Estates of Holland, one of the prince's most zealous friends, and his confidential agent in important affairs. He was, moreover, a strong advocate of the prince's sovereignty under certain conditions, and of the union of Holland and Zealand with Utrecht so as to make a kernel of resistance in the north. After the prince's death, action was rarely taken without him. In the spring of 1586, though barely forty, he was chosen as advocate. This made him leader of Holland's policy at the critical period of Leicester's administration.

This post of " land's advocate " originated at the end of the fifteenth century, from the union of the offices of legal councillor of the Estates and that of secretary of their particular assemblies.[1] It was of great importance in the continual change of individuals which composed

---

[1] See Blok, *Holl. stad onder de bourg. heerschappij*, p. 373.

the Estates. The incumbents could be considered the persons of influence in Holland, and that Paul Buys had certainly been.

Oldenbarnevelt's instruction of March 6, 1586, differed in one particular from that of his predecessors. As legal adviser of the Estates, the advocate was specially charged with the maintenance of the provincial privileges and customs, and of the conduct of suits in behalf of the state. It was his duty to be present at the assemblies, to keep the minutes, to bring up unfinished business, to ask the opinion of the nobles, to count the votes, preserve the ordinances and despatches in the registers, and attend the meetings of the colleges of deputed councillors and those of finance and marine affairs. In the new instruction, it was further stipulated that the advocate should " ask the opinions, record each one, declare the majority, and draw up the resolutions accordingly,"—an important right that would necessarily increase his influence in the conduct of affairs. Formerly he had only to record the votes. But the office really derived its chief value from the eminent personality of its incumbent. He represented the principle of provincial state sovereignty, of the aristocratic form of government, of Holland's dominance in comparison to the other provinces. In this spirit, too, were his measures taken to strengthen the weakened governmental authority after Leicester's departure.

The council of state established by the governor was thrown into confusion at his going. On April 12th,[1] this council received a new instruction from the States-General, by which it was endowed with executive functions. It was still composed of representatives from the various provinces and the English commander, with two English colleagues, in virtue of the treaty with England. All the provincial stadtholders also had seats therein.

[1] Bor, iii., p. 236.

Existing circumstances, however, deprived this executive body of the importance which it might have taken in the union. The English members often blocked important matters, while the advocate had no seat and was often expressly excluded from the deliberations; the three Holland members had slight influence and a desire was aroused in Holland to restrict the council in its power. This animus is evident in the new instruction, which withdrew the conduct of marine affairs from the council and gave that of the war practically to the English commanders and to the three stadtholders, while there was an express prohibition from interference in provincial matters. On the basis of article 32 of the instruction, according to which, " in time of need or when national affairs demand it," the States-General and the separate provinces might act without reference to the council, other business, too, could be withdrawn from its oversight. And that actually happened. Foreign affairs, conduct of war, judiciary, police—all were withdrawn from the council within a couple of years and transferred to the States-General and to the provincial Estates. That is, all business was virtually placed under the influence of Holland and its advocate. In 1590, the English complained bitterly of this encroachment by the States-General.

Thus in place of an executive body composed for the purpose, the hydra-headed government of the States-General came into being, an assembly which made the very most unwieldy executive imaginable, as the deputies were all bound to the charges of the Estates, of which they were only deputies. It was only the dominance of a single province — Holland — and the personality of one States' official, whether he were stadtholder of one or more provinces, as the prince of Orange had been, or whether his personal influence were powerful, like Oldenbarnevelt's, which could secure the necessary force to wield the central government.

There were loud complaints at the encroachments made both by Holland and Oldenbarnevelt. But all protests were futile. The advocate waved aside obstacles from the way which could balk the aristocratic govern- ment principle. "Better overlorded than ruled by a mob," was the maxim of the advocate, who was de- termined that the commonalty should have no voice in the administration.

There was only one province, or rather one town, where democracy was still strong — Utrecht. In the autumn of 1588, here, too, vanished the survivals from Leicester's time, to give way to the government of the aristocratic rulers. Deventer had kept the reins in hand after Leicester's departure. In the spring of 1588, the state council made an attempt to put down the disturb- ances, which failed, as did an effort of the Estates and the stadtholder Nuenar to regarrison the city. As long as Leicester lived and his return seemed possible, the democratic party held on. In September, however, the death of the ex-governor strengthened the States' au- thority.

When the election for council took place there was great excitement. On October 5th, a fight ensued which ended in the defeat of the democrats, who in vain asked the aid of the English troops still in Utrecht. Deventer, Trillo, and a number of their adherents were taken prisoners, and on the following day a new election, directed by Nuenar with the approval of the deputies of the province, put an end to the democratic spirit which had ruled for three years at Utrecht. The exiles were recalled, the former schout of Utrecht, Nicholas van Zuylen van Sevender, was restored to office. Deventer was imprisoned, tried, and sentenced to banishment (July, 1589) from Utrecht, and declared, moreover, ineligible for any office. He went to England for a time, and when he returned he found his part was played out. In the new state there was no place for a man of his opinions. From this time, city and province of Utrecht "held good correspondence with those of Holland." [1]

Until Leicester's death, his influence was felt in the Netherlands. Even among those who could not be suspected of conspiracy with England, there were many who had serious grievances against the system which had gained the upper hand. In Friesland the Leicester faction remained strong, and there was special dislike to Holland's dominance. In Holland itself, there was a very serious movement in 1589, closely allied with the plans of the Leicester faction. This was the matter of the separate government in West Friesland desired by Sonoy and his party. It had seemed pushed into the background by Leicester's fall. Under the leadership of François Maelson, the able pensionary of Enkhuizen, the three cities, Hoorn, Enkhuizen, and Medemblik, demanded a separate government. The claim was that, owing to West Friesland's earlier relation to the countship, it was fully as sovereign as Holland, and should rank as a separate province. The other cities of the north quarter were not in sympathy with this, as they were afraid of being excluded from the Estates. Concessions were made by allowing the college of deputed councillors of the north quarter to remain in existence, and to assure the three West Frisian cities proper the same rights as those enjoyed by Alkmaar and the others.

There was much difficulty in the establishment of the new council of his Excellency. Not until January, 1590, were two bodies created — of deputed councillors of the stadtholders and of the Estates, respectively. The first was to be responsible for defence, and consisted of four members, one from the nobles and three from the cities,— the most respected and ablest statesmen. The other was

[1] Bor, iii., p. 347.

purposed to direct finance and justice, and to execute the resolutions of the Estates. The first college, where the advocate was little influential, fell speedily into disuse, and its powers lapsed partly to the stadtholder and partly to the deputed council.

In church matters, too, Oldenbarnevelt pushed his opinions. In 1591, he convened an assembly of eight clerical and eight lay persons, among whom he himself, the moderate Uyttenbogaert, and Arminius were the most influential. This body drew up a ritual which confirmed the power of the States in church matters, but it excited so much opposition that it was not introduced, and, for the time being, there was no readjustment of church matters. The Hague Church Order of 1586 remained in vogue with virtual maintenance of the supremacy of the provincial Estates in church matters. From this time there was a strong church party—the "precisians "—in opposition to the advocate, who wished to keep the church under State control. Oldenbarnevelt was hated as their most powerful foe, whose motto, "*Nil scire tutissima fides*," was diametrically opposed to their opinions.

Opposition was, however, temporarily silenced, and Oldenbarnevelt was undeniably the soul of the government. At this period Count Maurice was still in the background and still willing to accept the direction of his father's proved friend. He lent the States' party the aid of his name and of his arm, especially in the troubles with Sonoy.

At the time of Leicester's departure, the young count of Nassau was twenty years of age, silent and reserved, intelligent, and prematurely developed by circumstances. Son of Anne of Saxony, the unfortunate second wife of Prince William, he had passed a very restless youth.[1] Born at Dillenburg in exile, in the midst of the troubles

[1] Van der Kemp, *Maurits van Nassau*, p. 1.

that had driven his family out of the Netherlands, he had remained, after his father's departure in 1572, with his sisters in the ancestral castle under the paternal care of his uncle, Count John.   When still very young, Maurice accompanied his cousins, the sons of Count John and of the Count van den Bergh,—these latter were later his opponents on the Spanish side,— to Heidelberg.   In 1577, when his father again had a settled household, he was summoned to Breda.   His step-mother, Charlotte of Bourbon, gave him a careful supervision for five years, when, at the pressure of the provinces Holland, Zealand, and Utrecht,— and at their expense,— he was sent to the University of Leyden to be prepared for the task which was expected to fall to him later, owing to his brother's detention in Spain.   There he stayed until his father's death forced him to leave his theoretical studies and devote himself to the service of his country.   The expectations entertained of him, the reputation of his name, the necessity of maintaining the freedom of Holland and Zealand as against the authority of the English governor,—all together induced the two provinces to offer him the dignity of stadtholder.   Supported by his intelligent, high-minded step-mother, Louise de Coligny, depending on Oldenbarnevelt in political matters, on Hohenlo for military advice, he succeeded in expressing the opinions of the States' party without wholly alienating the suspicious governor and the English queen.

Maurice was far from possessing his father's broad views either in politics or theology.   He had not the slightest patience with liberty of conscience for Catholics and those of other opinions.   It was to him an unbearable idea that papists and all other heretics could have the same privileges as the Reformed.[1]   Still, under the existing circumstances, this difference between Maurice

[1] *Archives*, 2d series, i., p. 82.

and the Libertines was not formulated, any more than
that between the young stadtholder and the States' government, which was rather superior to, than equal with
him.

Maurice was, above all, a soldier.   His first experience
of war was the siege of Antwerp.   In the succeeding
years he made successive campaigns, accompanied by
Hohenlo.   He was intimate with his cousins William
Louis and Adolph of Nuenar, especially with the first,
who, even more than Hohenlo, was his instructor in
military tactics.[1]   As children they played with tin
soldiers.   Maurice's later pursuit of mathematics, under
Snellius and Simon Stevin, was very serviceable in
strategical plans.   The brilliant skill in sieges, manifested
later by Maurice, the rapid mobility of his troops, were
all the results of these industrious studies, of his theoretical preparation for his future practice.   " *Tandem fit
surculus arbor*," his favourite maxim, is the true symbol
of his being in those days.

Now in default of a vigorous central-government body
—a name not applicable to the States-General—Maurice
was an excellent personification of an executive force,
and Oldenbarnevelt was clever enough to use him, his
name, and his reputation.

Friesland was assured by Count William, although care
was taken to prevent the Frisian stadtholder from becoming too powerful in the union.

The accidental death of Nuenar (October, 1589) left
vacant the stadtholdership of Utrecht, Gelderland, and
Overyssel.   These provinces had shown an inclination
to resent Holland's preponderance.   Oldenbarnevelt
therefore seized this opportunity to suggest his " Excellency of Nassau " for this important office.[2]   Overyssel at
once offered the title to Maurice (February, 1590).   Utrecht
finally followed suit, without, however, recognising the

[1] Van Reyd, p. 161.   [2] Van der Kemp, i., p. 295.

necessity of the approval of the States-General or of
the council of state.¹ After much delay the Estates
of Gelderland sent in nominations of Maurice and the
count of East Friesland to the council of state, whereon
(May, 1591) the council selected Maurice. The States-
General naturally approved the choice, and in their
sovereign capacity gave the new stadtholder his commission.

Thus Holland's influence was confirmed in the three
provinces. From August, 1588, captain-general and
admiral of the union in behalf of the States-General, and
stadtholder of five provinces, closely allied, too, with the
stadtholder of Friesland, Maurice was the man in whom
the coöperation of all the provinces of the union was
personified.

Still all these difficulties, smoothed over though they
were by the advocate's skilful policy, by give and take,
by sacrificing form for reality, showed how, from the
beginning, the States-General were on an uncertain basis
in regard to the council of state and to the provincial
Estates, apart from the great fault of the new States' institution — the weakness of the central government.
Under Oldenbarnevelt, backed by Maurice, these serious
faults were not so apparent, and the government of the
States-General had a chance to develop vigorously
enough. From 1593, they were in permanent session, a
fact plainly showing their executive character. That
the sovereignty had this chance to develop was owing to
the fortunate turn which the war against Spain had
taken.

During the whole year 1587, Philip had poured all his
resources into his preparations for the great Armada
destined to invade England. The Netherlands were
neglected, and Parma left without supplies, while an
especial appropriation of seven million ducats was made

¹ Kluit, *Gesch. der holl. Staatsreg.*, iii., pp. 109-114, 456-458.

for the new venture, and another million was pledged by the pope.   Parma was ordered to be ready to land thirty thousand men in England, and await the arrival of Santa Cruz, who had been appointed admiral of the invading fleet.   In a letter of December 24, 1587, Philip told Parma that he was hourly expecting news of his departure.   But Parma was far from ready.   He could squeeze no more supplies from the exhausted provinces.   His ports, too, Sluis, Sas van Gent, and Antwerp, were practically isolated, and Holland and Zealand freebooters were guarding the coast.   He declared, in the last days of 1587, that he could not take the initiative.   If Santa Cruz were once in the Channel, he might coöperate with him.   In England there was no real belief in the Armada. Only a few skilled seamen, Howard, Drake, and Hawkins, were anxious about the neglect to take precautions.

In Holland they were not so tranquil.   Maurice made every effort to collect craft, great and small.   Twenty States' ships were to be placed under the command of Cornélis Loncq, as an adjunct to the English fleet at Dover.[1]   At the end of May, 1588, the great fleet actually sailed out of Lisbon harbour, but not under the veteran Santa Cruz.   He had died in the early spring. The duke of Medina Sidonia was commander of this famous expedition, and he had no experience of the sea, no understanding of the conduct of war, and had tried his best to evade accepting the weighty responsibility. The fleet consisted of 150 big and little ships, 10,000 sailors and galley slaves, 20,000 landing forces, and about 2400 pieces of artillery.[2]

[1] Compare, for the part taken by the Netherlanders, Scheltema, *De Onoverwinnelijke Vloot*, pp. 118–176 (Haarlem, 1825), and the publication of the Navy Records Society, *The Defeat of the Spanish Armada*, ii., p. 230 (Laughton, 2 vols., London, 1895).

[2] Compare Motley, ii., p. 458 ; a more detailed narrative by Tilton, *Die Katastrophe der Spanischen Armada*, Freiburg, 1894, mainly from Duro, *La Armada Invencible*.

Slowly, very slowly, did the Armada sail against the wind along the Portuguese coast.[1]   A heavy storm caused great damage, and the vessels were detained a month for repairs.   It was July 22d when the Armada finally left the port of Corunna for the " holy war " dreamed of by the king and Medina Sidonia — a religious conception shown by the prayers and the strict stipulations concerning order and discipline, and in the flags decorated with Catholic emblems and standards.   Seven days later the fleet appeared off the Lizard in the Channel, to the great terror of the English, who had slackened their preparations after receiving the news of the storm.

Nevertheless, about two hundred ships of varying size were ready.   These were manned by some fifteen thousand men, — skilled seamen.   All the seaports lent aid.   Drake, Hawkins, Winter, and Frobisher, terror of the sea, hastened to Plymouth.   By July 30th, about sixty craft sailed out gaily to meet the enemy.   The following week was full of disaster for Spain.   All Philip's hopes of conquest were crushed.   Parma was effectually prevented from lending any aid.   There was a memorable series of skirmishes; fire-ships effected some damage; winds and storms were allies to the English.   On Monday, August 8th, a long, fierce engagement took place off Gravelines.   In spite of lack of ammunition, the English succeeded in sinking several of the biggest ships of the reduced fleet, while suffering little damage themselves.   The Spaniards had just enough heart to gather their ships together and sail off to the north, followed by the English.   A stiff wind drove the Armada towards the Flemish coast, where the States' ships under Van der Does sank a few galleons or forced them to surrender. Thus, as Howard wrote, they plucked the Spaniards' feathers piece by piece, until the Armada was almost on

[1] Motley's account of the deeds of one David Gwynn is based on false information.   See Laughton, *The Defeat*, i., p. lxxvii.

the Flemish coast and the English powder was almost exhausted.

The end of the Armada seemed near. A rising south-west wind drove it from the sandbanks and into the North Sea, while a portion of the English fleet under Howard and Drake pursued them, and another portion sought safety in the mouth of the Thames. The Spaniards' terror prevented them from turning on their pursuers. They determined to return to Spain around the north of the British Isles.

For three days the English followed, spoiling for a fight, but there was no conflict.

On August 12th, Howard and his crew caught the last glimpse of the Invincible Armada. On August 14th, a terrific storm overtook those ships which had reached the Scottish shore. They were driven, top-heavy, helpless as they were, on the bare rocks of the Hebrides, the Orkneys, the Faroes, on the Irish and Norwegian coasts, in the midst of an inhospitable nature and a rapacious population. Scarcely a third of the mighty flotilla ever saw a Spanish port. Thousands of sailors and soldiers perished, and nearly every family on the Spanish peninsula was thrown into mourning. Parma's darkest forebodings were realised. Where was he while the Armada fought ? When the first tidings of their approach reached him, he had hastily shipped his troops into bottoms lying at Nieupoort and Dunkirk, but contrary winds and the Dutch fleet on the coast left him impotent.

It was not until September that the returning English ships brought certain tidings of the destruction of the danger which had menaced the lands on both sides the Channel. Thanks were offered in the churches for the safety of Protestantism. England and the storm had scattered the Armada. The Hollanders and Zealanders had prevented Parma from aiding his compatriots.

Meanwhile the war on land continued, but nothing

important took place.   Maurice laid siege to Geertruidenberg, which had steadily refused to recognise the
authority of the States, but it was treacherously sold to
Parma by the English garrison.   This was a heavy loss,
and, too, the lack of confidence between the allies was
revealed.

In Spain the failure of the Armada was a bitter disappointment.   Parma was blamed for his failure to assist
the enterprise.   He was even suspected of a secret understanding with Leicester.   So serious were the accusations
that the duke considered it necessary to send Richardot,
member of the council of Artois, to defend his conduct
against the complaints of Medina.   Crushed and discouraged by the strained relations with Spain, he fell into a
serious illness in the spring of 1589, and was incapable
of effective action.

In France, events had taken a wholly new turn.   In
August, 1589, the king — who, as a protest against the
rule of the Guises, had thrown himself into the arms of
the Huguenots — died, and the crown passed to Henry
of Navarre as Henry IV.   This was an accession naturally
unacceptable to Philip, and he was willing to expend all
the strength that was left to him after his disastrous
encounter with England in establishing a new Catholic
dynasty in France.   The state of affairs in the spring of
1590 offered the States a favourable opportunity of changing the character of the war.

Some time had elapsed since Count William Louis had
conceived the idea of turning the defensive into an offensive war.   He presented a detailed plan for making
Groningen the base of operations, and thence strengthening and defending " the garden of the United Netherlands." [1]   This advice did not fall on fertile ground.
The States were afraid lest the enemy might turn from
France and make a new attack upon the Netherlands.

[1] See Van Reyd, p. 160

Maurice was of different opinion, and Parma's absence in France where he was ordered to lay siege to Paris, offered a favourable opportunity.   Elizabeth and Henry IV. both urged the States to action, both desirous of diverting Parma from France.

After an unsuccessful attempt to surprise Nimwegen, in September, Maurice made a sudden manœuvre, and succeeded with a tiny force in wresting Hemert, Crève-cœur, Hedel, Ter Heyde, Steenbergen, Oosterhout, and the redoubt at Rosendaal from the unsuspecting foe. This success gave encouragement.   A raid in Brabant, disastrous for the inhabitants, served to divert the enemy's attention from an expedition against Zutphen and Deventer, which proved successful.   The two cities fell into the hands of the States.   This was the beginning of a series of duels between Parma — handicapped by the war in France—and the States' troops under a new system of tactics vigorously pursued by Maurice and William Louis of Nassau.   Alexander Farnese was more than capable of meeting this new development of military science, but Spanish policy held him back.   His representations of the necessities of the situation in the Netherlands were met by cold suspicions of his own fidelity to his sovereign. The lack of restraint among his troops, who raided the lands to compensate themselves for their dearth of wages, began to be compared with the strict discipline enforced by Maurice.   There was a reaction in the southern provinces towards the league of the north.   In December, 1592, Parma's death gave the party of opposition an important advantage.[1]   He had hastened to Arras to meet the count of Fuentes, whom Philip had sent to the Netherlands to order his lieutenant to lay down his charge and return to Madrid.   The king, ever ready to suspect his faithfulest servants, had become convinced

[1] See the letters of Torrentius, *Compte-rendu de la Comm d' Hist.* 2d Series, 7, p. 273.

that Parma wished to create an independent sovereignty
in the provinces.   The envoy did not deliver his message,
for death suddenly claimed the duke, who thus died
under the displeasure of the sovereign whom he had faithfully served for sixteen years.   Just before he expired he
appointed old Mansfeld as his successor.   Fuentes at
once confirmed this choice.

Meantime, in France, Philip's scheme of placing his
daughter on the throne as the true Catholic heir of the
house of Valois had been defeated by Henry's formal
adoption of the ancient faith.   Paris opened her doors,
and he was recognised as Henry IV. (July, 1593).

During the year 1593, Maurice distinguished himself
in several feats, which showed *la restauration de la vieille
art et science militaire.*[1]   He seized Geertruidenberg by
a sudden movement when Mansfeld was expecting an
attack upon Groningen.   Then followed campaigns in
Friesland.   Count Mansfeld learned that he was not an
adept in the new science of war as studied by Maurice
and his cousin.   Coevorden fell after a siege of forty-
one days; Groningen on July 22, 1594, two months after
Maurice's arrival before its gates.   The conditions of
surrender, known as the " Treaty of Reduction," formed
the basis of the relations of the city to the union.   Groningen was coupled with the Ommelands, and the new
province, known as City and Land, under William Louis
as stadtholder, was received into the union with the
same rights as the other provinces.   Drenthe was placed
under the same stadtholder without receiving any individual seat in the States-General.

In these provinces the Catholic religion was barely
suffered by the victorious party, while the ultra-Calvinist,
William Louis, organised there the Reformed Church,
whose interests lay very near his heart.

There was universal rejoicing when Maurice returned

[1] *Archives*, 2d Series, i., p. 245.

triumphantly to The Hague through Friesland and Holland. What William Louis had predicted four years before, as the result of an offensive campaign, had actually been realised. Nassau's heroes had won an European reputation for their military talents. The series of fortunate enterprises — planned with care and judgment, executed with energy — really enclosed " the garden of the Netherlands."

The political path was far from plain travelling. Often Maurice in Holland, William Louis in Friesland, had the greatest difficulty in allaying jealousies, in obtaining the necessary grants, in collecting the needful ammunition. How many memoirs were drawn up at that period, how many conferences were held to persuade the provincial Estates to loosen the cords of the purse they held so fast! Holland still bore more than sixty per cent. of the general expenses, and the burden was a heavy one.   In 1593, Holland, Zealand, Friesland, and Utrecht supplied monthly two tons of gold, and nine tons down as an extraordinary grant, besides thirty thousand florins monthly as subsidy for France.   In addition, there were the revenues from the convoys and licenses, from the contributions levied in the States' parts of Gelderland, Overyssel, and Groningen, the forced contributions from the districts subject to the enemy,—altogether five tons of gold annually.   With this they supported about 100 ships of war, 150 companies of foot soldiers, 58 cornets of cavalry.[1]

Thus a small but fine army was formed.   The soldiers were no longer mutinous bands—worse plague to the inhabitants than to the foe—as in Leicester's time.[2] There were perhaps only half as many troops as formerly, but they were regularly paid and fed, accustomed to military discipline, continually exercised in marches and

---

[1] *Archives*, 2nd Series, i., p. 222.

[2] Fruin, *Tien Jaren*, p. 86 ; L. Mulder, Introduction to the Journals of Anthony Duyck, fiscal of Maurice's army.

evolutions, and transformed from a heavy mass into an easily mobilised whole. Armed with pikes and with muskets, which were replacing the former, and served conveniently as spades; provided with an excellent artillery, and directed by a remarkable military genius, Maurice's army was the admiration of Europe. Maurice's camp actually became a military school whither the young French, English, and German nobles came to learn to be professional soldiers. In addition to personal courage, Maurice's skill, developed by systematic work, was very marked,—a skill necessary, indeed, to guide the rough elements, often the very sweepings of society, English, French, Walloon, German, Dutch, which composed the then existing armies. It was all dominated by Maurice's real military genius.

The unit of Maurice's army was a company, about 120 strong, officered by a captain, a lieutenant, and a standard-bearer. A varying number of companies, sometimes six, sometimes twenty, formed a regiment. Maurice armed about two-thirds of every company with the musket introduced by Alva in the Netherlands — a heavy weapon that had to rest on the fork for shooting, —and with the lighter arquebus, which, like the musket, had to be provided with a flint. Thirty pikemen, armed with the eighteen-foot pike and a dagger, made up the rest of the company. Three of these were provided with shields, and charged with protecting the captain in action. The cavalry was armed with carbines, and divided into squadrons, of 120 men (after 1591). They took a subordinate place, as Maurice's method was rather directed to sieges than to pitched battles. The artillery was accordingly of greater importance, especially the siege artillery — heavy cannon which threw balls of forty-eight pounds, and half-cannon. Further, there were fieldpieces which could throw bullets less than half as heavy as those of the cannon. In addition to these, Maurice made much use of heavy mortars, whence stones and fire-balls were projected. He excelled, too, in ditch- and bridge-work, for which no particular divisions of troops were detailed. He effected great improvements in the administration of the camps, especially in regard to the payment of the men, by suppressing the shameful mis-use of " blind names,"—soldiers on paper whose wages flowed into the officers' pockets.

All these changes were brought about by the twenty-four-year-old Maurice in a couple of years, often to the great vexation of the veterans who had served under Hohenlo and other commanders of the old stamp, and missed the former financial perquisites. They ridiculed the ditch- and fortification-work, for which formerly country people had been employed, deeming it a degrad-ing occupation. The exercises, too, seemed to them absurd. But the commander, supported by William Louis and his other cousins, by Cornput, the brothers Vere and Bax, and others, succeeded in silencing the scoffers, and calmly proceeded with the task he had set himself. Success rewarded the reserved, simple, rather rough, intrepid, reckless, indefatigable soldier who felt nowhere more at home than in the midst of his troops, in the circle of his officers in camp, and whose favourite amusement was chess, the game of the thinkers, of the great strategists, among whom his name is a brilliant one.

CHAPTER VIII

THE ALLIANCE WITH ENGLAND AND FRANCE

AT last the time seemed come when Prince William's dream was to be realised, when the neighbouring states would openly recognise the Netherlands in the struggle they had maintained for thirty years. Just when Maurice's success seemed about to dissipate Spanish authority in the north, certain reasons inclined both France and England to make an alliance with the Netherland rebels.

Elizabeth personally was not so inclined. She had been willing to aid the Netherlands in order to check Spain's dominance in Europe. But now that the States had become the offensive party, and were, in their turn, assisting Henry IV., she demanded a return for her loans —a most inconvenient demand. Moreover, the tone in which this merchant-folk ventured to oppose her will irritated her excessively. Relations were decidedly strained in 1595–96. Nor was she as favourably disposed towards Henry IV. of France as she had been towards the homeless Henry of Navarre.

For his part, Henry was quite ready to make a close alliance with the States. In January, 1595, he formally declared war against Spain, that goal for which Orange had striven for so many years.

There seemed little chance of other allies at the moment. The Calvinist John Casimir, and the Lutheran leaders, William of Hesse and Christian I. of Saxony, had all died, one shortly after the other. John of Nassau was one of the few German lords who appreciated the fact of the revival and new life of Catholicism. He would have liked to erect a strong Protestant bulwark against the menacing danger, but the quarrels between Lutherans and Calvinists prevented all effective coöperation. The state of affairs on the lower Rhine, where Ernest of Cologne had wanted Parma to defend the Catholic interests, was deplorable; but still the Protestant princes neglected all precautionary measures. Commerce was practically annihilated in the region, and all the neighbouring towns suffered.

But neither empire itself under the impotent emperor, Rudolph II., who shut himself up in his castle at Prague and forgot imperial interests, nor Protestant nor Catholic princes, evinced the slightest inclination to protect German interests and end the contest between the militant parties. And there was no thought of action in behalf of the Netherlands. The South Netherland provinces were alarmed at Henry's declaration of war. They would be placed between two fires. Archduke Ernest, now governor of Philip's shrunken possessions, was also alarmed, and Philip, finally convinced of the desirability of a cessation of war, gave the archduke permission to conclude a peace upon easy conditions. The archduke at once sent a proposition to The Hague for a peace on the basis of the Pacification of Ghent. It was roundly refused, partially because an attempt on Maurice's life was discovered in which the government at Brussels seemed involved. Distrust was too deep. The archduke's difficulties were increased by a violent disturbance among his unpaid troops.

As a last resort, he convened the States-General of the loyal provinces. At the head of the discontented party among nobles and clergy—the cities were not invited to the assembly—was the duke of Aerschot, the prince's old opponent, who delivered a violent speech against the unendurable tyranny of Spain.[1] The archduke asked what he ought to do, and received in answer a detailed complaint of Spanish rule, interesting from the fact that it expressed the unanimous opinion of the assembly.[2] The document declared that the condition of religion was very satisfactory. There was practically no more heresy, but the lawless army needed reorganisation. There were masses of soldiers on paper only, payment was very uncertain, discipline was slack, superintendence faulty. The fortresses were out of repair, especially on the French frontier. Finances were in utter confusion, and no means of improvement could be indicated, because there was practically no cash on hand. Further, this document contained thirty-eight points of direct heart-rending complaints. In addition to charges similar to those expressed periodically during so many long years of discontent, there was the new charge of sacrificing the Netherlands to disastrous French schemes. *Il ne reste quasi plus riens, sinon ung tres grand crèvecœur et désespoir, menassant la dernière ruyne et confusion.* The conclusion was a petition for a truce. This document, signed by the archbishop of Cambrai, the bishops of Arras and St. Omer, the abbés of St. Vaast and Maroilles; Aerschot, his brother Havré, his son Chimay; the counts of Aremberg, Bossu, Berlaymont, Ligne; by La Motte and other governors; by Assonleville and Richardot, shows plainly the sentiment in the south.

A month after the presentation of this appeal, Archduke Ernest died, and Fuentes again assumed the reins of government temporarily. He had a difficult post to fill. The alliance had been completed between Henry IV. and the States, and hostilities were active.

[1] Van Meteren, p. 326.
[2] Gachard, *Actes des États Généraux de 1600*, p. 415.

Fuentes succeeded in thwarting a combined attack of the allies upon Liege territory and Luxemburg, but the States surprised Huy, which secured coöperation with Bouillon.[1] Fuentes showed himself equal to the situation. He used supplies that came from Spain to pay his men, restored some discipline, put three armies on their feet, and redeemed some of his losses, regaining Huy among other advantages. At an engagement in which Mondragon relieved Groenloo, besieged by Maurice, Philip of Nassau and his cousin Ernest of Solms both fell, while Ernest Casimir was taken prisoner. The loss of Philip, who had shown himself a valuable officer, was a serious misfortune to the States.

While Fuentes was thus retrieving Spanish losses to some extent, he let the marquis of Havré negotiate at Middelburg with the States in order to please the south Netherland provinces. This was done nominally in the name of the disaffected. The effect was vitiated, however, by the contents of two intercepted letters, which proved Fuentes to be privy to the transaction and showed his real aims. The States at once published the letters, with an explanation by Justus Lipsius, who had fled to Louvain from Leyden. Fuentes urged the Brussels government to make a truce. In his opinion, the immediate result would be an outburst of theological and political differences in the north, which would give the Spanish government a chance to fish in "troubled waters."[2] This evident duplicity immediately affected opinion in the north. The most ardent advocates of peace had to acknowledge that there could be no accommodation with such a foe. Everywhere the conviction gained ground that "for a hypocritical peace a good war is to be praised," as the rhetoricians put it, who held a prize contest at Leyden, in May, 1590, when this phrase was the subject of the poems.

[1] See Fruin, *Tien Jaren*, etc., p. 165.   [2] Van Meteren, p. 336.

In January, 1596, Fuentes was replaced by the Cardinal Archduke Albert of Austria. He had been educated at the Spanish court under Philip's eye, and treated like that monarch's own son. He had shown ability in his administration of Portugal, whither he was sent immediately after its conquest, and it was at his own request that he was transferred thence to the Netherlands, where his brothers Matthias and Ernest had played out their parts. Cardinal though he was, the plan was conceived that he should resign his ecclesiastical dignity and marry the Infanta Isabella, Philip's favourite daughter. Then Albert and Isabella, children after the king's heart, should undertake a joint regency over the Netherland provinces and put an end to the revolt by means of gentle measures,—if need were, by some concessions.

There was no doubt that Spain's capacity of waging war was utterly exhausted. She had no credit. Agriculture, commerce, manufacture, had suffered grievously, both from ill-judged governmental measures and from the raids of English and Holland pirates. The population of the Spanish realm deteriorated in numbers and prosperity. Every resource seemed exhausted. The financial condition was such that the state revenues were mortgaged four years in advance, while the debt, which aggregated thirty-four million ducats in 1575, amounted to one hundred million in 1596. The position was simply untenable.[1] Peace was an absolute necessity.

As an evidence of reconciliatory measures, the unfortunate Philip William of Orange was at last released from his half-imprisonment, his father's estates were restored to him, and he returned in the governor's train to his never-forgotten native land, whose soil he had not touched for almost thirty years. It was hoped that this prince, now forty-two years old, devoted as he was to the Catholic faith and educated in fidelity to the king, would

[1] Häbler, *Die wirtschaftliche Blüte Spaniens*, p. 129.

act as mediator between the government and the party of opposition, and that he might exercise a good influence upon Maurice, upon his Nassau cousins, and upon his father's old adherents, as the head of the family. With this end in view, the young prince had been well treated though carefully watched.   At the Spanish court he had been received with honours due to his rank.   He kept himself, to be sure, in the background, unmoved in the midst of opposing winds, as his device ran; giving heed to the wish of the States not to come to the northern provinces, but remaining true to his religion and his lawful prince — a tragic figure in the history of the house of Orange, holding aloof from every act which could place him in opposition to his brothers, but also from every act of hostility towards Spain; honouring the memory of his murdered father,—whom he resembled closely in appearance,—both with the king who had caused the murder, and also with Philip's opponents, his father's friends, while he could not approve their tendencies and actions.

A second conciliatory act, in the spring of 1595, was the liberation of the Holland and Zealand ships detained in the Spanish and Portuguese ports.[1] Four or five hundred ships with a force of five to six thousand sailors, about two-fifths of the whole merchant fleet of the northern Netherlands, had fallen into great danger, and many commercial houses were threatened with ruin. But Spain could not spare these traders, who brought corn and wood from the North Sea, and it was in her own interest that they were set free.   There was general joy at the return of the ships, especially as a report had been bruited that this seizure was the precursor of the despatch of a new Armada against England and the Netherlands.   Instead, however, of a new Armada's sailing out for offensive operations, a united Anglo-Netherland fleet, under Howard and the Dutch admiral

[1] Van Reyd, p. 262.

Duivenvoorde, destroyed a Spanish squadron in Cadiz harbour, and returned home in August laden with booty. In the Netherlands, Fuentes soon found that peace was not to be thought of, while war was very difficult, as the old generals were dead. He found at last an able commander in the French nobleman, De Rosne, who succeeded in reducing Hulst after a valiant siege, while Fuentes was still vainly hoping for the coöperation of the hoped-for Armada. Sixty ships did finally set sail with about eight thousand men, but they were overtaken by a storm off Finisterre, and scattered with a loss of about half.

Philip II. never learned by misfortune. In this same year he had recourse to a measure which had had fatal results in 1575,[1]—the issue of a financial decree whereby the pledges to all creditors of Spain were taken from the State revenues. The Fuggers were not included in this decree, in the hope that they would hold out a helping hand in the stress. But they were in difficulties themselves, and could do nothing. The government was speedily forced to treat with the injured creditors, especially with the Genoese, who were obliged to be content with five per cent. on their loans, a very low interest for the times. This bankruptcy gave a slight temporary relief, but inflicted a serious blow on Spanish credit. Many Spanish statesmen foresaw the consequences, which were not slow to show themselves. ·The governor in the Netherlands could raise no loans at all, and was at once blocked in the military schemes. This was an important fact, inasmuch as England had finally consented to make an alliance with France against Spain, in which the States were also accepted as a party. Two treaties were concluded, one open and the other secret. In the former it was agreed that England should furnish four

---

[1] Häbler, *Die Finanzdekrete Philippe II.*, in *Deutsche Zeitschrift*, 1894, p. 297.

thousand men, the cost for whose maintenance France should repay later. In the secret treaty, this number was limited to two thousand, who could only be used in Picardy.[1]

The States hoped that alliance was the basis of another which should include the king of Denmark, the German princes, and certain Italian potentates who feared Spain. England made some difficulty about admitting the States to an equal footing. They regarded their rise with jealousy, and could not forget their independent attitude in the time of Leicester and later, but Henry IV. insisted so strongly upon this point that Elizabeth had to yield.

This recognition was an important one for the States, but they had to pay dear for it. At the request of the two allies, they not only promised to support troops in France equal in number to Elizabeth's, according to the term of the public treaty, but they also pledged themselves to oppose the foe on their own borders with eight thousand men. Moreover, they now agreed to renounce a cherished privilege which they had defended so vehemently in the days of Leicester — that of free trade with the enemy.

The Estates of Holland assented to this provision with great reluctance.[2] The merchants, especially those of Amsterdam and Rotterdam, protested vehemently. In response to the complaints of England and France that the ill-armed Netherland merchantmen were simply prey to the foe and used to strengthen their fleet, to the assertion that Spain by this continuous supply was saved from dearth of grain, ammunition, and sails, Amsterdam urged that commerce and industry would vanish from the lands; thousands of boatmen, cast adrift without employment, would be a serious source of disturbance; that the convoys and licenses which formed the basis of the

---

[1] Fruin, *Tien Jaren*, p. 321.
[2] *Res. Holl.*, *1596*, pp. 415, 430, 459, 598.

financial resources of the admiralty would suffer. But the sacrifice seemed needful to secure the alliance. Some people even ventured to express the opinion that these territories were not solely dependent upon the merchants, and Amsterdam's opposition was fruitless. The only result of the prohibition was, however, that the trade was carried on secretly instead of openly.

Nor did the much-desired alliance fulfil expectation. No other princes or lords joined in. It was soon evident that England and France were looking only after their own interests, and, moreover, in the following summer,[1] the above-mentioned secret treaty came to the knowledge of the States, while it was also evident that France was coquetting with Spain, and the pope was giving his services in the negotiations.

There were some slight military gains for the States during the winter of 1596-97, and great preparations were made for a spring campaign, when Henry IV. was to attack Amiens, lately conquered by the Spaniards, while Maurice assailed it from the Netherlands.

This proved successful. The governor employed all his forces in Picardy, and Maurice seized the opportunity, with scarcely eight thousand men, to subdue Rijnberk. The fortresses in the Achterhoek and Twente were thus cut off from the southern provinces, and Maurice was free to turn against the last Spanish strongholds. Groenloo, Bredevoort, Enschede, Ootmarsum, Oldenzaal, and Lingen were the prizes gained in this brilliant campaign which freed Gelderland, Overyssel, and Drenthe from the foe, and put an end to Spanish raids on the open country. These gains were some compensation for the failure of another Anglo-Dutch sea expedition to the Spanish coast, when all plans failed, and the fleet was scattered by a violent storm. This same storm prevented the new Armada, which was really collecting, according

[1] Bor, iv., p. 325.

to rumour, in the harbour of Ferrol, from completing a scheme of landing in Ireland.

Circumstances were inducing Henry IV. to conclude his peace with Philip, disappointed in all his ambitious schemes, old, and enervated.   The States exerted themselves to hinder this step, and despatched two embassies —one to England, one to France—to urge the maintenance of the league.   Oldenbarnevelt undertook the first himself, accompanied by Justin of Nassau,—a proof of how important the matter was considered.   At the head of the English embassy stood Admiral Duivenvoorde, who was highly respected in the English court.

There was much parleying, but France formally concluded the treaty, as was to have been expected.   Henry IV. assured his allies that his plan was to resume the war after his country was restored by a few years of peace. The treaty was signed May 2, 1598, at Vervins, and practically confirmed conditions existing at the peace of Cateau-Cambresis, thirty-nine years earlier.

Much as England wished peace, she could not obtain sufficiently good conditions now that Spain was freed from fear of France.   Elizabeth, therefore, agreed to continue the war with the States on pretty stiff conditions.   Oldenbarnevelt went to England to try to obtain easier terms, but was unsuccessful.[1]   The States promised to pay the eight hundred thousand pounds which Elizabeth had advanced, half being paid in annual instalments of thirty thousand pounds, and the other half later, while they pledged themselves to assist England with five thousand infantry, five squadrons of cavalry, and at least thirty ships if Spain attacked the island realm.   These were the only provisos on which England would relinquish her plans of peace.   It was important, however, that Elizabeth promised henceforth to be content with one representative in the council of

[1] Van Deventer, *Gedenkstukken*, ii., p. 236.

state, and that her soldiers, even in the pledged cities, were to swear fealty to the States alone, and thus only owe obedience to them.[1]

At the same time that he concluded the peace of Vervins, Philip came to the execution of a plan which had been considered by the Spanish government as a means of paving the way to a definite regulation of Netherland affairs according to the advice of the south Netherland provinces themselves.

It was resolved to erect the Netherlands into a separate realm, nominally independent of Spain, under Isabella and Albert. Stipulations in the contract show that it was intended to keep the provinces subordinate to Spain in order to retain the position that kingdom had held in the north since the times of Philip the Fair.

Still plainer was the intention seen in the secret agreement, whereby the chief fortresses were to be held by Spanish troops. It was evident that the king wished, as the States-General of the north declared to the emperor a year later, to hold the Netherlands as a Spanish fief or under tenure, with an appearance of independence.

This prospect did not attract the States in revolt to accept the archduke as their overlord. There were fair promises that all should remain *in statu quo* in the north, if only the new sovereignty were nominally recognised. But radical differences upon theories of government and of religion had grown up. Catholics were shut out from the government in the north; in the south, the heretic Anna van den Hove was buried alive as late as 1597. Albert's letter to the States-General remained unanswered, but a reply was sent, in March, 1598, to the States of the south, that the body in the north still deemed that war was the only way to expel the Spaniard, and they wished their brothers in the south would coöperate. The numerous pamphlets and documents protesting against

[1] Arend, *Gesch. der Vaderl.*, iii., p. 274.

peace, which were disseminated, show the opinion in the
north.   The States of the south were not particularly
well pleased with their new regent and the new conditions,
and asked to be convened as soon as the projected marriage between Albert and Isabella was concluded, to discuss general measures to be taken.   Albert answered
evasively, and made ready to fetch his bride.   He
formally resigned his cardinalship, charged his cousin
Andrew of Austria with the administration during his
absence, and hastened to Italy by way of Austria.   In
November, he was wedded by proxy to the Infanta at
Ferrara, she being still in Spain.

Meanwhile the Spanish king, long a chronic invalid,
had died.   Gout tormented him during his last years.
His spirit was broken by disappointment.   Then a frightful malady overtook him.   Covered with malignant boils
from which worms crept, he dragged on several months,
until death relieved him of his horrible sufferings on
September 13, 1598.

Thus died the man who had once been the mightiest
prince of the earth, who had dreamed of universal sovereignty, ever hampered in his ambitions and comprehensive plans by the weakness of the means as well as by the
narrowness of his spirit.   The universal sovereignty of
Spain and the supremacy of the Catholic Church—these
were the two ideas for which he had lived, uniting the two
in his spirit to one coherent maxim.   From morning to
evening, the sombre, reserved man had striven more than
forty years long for the realisation of this aim, exerting
his indefatigable activity, devoting himself in his lonely
study to the great goal to which he was ready to sacrifice
everything, and did sacrifice much — his own happiness,
that of his own family, the prosperity, the riches of his
state, the lives of thousands and thousands of his subjects.
And when he died he was farther than ever from his goal.
He left his successor an exhausted treasury and a state

ruined by a war which was not yet finished. The curse of posterity was on his memory for centuries after his death, casting suspicion on his best feelings, his zealous belief, and his love for his children, as though they were hypocritical. Not until our time has it been made clear that in the heart of this politician, full of political cunning, of devilish revenge, of low craft,—in the heart of this little-spirited, narrow, sombre, bitter king,—there were also great world-wide thoughts, noble feelings of belief, hearty love, rich artistic feeling, and devotion to higher ideals.

CHAPTER IX

INDIAN COMMERCE—WAR WITH THE ARCHDUKES

THE new government at Brussels cherished a brief expectation of peace throughout the Netherlands. Futile hope! Even had the archdukes acknowledged the complete independence of the north,—a necessity they did not yet realise,—serious difficulties lay before the States. Without acknowledged independence, however, there could be no peace for the north, now accustomed to political freedom.

In time of war, the supremacy of Holland and Zealand, the soul of the union,[1] had been endured. In time of peace, jealousy would be excited by this dominance, and the lack of a strong central government would become more patent. Moreover, the Calvinist minority now in power would have to yield, more or less, to the majority composed of nominal Catholics, of libertines, and of indifferent people. The house of Orange, whose reputation Maurice had sustained during active hostilities, might find its influence weaken.[2] Maurice could not stand in his father's shadow as statesman, and wholly lacked capacity to revise the articles of union. Thus there was much ground for reluctance to make peace.

Moreover, the war had become a source of commercial prosperity, which could not be checked without affecting the existence of many thousands. In the early stages

[1] *Lettres de Busanval*, p. 7, ed. Vreede. Leyden, 1846.   [2] *Ibid.*, p. 300.

of the conflict, great profit had been reaped from trade
on hostile and neutral ground as well as from piracy.
Numerous ships sailed yearly from Holland, Zealand,
and Frisian ports to Spain, Portugal, Flanders, and Brabant,—to neutral lands. The new pathway to India had
proven, too, a source of profit. Peace would prevent
this. Had Philip not cut off the Netherlanders from the
Portuguese marts, had he not hampered them in their
trading trips to his territories, it would probably have
been long before they would have relinquished the profits
from these easy trips, in order to undertake dangerous
voyages to the far coasts of east and west.[1] Philip was
warned that his prohibitory measures might induce the
enterprising seamen to seek India. But the king hoped
for booty from captured ships, he trusted Spanish might,
and he threw the warnings to the winds. The expansion
of Netherland navigation would have suggested future
possibilities to a wiser man. A certain Antwerp merchant, Balthasar de Moucheron, established at Middelburg after Antwerp's fall, carried on a traffic to the White
Sea, which had begun as early as 1577. His factory at
Archangel, built in 1584, was the Netherland headquarters in that region.[2] Netherlanders sailed through
the Straits of Gibraltar to Italy, and brought corn from
the Baltic. Netherland merchant traders first appeared
at Venice about 1590. They were to be found, too, at
Alexandria, Tripoli, and Constantinople, although it was
only by stealth until 1598, when the sultan gave them
permission to trade under French auspices. This French
intervention in favour of their Netherland friends was a
great annoyance to the English, who disliked these dangerous rivals in the Levant.[3] Meanwhile some of the

[1] See the introduction to the work " Begin ende Voortgangh der O. I.
C.," Velius, *Chronyck van Hoorn*, p. 261.
[2] Scheltema, *Rusland en de Nederlanden*, i., p. 37.
[3] Van Meteren, p. 371.

Dutch merchantmen sailed on as far as the Cape Verde Islands and the coast of Guinea. About twenty-five anchored together on this coast, traded with the blacks, and pushed out the Portuguese while they penetrated up the rivers far into the interior.[1] Under these circumstances it was not surprising that the twenty-seven hundred merchantmen in commission on the approach of the Armada in 1588, were augmented with many hundreds more, that shipbuilders were busy, and that, at the end of the century, the number of sailors who subsisted entirely on the trade to Spain and Portugal was twenty-five to thirty thousand.[2]

That trade checked, this army of merchants determined to export directly from the Indies and America.

Netherland sailors had been employed on Portuguese ships and knew the way eastward well. The passage to America was even more familiar because, before the conquest of Portugal, Spain had preferred to employ Netherland rather than Portuguese sailors, from fear of the competition of Portugal in the Antilles. The information, published, 1595, as *Reys geschrift van de Navigatien des Portugaloysers in Orienten,*[3] by the seaman, Jan Huyghen van Linschoten, about the course of navigation and the commercial relations of the Portuguese in the east, was of great value.

Soon these hardy seamen were found on the course around the Cape of Good Hope, dangerous though it was from the enemy's armed ships. The experiences of Moucheron and others in the lands of the White Sea turned attention to the northern passage from Europe and Asia, where there was, according to Mercator, an open sea. The promise of this shorter passage, safer, too, from hostile attacks, led to the formation of a company

---

[1] Van Reyd, p. 350.
[2] *Lettres de Buzanval,* p. 121 ; compare Fruin, *Tien Jaren,* p. 203.
[3] De Jonge, *De Opkomst van het Nederl. gezag in Oost-Indie,* i., p. 35.

by Moucheron. He discussed plans with Prince Maurice, with Oldenbarnevelt, with Warmond, and several
members of the States, and in December, 1593, laid a
project before the Estates of Holland and Zealand as
to how the northern course could be developed. He
was willing to bear a quarter of the expense in consideration of a quarter of the products of the import
and export duties upon the wares carried.[1] This offer
was refused for various reasons, but the Estates fitted
out two ships, and the Amsterdammers added a third,
all to be placed under command of Linschoten. At
Amsterdam, the learned preacher, Petrus Plancius, an
able astronomer and geographer, aroused sympathy in
the project.

In July, 1594, the little fleet sailed out, accompanied
by a yacht from Terschelling, commanded by William
Barendsz, native of that place. They found open water
in the Waigat, which raised their hopes of success, but
owing to a lack of supplies they were forced to relinquish
further investigations for the time. A year later a fleet
of seven ships, equipped by the States-General, sailed in
the same direction, but were driven back by storms and
icebergs. The next adventurers were Jacob van Heemskerck and Jan Cornelisz. de Rijp, sent out by the Amsterdam government at the instance of Plancius (May,
1596), to win the prize of twenty-five thousand florins
offered by the States to the discoverer of the passage.
De Rijp was forced by the ice to return to the coast of
Lapland. Heemskerck, who had sailed eastward, guided
by the courageous William Barendsz, was frozen into the
ice and forced to winter in Nova Zembla, whence he
returned home at the end of 1597, after suffering frightful privations, to which a portion of his crew succumbed.
Barendsz, too, died on the journey, and the pitiful story
of the survivors discouraged further expeditions. It

[1] Van der Chijs, *Gesch. der stichting der V. O. I. C.*, p. 22. Leyden, 1856.

was evident that the passage was not feasible for regular trade traffic, at least with the means at hand.

The one advantage gained from these voyages was a better knowledge of Nova Zembla and Spitzbergen, where Netherland names of capes, straits, and islands show the dauntless courage of the mariners who gave the first data for scientific knowledge about the north—its temperature, its currents, its natural phenomena. The name of the Terschelling sailor is still famous as one of the first North Pole travellers. A century later the memory of Barendsz incited his descendants to new voyages. The modern art of navigation finally overcame the difficulties, and the passage north of Asia to the Pacific Ocean was opened.

Contemporaneously with Barendsz's last voyage, others had made their way around the cape. One Cornelis Houtman of Gouda, and Linschoten were able to give valuable information respecting the route, which induced several enterprising Amsterdam merchants to equip a fleet destined for India.

A " *compagnie van verre* " was organised by such men as Hendrik Hudde, Reinier Pauw, Pieter Hasselaer, and seven other rich Amsterdam merchants.[1] From their own purses and those of certain " participants," and under the sanction of the States, this company fitted out four ships with 250 men. These set sail on April 2nd, under Houtman's command, and with an instruction from Maurice. They reached Madagascar without misfortune, were detained there five months by storms and sickness, and sailed thence direct for Java. On June 22, 1596, they arrived off Bantam. The Portuguese merchants had inspired the natives with distrust for these new-comers, hostilities ensued, and Houtman, the " captain mayor," was taken prisoner, and was only released on payment of a heavy ransom. He then turned his course toward

[1] See the above-mentioned *Inleiding;* compare V. d. Chijs, p. 33, and De Jonge, *Opkomst,* etc., vol. ii., p. 191.

Molucca, and reached Lombok, but one of his ships became unseaworthy, and his force was reduced by sickness to ninety men, so he yielded to the demands of the survivors and sailed back south of Java. It was not until July, 1597, that the plucky mariners reached the fatherland. They were only a remnant of those who had sailed forth so gaily, but they brought a cargo of Indian products, insufficient, it is true, to defray the costs of the expedition, but quite sufficient to show that great profits were to be gained from India.

Scarcely had this first fleet reached home, when a new company was formed at Amsterdam side by side with the old, which was speedily followed by another at Rotterdam under Moucheron and several others. Two companies were organised in Zealand, and they all vied with each other in equipping ships, aided by the Estates, for the profitable voyages. In 1598, twenty-two vessels sailed for the East Indies. Of a fleet of nine ships under Jacob van Neck and Wybrand van Waerwyck, equipped by the two Amsterdam companies jointly, four richly laden vessels returned after an incredibly short trip of fifteen months. In very truth the riches of India began to flow to Holland.

At the same time voyages were made to Guinea and to South America. De Moucheron, backed by the prince, sent an expedition to Guinea, which conquered and garrisoned Prince Island, but the enterprise had to be abandoned on account of heat and lack of provisions. Greater ships were built, stronger fleets sent out. Eighty great vessels sailed in that year east and west.[1] In 1598, two of these, under the enterprising Olivier van Noort, passed through the Strait of Magellan, and completed the circuit of the world with the prince's approval and his active coöperation. Rough were the mariners who attempted these journeys; rougher often were the captains

[1] Van Meteren, p. 371.

who led them. Piracy and license, wantonness, mutiny, and murder were the order of the day upon the fleets, but the rough customers paved the way for a regular trade that soon developed from these small beginnings.

Before the century was ended men ceased to mourn the loss of the trade with Spain and Portugal. The new ventures promised far greater profits than the old carrying trade could bring, and the States-General encouraged these early voyages by exemption from taxes, hoping for later revenues from the Indian trade. In 1598, intercourse with Spain and Portugal wholly ceased—an edict from Philip declaring all Netherland ships found in his ports forfeited and the crews prisoners. These commands were vigorously executed. Netherlanders who had lived thirty years in Spain were made prisoners and tortured to extort confessions in regard to Netherland property in the ports and warehouses. The corn-ships alone were freed, and under the pretext that they belonged to the Hanse, many Hollanders, too, were let go. Out of five hundred ships detained, about half were finally allowed to depart.[1] In February, 1599, a placard was published wherein all commercial relations between Netherlanders under the States and under the archdukes were forbidden, a measure which caused at once dearth of corn, salt, herrings, cheese, butter, and other articles in the south. The Spanish and south Netherland governments were determined to maintain these rigorous stipulations as long as possible, so as to ruin the trade of the States. How little they succeeded is shown from the fact that in spite of the closing of Spanish ports, in that very year 640 ships, mainly of large tonnage, brought wares from the Baltic lands to Amsterdam.[2]

At last the receipt of substantial financial support from

Spain enabled the archdukes to collect a force of twenty-five thousand men to prosecute the war against the government of the States. Mendoza was placed in command, with Frederick van den Bergh and Don Luis de Velasco as lieutenants. In order to spare the southern provinces as much as possible, it was decided to make the easterly quarter of the northern Netherlands the point of attack. There the people were mainly Roman Catholics, and ill inclined to accept the dominating Calvinism.

In Groningen there was much discontent at the manner in which the States-General tried to settle troubles in the new province of City and Land by the stadtholder, William Louis, and his fellow-commissioners. In February, 1595, a decision was made regarding the new organisation which was little to the taste of both parties. The Ommelands rebelled at being united to the city, *tot een corpus*.[1] They disliked the subordination which resulted, while the city complained of loss of its ancient privileges in the country. Count William's efforts at mediation were only met by ingratitude from both sides.

There was soon greater cause for discontent. It was stipulated in the "Treaty of Reduction" of Groningen that all questions pertaining to the staple, to brewing, and to justice were to be settled by the States-General. Nine jurists from all the provinces appointed by that body issued a decision in which the nomination of four of the eight members in the "Captain's chamber" was given to the city. Groningen beer had the monopoly in the Ommelands, and the staple for all exports, especially cattle and grain, was maintained within Groningen, while foreign wares —clothes, wood, iron, stone, chalk, salt, etc.—were made wholly free. But the execution of these stipulations had neither heel nor foot in the earth. The Ommelands were. inclined to obedience, while the city was vehemently opposed. Spanish sympathisers began to manifest them-

[1] Van Reyd, p. 257.

selves. Some of them were admitted to the government, and tried to restore the old condition in the city.

There was no possibility of exacting payment of the contribution levied on the newly erected province. Friesland, too, was very lax in this particular. Party spirit was still rampant there. Roorda's faction was subdued, but was still strong enough to annoy the stadtholder continually both in the diets and in the quarters. There were many Spanish sympathisers in Drenthe, Overyssel, and Gelderland. Even the city government was far from being entirely harmonious with the States' government, while the nobles complained bitterly about their loss of influence. Moreover, the fortresses in the east were weak and neglected, for no attack was feared from the neutral German side after Maurice had wrested the last stronghold there from Spain, and the force of the foe seemed broken.

In Germany, however, the existing circumstances were such that little opposition could be expected even if imperial territory were invaded.[1] A strong Spanish party had arisen, of which Ernest of Cologne, the declared foe of the States, might be considered the soul. In the duchies of Cleves, Jülich, Berg, and Mark, was a half-insane prince, Duke John William, in whose name his Spanish-sympathising Catholic council wielded the power after they had set aside his wife. They wanted nothing more than Spanish help. An imperial ban was published against the imperial city of Aix at the instance of the Brussels government and of the elector Ernest. The duke of Cleves and Archduke Albert were intrusted with the execution of this edict, and forced the city (August, 1598) to suppress Protestantism completely.

Even in Protestant East Friesland Spanish influence .gained ground. The wife of Count Edzard II. was the sister of the king of Sweden, the Catholic Sigismund Wasa, and hope was entertained that the count might be

---

[1] Compare Ritter, *Deutsche Geschichte*, ii., p. 126.

converted to the ancient faith.   Quarrels between him and the city of Emden prevented the realisation of these hopes, but a Spanish faction sprang up, consisting mainly of merchants trading with Spain, who perceived advantage to themselves from the exclusion of the States from the Spanish ports, and on that account were ready to espouse the party of Spain.

There was, too, some anxiety lest Elizabeth might offer the cautionary cities still in her power, to the enemy as bait for an advantageous peace.   She was already wishing to withdraw her best troops from the provinces for a use in Ireland.   France, too, raised many difficulties about furnishing her annual subsidy in spite of Buzanval's representations of the urgent need.   That ambassador wrote to his king,[1] " I believe, sire, that this year will see the crisis in this state," a natural opinion in view of the difficulties in which the young nation was swamped. That it emerged successfully was due to the masterly leadership of Maurice and of Oldenbarnevelt, supported by the sacrifices and energy of Holland statesmen.

In September, 1598, Mendoza opened his campaign by crossing the Meuse, taking possession of all the ships on the Rhine, and gaining the town of Orsoy.   A delay between the choice of two courses—Mendoza was not a commander of the first rank—gave Maurice a chance to take defensive measures and to assemble a force at Arnhem. Mendoza now pressed on into Cleves.   Rijnberk, Wesel, Rees, Emmerich, Xanten, were all besieged by the Spaniards with greater or less military success, but with terrible result to the land, where Mendoza's troops lived for months at the expense of burghers and boers of Cleves and Munster.   The army was wintered in the German cities and villages, and levied on the surrounding country.

This began to be very disastrous for the empire.   In the early spring of 1599, some steps were taken to repel

· [1] Buzanval, p. 107.

the invader, but both Maurice and the States-General were fully convinced that they could not count on any efficient aid from Germany. John of Nassau was deeply discouraged at the small-spirited quarrels and slow negotiations which impeded all action in imperial territory.

The States had to depend on themselves to rebuff the foe who were thus expecting to attack them from the German frontier. The " state of war " in the spring of 1597, the budget for the following year, showed plainly that the danger was realised. For a time the States were inclined to avoid the expenses of offensive war, but they were finally persuaded that such would be false economy. Before 1599, two and a half millions were made available.[1] Permission was asked and obtained from France to levy two regiments of foot and some cavalry. The latter was to be placed under the sixteen-year-old Frederick Henry, and the young prince was summoned from the French court, whither he had been sent a year previous to this. Troops were also levied in Scotland, and the army was increased to about sixteen thousand men. Funds were raised by new duties on commerce and by an assessment which in Holland was imposed upon property,—a very unpopular tax. By early spring all was ready, and the prince could betake himself to menaced Gelderland.

At the same time a fleet of about seventy ships was equipped and well manned. The crews were rough fellows, thrown out of work by the cessation of trade with Spain, all eager to take up privateering as a means of livelihood. They gladly took service on this fleet, which was intended to seize some port on the Portuguese or Spanish coast, as Drake and Essex had done, and from that as headquarters to harry all commerce—even of

[1] Buzanval, *Lettres*, p. 30; compare the complaints of Oldenbarnevelt in *Lettres et Negociations de Busanval*; *Hist. Gen. Cod. Dipl. Neerl.*, 2nd series, i., p. 177.

neutral powers—with the peninsula.   At the head of this
fleet, with its force of about eight thousand sailors and
three thousand soldiers, Pieter van der Does was placed
as admiral.

Both outfit and plan showed consciousness of power in
the young state.   It dared to prescribe laws to English,
French, and Hanseatic commerce and to defy the neutral
powers.[1]   Further, the States urged France to change
Calais into a great free port as headquarters for trade in
that locality.   It was hoped, too, that the loyal provinces
in the southern Netherlands would be cut off from supplies.[2]   In March, the prince was in the field and obtained
some advantages during the summer.   Mendoza was
finally forced to relinquish the siege of Bommel and retreat over the Meuse.   The mutiny among his men, disappointed in their hope of booty, prevented him from
further aggressive action, so that danger from his quarter
was averted.   On the approach of winter, Maurice dispersed his army, but retained sufficient to overpower
Crèvecœur in March, 1600, and to surround the fort of
St. Andrew which Mendoza had begun to build.   The
Spanish garrison were in a mutinous condition, and were
easily persuaded to deliver over the newly built fort to
the States' troops for a considerable sum.   This possession of St. Andrew " closed in the Holland garden."
The Spaniards themselves had built " the last gate "[3] in
the Bommeler district, which had always been a dangerous point.

The great fleet was less successful.   Corunna was too
strong for them, so they sailed down to the Canaries,
where Van der Does hoped to encounter the Spanish
fleet on its homeward voyage from America.   Here the
crews were attacked by a serious illness which carried off

[1] Buzanval, *Lettres*, p. 359.
[2] *Codex Dipl. Neerl.*, pp. 180–185 *et seq.*
[3] Van Reyd, p. 414.

many. Van der Does sent part of his ships home, and proceeded towards Brazil. But a new sickness appeared. The admiral was among the victims, and the remnant reached the home ports in a sorry state in the spring of 1600.

This was a bitter disappointment. Great hopes had been staked on the booty expected. The heavy expenses of the year pressed especially hard upon Holland. Zealand could contribute almost nothing on account of the cessation of trade to the southern provinces, and showed a deficiency of forty thousand florins monthly. Zealand, indeed, was almost inclined to negotiate with the archdukes.[1] Her trade, too, suffered greatly from the depredations of a Genoese privateer, Frederick Spinola, who established himself at Sluis. Friesland complained bitterly of the offensive war and of Holland's influence, while she virtually contributed little. Groningen brought almost nothing. Utrecht, Gelderland, and Overyssel were also unable to contribute, while they needed help against the enemy. Thus Holland had practically to meet the financial obligations alone. In 1599, it was said that she had furnished more than five millions to the national cause, while her debt had amounted to several millions, and was still increasing.

It was highly necessary for the general good that an end should be put to the irresponsible state of affairs in City and Land and in Friesland.

In Groningen the opposition emanated less from Spanish elements than from some of the citizens who, although Calvinists and States' sympathisers, complained of favouritism shown to the Ommelands. There was no inclination to negotiate with the Spaniards,—only an objection to accept the central government. Contrary to the advice of Count William Louis, the States-General determined to send a force of fourteen companies, horse and foot,

[1] Van Reyd, pp. 397, 404, 410.

under Oliver van den Tympel, to suppress this opposition. William Louis finally consented to admit these troops to Groningen, against the sentiments of the municipal government. The envoys of the States-General and the stadtholders demanded the arrears of the contributions of the last five years, 625,000 guilders, and the two members of the state were admonished to keep the peace. The Ommelands yielded, but the city was disinclined to meet the demands of the States-General in regard to their relation with the Ommelands. The deputies went so far as to arm the citizens, while the leaders of the opposition were sent to The Hague. After all opposition was broken, a citadel was begun by the garrison which, in spite of the protests of the city, was finished within two years. This decided action on the part of the States-General, instigated by Oldenbarnevelt, was successful in restraining the rebelliousness of the Groningers. It excited both admiration and criticism.[1]

In Friesland, at about the same time, Roorda began to make his faction heard. There were various attempts to magnify the local governments at the expense of the central. On her own authority, Friesland had reduced her share in the war contribution by one-half — not less than four tons of gold — without troubling about the effect upon the national cause. Certain noble families made leagues among themselves, elected their members " great men," or elders, and these " great men " threatened to become the rulers of the whole province and to create a ruinous oligarchy in Friesland.

The existing condition was almost a state of civil war. Matters were smoothed somewhat, but the " kuiperij "[2]—the family cliques—continued to be an abuse. In 1601, certain regulations were made wherein it was

---

[1] See Van Reyd, p. 414 ; *Archives*, 2nd series, ii., p. 56.

[2] Slothouwer, *Oligarchische misbruiken in het Friesche Staatsbestuur* in Fruin's *Bijdr.*, 3rd series, i., p. 73 ; Van Reyd, p. 458.

stipulated, for example, that no high States' official could hold two important offices; and at the same time the term during which one person could enjoy the same office was limited to two or three years, while it was expressly forbidden to vote for oneself or for a blood relation.

The States-General also made an effort to mediate in East Friesland, as the quarrels between Count Edzard, and, later, his son Enno with the city of Emden, rendered adjacent territories insecure. This was only temporarily successful. In the south, the general opinion seemed to incline more and more to peace. At the end of 1599, Albert and Isabella arrived, and were received with all the old-time solemnities. The Estates of the loyal provinces, however, demanded three points before giving homage: dismissal of the Spanish garrisons, removal of all foreigners from office, peace with the United Netherlands. The archdukes refused to pledge themselves, but promised to maintain the privileges, and gave, moreover, certain private assurances about the other points. Accordingly, homage was offered for Brabant at Louvain after solemn sealing of the *Joyeuse Entrée* had taken place, followed by similar ceremonies in the remaining provinces of the south. In accordance with these secret promises, the archdukes convened the States-General in April—a very important assembly, which showed what the loyal provinces had to expect from the new government. Philip William, prince of Orange, who had accompanied the archduke on his wedding journey, the duke of Aerschot, and the count of Aremberg were taken into the council of state. Aremberg was appointed admiral; Havré, head of finance; Egmont, the stadtholder of Namur; while all these gentlemen received the order of the Golden Fleece from the king of Spain. The times of Margaret of Parma seemed returned without a new Granvelle. The names of the members of the government were almost the same, though the individuals were differ-ent.   A national government seemed attained.[1]

The soldiers in the Spanish Netherlands were becoming a more serious problem to their masters than to their foes.   Since the defeat of Mendoza's army, mutinies had increased.   Regular *elettos* had been chosen at Ghent, Antwerp, Lier, and elsewhere.   Their ravages were ter-rible to the country already suffering keenly from their loss of trade.   Government and population were both anxious when they recalled the frightful results of similar conditions in 1576.[2]

The archdukes were therefore willing to agree that the loyal States should invite the States-General of the north to a conference.   In June, a deputation set out for Antwerp with a letter translated from French into Dutch,[3]—for some time the northerners had declined to receive French letters,— but achieved no results.   The Hague States refused passports for the time, and insisted on complete separation also of the southern provinces from Spain, but declared their readiness to entertain later propositions if they were addressed to them as the States-General, as other powers entitled them, while in the let-ters of the southerners they were always named " the deputies of the States-General."

Sentiment in the north was only half inclined to peace. Discouragement, misery, and mutiny in the south seemed to offer a favourable opportunity to strike a mighty blow and to bring the foe to extremities.   The States began to turn their attention to Dunkirk, a dangerous pirate's nest for years, which had inflicted great injury on Nether-land trade.

In 1583, Parma, preparing for the attack upon England, had erected an admiralty in Dunkirk and favoured the

[1] Gachard, *Actes des États-Généraux* (1600), p. v.
[2] *Ibid.*, p. lxxxvii.
[3] Gachard, *Collection de documents inédits*, i., p. 456.

equipment of private craft, ready to prey on Holland and Zealand merchantmen and herring-boats.[1] Four years later these pirates had become so dangerous that the States-General ordered no mercy to be shown to them when captured. As soon as they were brought into Zealand or Holland ports, the hangman was ready to hang master and men—very rarely were any spared on account of youth. It was a war to the death between Dutch and Dunkirkers, a war which lasted sixty years. Regular watch-ships were posted off the Flemish coast and the Scheldt to keep an eye on the pirates. Merchantmen and fishing craft were protected by convoys, or armed themselves. This strife became the chief duty of the Zealand admiralty. Still the Dunkirkers often succeeded in overcoming four or five States' ships together, even men-of-war, and saving themselves and their booty behind the dangerous Flemish sandbanks.

The States, incited by Oldenbarnevelt, now urged offensive operations upon Dunkirk. Some of their reasons were good, but Maurice and William Louis raised objections. The prince did not desire to be bound by a definite plan of the States. However he finally yielded, though reluctantly.

By June, twelve thousand foot and three thousand horse, with thirty-seven pieces of artillery, were ready on the island of Walcheren. Leaders and soldiers were alike picked men. The young Frederick Henry, made member of the council of state in the spring, Louis Gunther, and Ernest Casimir of Nassau shared the command with Sir Francis Vere and the count of Solms, all under Prince Maurice. Numbers of distinguished young French, English, and German nobles flocked around the famous commander. It was the most brilliant army ever mustered by the Republic. Oldenbarnevelt himself, Van der Dussen, De Huybert, and other leading Netherland

[1] De Jonge, *Gesch. van het nederl. seewesen*, i., p. 226.

statesmen accompanied the expedition, to the no small annoyance of the prince, whom they wished to supervise, and who was fully conscious of the fact.[1]

The archdukes succeeded, to the great disappointment of the States, in pacifying the mutineers by a passionate personal appeal and by holding out hopes of booty. They put a strong body into the field, surprised the States' troops at Nieuwpoort (July 1st). There was an engagement. Three thousand men were lost by the States, and then a discussion and delay gave Maurice opportunity to recover himself.[2] On July 2nd, the tables were turned. At first the States' troops were forced to yield dune after dune. Their retreat was indeed almost a flight, only stayed for a moment by the exhaustion of the conquerors. The prince, distinguished by his orange plume in the thick of the fight, tried to put heart into his men by declaring, rapier in hand, that they should conquer or all die together. Then came a moment of relaxation on the part of the foe, of renewed courage on the parts of the States' troops. Maurice seized that moment to throw his reserve cavalry upon the hostile infantry. At the same instant the main force of cavalry under Louis Gunther made a mad charge. The enemy was thrown into confusion and fled. The battle was won. Albert himself barely escaped, and left his sword and arms in the hands of the States. Six thousand dead were left upon the field, and seven hundred prisoners in Maurice's power. A hundred standards fell to the victors. Still the danger was not over, and Maurice did not venture to press farther, the more that Albert collected his army and camped near Dixmuiden. The siege of Nieuwpoort was begun and abandoned. There seemed little advantage to be gained near Ostend, and, contrary to the opinion of the States, Maurice decided to return

[1] Fruin, "De slag bij Nieuwpoort," *Bijdr.*, new series, v., p. 65.
[2] See the narrative of Louis Gunther of Nassau, *Archives*, ii., p. 23.

without making any attempt against Hulst or Sluis. Towards the end of July, he embarked his troops at Ostend and betook himself to Middelburg. The troops were apportioned to the fortifications on the boundary.

This costly enterprise, which had cost tons of money, had no other lasting consequence than the impression of a victory on friend and foe, and the memory of the first serious quarrel between the States and their great captain, between Oldenbarnevelt and Maurice. The prince's friends complained bitterly of the recklessness of Oldenbarnevelt and his "long-coats." On their side, the States criticised the obstinacy of the general and his evident disinclination to execute their plans, especially now that the real aim of the dangerous campaign was not attained by the victory. Henry IV., too, took the prince's retreat in ill part and supported the States in their unfavourable opinion of Maurice's leadership.[1] The prince remained obstinately fixed in his own opinion. He was determined to employ his own methods, as he had done since 1590. The difference ran so high that Elizabeth sent an envoy extraordinary, Noël de Caron, together with the Netherland ambassador in England, to urge unity. There was no open quarrel, only a deep-lying difference of opinion.

Meanwhile peace negotiations with the south, begun before the battle of Nieuwpoort, were opened by envoys from the south, but they were fruitless. The north did not now want peace at any price.

The archduke's energetic measures, too, began to inspire confidence in the south, and the sum of three hundred thousand guilders was furnished him to avert the dangers pressing from the States at Ostend and in Brabant. The States found themselves obliged to take measures of defence at Ostend. Elizabeth promised five thousand men, Henry IV. held out hopes of his

[1] Van der Kemp, ii., p. 79 ; compare *Archives*, ii., p. 14.

coöperation, and Maurice was not disinclined to undertake a new expedition with these chances of foreign aid,
especially as the piracies were continuing from Sluis and
Dunkirk.

In 1601, Maurice opened a campaign by laying siege to
Rijnberk, either for the sake of the city or to lure Albert
from Ostend to the Rhine, when he intended to hasten
to Flanders. Albert did not take the bait, but began to
besiege Ostend. Maurice found himself forced against
his will, at the express command of the States, to despatch Vere from this army to the menaced spot. With
the remnant, he took Rijnberk and Meurs, and tried
Bois-le-Duc, but there the Spanish garrison was evidently
too strong for him. The siege of Ostend proved no
summer campaign. Three long years did it last, years
full of hardship to besieged and besiegers. The dikes
were cut, the sea brought as an ally, one wall after
another fell, the canals were filled by the ruins. For a
time, too, it seemed as though mutiny—the old friend of
the Netherlanders—was about to break out in the Spanish camp, but that was checked by the energetic hand of
Ambrosius Spinola; and finally the besieged, driven
back to their last bulwarks foot by foot, were forced to
surrender on September 22, 1604.[1]

During these three years, the States had repeatedly
endeavoured to divert the foe by attacks in other quarters. In the summer of 1602, the prince crossed the
Meuse and penetrated far into Brabant to St. Trond,
where Mendoza, who had been exchanged for all Netherland prisoners and a heavy ransom, had established an
observation camp. A brilliant raid of Count Louis Gunther upon Luxemburg caused a panic in the south, where
a fresh mutiny among Mendoza's troops, too, had excited

[1] For details of this siege, important for the military history of the time,
see C. A. van Sypesteyn, *Het merkwaardig beleg van Ostende*, 's Gravenhage, 1887.

confusion. Finally, after a career of plunder, the mutineers threw themselves into the arms of Maurice, who had
collected an army near Oosterhout.

Meantime the States urged Maurice to a new campaign
in Flanders, and after vain efforts to take Bois-le-Duc and
surprise Maestricht, the prince finally consented to make
an attempt to relieve Ostend. In April, 1604, he led an
army of some eleven thousand men to the then island of
Cadzand, possessed himself of several Spanish strongholds, and laid siege to Sluis on May 19th. Just three
months later, the city yielded to him.

The next step to be taken caused new discussions between the two generals, Maurice and William Louis, and
the members of the States-General and the council of
state, all assembled at Sluis. The generals, as " servants of the lord States," finally accepted their dictum,
and consented to attempt to relieve Ostend. Before
they did so, however, Ostend had fallen.

The position of the States was greatly strengthened by
their possession of Sluis. It was made the headquarters
for a series of raids. Frederick Henry was appointed
governor of States-Flanders. Well might Ernest Casimir
of Nassau write in commenting upon their deeds of arms:
" I do not think there is a place in the world where a
professional soldier could learn so much as in our low
lands." [1] Officers flocked from neighbouring countries
to Maurice's camp. He was an acknowledged master in
the art of war. He was continually inventing new
methods, new ideas, aided by a valiant band of princes
from the house of Nassau, among whom William Louis
undoubtedly took the first place.

The understanding between Prince Maurice and the
States was not improved by the differences regarding the
details of the Flemish campaign. There were other
causes, too, which had tended to alienate the prince and

[1] *Archives*, ii., p. 307.

the States.   The political relation between this servant of the States, highly honoured and influential on account of his brilliant military genius, and his masters was far from being well defined even at the beginning.

The combination of sovereign rights with the duties of an official gave rise to many complications.   On the one hand, Maurice seemed the head of the state and occasionally acted as such at the desire of the States, as, for example, by receiving the princes of India who came to offer him homage.[1]   In official letters, his name stood first. On the other hand, the States were careful not to allow their servant to appear as sovereign within the state. In Zealand his influence was great.   He maintained his rights to the office of First Noble against his brother-in-law, Hohenlo, the deputy of his brother, Philip William. In Gelderland and Overyssel, where the nobles disliked the burgher ascendency in the States, a movement was set afoot to make Maurice count or duke.   The army and the populace would undoubtedly have rejoiced at such an elevation, devoted as they were to the prince's person.   And he was not averse to the idea.   He always felt some claim to the offer made his father, and not fulfilled on account of the prince's death.   The circumstance that in 1601 Maurice asked the States' permission to make conquests in the southern Netherlands at his own expense, and to enjoy the monopoly of the trade in pepper and ginger in order to obtain funds for the purpose, reveals the prince's own inclination.[2]   But a limited authority, like that demanded by his father, was not at all to the taste of Maurice, accustomed as he was to command.   Once sovereign, he would not allow his hands to be tied by merchants and burghers in the way which his prudent father would have forced himself to accept.

[1] Van Meteren, p. 480.   The embassy from Atjeh in the camp before Grave.
[2] Arend, *Gesch. des Vaderl.*, iii., 2, p. 16.

Maurice had none of William's political genius, which would have enabled him to retain actual power with constitutional limitations.

In 1602, secret conferences were held in Zealand about an offer of the sovereignty to Maurice. Oldenbarnevelt expressed himself upon the subject with great reserve. Finally the little conclave of Holland statesmen summoned to discuss the scheme, decided that "at this time" it would not be good or serviceable for his Excellency. The prince let the matter pass temporarily, but he always considered that Oldenbarnevelt had opposed his interests.[1]

Thus Oldenbarnevelt was universally acknowledged as the political leader of the United Netherlands, which were gradually becoming a republic, although he had no official title thereto. It was under his influence that the East India Company was established, that great commercial body which laid the foundation of the commercial prosperity and of the colonial possessions of the Netherlands.

From 1598, the number of little companies for the India trade increased, in spite of the great losses suffered by many of them. In 1600 there were five companies existing at Amsterdam, two at Rotterdam and in Zealand, one at Delft, another at Hoorn and at Enkhuizen. How great were the losses at the outset is difficult to tell, but it is certain that barely half of the twenty-two ships equipped in 1600 returned home.[2] The States-General soon perceived the desirability of abolishing the competition between the various companies and of forcing cöoperation, but the merchants rejected several propositions of this nature made by the Estates of Holland in the following year. The "old" company was especially averse to such a consolidation, although it suffered from the

[1] Buzanval, *Cod. Dipl. Neerl.*, i., p. 303.
[2] Van d. Chijs, p. 79.

results of competition in the Java and Molucca markets, where, in consequence of the demand, the prices were increased eightfold, [1] and the island princes hampered trade by tolls, etc. Every ship that returned brought news of the lamentable results of the excessive competition. The Estates of Holland considered the question seriously. A commission from Holland investigated the matter, and advised a union of the companies under the protection of the States-General. The merchants themselves finally perceived their own interest in the matter, and the companies at Amsterdam, as well as the two at Middelburg, were consolidated with the coöperation of the municipal government, while exclusive right of trade to India, so far as these cities were concerned, was guaranteed to the consolidated body.

At the end of 1601, the States-General, following the example of Holland, advised by her advocate, convened the deputies of all existing companies to " consider an advisable policy for navigation and commerce for some years." The affair miscarried from the opposition of the Zealanders, who were afraid of the domination of richer and more powerful Holland.

But the government did not allow itself to be driven from the field. Again the merchants were convened under the direction of Oldenbarnevelt.[2] The advocate presented the advantage which would accrue from an effective coöperation. Obstacles of all kinds cropped up. Provincial jealousy, the quarrels of the Zealand and Holland cities, the obstinacy of the representatives of the North Quarter and of Zealand, all delayed the affair. The prince in Zealand, the advocate in Holland, exerted themselves to smooth over the difficulties. The plans were discussed in the States-General on March 18th, 19th, and 20th. Finally, on the afternoon of the third

[1] *Res. Holl.*, March 20, 1602.
[2] *Gedenkst. van Johan van Oldenbarnevelt*, ii., p. 311 ; iii., p. 47.

day, the United East India Company received a charter for twenty-one years, in accordance with the vote of the majority.

This important charter [1] comprised forty-six articles, the first of which stipulated that in every equipment the chamber of Amsterdam should bear half the expense, that of Zealand one quarter, those of Delft, Rotterdam, and West Friesland together one quarter. The chambers were the former small companies incorporated into one body.

The second article created a chamber of seventeen as a general assembly, an executive college, wherein Amsterdam had eight members, Zealand four, the Meuse and North Quarter each two, while the last member was to be elected by a majority of the three last mentioned. The seventeen were to sit for the first six years at Amsterdam, the next two in Zealand, and so in rotation. As " participants," all inhabitants of the province might invest as much capital as they desired, provided that they signified their desire within five months after April 1st. The capital was to be placed in three terms within three years, which was modified later so that the last instalment was paid at the end of September, 1606. [2]

Each chamber was to have supervision over the ships sailing from its ports. All vessels had to return to the port whence they sailed. The chambers were obliged to send bills of lading on demand to the provinces or cities whose inhabitants had invested fifty thousand guilders. Dividends were to be declared as soon as there was five per cent. of profit on the invested capital. All directors of the little companies were reappointed in the great one. On occasion of death or removal, the chamber of Amsterdam was gradually to be limited to twenty, Zealand to

---

[1] Van der Chijs, p. 118.

[2] Klerk de Reus, *Geschichtlicher Ueberblick der administrativen, rechtlichen und finanziellen Entwicklung. der Niederl. Ostend. Compagnie*, *Verhand. Batav. Gen.*, vol. xvii., 3rd part, 1894.

twelve, Delft and Rotterdam to seven, Enkhuizen and Hoorn to seven members. Vacancies were to be filled within three months by the Estates of the province wherein the chamber lay, from a nomination of three persons made by the remaining directors of the chambers in question. Later, every director had to possess at least one thousand pounds Flemish (six thousan'd florins) capital in the company, except in Hoorn and Enkhuizen, where half of that sum sufficed. They received all together one per cent. of the costs of equipment and one per cent. of the profits, out of which a bookkeeper, a cashier, and a custodian were to be paid. Article 34 gave the company the full monopoly for twenty-one years, a number adopted from an earlier stipulation, providing that after 1603 account should be taken every ten years, when any capitalist might withdraw from the company. The monopoly affected the other inhabitants in provinces as regarded commerce " east of the Cape Bonne Espérance or through the Straits of Magellan." According to article 35, the company might, in the name of the States-General of the United Netherlands, make treaties with princes and potentates, build forts, appoint governors and judicial officials, and levy troops. All officials and troops were obliged to take an oath to the States-General and to the company, to the last " in respect to trade and traffic." The chief officials were not to be prevented from making direct complaints to the States-General. In capturing treasure ships the union was to have a specified share in the booty. Taxes upon spices, silks, and cotton were not to be raised. Returning commanders of fleets and ships must present a report to the States-General if necessary, in writing.[1] Twenty-five thousand pounds were paid to the States for the charter, but the whole sum was promptly invested in the company and considered in the light of an ordinary share.

[1] V. d. Chijs, p. 137.

Thus the dangers of a monopoly were substituted for those of competition.

Oldenbarnevelt himself only advised this measure as one of need. Besides the monopoly, the permission granted the company to possess territories, strongholds, and sovereign rights seemed hazardous, but still something that the national government must permit temporarily to avoid undertaking risks in distant provinces. Moreover, it was urged that the charter was for a limited time in that respect, while an oath to the States-General had to be taken by officials and troops. Also it was urged that profit accrued to the state from the company's ships and artillery. On the other hand, a dark side of the charter was the power of the directors as against the shareholders.

The capital of the company reached six and a half million guilders, divided into shares of unequal value. For the present, naturally there was no question of dividends. The fleets had to be equipped and commercial relations established. It would be enough if the costs were covered in the first years.

A very few days passed before the company went into active operation and before her first ships were despatched in a great fleet of seventeen bottoms, under Wybrand van Waerwyck as admiral and Sebald de Weert as vice-admiral. The fleet was away fully five years.[1] De Weert fell upon Ceylon, where he had at first been well received, and lost his life. His successor, Cornelis Pietersz., overcame the Portuguese near Djohor. Admiral Waerwyck sailed farther, and obtained permission to build a factory at Bantam, where he left a supercargo and several other officials with some capital and directions for administering justice and developing trade. He sent his ships to all quarters—through the archipelago to Banda, Atjeh, Djohor, Borneo, and finally to Siam and China, where he vainly tried to obtain free trade. In June, 1607, he

---

[1] De Jonge, *Opkomst*, iii., p. 1.

ɪᴄturned home with his last ships and rich cargoes. Others
of his vessels, also well laden, had returned earlier.

Meantime a new fleet of thirteen armed ships under the
Admiral Steven van der Hagen were sent out by the
Seventeen to harry the Portuguese in India.[1] This fleet
sailed first to Mozambique, but found no booty, and so
turned to Goa and the other Portuguese settlements on
the coast of Malabar, where Van der Hagen made a
friendly treaty with Calicoet. News from Ambon, where
he himself had built the *Kasteel van Verre* in 1600, the
first settlement of the Netherlanders in India, retaken
by the Portuguese shortly before, attracted him to Molucca. Here he reconquered the fort and placed Frederick de Houtman there as governor, and built a factory.
His ships visited many an island of this spice-bearing
archipelago, while others on the coast of Coromandel laid
the foundation of a flourishing trade in India rugs,
and brought the first reports about New Guinea and
New Holland. When Van der Hagen touched at Mau-
ritius on his homeward voyage in 1606, he encountered
the company's third fleet, which, eleven ships strong, had
sailed in the previous May under Cornelis Matelief.

Matelief entered the Moluccas and the Straits of Malacca, according to orders, and succeeded in defeating the
Portuguese fleet repeatedly, but had to relinquish the
siege of the city on account of the weakness of his fleet.
He had some thought of making a permanent fort at
Atjeh, to which the sultan agreed, but for the time Bantam remained the centre of Netherland commerce in that
locality. In Molucca, Matelief regulated affairs, and
placed an instructor at Ambon at the request of the
islanders. He gave permission for marriages between
Europeans and native women. Afterwards he confirmed
the authority of the company on Tidore and Ternate.
In China he never succeeded in gaining foothold. Finally

[1] De Jonge, iii., p. 26.

he returned home by way of Bantam, after leaving the completion of his task to Paulus van Caerden, lately arrived in India with ten ships.

This new commander was unsuccessful in his efforts to repel the Spaniards, who tried to control the Moluccas from the Philippines. On the contrary, he was himself taken prisoner, and remained in the hands of the foe together with his crew.

His defeat showed that the enemy were still doughty in these eastern waters. They continued to concentrate forces in Goa, Malacca, on the Philippines, and at Macao. The States-General finally took alarm, and, in 1606, sent two fleets to the Portuguese coast to check their preparations. The first time the mariners obtained a big haul of booty, but the second time they were defeated and fled, while the valiant vice-admiral of Zealand, Reinier Claeszen, set fire to his own ship and was blown up. In the following year, a new fleet under Heemskerck inflicted serious damage upon the enemy.

During the succeeding two years there were several encounters in the eastern seas, mainly to the advantage of the Netherlanders, when news arrived, April, 1609, of a European truce, with the chance that negotiations with Spain were to result in a peace. It was to be expected that *in statu quo* would be taken for India, and the directors desired to extend the company's rights as speedily as possible. Their commanders were instructed accordingly.

The condition of the company was far from brilliant. It had started off well. Immediately after the incorporation, the shares had been sold on the bourse at fifteen per cent. premium. The first good news advanced the price to 130, yes,—after the arrival of the first ships,— to 140. But very soon the prices of the spices, especially pepper, fell, owing to over-importation, and the storehouses were filled with unsalable wares. Bad news came then from the east, and the shares fell as low as forty-eight per cent. The directors saw their capital melting away and began to run in debt, while, too, they were forced to borrow ammunition, etc., from the States. Clever speculators took advantage of the opportunity. Foes of the company and of monopoly, ill wishers at home and abroad, undermined their credit in every possible way, both by throwing shares on the market and by false reports. Some shareholders were in arrears, others complained of the conduct of affairs. There were grave doubts about the company's tenure of life. Rivals, too, sprang up. De Moucheron, who had ventured much and lost much, finally declared bankruptcy and fled to France, where he suggested to Henry IV. the establishment of a French East India Company. One Pieter Lyntgens, an Amsterdammer Baptist, withdrew his capital from the Dutch company, went to France, and worked secretly to the same purpose. And there were also many domestic foes, "libertines and mennonites," as Oldenbarnevelt said contemptuously, who were quite ready to balk the company. Isaac Lemaire was one of these. He allowed himself to be persuaded by the ambassador Jeannin, in 1607, to lend his aid to the establishment of a French company.

The States-General conceived a plan of diverting Henry's attention from the east by suggesting, through their French ambassador, François Aerssens, and François Francken, the establishment of a West India Company. Francken had repeatedly discussed this with the able navigator and merchant, William Usselincx, with Linschoten, and the learned Plancius. Oldenbarnevelt was ready to adopt a plan of a West India Company with Holland capital and French support, as he saw an opportunity of inflicting injury in Spanish America. But in 1607, practical difficulties seemed too great to warrant the execution of this plan. Merchants were afraid to

risk their capital; the increasing hope of peace decided
Oldenbarnevelt and other statesmen not to add to their
difficulties in East India.   The matter was temporarily
dropped, to the great annoyance of the zealous Usselincx,
who thought that this company promised the " greatest
traffic in the world." [1]

In spite of all disadvantages, the shareholders of the
East India Company had received, since 1605, large sums
in return for their expenditure, first from the ships despatched by the old companies before the incorporation
of the new.' In February, 1606, this amounted to fifty
per cent., in the spring of 1609 to twenty-five per cent.,
which was paid a year later.   These first " dividends,"
although they amounted to a capital within six years,—a
fact that did not appear wholly extraordinary to merchants
accustomed to gross receipts,—proved little as to the
durability of the business.   They served to send the
shares up in the market, which happened more quickly
because the public did not know the origin of the
divisions.   It was very questionable what effect the proposed peace would make upon the company.

The defect in India at this time was lack of direction.
The bureau on the coast of Coromandel, whence trade
was transacted with Ceylon and the coast of Bengal and
farther India, the relations with Calicoet, with Djohor
and Atjeh, the bureau at Patani for trade to China,
Japan, and Borneo, had little connection with the headquarters of the company at Bantam, where Jacques
l'Hermite conducted the factory for years and lived to
oppose the sultan's attempts at taxation.   Between
Bantam and the bureaus at Ambon, Banda, Ternate,
and Matsjan in the Moluccas there was just as little connection, while even the understanding between the officials settled there was unsatisfactory.   There was need
of one centre, with one official who would be paramount

[1] *Gedenkst.*, iii., p. 75.   ' Klerk de Reus, p. 178.

to all others, and endowed with sufficient power to repel Portuguese and Spaniards and to compel obedience from his underlings. ᛁ

Meanwhile the war in Europe had been laxly waged, partially owing to the States' exhaustion after the siege of Ostend, which had cost one hundred thousand guilders monthly and forced Holland to great financial sacrifices. Spain, on the other hand, had been enabled by circumstances to take a more vigorous stand than she had for years. In 1604, the conclusion of peace with James I., Elizabeth's successor, left Spain's hands free on that side. In spite of all his promises, the new king did not show any disposition to be hard on his Netherland neighbours, who feared at first lest he might deliver the cautionary cities to their enemy. The embassy of the States, in which Oldenbarnevelt and the young Prince Frederick Henry took part, was well received; their agent, Caron, was made ambassador. At the same time James promised Spain not to aid the States from the cautionary cities. Oldenbarnevelt did not think, with this weakening of all support from England, that the Netherlands could maintain the war.

In Spain, it seemed as if the government's intention was to wage war more vigorously in the Netherlands with the intent to force peace. The archdukes were longing to bring all opposition to a conclusion, and they had a general who called to mind the capacity of Alexander of Parma. Ambrosius Spinola had speedily risen to the first rank through his conquest of Ostend and from his evident talent. He was a fitting opponent to Maurice. Undaunted, strong in his discipline, clever, cultivated, and endowed with political insight, the scarcely thirty-three-year-old Genoese was well adapted to reconcile the inhabitants of the southern provinces. A journey to Spain in the winter of 1604 gave him opportunity to obtain sympathy for his plans.

After his return to the Netherlands, charged by the archdukes with the full conduct of the war, he made ready (1605) for offensive measures. With two armies, formed from Spanish, Italian, German, and English regiments, he was planning in part to protect the southern provinces, in part to attack the States. Fresh supplies, the title of commander, and the order of the Golden Fleece from Philip III. placed Spinola in a position to act. Haultain, to be sure, succeeded in annihilating a great portion of the transport ships containing the regiment sent from Spain, but Spinola proceeded to the execution of his plan, which was to attack the States' territory from the east. After some preliminary movements in 1605 in this quarter, where he met some success and some reverses, he collected an army of twelve thousand men in the early summer of 1606, and invaded Overyssel, while his general, Bucquoy, appeared near Mook with an equally large force. His aim was to force the Yssel and the Waal at the same time and to repel Maurice's much smaller army. Maurice, however, succeeded in thwarting him and saving the threatened provinces. He gained some ground by taking Lochem, but was hampered in his further plans by a sudden attack of the enemy from the Lippe. He was forced to break the siege of Groenloo on their approach, partly, too, on account of the ravages of a fever in his camp, and partly to avoid a decisive battle.

In general, Maurice's reputation was not increased by this action. Exaggerated fear of pitched battles was urged as the cause of his repeated retreats. On the other hand, Spinola's courage was universally admired, and nothing but the lack of money, the canker of Spanish government, and the result, a mutinous spirit, spoiled his success.[1]

[1] Compare, for these campaigns, Van Meteren, p. 496 ; Vervov, *Gedenkw. Gesch.*, p. 195 ; Giustiniano, *Della guerra di Fiandra* (Antwerp, 1609). p. 149 ; Carnero, *Historia de las guerras civiles*, p. 519.

Exhaustion was evident on both sides, and in the spring of 1607 all action was restricted to raiding. Frederick Henry surprised Erkelens and plundered the environs of the city. The cavalry of Grobbendonck harassed the Bommeler region and made Bois-le-Duc the centre of hostilities on the border of the States' realm. Prince Maurice, urged by the States to repel the enemy from the rivers, refused, on the advice, too, of William Louis[1] and his brother, Count Casimir of Nassau, to stake the fate of the States on a pitched battle, and, conscious of his own weakness, contented himself with a defence of the threatened regions.

In compensation for this moderate success on land, Spain suffered a lamentable defeat of her fleet in her own ports. Fear of an expedition from Spain to the East Indies had led to the despatch of fleets to the Spanish coasts. At this time a force of twenty-six well equipped warships, under Jacob van Heemskerck, sailed to Portugal. When they did not find the enemy, they proceeded to Gibraltar, where lay a fleet of twenty-one great ships under D'Avila. Under the protection of the city, the admiral attacked the enemy on April 25th, sailing into the bay himself and thus giving the example of courage which he paid for with his life; but the captain of his ship, Verhoeff, who later commanded the fleet to India, continued the fight with the vice-admiral, Alteras. D'Avila perished, too, and the Spanish fleet was scattered, routed in confusion, half the ships being destroyed, half reaching port. About one hundred Netherlanders perished, while not less than two thousand Spaniards met their death. Nothing further was gained, as no landing could be effected, but the impression of the brilliant victory was powerful enough to give a strong impulse to the newly opened negotiations.

This was the last military event of significance which

[1] *Archives*, ii., p. 378.

took place before the long truce. The expenses of the interminable war could be borne by the northern provinces no longer. Holland's debt alone was twenty-six millions, and the military leaders were continually demanding more money, estimating that effective work could only be done with an additional sum of four or five millions. Heavier taxes could not be imposed. An investigation by a commission appointed by Oldenbarnevelt, and pledged to secrecy even toward Prince Maurice, declared on August, 1606, that it was impossible to prolong the war.[1]

In 1598, France, on the earnest petition of the States, had increased the subsidy to two millions a year; but no more than that could be expected, and even this sum now began to decrease. The Huguenots, legitimated since 1598, made themselves felt in everything to the annoyance of the orthodox Catholics. There were, too, various rumours of attempts on the life of the king, which brought the Protestants into ill repute and induced disinclination to aid another Protestant state. Nor was aid to be expected from James of England or the German princes. The Netherlands had lost their most faithful friend in the empire, old John of Nassau, who had given all he had to their cause.

There was no more possibility of an offensive war, such as the prince and Henry IV. had planned.[2] Oldenbarnevelt thought some desperate resolution would have to be taken as a last resort, either a new offer of the sovereignty to France, or submission to the archdukes. There were frequent discussions about the former point at this time, and in the spring of 1607, Henry IV. asked Aerssens to go to the States so as to be able to inform him on what conditions they would acknowledge him as sovereign.

---

[1] *Gedenkst.*, iii., p. 83.

[2] Compare, for this, Van Rees, *Staathuishoudkunde* ii., p. 245 *et seq.*, *Gedenkst. van Oldenbarnevelt*, iii., *passim*, especially pp. 69, 83.

Oldenbarnevelt lost heart completely, and wanted to resign from public affairs. He knew that his desires for peace had placed him on a dangerous path. He, the powerful and haughty leader, had many personal foes who complained of his ambition, accused him of selfish intentions, and tried to undermine his influence. The French envoy found that Oldenbarnevelt was embarked on a perilous game. But the advocate did not easily give up a fixed conviction, although he was conscious enough of the obstacles. Was it possible that a truce would incline the people of the northern provinces to submit to the claims of the archdukes ? Was the organisation in the north suited for peace ? Would the Catholics submit to the domination of the Calvinists ? Would the army, would the prince himself, accept a peace or even a truce which would doom the military power to inactivity and to the loss of the profits of the war ? Moreover, could the provinces hope to retain their independence permanently as against France and England ?

All these questions obtruded themselves on the statesman in the consideration of the future. He was aware of the risk to his personal influence by his espousal of an unpopular policy, but the fear of the ruin of the state was stronger. And there were many, especially among the magistrates, who agreed with him.[1] The old " hearty men " who had felt the Spanish yoke were dead. The new generation was weary of war and wanted peace, permanent or temporary. Such was the inclination of the majority in the Holland Estates. The provinces exposed to the foe were still more eager. The state of finances, especially in Holland, has been shown. Thus a wind was blowing in the north which spread thoughts and expectations of peace. This wish had prevailed in the south for a still longer period. In 1600, the States-General at Brussels had expressed themselves plainly,

[1] *Archives*, ii., p. 380.

and the archdukes were not disinclined to yield to the demands of their subjects.   Even Spinola desired a time for repose.   And in Spain, Lerma's party wanted nothing more than peace in order to enjoy their sovereignty.

Maurice and William Louis, on the other hand, were strongly opposed to any such scheme.   They thought they would be plunged into an abyss of misery.   They considered the offers nothing more than craft and deceit, —an attempt to dominate by sowing discord, and, under the pretence of peace, to gain a domination of the north which Spain had failed to conquer by war.

In Spain there was a party of opposition to any peace which would imply an acknowledgment of the rebels' independence.   Such an acknowledgment would be contrary to all traditions, in conflict with Castilian pride, with the dignity of a state like Spain.   All the old servants of Philip II. could not bring themselves to accept Lerma's peace policy which shadowed, to their mind, the end of Spain's greatness.

CHAPTER X

NEGOTIATIONS FOR THE TRUCE

IT was the archdukes who took the first step towards serious negotiations. In May, 1606, secret overtures were made, abandoned in a short time, and again renewed in the early part of 1607. One Cruwel, a bankrupt Brussels merchant, related to Cornelis Aerssens, and Father John Neyen, the archduke's confessor and commissary-general of the Franciscans, obtained access to Oldenbar-nevelt and Maurice by means of Aerssens. From that time the parleyings were mainly conducted by Neyen. The chief fear entertained by people at large was that the independence of the States would not be recognised, and that the prosperous trade with India would be hampered. There were many undercurrents, too, which rendered plain sailing very difficult.

It was clear at a very early stage of the negotiations that even in the bosom of the state colleges there were persons who were in secret communication with Spinola and the archdukes. It was even clear that certain people from Utrecht had been to Spinola's army and given information. The well-known circumstance that with the many-headed government in the Netherland provinces, it was always possible to buy state secrets, and that many a member of the sovereign assembly was not proof against money even from the enemy, was a warning to prudence. The French ambassador, Buzanval, did not think it incredible that Oldenbarnevelt might be won over to accept certain French plans even if he could not be bought by Spain. Prince Maurice was the only one among the Netherland leaders who was considered wholly above corruption. He was unflinching. A more fell, at the same time honourable and upright, foe Spain did not have in the provinces, to whose weal the prince was devoted heart and soul.

At the very beginning of the discussion of terms, duplicity was evident in the use of phrases, and distrust excited, but in spite of all, on April 11th, a preliminary resolution was actually taken for an armistice which Spain was to accept within three months. She was also to recognise the northern provinces as an independent state.

At Neyen's instance, but much against the will of Prince Maurice and with opposition from Zealand, it was stipulated that Heemskerck's fleet should be recalled from the east, and all hostilities should cease on the Spanish coast and in the Mediterranean. An official proclamation of the States-General announced these points to the provinces and begged them to hold a general fast in consideration of the great importance of these negotiations.

Many besides Maurice and William Louis were ready to shake their heads, and did not rejoice at the prospect of peace. Was there not indication in the wording of the convention that only a *quasi*-independence was recognised? asked Jeannin. James I., too, was incredulous. In Germany, it was asked whether it were not a Spanish rule that faith need not be kept with heretics. Henry IV., Christian of Anhalt, and others gave warnings. The strict Calvinists were alarmed. Others besides the prince feared civil strife, and the condition of affairs in Groningen and Friesland showed that these last fears were not altogether baseless, while newer differences between two schools of moderate and strict Calvinism, as

represented by Jacobus Arminius and Franciscus Gomarus opened new possibilities of dissension.   There had
been serious dissatisfaction in relation to the stipulations
of the States-General regarding a national synod.   The
Estates of Holland had shown their sympathy for the
liberal wing of the church party.   The close connection
between church and political affairs in a state like that of
the United Netherlands afforded continual opportunities
for rubs.   In Utrecht, as well as in certain Holland cities
and in Friesland, the adherents of the old democratic
party made themselves evident, conscious of the rôle
which they had once played in connection with church
quarrels.

Oldenbarnevelt pushed matters to this point in spite
of all difficulties, but at the cost of serious quarrels with
the prince and calumnies from his numerous foes.   Even
Buzanval thought that he wished to protect his own
property by peace.   Aerssens, the envoy at Paris, took
pains to repeat all the rumours current there.   He himself was playing a double game, wishing to keep both the
advocate and the prince as friends.

Not until October did the desired papers arrive from
Spain.   The king informed the archdukes and Spinola
that in return for his recognition of the independence he
should demand religious freedom for the Catholics for
the time of the truce or until peace should be concluded.
Then the negotiations could begin.   On February, 1608,
the envoys of the enemy arrived in Holland by way of
Rotterdam, and were received by the prince himself on the
Hoornbrug by Delft.   These were Spinola, the Spanish
negotiator, Don Juan de Mancicidor, the south Netherlander, Richardot, besides the two earlier envoys, Neyen
and Verreyken, with a suite of 166 brilliantly attired
nobles, masses of servants, and rich baggage.   Not less
brilliant was the train which received them, Prince Maurice with William Louis and Frederick Henry, supported

by a number of renowned commanders and statesmen. An enormous crowd had flocked between Delft and The Hague to enjoy the remarkable spectacle of the meeting between the two greatest generals of their time. Maurice's state couch conducted the distinguished visitors to the dwellings prepared for them.[1] This splendour on both sides was not wholly agreeable to the people. There was much fear of secret plots of the Jesuits.

After a few days of solemnities and visits, the negotiations began in the so-called Treves chamber of the Binnenhof. The States-General was represented by one member from each province under direction of Oldenbarnevelt, who, together with William Louis and the Hollander, Walraven of Brederode, acted in behalf of the central government of the united provinces. Envoys of the friendly powers, France, England, Denmark, Brandenburg, and the Palatinate, took part in the negotiations.

Difficulties arose at the beginning. The archdukes used the seals of the seventeen provinces, which the States objected to. The question as to language resulted in the use of both French and Dutch in discussion, with the documents printed in both tongues.

Then more serious difficulties came to the fore. For weeks long, Indian trade was discussed point by point, and no conclusion was reached. Religion was avoided in the main, as that was the rock on which all previous conferences had been wrecked. Thus April, May, June, and July passed. The States were impatient. The Danish envoys left, and the Germans began to prepare to follow. The time of the armistice first announced by the States-General—April 3, 1607—was prolonged. Further delays ensued. Messengers travelled to and fro from Spain, and the progress of proceedings was criticised

[1] The official report in *Gedenkst.*, iii., p. 168, in Oldenbarnevelt's handwriting.

freely by the people not only in private conversations but from the pulpits, where the ultra-Calvinists protested vigorously against peace with any recognition of the ancient faith, and also in masses of pamphlets. There were rhymed " conferences " between the pope and the king of Spain, so-called letters from bakers and other burghers to the pope, " echoes " of " the present peace negotiations," etc. A dialogue was a very favourite form for these publications. The pamphlet, *Een oud schipper van Monnickendam*, a memorial on the valiant Cornelis Dirksz., who won the first sea-fight against the Spaniards, is one of the best-known writings of this nature. A clever, sharp *brochure*, whose frontispiece showing a Holland sailor and a Spaniard on a stick which represented India, revealed plainly where the shoe pinched. In 1608 the directors of the East India Company published a " discourse in form of remonstrance," handling the necessity of East-Indian navigation, which was repeatedly reprinted. The indefatigable William Usselincx tried to direct public opinion, too, to the importance of free passage to the West Indies, and to point out the advantages of the war. Nearly all these pamphlets were directed against the negotiations, and were full of warnings of Spanish craft. *The Spider and the Little Bees*, *Spinola and the States*, and *The Netherland Hive*, besides a collection of forty more, all attacked the peace at this time. Van Reyd's history, published at this time, revived the memory of the Spanish cruelties from the days of Alva, as that of Van Meteren had done a little earlier, and found ready purchasers. The well-known letter of Justus Lipsius was published at Dusseldorf as a warning to the promoters of peace, and scattered by thousands through the Netherlands.

All official documents exchanged on both sides were given to the public by the States, in the midst of the popular excitement, without comment. The advocate did not lose heart, although he was the central point of calumny and attack.   Meanwhile the prince and his party were fixed in their opinion that any truce would be a serious injury to the provinces, especially one of four or five years.   " Commerce," they said, " would be ruined; Protestant religious services would suffer from the increased freedom to the Catholics, which the enemy would certainly demand; heavy sums would have to be paid out for retaining soldiers; the enemy would sow dissension." They tried to prove from the action of the envoys during the negotiations that the words of the enemy were untrustworthy, especially that his recognition of independence in the little word " as " contained an ambiguity which became more and more evident in the later assertions.   The prince begged the States, on the strength of his own proven services, on his office as stadtholder, to maintain " good correspondence " with him against the attempts of others.   On the other hand, the advocate argued the impossibility of waging war on the present footing, and that a well-protected truce offered less danger than the opposition claimed, even if improvements were at once necessary in the government, since up to now it had been arranged for defence only.

Thus the parties stood opposed when something unexpected turned the scale.   In September, an intermission of three weeks was taken.   On the 30th, the archdukes' envoys returned to Brussels.   In a table-drawer of the lodgings where Richardot had lived was found an instruction from the archdukes.   Possibly Richardot had conceived the plan to convince the government of the northern provinces of the archdukes' sincerity, which was evident in this paper, and of the uprightness of the emissaries of the foe in their demands made at the instance of Spain.   The prince thought, on the other hand, that this instruction proved that the point of religious freedom was deemed a prime point by the

Catholics, and that the envoys had reckoned on French help for obtaining it. The document was first brought before the States-General and then printed and disseminated.

The two leaders now exerted themselves to obtain their desired ends. Oldenbarnevelt, moreover, defended the purity of his own motives eloquently in the States-General, and no one ventured to take up the gauntlet against him.

Finally, on November 19th, Maurice and the advocate were persuaded to meet and discuss the question. Oldenbarnevelt swore to the prince that he had in mind only the welfare of the country, and promised to consent to Maurice's retaining thirty thousand men for 1609, to temper the prince's distrust. The French envoy, Jeannin, who had been indefatigable in all the negotiations, urged Maurice to withdraw his opposition. In addition to his own representations, he showed him a letter from his sovereign, in which Henry IV. threatened to withdraw all support from the Netherlands in case the truce was rejected. William Louis, Louise de Coligny, and the influential court chaplain, Uyttenbogaert, tried to convince Maurice of the advocate's good intentions.

By the end of November, Oldenbarnevelt had brought over the majority of the Holland cities and nobles to his sentiments. Amsterdam and Delft delayed, but finally gave their consent in December. No opposition was to be expected from the other provinces, except Zealand, and finally it was won over by Maurice's advice. The matter was decided on the one side, and popular agitation —which had been very threatening—began to abate now that the prince had given the example of concession.

In early February the envoys went from The Hague to Antwerp, now appointed as the place for the negotiations. There Spinola and Richardot with their colleagues received them. For the time being Jeannin conducted the

negotiations.   The States-General were not to send their
deputies until later.   Points were finally settled, and on
March 25th, a formal deputation from the States-General,
who were assembled at Bergen op Zoom, went to Antwerp to finish the negotiations.   It consisted of Oldenbarnevelt and other gentlemen who had conducted the
negotiations at The Hague.   A few days later William
Louis joined them to protect the interests of the house of
Nassau.   On April 9, 1609, a truce of twelve years was
solemnly signed.

   Thus the tedious negotiations came to a happy conclusion, thanks to the efforts of the able Jeannin and to the
need for drawing breath felt by both parties, especially
by the archdukes.   On April 16th, the deputies of the
States embarked from the Antwerp quay in the midst
of cannon salutes from the warships on the Scheldt and
the forts, and left the city where they had completed a
difficult and important task, as the advocate wrote with
truth, and to him and to Jeannin was all honour due.

   The treaty thus concluded comprised thirty-eight
articles besides the added acts.   The first declared that
the archdukes in their own name and that of the king
concluded a truce for twelve years (Article 2) on the basis
of possessions at the time (Article 3).   The fourth article
provided a universal cessation of hostility both for territory within and without Europe.   As regarded the latter,
this would not go into force within a year (Article 5), on
account of the distance, and with the general stipulation
that there should be mutual freedom of trade, while in
the Spanish possessions within Europe the inhabitants of
the provinces could not trade without the king's express
permission, but outside of them should be allowed full
freedom of entry.   In a secret article, this permission
herein mentioned was expressly given by the deputies
from the enemy in the name of the king and the archdukes, " on condition that the trade be free and assured."

The following articles had to do with tolls, taxes, etc., which could not be increased for their respective subjects. Article 7 gave the inhabitants of the northern provinces trading in the lands of king or archdukes the same rights and same obligations as had been given to and imposed upon the English in 1604, especially as regards freedom of conscience and of respect for the Catholic religion. Article 13 stipulated restoration of confiscated property on payment of debts resting thereon (Article 16), with exception of houses sold in the cities (Article 17), which would make too much complication, and only for the period of the truce, so that nothing could be alienated. Article 20 stipulated the same thing for ecclesiastical property in so far as it was not alienated before January, 1607, in which case a yearly rental was to be paid, all for the profit of churches, colleges, and persons who were submissive to the archdukes and had possessions in the north or who were under the States, and rightfully entitled to property in the south.

Article 29 decreed that no new fort could be erected; Article 30, that the house of Nassau could not be sued on account of the debts incurred by Prince William after 1567; Article 34, that all prisoners on both sides should be freed without ransom.

The treaty was signed by the ambassadors of France and England as mediators, afterwards by the envoys of the interested parties. Then followed the above-mentioned secret stipulation. A second codicil comprised the declaration of the French and English ambassadors, under Article 3, that all territories belonging to the marquisate of Bergen op Zoom, the barony of Breda, and the land of Grave with Kuik, should lapse to the States; further, too, that trade to Spanish possessions in India should be subject to the permission of the king of Spain, and that to the States' possessions to the permission of the States. In a third act the French envoys promised

the archdukes and Spain, in the name of the States and Prince Maurice, that in Brabant territory under the States nothing should be changed in respect to religion, and consequently Catholicism should be maintained. Finally, in an additional article, the archdukes promised to pay the heirs of Prince William three hundred thousand guilders, which the prince still claimed from the national government.

The ratification of the archdukes came without difficulty. Three months later came that from the king of Spain, who added that he hoped that the States would be kind towards the Catholics who went among them during the truce.[1] Finally, the two mediating powers, France and England, promised (June 17th), at the States' instance, the maintenance of the truce in connection with the treaty of 1608, also in case that trade in India was harassed by, or on account of, the king of Spain. An attempt to attain in the treaty of guaranty a full acknowledgment of the independence of the States by the allies failed. Both feared embittering Spain, although they had long since acknowledged the justice of the abjuration of 1581.

Thus the wish entertained for years by Oldenbarnevelt was realised, and Jeannin could write it to his government, " to the great satisfaction of everyone, even of M. the Prince Maurice."

The treaty was very advantageous for the north. Dangers of a surprise like that in 1605–1606 were past; the increasing retrogression of the finances was ended. The troops did not need to be increased; extraordinary protection would not be needed for navigation; every domestic disturbance could be suppressed by force; sinking credit could be restored; national debts, which amounted to twelve millions, and paid ten to fourteen per cent. could be liquidated; with France, who could demand

[1] Van Meteren, p. 579, v.

fourteen to fifteen millions, they could treat about pay- ment ; the peace would further trade and industry ; eastern neighbours could be better watched—a matter of importance now that the duke of Jülich, Cleves, Berg, and Mark had died in March, and serious troubles had arisen over the succession.[1]

But the good understanding between the prince and Oldenbarnevelt had suffered seriously, and the temporary reconciliation had not restored the prince's earlier con- fidence in the national advocate.   Moreover, the advocate had triumphed over his friends, but they did not cease to calumniate him, and many continued to think that the truce was a serious disadvantage to the country, espe- cially when it was rumoured that in the south the treaty was considered a salvation, as they were not in a position to wage war longer, and would have been helpless in case of an attack from the States.   For the moment, re- joicings over the peace had the upper hand, and the thanksgiving day of May 6th was universally celebrated in the north, as men in the south rejoiced over the truce, which was regarded as preliminary to a permanent peace. Richardot doubted whether after twelve years of peace either means or inclination for prolonging the war would exist in the south, and thanked God for the treaty.

Thus the war which had wrought confusion in the Netherlands for more than forty years was ended for the time being.

[1] *Gedenkst.*, iii., p. 311 ; *ibid.*, 368.

THE TRUCE

1609–1621

CHAPTER XI

THE NETHERLANDS IN 1609

THE differences that had grown up between the conditions of the provinces of the north and those of the south have been clearly indicated in the preceding chapters.[1] Antwerp had become a deserted harbour through the closing of the Scheldt. It was a decayed country town, numerous still in population, but even in that point suffering a daily loss from emigration. Instead of the forty Genoese counting-houses, there were only two, instead of the numerous German, Portuguese, and English firms, there were only a few here and there.[2] A mass of native merchants and workmen had left the poverty-stricken city on account of their religious convictions or because of the turn of affairs, or for both reasons, and betaken themselves to the flourishing cities of Holland and Zealand, to Hamburg and Bremen, to London and Rouen. And the merchants who remained were in constant terror not only of the Zealand pirates on the Scheldt, whose outposts, the fortresses Lilloo and Liefenhoek, were like knives at Antwerp's throat, but also of the heavy taxes imposed by their own government. Middelburg, Breda, Bergen op Zoom, Lilloo, attracted

[1] See Overbury, *Observations upon the Provinces United and the State of France in 1609.* (No place of publication, 1626.)
[2] See the proof published by De Ram in *Bull. Comm. d'Hist.*, 2nd series, pp. 8, 297 *et seq.*; Mertens and Torfs, *Geschiedenis van Antwerpen*, v., pp. 329, 349.

much of the city's commerce.   Nothing remained but a little traffic with the impoverished interior.   The hope of a revival of commerce after the truce was crushed by the conditions.   Export and import were both dependent upon the Hollanders and Zealanders, who drove an import trade with Flanders in hundreds of tiny ships.[1] They commanded the mouth of the Scheldt, and all international intercourse was forbidden to the provinces loyal to Philip.   The tranquillity that came with peace gave the blood-drenched country districts of Flanders, Brabant, Namur, Hainaut, and Luxemburg, opportunity to recover themselves somewhat, but as commerce and manufactures made no outlet for production, the Flemish and Brabantine manufacturing centres declined to the rank of petty places with a certain industry just sufficing for local needs, and confined, moreover, to narrow limits by oppressive mediæval guild regulations.   Certain manufactures—lace-making, weaving, brewing—lingered on in the decayed cities, barely holding their own locally against foreign competition.

A faithful subject of the archdukes could have found, however, one bright spot in the dreary state of affairs in the south in connection with the submission to their ancient overlord—the complete victory of the Catholic church in the very provinces which had formerly been the most seriously stained with heresy.

In Artois, in the adjacent parts of Flanders, Brabant, and Hainaut, where the movement had originated, there was no trace of Calvinist sympathies.   On the contrary, the young university of Douay and the Jesuit seminary at St. Omer formed in the region the kernel of a strong Catholic reaction, which made itself felt in a wide circle. At Valenciennes and Cambrai, at Bruges and Ypres, at Brussels and Mechlin, there was no evidence of the ancient heresy.   The close oversight of the Louvain

[1] *Bijdr. en Med. Hist. Gen.*, xix , p. 35.

theologians watched for every questionable utterance of priest or layman.

The court at Brussels, modelled, by the former cardinal and his consort, on forms that were almost conventual, presented a striking contrast to the luxurious courts of the ancient Burgundians, of Margaret and Mary of Austria. And they gave the tone to the aristocratic and burgher circles of the Brabantine capital.

The clergy of all degrees devoted themselves to their duty zealously. Nowhere, except perhaps in Bavaria and Austria, was the Catholic counter reformation, whose soul was the Jesuits with their profound zeal of belief, so vigorous and effective as in the Low Lands,—the *Pays-Bas*, as the archdukes' realm came to be called. After the fall of Ostend, heresy disappeared from the Flemish coast and the north-western region of Flanders. It lingered on a little at Nieuwpoort, Ghent, and Antwerp, but the clergy, supervised by intelligent bishops and lay workers among the Jesuits and Dominicans, were unceasing in their efforts to eradicate it entirely, and their efforts met with success.[1]

A certain lethargy had replaced the turbulence which had characterised the Flemish Brabantine people a century earlier. The pressure exercised by the Spanish officials and by the weakened army—there were only a couple of tercios—did continue to arouse some dissatisfaction, but the great personal popularity of the archduchess, who was more successful than her husband in gaining favour, kept this discontent in check, and the tranquillity and peace at the time of the truce militated to the spread of the spirit of resignation. Many in the south were apprehensive about the expiration of the truce. They feared a renewal of hostilities. And what would then become of the faithful south ?

This question was also asked anxiously by the southern

[1] See Bentivoglio, *Relazione di Fiandra*, pp. 157, 192.

States-General.   The upper nobles complained that they were ignored for the haughty Spaniards.   Spinola, an Italian, was somewhat looked down on by the archdukes' favourites, though he was grandee of Spain, knight of the Fleece, commander of the camp, and superintendent of Spanish finances in the Netherlands.   Don Juan de Mancicidor, a Spanish statesman of the old type, and the archduke's confessor, Fra Inigo de Brizuela, were, with Spinola, at the head of the government.[1]   Native statesmen, like the state secretaries Verreyken and Pratz, the councillors, found themselves reduced to second rank.   It was due to these last, skilled jurists as they were, that the jurisprudence was improved by a perpetual edict issued in 1611, wherein the varying ordinances of earlier and later times were brought into accord with the existing privileges, and the civil law was enriched with a new national law book, while the older and newer stipulations of the criminal law were collected.[2]   This, and care for the long-neglected dikes, and for the restoration of the plundered and desecrated churches, for the establishment of cloisters that rose at this period under the protection of the pious archduke, and aid offered to certain scholars and artists—this was the good brought to the south by the government of Albert and Isabella at the time of the temporary peace.[3]

The new government could not, however, stem the poverty, the retrogression, the misery that was dominant everywhere in every realm.   Material and intellectual enervation went hand in hand.   The Louvain university, shortly before proud of Lipsius and his pupil Puteanus, had fallen into decay, and Douay did not inherit the ancient reputation of the Brabantine sister institution.   The study of theology—of Catholic theology—was

[1] Richardot died in 1609.
[2] Edmund Poullet, *Histoire du droit pénal Brabançon*, p. 248 *et seq.*
[3] Compare Juste, *Histoire de Belgique*, ii., p. 235.

fervently pursued, but no single man in the first rank was heard in the scantily frequented lecture-rooms after the death of Lipsius in 1606. Outside of the university life there was the mystic physician, Van Helmont, at Vilvoorden, one of the founders of chemistry and the new science of healing; the learned Jan Bolland at Antwerp laid the foundations of the famous collection of the *Acta Sanctorum*. But the majority of the learned men,—Heinsius, Vulcanius, Dodonæus, Clusius, Simon Stevin, —although born in the south, preferred the fresher spritual atmosphere of the north to their heavy native air. Literature could not free itself from the stifling confines of the antiquated rhetoricians' poetry, which had lost her last men of name in Houwaert (died 1599) and his contemporary, Van der Noot. From that date, Flemish letters sank back to a condition of numbness which lasted more than two centuries. Van der Noot had heralded the coming of a new day which never dawned, for no poet followed his steps, and the poetical forms of the French Renaissance were detrimental to poetry. The Flemish prose, that had appeared about 1580 in the versatile painter-poet, Karl Van Mander, an equal of Coornhert, deteriorated from 1600 on. Van Mander himself went, like the best of his compatriots, from the south to Holland. Flemish in general, less than half a century previous the speech of cultivated people, fell, with the intellectual gauge of the nation itself, to a depth that made it scarcely worthy of the name of a language in comparison with the purer speech of the north or her brilliant rival, French. Soon Flemish was little more than a dialect, debased by lack of solid literature, by lack of rule and regulation or scientific study. It became the language of the peasant and the small burghers, despised by the cultivated, and its very existence menaced by the introduction of debased French. Flanders and Brabant had to live on a few crumbs that fell from the richly provided table of the north, and only such crumbs as were suitable for an exclusively Catholic population.

Flemish art had a period of brilliancy in Peter Paul Rubens, who permanently settled at Antwerp in 1608. For thirty-two years this truly Flemish painter wrought at Antwerp,[1] leaving more than fifteen hundred known works. Great artist, talented draughtsman, engraver, and etcher at the same time, he formed a remarkable school of versatile artists who kept up the reputation of Flemish art even at a period when that of the north began to surpass it. His equal and pupil, the Antwerp Anthony Van Dyck, the greatest portrait painter of his age, only worked a short time in his native city. In his youth he wandered through Italy and France, and later was established at the court of Charles I. in England. Besides Rubens, there lived at Antwerp the famous " velvety " Brueghel, painter of landscapes, animals, genre pieces, an engraver of note, in high favour with the archdukes, and head of an important school. Under the leadership of these two masters many artists were developed,—the artists Van Baalen, Vrancx, Franken, Seghers, Rombouts, Jordaens, Neeffs, the engraver Wierix, and others, who, through them, were connected with the older Flemish schools from the middle of the sixteenth century,[2] whose kin they are—Catholic realists in the old Flemish fashion, but coming gradually under the influence of the art schools of the north.

The keen interest of Albert and Isabella in art made Rubens and his pupils create many a masterpiece, and the palaces at Brussels, Tervueren, and Mariemont remind one, in this regard at least, of the old dwellings of the Burgundian princes,—art patrons, like those whose footsteps they wished to follow. But these few exceptions

[1] His father did not die until 1587. See p. 58.
[2] Compare for all, Van Vloten, *Nederlands Schilderkunst*, p. 97 *et seq.*

to swing their swift wings through the air. In Zealand, Walcheren alone made any show. Middelburg could compete with the Holland cities in commercial enterprise; the harbours of Flushing, of Arnemuiden, and of Veere were filled with trading and fishing craft, and held their own with the Holland ports across the Y.

The extensive draining and diking operations undertaken at this time in these two provinces were also evidences of their prosperity.[1] A fertile clay bottom was redeemed from the old peat bogs, and furnished land for the increased population which flocked thither. Thus an outlet was provided, to the great advantage of the little cities Alkmaar, Purmerend, and Edam. But there still raged on the borders of the present north and south Holland the grim water-wolf. Haarlem Lake was at that time united to three other lakes in the neighbourhood, together covering about 15,000 acres, and, continually overflowing the outlying parts of Rhine- and Amstelland, was a menace to the whole region. The renowned "mill maker and engineer," Jan Adriaansz. Leeghwater, from the Rijp, was summoned as an expert. He had done excellent service at the impoldering of other meres at home and abroad, at Bordeaux and Metz, and as far east as Holstein, and perceived that this sheet of water was steadily encroaching on the land. It had increased three and a half times in a century, and threatened the existence of Amsterdam, Leyden, and Haarlem.[2]

Thousands of acres, for the most part of excellent ground, were made arable. At about 1640, the reclaimed land in Holland and Zealand reached 80,000 acres, sowed in part with rye, wheat, barley, oats, buckwheat, beans, peas, etc., in part grazed by thousands of cattle, and in

---

[1] In 1597 the Zype was embanked, in 1610 the Beemster ground drained, in 1622 the Purmer ground, etc.

[2] These and other details are taken from Leeghwater's *Haarlemmermeer boek*, 1641.

more than 100,000 inhabitants, and was still increasing, he calls " the greatest commercial city of Christendom," whence "forty ships" were regularly on the route to India, and whence, too, twice a year fleets of 800 ships sailed to the Baltic, apart from the numerous freight transports to the English, French, Spanish, German, and Italian coasts, as far as the Levant.   And besides Amsterdam, other cities of Holland began to show a high state of prosperity.   Rotterdam gradually became the second commercial city of the provinces, also as a result of Antwerp's decline.   Dordrecht flourished from her renewed wood and wine trade along the Rhine and to France. Leyden became again a centre of the cloth industry, owing to the steadily increasing stream of Walloon and Flemish immigrants.   Haarlem, Delft, Gouda, all developed manufactures, while, too, they became industrial centres of great importance.   Nearly all the cities were obliged at this period to extend their walls and increase their territories, while their population reached a figure of twenty, thirty, forty thousand souls and more, to the amazement of the stranger, who had seen nowhere else in the world so many flourishing cities in so small a space.[1]   The total population of Holland can be estimated without exaggeration at 600,000 souls,[2] almost half of that of the seven provinces together, which did not reach two millions at the end of the eighteenth century.   In North Holland, across the Y, the old country town, Alkmaar, though prosperous in the midst of a well-to-do peasant population, was surpassed by the seaports Enkhuizen and Hoorn, outposts, as it were, of mighty Amsterdam, and flourishing from shipbuilding, fishery, and commerce. Shipbuilding made villages such as those on the Zaan the centres of a lively industry, where from the end of the sixteenth century the numerous saw- and oil-mills began

[1] Trevisano, *Bijdr. en Med.*, *Hist. Gen.*, p. 408.
[2] Compare Fruin, *Tien Jaren*, 4th edition, p. 206, note 6.

to swing their swift wings through the air.   In Zealand, Walcheren alone made any show.   Middelburg could compete with the Holland cities in commercial enterprise; the harbours of Flushing, of Arnemuiden, and of Veere were filled with trading and fishing craft, and held their own with the Holland ports across the Y.

The extensive draining and diking operations under-taken at this time in these two provinces were also evid-ences of their prosperity.[1]   A fertile clay bottom was redeemed from the old peat bogs, and furnished land for the increased population which flocked thither.   Thus an outlet was provided, to the great advantage of the little cities Alkmaar, Purmerend, and Edam.   But there still raged on the borders of the present north and south Hol-land the grim water-wolf.   Haarlem Lake was at that time united to three other lakes in the neighbourhood, together covering about 15,000 acres, and, continually overflowing the outlying parts of Rhine- and Amstelland, was a menace to the whole region.   The renowned " mill maker and engineer," Jan Adriaansz. Leeghwater, from the Rijp, was summoned as an expert.   He had done ex-cellent service at the impoldering of other meres at home and abroad, at Bordeaux and Metz, and as far east as Holstein, and perceived that this sheet of water was steadily encroaching on the land.   It had increased three and a half times in a century, and threatened the exist-ence of Amsterdam, Leyden, and Haarlem.[2]

Thousands of acres, for the most part of excellent ground, were made arable.   At about 1640, the reclaimed land in Holland and Zealand reached 80,000 acres, sowed in part with rye, wheat, barley, oats, buckwheat, beans, peas, etc., in part grazed by thousands of cattle, and in

[1] In 1597 the Zype was embanked, in 1610 the Beemster ground drained, in 1622 the Purmer ground, etc.

[2] These and other details are taken from Leeghwater's *Haarlemmermeer boek*, 1641.

part covered by orchards. The Beemster alone brought in 250,000 florins clear profit annually. Hundreds of peasants found good subsistence there and on the other polders. The villages doubled in compass, the little cities and ports in the neighbourhood flourished. Watermills were seen everywhere in the land that had known nothing of the works 175 years previously.

In Zealand and on the South Holland islands where the great flood of 1570 had wrought dreadful devastation, and the condition of warfare of the following years had left little opportunity for the restoration of the damage, diking operations were again in full swing by the year 1580, after the expulsion of the Spaniards. Gradually the inundated territories upon the islands in the mouths of the Meuse and the Scheldt emerged from the flood. The island of Dordrecht was little more than the city until it was extended by dikes in 1589. Willemstad rose between the low-lying lands, and many an acre was gained by the Moerdijk. After 1614, Schouwen and Duive-land began gradually to approach each other, and many other important reclamations were made.

Relations between sea and land changed unceasingly, and the ancient foe was held at bay to the great profit of agriculture and of cattle-breeding, the chief industries of the Holland and Zealand polder peasant. In the neigh-bourhood of Leyden and in the Westland there was more tillage, while around Gouda nurseries flourished.

Holland and Zealand had thus been able to develop their own resources for about twenty years, protected from actual hostilities by the other provinces. Then, too, they enjoyed the profits of commercial relations with the world, a trade that soon surpassed agriculture and manufacture in importance.

Up to 1609, the condition of the East India Company remained very precarious. After the Truce, thanks to the secret stipulations regarding India trade, the directors began to extend their activities. At the end of 1610, Pieter Both was appointed head of the council of India on the recommendation of the directors. He succeeded in greatly improving the coöperation between the Indian offices. In 1614, Jan Pieterszoon Coen had become director-general of all the offices and member of the council. He had already gained experience in Indian affairs, as he had been bookkeeper-general and head of the important bureaux at Bantam and Jacatra. The head-quarters of Netherland authority gradually became fixed on West Java. Meanwhile a bitter contest was constantly going on with the English, now the most dangerous rivals of the Netherlanders in the Eastern seas. Spanish and Portuguese both lost ground. Coen considered that the expulsion of the English was necessary to confirm Nether-land authority in the archipelago, and therewith the establishment of the company's monopoly. He was resolved not to rest until that goal was attained, and was only hampered in his action by the timidity of the direc-tors at home who were afraid of risking their money. They urged, not unjustly, that the company was not designed to create an Indian realm under Netherland sovereignty. Its purpose was to acquire wealth, as the directors tried to impress upon their officials, roundly as well as in covert terms; they did not fully understand that, in the existing circumstances, conquest was the in-dispensable condition of profit. They regarded Coen's efforts as evidences of the desire for power and authority on the part of an official really their subordinate, although virtually very independent.[1] Dividends were their war-cry. Such dividends then actually resulting from the company's repeated gains were also paid from 1610–11.[2]

[1] See Heeres's article, "Compagnie," in the *Encyclopaedie van Nederl. Indie.*

[2] Klerk de Reus, *Geschichtlicher Ueberblick*, p. 178 *et seq.*

There were earlier distributions from the profits of the fleets before 1602, which were properly to the advantage of the old companies, not to that of the shareholders in the new association.

The payments of 1610–11 amounted in products and money to not less than 162 per cent. These enormous payments, added to the almost as great joint dividends from the above-mentioned earlier gains already acquired at that time, greatly improved the company's credit; more than 30 per cent. annually was paid out to the shareholders, and although no new distribution was to be expected until 1620, the shares soon rose, after some uncertainty, to 300 per cent. The company had disappointed the hope of her numerous home and foreign enemies for ever, and had become one of the pillars of the commercial prosperity of the Netherland provinces.

The States-General protected it against its enemies. The enterprising Isaac Lemaire, who, in 1609, making use of an issue of shares, attempted to depress the prices by throwing suddenly a great number on the market, and was imitated by other speculators, found himself checked in his projects by an edict of the States-General, issued at the request of the directors, and although " freedom of trade "[1] prevented the actual publication of the edict, he was forced to leave Amsterdam and to abandon his plans for the time being. He looked round for other pathways of commerce and founded an " Australian " Company. He hoped by the discovery of a new route to India, around South America, to evade the conditions of the octroi of the East India Company, and at the same time to open up a new realm to commerce—the great unknown Southland, or Australia. In 1615, his son Jacques sailed with two ships and discovered, south of the strait of Magellan, the strait named after him, and Cape Horn. He actually reached the Moluccas

[1] L. Aitzema, *Saken van Staet en Oorlogh*, i., p. 261. 's Gravenhage, 1669.

by this route, but his ships and cargoes were detained by Coen. Young Lemaire died on the homeward voyage from disappointment; his father brought a suit before the high council of Holland against the company regarding the seizure of the ships, which he won, but the company had attained its end, and its opponent, disheartened by the injury he had suffered, died in loneliness at Egmont.

The fate of Lemaire was that of Usselincx, who fought unceasingly for the establishment of a West India Company. The plan was opposed by the East India Company from fear that it might affect their monopoly, and by Oldenbarnevelt, who dreaded lest new difficulties might arise with Spain.[1] When the truce was concluded, Usselincx saw that the matter could not be pushed, and invested his money in the reclamation of the Beemster. But he was too restless to submit to defeat. Soon he took up the subject again and carried it so far by 1614 that the Estates of Holland finally gave ear to his representations. But the opposition of Oldenbarnevelt and the East India Company again caused the failure of his plans, and Usselincx went back to the Beemster, where he lost his whole fortune before the polder brought returns, and became bankrupt. Nevertheless he attempted to realise his cherished plan on a more ambitious scale than at first in connection with emigration to fertile Guiana and the offer of help against Spain to the natives of the silver-bearing lands of Chili and Peru. Neither the Estates of Holland nor the States-General were inclined to aid these plans for the formation of a new colonial empire, and Oldenbarnevelt, prudent statesman and little inclined to adventure, showed a constantly decreasing sympathy for the schemer, who threatened to endanger his peaceful policy towards Spain by new enterprises in Spain's richest colonies.

And not alone Usselincx had turned his attention to

[1] Compare Van Rees, *Gesch. der Staathuishoudkunde*, ii., p. 96.

the West, but the East India Company itself was continually seeking a shorter way to India by way of the
Western hemisphere.   The sturdy English seaman, Hudson, undertook, in the service of the company, a voyage
to North America in 1609, in order to look for a north-
west passage to East India, a plan that failed for the
time, but which attracted attention to the American
coasts and excited many a new voyager of discovery.
In Guiana, too, and in the Antilles, even before 1609,
Netherland ships made their appearance to obtain to-
bacco, sugar, coloured wood, etc., in return for which
they carried African blacks for the plantations, and manufactures,—spoons, forks, knives, wines, cheese, butter.
Moucheron and others, inspired by Usselincx, gained large
profits there.   Enterprising merchants tried to establish
colonies (1613) on the wild coast of Guiana, the first
beginnings of a settlement in Essequibo and Berbice.[1]
The publication of a placard of the States-General in
1614, wherein a forty years' commercial monopoly in the
localities was offered to those who should discover '' any
new passages, ports, lands, or localities,'' aroused a still
greater zeal of discovery in the West.   A Company of
New Netherland was founded.   This established Fort
Nassau and another fort on the island of Manhattan at
the mouth of the Hudson, while the American coast was
further explored, and the voyages thither continually
increased.[2]

Voyages were made, too, to Brazil and Guinea in ships
of the Holland and Zealand shipowners, who banded
themselves into companies and had already before the
Truce supplied more than two hundred ships, which
brought rich cargoes of wood, ivory, gold, gum, salt, and

[1] Netscher, *Geschiedenis van de Kolonien Essequibo, Demerary, and Berbice*, p. 30.   's Gravenhage, 1888.
[2] Compare Berg van Dussen Muilkerk, *Bijdragen tot de geschiedenis onzer
kolonisatie in Noord-Amerika*.   De Gids, 1848.

other products of these coasts,[1] purchased there for knives, spoons, linen, and so-called Nuremberg wares. The salt trade, so important for fishery, kept thousands of craft and thousands of hands busy, to the great profit of Enkhuizen and other places. Now that Portugal was in Spanish hands, the west coast of Africa, where salt could be easily obtained, became the chief headquarters of this industry, which was shared even by the natives.

Among the little short-lived companies established at that time, the North Company was conspicuous. The Netherlanders, who had first appeared in the northern ice seas at the end of the sixteenth century, began in 1612 to devote themselves to whale fishery, undertaken by the English a few years previously.[2] Hot quarrels ensued between the English Muscovite Company, which held the monopoly from their government, and the Holland shipowners; the Hollanders were at last driven out with force, and, for self-preservation, formed a Northern, or Greenland Company, which obtained a charter in 1614. They speedily had a score of well-armed ships, each provided with two sloops, and proceeded to exploit this new branch of industry. This Northern Company, especially after its consolidation (1622) with a couple of little companies of the same kind, was really a prototype of the great " trusts " of to-day. The aim was to destroy competition by mutual coöperation, and then, by combined regulation of production and prices, to control the market of supply completely. Care was taken to maintain the independence of the parties both in the management and in commercial details, while the division of the profits was made according to the capital of the firms.[3] They built at

[1] De Jonge, *Opkomst*, i., p. 40.

[2] S. Muller, *Geschiedenis der Noordsche Compagnie*, p. 72. Utrecht, 1874.

[3] S. Muller, *Sociaal Weekblad*, January 9 and 16, 1897 ; Kernkamp, in *Bijdr. en Meded. Hist. Gen.*, vol. xix., p. 265.

Spitzbergen their own huts for the blubber boiling, where the whalers and other sailors pitched their tents in the season, so that a regular village, Smeerenburg, sprang up, which was deserted on their departure.   The company made their interests so important that the States-General devoted several warships to their protection; walrus ivory, the fat of whales, walruses, and seals, the skins of the latter, train-oil, and whalebone, all became important articles of commerce.   Not only were trade and manufacture stimulated, but science, too, as every year new discoveries were made in these inhospitable and little-known regions.   Thus Holland enterprise was in every corner where valuable products were to be found or where purchasers waited for their wares.   A merry song[1] describing the ubiquitous character of the Hollanders and Zealanders was heard in many a strange place when the travellers met in foreign lands.   They outshone their old Hanse rivals.   For every twenty Hanse ships a thousand Netherland craft passed through the sound.   Coasting trips were frequent in addition to the more lengthy voyages.   One Cornelis Haga can be considered the founder of direct trade to the Levant. He won his spurs as diplomate by negotiations with the Swedish court, took some steps towards an alliance with Russia, and was sent (1611) by the States to Constantinople, where he concluded a commercial treaty, notwithstanding the opposition of his French and Venetian rivals.   This opened the way for Dutch merchants and freed them from the need of French protection hitherto needful in that quarter.[2]   A survey of the shipping of this period, based on a rough estimate of the

[1] "Daer vindt men 'tsij oock op wat ree
D'Hollander end' de Zeeuw.
Sij loopen door de woeste zee
Als door de bosch de leeuw," etc.
[2] Compare Chapter ix.

time,[1] will give some idea of the extent of Netherland shipping.

Destination	Number of Ships	Tons Burden	Crew
Baltic	3,000	300,000	38,000
Archangel	20	2,400	560
Denmark and Norway	500	45,000	10,000
Spain	2,000	200,000	50,000
Italy	600	78,000	15,000
Coasting voyages [2]	10,000	268,000	40,000
Canary Isles	60	4,000	1,320
Barbary	50	4,000	1,200
Guinea	10	1,250	400
St. Thomas	10	1,000	250
Angola	8	800	200
Brazil	15	1,500	375
S. Domingo	6	450	120
East Indies	7	4,200	2,100
China	3	600	300
Total	16,289	911,200	159,825 [3]

It is evident that with such a development of world-wide commerce the condition of exchange could not remain in the same state as it was in the previous century.

In the very beginning of the seventeenth century commercial intercourse suffered from the same inconveniences of currency which obtained in the later Middle Ages.[4] Foreign coins were current at changing values, the good at high rates of exchange regulated in the mint ordinances, the bad, in spite of all stipulations to the contrary.[5] At

[1] *Bijdr. en Med., Hist. Gen.*, vol. xix., p. 15 *et seq.*

[2] To the coasts of France, Germany, Spain, Portugal, and Flanders, carried on with little ships called smacks.

[3] In comparison with note, p. 323, this total is far too high, as evidently several items, such as Spain, Denmark, and Norway, are counted again under coasting voyages. For details compare *Bijdr. en Med., Hist. Gen.* 12,000 ships with 60,000 tons burden, manned by 100,000 men, is not too low an estimate.

[4] Compare Part II., p. 340.

[5] Mees, *Proeve eener geschiedenis van het bankwezen in Nederland*, p. 1, etc. Rotterdam, 1838.

the banks of the exchangers in the various cities, after Leicester's Ordinance of 1586, issued by the generals of the mint at the instance of the city governments, were "manuals for money-changers for instruction on mint ordinances," according to which they were compelled to change coins or bullion.   Within a fixed term they were obliged to turn over what they had received to the provincial mint.   The attempts made by Maximilian, by Charles V., and by Philip II. to improve Netherland coinage all failed.   In 1586, Leicester's ordinance enforced article XII. of the union of Utrecht, which provided for conformity with the other provinces ' in the matter of coinage, but the Netherland real (2.50 guilders), then established as an imperial coin, simply increased the coins in circulation, like the later imperial dollar (2.40 guilders) and the lion dollar (1.90 guilders).   The so-called imperial cities of the eastern provinces troubled themselves little about the general regulations, and coined at will, while the provincial coinage was in vogue elsewhere.   The mint ordinances of the Estates of Holland (1603) and of the States-General (1606) rest upon exactly the same theories as those of Maximilian and his successors.   It is therefore not surprising that we find continuous complaints on the subject, abuses of money-changers and goldsmiths, who were in the habit of driving a trade in coins.   Attempts to regulate this failed, too, in Amsterdam, where the need was great.   The depreciation of the guilder of 396.6 azen [1] fine silver in 1542 to 225.2 in 1606 is a proof of the degeneration in the currency.

The government vainly tried to prevent all trading in money.   In 1608 the Amsterdam government, anxious about the increasing confusion and the rise in value of certain coins, threw the whole blame on the ruinous operations of the bankers, and forbade their entire

[1] The ass was a small weight equivalent to about ⅜ grain.

business by a statute which had to be revised a fortnight later, as it was evident that commerce could not dispense with these middlemen. At the same time all transactions in bills of exchange and bonds, introduced from Antwerp at the end of the sixteenth century, were prohibited. Cash alone was legal for any payment. This, too, had to be rescinded, for bills of exchange had been adopted as medium of payment and of credit. Other methods of regulating the medium of exchange were then made the subject of investigation for a couple of years.[1]

After the fall of Antwerp a commercial bourse had been established at Amsterdam. It was held first in the open air on the New Bridge, or in rainy weather in the church, but after 1613 in a fine new building constructed by Hendrik de Keyser.[2] Side by side with this a commercial bank came into existence, developed from the bank of exchange established in 1609. This bank was intended to replace all offices and banks of the kind. There, and there alone, could money be legally exchanged for other coin, and bullion be received and paid for by means of money orders on the bank commissioners, either by transfer of a sum of money to another name or by cash payments. In such payments no one could give higher " assignments " or money orders on the bank than his own deposit or his credit at the bank amounted to. The government favored the development of its bank of exchange into brokerage by guaranteeing all money brought in and by forbidding all competition, finally by making all bills of exchange on Amsterdam payable there alone when they amounted to six hundred guilders and over. All city exchanges, all brokers' offices, outside the great city bank, were strictly forbidden, while, for the

[1] Mees, p. 37 *et seq.*
[2] Ehrenberg, *Die Fugger* (Jena, 1896), ii., p. 291 ; Wagenaar, *Amsterdam*, iv., p. 89; P. L. Muller, *Onze Gouden Eeuw* (Leyden, 1897–98), i., p. 276.

convenience of the merchant in the city, outside receivers of the bank were established, who had to account for their receipts within three days.   Neither private changers nor brokers could be wholly suppressed, but the Amsterdam bank, guaranteed by the government, soon became the chief institution of credit—a powerful ally to Amsterdam commerce.   The deposits in the bank, aggregating a million in 1609, amounted to four millions by 1626.[1] The confusion in the coinage was not avoided by the establishment of this exchange bank.   More radical measures were needed for that.   But the bank was useful to the merchants who had to pay their debts in good specie, since they could be sure of obtaining that from the bank, which was provided only with good coin and bullion appraised officially.

The old branches of manufacture, cloth-making, beer-brewing, and others, which had existed from the fourteenth century, were still in being and prominent ; beer was still the ordinary drink among the people, and cloth manufacture gained by the emigration of many workmen from Flanders and Brabant, especially to Leyden, Amsterdam, Haarlem, and Delft.   The industry remained confined, as previously, by the guild regulations concerning tools, wages, number of workmen, quality, prices, etc.   Small establishments with a couple of workmen were the rule; the halls[2] for the various articles had to maintain a supervision on manufacture and sale.[3]

In addition to the ancient manufactures and a few others, like tile-making, which began to develop at this period in Utrecht and Delft, lace-making at Dor-

[1] Mees, p. 61.
[2] Used for the guilds. Hall-mark means the stamp of approval.
[3] Compare Part II., pp. 3, 497, and 510.   Pringsheim, *B.iträge sur wissenschaftlichen Entwickelungsgeschichte der Vereinigten Niederlande*, (Schmoller's *Forschungen*, x. 3), p. 29.

drecht, the gobelin industry, etc., new trades rose in connection with the shipping: shipbuilding came to the fore on all sides; sawmills flourished on the Zaan; sail-making and rope-making kept many hands busy in all the ports and far inland, too; smithies and metal foundries worked on a large scale; the waterland villages Jisp and Wormer were the centres of biscuit manufacture for ship provender; the salting of provisions for the same purpose, salt trade in general for the herring, the very packing of the articles, gave a subsistence to thousands; masses of petty industries all sprang from various necessities of navigation.

According to Oldenbarnevelt, the herring fishery was still the chief means of existence of " many thousand households in the land, and exercised with great risks and slight recompense, as I have good reason to know." [1] According to the States themselves, it was " one of the chief mines of the United Netherlands." The number of those subsisting upon fishery in Holland and Zealand was reckoned at from 50,000 to 60,000, 40,000 of whom were sailors; in the whole republic at about double that number.[2] In 1601, 1500 doggers sailed from Holland and Zealand to the herring fishery,[3] four times as many as half a century earlier. Not only the ports, but also little inland towns, like Oudewater and Woerden, shared in the profits of the herring fishery[4] by their rope-making, sail-making, etc.

[1] Minutes, Oldenbarnevelt, October 6, 1616, Royal Archives.

[2] Muller, *Mare Clausum*, p. 4; Fruin, *Tien Jaren*, p. 206; *Bijdr. en Med., Hist. Gen.*, xix., p. 14.

[3] Van Meteren, p. 437.

[4] It must be remembered that these numbers are as a rule much too high. For example, the fishers and boats mentioned under the head of herring fishery are also included under cod fishers, etc. An estimate of 3000 ships and 35,000 to 40,000 fishers is probably not far from the truth. Compare *Bijdr. en Med., Hist. Gen.*, xix., p. 14. Semeyns, in his brochure, *Eene*

Both the commerce and fishery of Holland and Zealand were objects of jealousy to the competing English. The exaggerated figures which famous voyagers and economists like Walter Raleigh placed before their fellow-countrymen at this time, to warn them against the dreaded Hollanders, are very interesting. The Netherlanders, or rather more truly, the Hollanders, were " masters of the sea," and England's aim was to wrest that mastery from them. This was the reason why haughty Albion at this period brought anew upon the *tapis* their old demand of the *Dominium Maris*, the sovereignty over the waters around the English and Scottish coasts, and formulated it in clearer terms than before.[1] In the Middle Ages this sovereignty had only been applied to the Channel, and confined to the universally acknowledged right of all nations situated on the sea to the immediate surroundings as far as one hundred miles out from the shore, but in later years the English government began to make claims to the North Sea, the terrein of the Holland fisheries, which extended from the Faroë Islands as far as off Yarmouth. The publication of De Groot's *Mare Liberum*, in 1609, really written with the purpose of proving the right of the Hollanders to navigation to India, as against Portuguese pretensions,[2] furnished the Hollanders with good arguments against these English claims, and gave rise to a fierce war on paper.

The interests involved were very important; not only questions of commerce and manufacture, but also those of state revenues dependent in great part upon them. Our above-mentioned informant reckoned that the revenues from the convoys and permits on marine commerce

corte visscherye in Hollandt (1640), says that Holland alone had 700 large boats of 16 tonnage, of which Enkhuizen alone had 400 to 500, besides 170 smaller ones of 7 or 8 tons for fishing on the Zuyder Zee. He reckons those who subsisted on fishing at about 100,000.

[1] Compare Muller, *Mare Clausum*, Introduction.
[2] Fruin, De Gids, iv., p. 25. 1868.

and fishery from which the state profited, could be estimated at not less than 26,000,000 and 5,000,000 guilders
respectively, while the sum needed for protection by warships, to be subtracted from the profits, amounted to
about 3,000,000 guilders—figures, however, which are
undoubtedly far too high.   Each one of the 80 warships
—of which 25 were employed against the Dunkirkers,
20 to protect the fishery, 8 for guarding the Channel,
10 for the Baltic, 9 for watching the French and Spanish
coasts, 8 for the coasts of Denmark and Norway—cost,
according to this statement, 3000 guilders monthly.[1]

Holland fishery on the English coast was guaranteed[2]
by old treaties that dated back to the thirteenth and fourteenth centuries, and confirmed in its rights of free exercise of the trade by the *Groot-Entrecours* of 1496, which
regulated the commercial relations of the Netherlands
with England; fishing along the Scottish coast did not
rest on similar agreements, although the very silence
about the fishery right can be adduced as an argument
for the complete freedom of the industry.[3]   At the end
of the sixteenth century English fishery began to develop,
and quarrels ensued between English and foreign fishers,
especially as the more numerous Hollanders gained the
upper hand from time to time, and as a result the English
fishery began to deteriorate.   James I., urged by jurists
and economists, and especially by the injured seaports,
issued a placard (May, 1609) forbidding the fishery along
his coasts and in his waters to foreigners, unless they paid
a tax for the privilege.   This decision excited a great
commotion in the Netherlands; complaints, protests,
and diplomatic discussions resulted.   In the following
year a considerable embassy went to England in order to
defend one of the greatest native interests against the

[1] *Bijdr. en Med., Hist. Gen.*, xix., p. 14 *et seq.*
[2] Muller, p. 26 ; compare Part II., p. 345.
[3] Muller, p. 36.

sinister interpretations of the ancient treaties.   They did succeed in suspending the placard, owing to the difficulties of the then existing political conditions, which forced James into relations with the States, but Raleigh's remonstrances and Gentleman's and Welwod's arguments against De Groot's theories aroused public opinion in England, and fixed attention on the *Dominium Maris.* Popular pamphlets, like the famous *Trade's Increase,* wherein English commerce and fishery and the growing competition were pictured,[1] added their weight; and in June, 1616, James returned to his original decision: a toll was suddenly exacted from all the fishermen, and, at the beginning, paid without much difficulty to the collectors who appeared in the Netherland fleet, until a couple of Holland convoys drove them off, an act that excited great bitterness in England.

In the following year matters became worse: the fishermen, one and all, refused to pay the tax.   The royal officials charged with collecting it were attacked and carried to Holland.   Violent quarrels, destruction of fish-nets, and finally, actual outbreaks between fishermen of Netherland, English, and Scotch nationality ensued, and it was only with great difficulty that an open breach was avoided between England and the States.   A new embassy (1618) attempted to settle the continuous differences in general and especially those concerning the Northern and East India Companies.   About the so-called " great," or herring fishery, the cloth trade, etc., there was much discussion, but the matter was checked for the time being on account of the threatening state of provincial affairs, until the difficulties should be past and a renewal of the ancient treaties could prevail.   A compromise was made in regard to the East India Company.   Thus the matter of the fishery remained at a standstill, although it was hardly to be expected that English claims were definitely silenced.

[1] See Muller, Introduction.

It must be remembered that these foregoing statements can be applied to Holland and Zealand alone. Activity in trade was confined to them. Not only the East India Company, but all the petty trading monopolies had their headquarters there, and there found by far the major part of the needful capital. The trades and industries dependent upon this commerce and the fishery naturally were there. Friesland is the only one of the other provinces which occasionally reaped advantages from the industries and the trade plied with Terschelling, Ameland, and Schiermonnikoog. It contributed a fairly numerous contingent for the manning of the trading craft, and took some part in the fishery. Holland and Zealand, containing about half the whole number of inhabitants in the united provinces, and paying seventy per cent. of the taxes, thus, not unnaturally, assumed a somewhat dominant attitude in the state.

This prosperity of Holland and Zealand did, however, undoubtedly exercise an indirect influence to the good of the other provinces. The interests of the maritime provinces, of maritime commerce, and industrial branches therewith involved, were usually taken into chief consideration in the common state, but the period of peace and quiet enjoyed by the other provinces after Prince Maurice's great campaigns gave them, too, an opportunity to recuperate from the condition of decay to which the long-enduring warfare had reduced them. The river commerce of the cities on the Rhine, Waal, and Yssel began to revive; the fields were again tilled regularly; cattle-breeding could again be pursued with good result in Friesland and Groningen. Still the prosperity of the country provinces from Utrecht to Groningen could not be compared with that in Holland and Zealand. States-Flanders and States-Brabant were so reduced they had to submit to be governed like conquered provinces.

Horses, butter, and cheese were exported from

Friesland, and there was some slight commercial exchange between Amsterdam and the cities on the Zuyder Zee, but as a rule the cities of the country provinces became mere local market-places, or the seats of garrisons. Occasionally some industry, like peat - digging, was developed, but as a rule they remained stationary in enterprise and in population. The old mediæval life went on within their walls, only slightly enriched by newer ideas, and the citizens participated little in the great economic or intellectual movements in which Holland and Zealand played a part.

From about 1590, intellectual life began to revive in the two commercial provinces. Art, letters, and science made Holland a focus of intellectual development. In the early years of the century, to be sure, the university of Louvain, the episcopal court of Philip of Burgundy at Wijk near Duurstede, Utrecht itself, and such cities as Groningen, Deventer, and Zwolle, under the leadership of cultivated clergy and laymen, ranked as centres of active intellectual life; as the century drew to a close it was the prosperous cities of rich Holland, where the citizens themselves became interested in cultivation and tried to foster it, emancipated from ecclesiastical guardianship, freeing themselves, too, from the swaddling bands of the rhetorician or rousing them to a new life. The use of the vernacular was developed, and Latin was left more and more to learned circles. To be sure, the " world wonder," young De Groot, still wrote his numerous scientific works in classic Latin, the volapuk of science, —his *Mare Liberum* (1609), his *De jure belli ac pacis* (1613), his classical studies, his *Tragœdiæ sacræ*, his *Poemata* (1617), his later published *Annales;* but in addition there was a series of his polemical writings in the vernacular, his famous Introduction to Holland Law (*Inleidinghe tot de Hollandsche Rechts-geleerdheid*) proving that this science, too, could be handled in the language which he proudly names " our Dutch mother tongue." [1] Emmius, Boxhornius, Meursius, and Baudius still wrote their historical works in Latin, but Baudartius in his important work about the Truce, followed the example set (c. 1600) by Bor, Van Meteren, and Van Reyd of presenting history in the vernacular. And the burghers read the tales of their forefathers with avidity, though the dry style of the good Utrecht Bor, with his laborious incorporation of numerous and important documents into the text, was, naturally, less popular than the clever narration of the Antwerp antiquarian or the brilliant brevity of Van Reyd. This latter was in the service of William Louis, and was thus initiated into many secrets.

The foundation laid by Coornhert and Marnix for Netherland prose was greatly strengthened by the scientific philological studies of Kiliaen in his famous *Etymologicon Theutonicæ Linguæ* (1583), and Plantijn's busy press brought to light various other works of the same nature whereby the knowledge of the rich vocabulary of the Dutch tongue was greatly enriched.

From Antwerp this movement in scientific philological speech spread to Amsterdam, where the ancient Chamber, *In Liefde Bloeyende*, established in 1584 as a result of the study of its members under the direction of Hendrik Laurentsz. Spieghel and the supervision of Coornhert, published a *Kort begrip leerende recht Duidts-spreken*, with the intention " of bringing their mother tongue again to her ancient honour," and to attain the " improvement of our Netherland speech " by cleansing it from the Burgundian stains of " the useless patches and foul embellishments." Also among the Latin-writing and -speaking scholars in the national university at Leyden, some attention was paid to the neglected vernacular, and although they did not yet enjoy knowledge in their native tongue,

[1] From the dedication to his children.

still a learned man like Daniel Heinsius no longer considered it beneath him to publish a collection of *Neder-duytsche Poemata* (1616) in conjunction with his Latin, while he had already issued a few of them in separate collections.[1]

Amsterdam became the centre of a school of Netherland prose and Netherland poetry. Roemer Visscher, the versatile merchant whose hospitable home was thronged by " painters, artists, singers, and poets," collected a considerable circle about him, wherein youthful talents like Coster and Brederoo, the knight Hooft and " sinjeur " Vondel, nobles and burghers, were spurred to action by the example of the lively Roemer, a so-called second Martial, and his two gifted daughters. Visscher's talented *Zinnepoppen* (1614) was more gain to the language than to the poetry. In his *Hertspieghel* (1618) Spieghel followed Coornhert's philosophical tendency, and showing real affection for " our tongue." At Amsterdam, " on whose stage a lost art again lived and breathed," as the learned Leyden prose writer and poet, Peter Schrijver, sang, the tone was given by the Rhetoric Chamber, the Old Chamber to which the singers belonged. The *Nieuwen Lusthof*, a song-book printed in 1602,[2] collected a number of the verses of the members. The popularity of the book is shown by five editions in a few years, while there were similar collections like *Den Bloemhof* (1610) and *Apollo* (1615).

At the time of the Truce there flourished at Amsterdam Dr. Samuel Coster and Gerbrand Adriaensz. Brederoo. The latter was a passionate love singer in his *Boertigh, amoreus en aandachtigh Liedtboeck* (1622), the poet of the best dramatic popular poetry of the period, of the *Moortje* (1615) and *De Spaensche Brabander* (1617), of

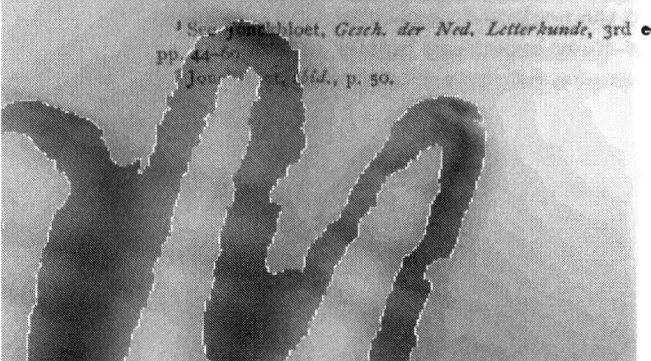

[1] See Jonckbloet, *Gesch. der Ned. Letterkunde*, 3rd edition (1881), iii., pp. 44-50.

[2] Jonckbloet, *ibid.*, p. 50.

various rough but witty *kluchten;* the former was a scholar of note, who soon turned to tragedy. The Old Chamber also included young Hooft and young Vondel in their early years. Hooft, the burgomaster's son, in 1609 drost of Muiden, was soon known as head of the poets, leader of the Chamber, and of a throng of poets, writers, artists, and scholars who collected at his castle of Muiden, especially after Visscher's death. Vondel, the burgher youth, who had outgrown his rank by dint of his genius, was graciously received in this circle, to which also Reael, Plemp, and others be-longed. It seems that the works of many of them were very suggestive of those of the old rhetoricians, al-though the individuality of the poets is evident, an important deviation from the old coöperation without individual manifestation.[1]

A strife, excited by the talented but vain and ambitious Antwerper, Theodore Rodenburg, knight and former di-plomate, distinguished, and arrogant towards the Amster-dam citizens, came to a crisis after 1614, and disturbed the friendly feeling between the leading members of the Amsterdam Chambers of Rhetoric. Cousin of Spieghel, Rodenburg had been a former member of the Old Cham-ber. On his return from a diplomatic embassy to Spain, where he won his knighthood, he reappeared in the Chamber and played an important part both on account of his rank and his services in literature. His works were more to the taste of the Brabant Chamber, founded by Flemish and Brabant immigrants, which existed alongside of the Old from 1585, than to that of the Amsterdammers proper. Coster and Brederoo were his bitter opponents, and the pugnacious Antwerper was not slow in reply. He criticised their writings pitilessly, although less roughly, in more polished form, than they did his. The

[1] See Kalff, *Literatuur en tooneel te Amsterdam in de seventiende eeuw,* p. 63. Haarlem, 1896.

Old Chamber divided gradually into two parties, and
so high ran the strife that Coster in 1617 carried out a
plan conceived earlier and founded a new Parnassus, the
Netherland Academy, the *Byekorf*, which was intended
to fulfil the aim of the Old Chamber more energetically than the latter had done of late, according to the
opinion of its founders.   And the New Academy wished
more.   It wished to break with the mediæval spirit
which was still too dominant in the Old Chamber.
Sons of revived Holland, they wished something better
in letters than what had contented their fathers, than the
work of the old rhetoricians whose heir the Chamber
was.[1]   It was the old and the new times that parted, the
spirit of freedom and majority against that of attachment
to old forms.   Both institutions found their zealous par-
tisans and their fierce enemies.   The Old Chamber and
the Brabanters who frequented it kept closer to the footsteps of the ancient rhetoricians, Coster's academy
emulated classical forms, popular cultivation in a broad
sense.   From the contest thus born came much good,
notwithstanding that the reformed church councillors
looked askance at their prosperity and thwarted the New
Academy.   Thus Amsterdam was the scene of a vigorous
literary life, and, in comparison, the activity in the other
cities is only to be mentioned in the second place.   At
Leyden lived the scholars Schrijver and Heins,[2] both
talented poets; Gerard Vos and Van Baerle, in close relation to the active Amsterdammers.   In The Hague,
young Huygens developed his talent, soon allied by new
ties to the Muiden circle.   At Leeuwarden, Jan Jansz.
Starter established a rhetoricians' chamber according to
the example that he, a Londoner by birth, had seen in his
second father city, Amsterdam, but he was speedily forced
to renounce his book trade, partly as a result of his wild

[1] Kalff, *Literatuur en tooneel te Amsterdam*, p. 9.
[2] Heinsius.

life. He then wandered for a time, and finally became a soldier, leaving his songs, *Friesche Lusthof*, as a proof of his great poetic talent.

In Zealand a circle was formed at Middelburg,[1] from which the " Zealand Nightingale " (1623) issued, and wherein young Jacob Cats was the dominant spirit; but this is rather a proof of the good will of " the Zealanders who shriek here," as they themselves put it, than of poetic talent and true artistic feeling.

An exception must be made for the pensionary Simon van Beaumont and Jacob Cats himself, first advocate and later landowner at Grijpskerk and pensionary at Middelburg, who was of the opinion still, in 1618, that in Zealand, " art is forgotten." They were connected with the Amsterdammers both by kinship and by common inclinations, and the clever Cats gave due honour to Hooft and Brederoo, Heins and Van Baerle, but preferred to imitate the more old-fashioned Anna Roemers Visscher or her father, and felt more attracted to the footpaths of the ancient rhetoricians than to the heaven flights of the more modern school. Nevertheless, although men like Cats show many traces of the old type in the realm of letters, it is very evident that by the beginning of the seventeenth century a new period had come for the Netherlands; that a new intellectual spirit was dominant; that the war of independence had given to a new people new ideals, new needs in intellectual ways.

Science, too, had a new birth. Leyden university attracted the best elements, and was the centre of learned studies. Lipsius emigrated to the south in 1590, but he was succeeded by the not less famous Frenchman, Joseph Justus Scaliger, the Huguenot savant, who, after some delay on account of his advanced age, accepted the call of the Leyden curators, among whom the old humanist

[1] Jonckbloet, *Gesch. der Ned. Letterkunde*, iv., p. 7 ; Frederiks, in *Oud Holland*, xiv., p. 1.

Dousa was the most prominent.   This brilliant new star attracted the most promising pupils; Hugo de Groot, Daniel Heins, the younger Dousa, Schrijver were all trained under him as classical scholars.   He was also eminent as a mathematician.   His pupils vied with him in reputation, especially the linguist, James Dousa; Heins, the pride of both Leyden and Holland after 1602, poet and scholar of European reputation, who, together with Lipsius and Scaliger, was one of the founders of the famous Leyden school of philology, which has continued in almost unbroken sequence to our time; the versatile jurist and historian, Paulus Merula; Raphel-engius, the distinguished orientalist.   Later came the learned Baudius; the clever Johannes Meursius; the famous manuscript-collector and antiquarian, Gerardus Vossius, regent of the college of the states; his col-league, Barlaeus; Scriverius, the orientalist; Erpenius —all these added lustre to the reputation of Leyden in the realm of philology, letters, and history, making the university one of the first in Europe.   Under their leadership was educated a mass of young students of classic lore, who introduced scientific methods into the municipal Latin schools of Holland and the neighbouring provinces and other universities of Europe.

Besides these studies in letters, much interest, too, was taken in theology.   It was the subject of a long dispute between Gomarus and Arminius.   Episcopius and Poly-ander à Kerchoven, Conradus Vorstius, the older Tunin-gius, the two Trelcatiuses, all followed this profession and attracted a mass of pupils, through whom they ex-ercised a great influence on contemporaneous thought. The learned Snellius, who was at the same time mathe-matician and naturalist, philosopher and linguist, aroused the admiration of all his contemporaries; the famous botanist, Paludanus, developed the university garden. Thus the youthful Leyden school, attended by eight hundred students, far surpassed the other institutions of the kind in the provinces.

The Frisian university, established at Franeker in 1585, was well represented in the realm of theology by the ardent Calvinist, Sibrandus Lubbertus, and his colleague, Martinus Lydius, but the number of the students remained limited to a couple of hundred.[1] Much smaller was the number at Harderwijk, where were at this time the learned Pontanus, physician, naturalist, and historian, and the theologian Thysius. An university was established at Groningen in 1614, whose first rector, Ubbo Emmius, the famous local historian, was the chief ornament, to whom was added the Leyden Gomarus, weary of the quarrels in the great university. About seventy new students registered annually at this young institution. Many Protestant foreigners — Frenchmen, Englishmen, Danes, Swiss, and Germans — thronged Dutch schools at this period, which numbered almost as many foreigners as native students.

Nor was learning confined to the universities. Preachers, such as Uyttenbogaert at The Hague, Plancius at Amsterdam, Menso Alting at Groningen, Boxhorn at Woerden, all did credit to their pulpits. François Maelson at Enkhuizen and William Usselincx were frequently mentioned as economists and adepts in the art of navigation. Cornelis Drebbel of Alkmaar was famous as one of the great inventors of his period; he lived at the court of the Emperor Rudolph in Prague, and later at that of James I. in London, honoured as mathematician and naturalist. Simon Stevin was mathematician and naturalist, engineer and military architect of European fame, and Prince Maurice's faithful aide, and there were other scientific architects and engineers, like the famous Leeghwater, who designed

[1] Boeles, *Friesland's hoogeschool*, i., p. 24. From sixty to eighty were registered annually.

the bridges, fortresses, and works of other kinds, drained
the polders, and built the dikes.   Our Latin schools
were renowned for the excellent instruction that was
given in them ; the invention of the telescope by Lip-
perhey at Middelburg [1] dates from this period.   The art
of navigation and allied sciences, astronomy, geography,
cartography, found numerous disciples both among mariners and landsmen.   The names of Plancius, of Linschoten, of William Barendsz., of Lemaire, naturally occur.

Certain branches of commerce and industry were closely
related to learned studies.   Countless mathematical and
navigation instruments, compasses, sextants, and tele-
scopes, were manufactured at Leyden and Amsterdam
which were used by the whole world.   The famous
booksellers, too, of those days, dispersers of Netherland
science, were also established there.   At Leyden, the
learned academical printer, Frans Rapheling, carried on
Plantijn's business, temporarily transplanted there; here
the energetic bookseller, printer, and academical beadle,
Louis Elsevier, established his famous printing-press
about 1590; his eldest grandson, Isaac, who began business in 1617, was the first to publish the duodecimos
which made the reputation of his family.   At Amsterdam, besides the numerous lesser printers and publishers,
the firms of the Van Waesbergs and Cloppenburch were
distinguished, as well as the famous globe and chart maker,
William Jansz. Blaeu, eminent publisher of good atlases
and maps, of works on mathematics and navigation, and
also of poetical and literary productions.   He was himself a man of great learning and known to his contemporaries as the prince of printers.   The numerous pamphlets
excited by events of the day, especially by theological
disputes, found very ready printers, who scattered thousands of copies over the land.   The interest of merchants
and of regents, of the citizens themselves in the political

[1] Not by Zacharias Jansen ; compare Frederiks in *Tijdsp.*, 1885, iii., p.
186 *et seq.*

condition of Europe, caused the publication of the first weekly journals at Amsterdam, which sprang from the local correspondence already very abundant in the sixteenth century. These letters were printed as pamphlets at irregular periods and widely disseminated, but it was not until 1609 that Broer Jansz., " ancient courier in the camp of his princely Excellency," published the " Friday Courant " regularly at Amsterdam.[1]

Holland took the same preëminence, too, in the realm of art. Painting and sculpture, music and engraving, attract our attention in high measure at this time. The schools of the Holland cities began to vie with Antwerp's great school, if not in richness of colour and ideal conception, at least in technique of portraiture, although the highest point of the Holland portrait school was not reached until half a century later. From this time, the beginning of a period of great prosperity, date the talented portrait-painters, the successors of Scorel and other realistic artists of the sixteenth century, as Cornelis Cornelisz. of Haarlem, who trained many pupils; the De Grebbers, living in the same city; Frans Hals, one of the greatest portrait-painters of any time; the little less known but undoubtedly inferior Michael van Mierevelt, who worked at Delft, and was the master of the famous Utrechter Paulus Moreelse, himself soon the head of an art school at Utrecht; Aart Pietersen at Amsterdam, the artist of the well-known picture of the members of a surgeon's guild around an operating-table; Jan van Ravestein at The Hague, the painter of the majority of military portraits which have come down to us from the days of Prince Maurice. Next to him ranks our first marine painter of note, Hendrik Cornelisz. Vroom, his rival Jan Willaerts, and many others of lesser rank. In all great cities of Holland schools of art grew up, whence

[1] Sautyn Kluit, " De Amsterdamsche Courant," in *Nijh. Bijdr.*, new series, v., p. 209 *et seq.*

issued a line of great seventeenth-century artists.   In the realm of engraving Hendrik Goltzius, of Haarlem, was still universally recognised as a master, although after 1600 he often used the pencil instead of the graver; his pupil, Jacob de Gheyn, like him established at Haarlem and rivalling him; his stepson Matham, clever etcher and engraver, and, like him, the father of a race of artists; the De Grebbers, both engravers and artists; Willem Jansz. Delff, Mierevelt's son-in-law.   A number of other engravers and etchers preserved paintings of their contemporaries on stone or copper, illustrated historical works, or produced independent engravings, mainly portraits. Architects and sculptors like Hans Vredeman de Vries, Cornelis Bloemaert, and especially Hendrik Keyser, who made the tombstone of William I. at Delft and Erasmus' statue at Rotterdam, and " gave life to marble and metal, ivory, alabaster, and clay," represented their time in this realm in a masterly fashion.   Thus in a very small region there was an animated artistic life in the midst of a prosperous society who had both taste and money for works of art.

The prevalent prosperity was especially advantageous to architecture.   In the well-to-do cities of Holland and Zealand, already rich in mediæval, ecclesiastical, and municipal buildings, council- and guild-houses, schools, halls, and other public buildings sprang up everywhere: the stadthouse and the Rhineland house at Leyden, the slaughter-house and stadthouse at Haarlem, the council-houses at Hoorn, Woerden, and Naarden, the poorhouse at Enkhuizen, the stadthouse at Delft, orphanages and almshouses everywhere, the Harborgate at Dordrecht, the Bourse, the South, North, and West churches at Amsterdam, besides many gates which were rebuilt in this period of enlargement of the cities, when in Amsterdam alone seven hundred houses were built in 1601; new Protestant churches were founded; the industrious burghers built new houses or decorated old dwellings. As a rule, the builders were simple carpenters. There were a few exceptions, like the wanderer, Hans Vredeman de Vries, who returned (c. 1600) at a great age to his native land, which he had left at the time of the revolt; like the famous Utrechtner working at Amsterdam, Hendrik de Keyser, and his aid, Hendrik Staets; like Lieven de Key at Haarlem and Leyden; like Danckerts and de Ry. These gave evidence of architectural knowledge and skill gained abroad and adapted to native architecture.[1] Other provinces, too, followed Holland's example, and erected monumental council-houses like those at Flushing and Brouwershaven, at Bergen op Zoom and Venloo, at Franeker—and especially the last, a remarkable effort of domestic architecture; municipal scala like those at Leeuwarden and Nimwegen, courts like that at Groningen, guard-houses like those at Zwolle, gates like the *Kerkboog* at Nimwegen, the Watergate at Sneek, beautiful façades on merchants' or regents' houses, many of which have lasted until to-day. A few names of the architects of these have been preserved, and here and there drawings and plans. The works on architecture of De Vries, De Keyser, Pieter Koeck, were zealously studied; the constructions of the masters of one city stirred those of others to emulation, and were taken as examples elsewhere. There was some dissatisfaction about these fine ornamental buildings, and as early as 1606, one writer speaks of the *magnifiques bastimens*, the *édifices somptueux* which the people complained were adding to the heavy burdens of the war. The stranger could plainly see how in these provinces there was superfluous expenditure by the magistrates themselves.[2]

[1] Compare Galland, *Die Renaissance in Holland* (1882), pp. 61 *et seq.*, and his *Geschichte der Hollandischen Baukunst und Bildnerei* (1890), p. 155.
[2] *Considérations sur le présent estat des Provinces Unies*, in MS., Bibl. Nat. (at Paris) fonds français, No. 3458, fol. 100.

As a matter of fact, luxury, the daughter of prosperity, began to be evident in the early years of the seventeenth century among the honest burghers. To be sure, the regents were still simple merchants[1] who honourably acquitted themselves of their task to care for the general interest, and distinguished themselves little in costume or manners from the people whom they governed. But we find frequent mention of sumptuous and solemn banquets[2] celebrated in the council-houses at the expense of the state. The moralists describe Amsterdam in the days of the Truce as a city of simple morals, with an industrious though excitable population, plain in speech, rough in tone, but little spoiled, cherishing an antipathy to the Spanish Brabanter who tried to imitate the foreign manners of the seigniors, but where Luxury had made her appearance[3] and the rich began to consider themselves better than the common citizens. Louise de Coligny introduced the first state chariot. In the Hague at the court of Prince Maurice there was a good deal of drinking, rough speech was heard, and rapiers were used freely in his military family, but in the household of his noble step-mother, where his brother Frederick Henry was at home, in those of the French and English ambassadors, of the chief statesmen of the young state, a fine taste began to be evident, borrowed from the upper French circles,[4] which was the standard gradually adopted by the members of the States which assembled periodically in the Hague. With more polished French manners came, however, certain objectionable accompaniments, like the duel, confined to military circles, but which became so serious an abuse that it was considered necessary, as early

[1] C. P. Hooft, *Memoriën en Adviezen* (*Werken Hist. Gen.*, no. 16), p. 106.

[2] "*Considérations*," etc.

[3] Compare Warener, *Tweede Bedrijf, Vijfde Tooneel*, Rykert's complaint about the distinguished ladies.

[4] Compare what we know of Constant Huygens's youth.

as the period of the Truce, to issue prohibitions of its indulgence.

Thus the Seven United Provinces were like a brilliant constellation that had risen in the political heaven of Europe, to the admiration of all who had watched its sudden rise. Is it any wonder that many asked whether this was a meteor about to vanish speedily, or a fixed constellation destined to keep its place in the political firmament ? There were many who doubted, friends as well as foes. Both turned their gaze upon certain phenomena of dissolution which manifested themselves plainly,—as the theological and political quarrels in the new community, dangerous for the young state. Bentivoglio with his Spanish sympathies, and the English, French, and Venetian ambassadors who were friendly towards the republic, both those who on account of this reason had objected to the Truce and those who had wished for it in spite of this obstacle, watched anxiously the progress of this unholy lack of unity, the heritage left by the struggle in the realm of religious and political principles. These quarrels and the doubt thereon dependent as to whether the state establishment could long endure — a government ill called a " democracy "— caused many to shake their heads at the future of the young state which already had a brilliant past, and through its brilliant present attracted observation.

The evil times were past when men sang:

" Happy is the Land
   Which God the Lord protects
   When with murder and fire
   The enemy is rampant."

The sword was, for the present, in its scabbard, and the Spaniard had fled " like the wind which blows," but a new foe was in their midst, more to be dreaded than the old one. Well might the rhetorician say warningly: " Beware of the Spanish truce," and pray the Lord to " guard the united land from domestic conflict." [1]

[1] Van Vloten, *Nederl. Geschiedzangen*, ii., p. 416.

CHAPTER XII

THE consummation of the Truce gave the United Netherlands peace, but not complete independence or " sovereignty." England and France made the young nation feel this fact.[1] If some end were to be gained, the Netherlanders were treated as responsible parties, but, at the bottom, the powers regarded the new State as a *protégé* who might and must be reminded of its duties towards its benefactors.

Two treaties bound the United Netherlands to France. One provided that in case of war during the Truce, Henry IV. should aid the States with 10,000, they him with 5000 men, and that no treaty should be concluded without respect to reciprocal interests. The second stipulated that two French regiments of foot and two companies of horse should remain for the present in the service of the States in consideration of the sum of 600,-000 livres annually. Treaties of 1585 and 1603 stipulated the relations with England. So close had these international relations been in certain features that, just before the Truce, it seemed as though pressure might be exerted to induce new offers of the sovereignty to Henry IV. or to James I., and it was to be expected that neither France nor England would again reject a tender thereof, as in 1584. The efforts of Oldenbarnevelt, leader in

[1] Compare Motley, *John of Barnevelt*, i., p. 38.

357

foreign policy, were, therefore, directed towards making both neighbours see their personal advantage in permitting the States to act as an independent republic. He hoped that fear of each other's dominance and their common interests in regard to Spain on account of commercial relations, would lead them to further this independence.

The sudden death of the duke of Jülich (March, 1609) without direct heirs introduced a new element into the situation. The duchy was too close a neighbour to the provinces to come under the control of Spain or of Spanish sympathisers without imminent danger to the States. In Germany the condition of affairs, too, was serious. Catholicism had revived under the influence of the Jesuits, and there was suspicion that secret plots of the pope and the house of Austria might be in progress. From these circumstances occasion was given to negotiations wherein the United Netherlands could make itself felt as a weight in the scale. The chief person on whom the eyes of both friend and foe were fixed was Henry IV. To carry out his plans, the aid of the United Netherlands was highly important, and he treated their envoys at Paris with great consideration. Aerssens,[1] as he was usually called, represented the provinces from 1598. In November, 1609, he was distinguished by the title of ambassador. At that time Aerssens was, apparently, in perfect understanding with the advocate and enjoyed the confidence of Sully. Henry himself did not fully trust him, and had asked for his removal.[2] The fact that, after his failure to effect this, he continued to show the envoy favour, shows his desire to propitiate the States, his principals, as does also the change of rank — envoy to that of ambassador. Aerssens was a talented but

---

[1] He called himself Françoys d'Aerssen or van Aerssen. His father, the clerk of the States-General, was known as Cornelis Aerssens. Probably the change was to give the ambassador the effect of noble descent.

[2] Jeannin, *Négociations*, i., p. 77 ; Ouvré, *Du Maurier*, p. 206.

imprudent and intriguing person, who secretly worked against the old advocate to whom he owed much, and manifested great sympathy for the most orthodox tendency of the reformed doctrine.

The complications which arose on the death of the insane duke of Jülich threatened to involve Europe in a general war, a war in which the Netherlands would necessarily be included. Not only the question of the mastery of the lower Rhine territories would be at stake, but also the supremacy of the house of Austria and of Catholicism.

The heritage of the duke of Jülich had been watched by possible claimants for a long time. John Sigismund, elector of Brandenburg, husband of the daughter of the late duke's oldest sister, and Wolfgang William of Neuburg, count palatine, son to the duke's second sister, both urged their claims. The duke of Deux Ponts, the marquis of Burgau, the elector of Saxony, and the duke of Coburg, all came forward as heirs more or less direct. The emperor, Rudolph II., appreciating the political significance of the contested lands as a balance of power, declared his intention of placing them temporarily under the administration of a ducal council and of the dowager duchess, assisted by a couple of imperial commissioners, until the rival claims were investigated. In this last proposition lurked danger lest the decision might award the duchy to the empire on the pretext that it was a lapsed imperial fief.[1]

The result was that Brandenburg[2] and Neuburg considered that their claims were sufficiently strong to ignore the imperial decree and to make a compromise with each other whereby they entered jointly into possession of the duchy. The " possessors," as they were termed, were

---

[1] Compare, for all this, Ritter, *Deutsche Geschichte im Zeitalter der Gegenreformation*, ii., pp. 29, 126, 199, 278, 283.

[2] Brandenburg obtained promises of support from the States-General. Ritter, *Briefe und Akte*, ii., No. 112.

recognised in their joint sovereignty by the Protestant Union at Heidelberg. But the emperor, urged on by his energetic cousin, the Archduke Leopold, bishop of Passau, refused to acknowledge the righteousness of this agreement. As imperial commissioner, Leopold took possession of the fortress of Jülich, and the inhabitants of the duchy were divided into parties, while neighbours on all sides delayed decisive action, each waiting for the other.

A personal motive finally induced Henry IV. to make preparations for war. Still amorous by nature, he was inspired by a violent passion for the newly wedded princess of Condé. The young couple fled to Brussels to escape the king. He demanded their return from the archdukes, who refused to listen to his request.[1] The relations between France and Spain were already strained, and this episode inflamed the fire so that there seemed every prospect of open war, with the Jülich succession as nominal cause.

It was a remarkable situation when the spring came. France pushed forward preparations vigorously, but was evidently prepared to pause on the surrender of the princess. Spain, the archdukes, the United Netherlands, were little inclined to resume hostilities either for the princess or for the Jülich question; the German Union was ready for everything except conflict, although Christian of Anhalt was active in his armament; the Catholic German League was just as little inclined for strife. Nevertheless the outbreak of a general war seemed imminent.

Henry IV. had urged that Oldenbarnevelt and Count William Louis should come to Paris to discuss with him and his council measures for a common campaign.[2] There

---

[1] See Henrard, *Henri IV. et la Princesse de Condé*, Brussels, 1870.

[2] Despatches of Aerssens in Motley, *John of Barnevelt*, i., 168, *et seq.;* Ritter, p. 321.

was some talk, too, of the king's visiting the Hague as a private individual.[1] In March, 1610, the war seemed to depend on the arrival of the envoys of the States at the French capital. Oldenbarnevelt and William Louis were unwilling to leave the land. The embassy which appeared at Paris in April consisted of the advocate's son-in-law, Van der Myle, and Walraven of Brederode from Holland, and Jacob van Malderee from Zealand. They were formally received with fine ceremonies, and there was no dearth of fair words on either side; but it was soon evident that the States, informed by Aerssens of Henry's real opinions, were not prepared to enter upon a dangerous war.

On their departure the king did not hide his discontent at their lukewarm spirit of coöperation, and spoke warningly of the great political interests which were at stake. As the embassy left, Béthune returned from a similar mission to the Netherlands, and his tidings also showed the disinclination of the States for hostilities, but Henry declared that he should take the field in May at the head of his troops, setting out for Jülich from Mézières, and counting on aid from Maurice.

His purpose was sustained by his indignation at the continued stay of the princess of Condé at Brussels, and by the prospect that, owing to the weakness of Spain and of the archdukes, he would be able to regulate Jülich affairs to his liking without serious risk.

A well equipped French army of 30,000 men was in readiness at Mézières; the States were to send 18,000 under Maurice to Dusseldorf; Anhalt had 10,000 collected from the Union; the duke of Milan was to conquer Milan with French aid; another French force was at the Pyrenees. During the king's absence, Marie de Medicis was to be head of a regency after her coronation, a ceremony which had been postponed until now. A few days

[1] Bentivoglio, *Relationi*, p. 112.

later the king was to set out.   In case that the archdukes refused to permit the passage of the French troops across their territory, Henry IV. was prepared to force it.   But they did permit it.

The coronation took place, as planned, on May 13th, but on the 14th Henry IV. fell by the hand of the fanatic Ravaillac.

The death of Henry the Great, as he was called by his contemporaries, brought about a sudden change in the political condition of Europe.   He was succeeded by an infant, in whose behalf a capricious, weak mother ruled with her favourites in the midst of intrigues and quarrels. France was doomed to years of inactivity abroad and lack of government at home.   The party of Spanish sympathisers again gained great influence; the Huguenots fell into the background.   The tie with the States loosened, although the queen-regent confirmed the treaty made in 1609.

The expected European war remained in abeyance when an embassy [1] went from the States to England to thank the king for his help in the Truce, to discuss the debts of the States, the fisheries on the English coast, and finally to suggest that England should, in the interests of Protestantism, lend a hand to the " possessing " princes in Jülich.   But James had turned his attention to a dynastic alliance between his family and that of the Spanish Hapsburgs, and did not wish to involve himself in Jülich affairs, although he promised financial aid.

In France, Sully had lost all influence.   A neutral policy was adopted towards foreign powers.   No one except the States was closely interested in the possession of Jülich.   The presence of the archduke in such immediate

---

[1] It was composed of Jan van Duivenvoorde, lord of Warmond, who died on the journey, the pensionaries of Dordrecht, Amsterdam, and Rotterdam, and Albert Joachimi from Zealand.

vicinity was a menace to the republic. In the early summer accordingly the States troops took the field. In the middle of June, Maurice marched into the duchy with a well-equipped force of about 16,000 men and laid siege to the town in a methodical manner. On September 1st, it capitulated. Leopold withdrew to Bohemia, the Jülich territories were left undisputed in the hands of the "possessors," and the armies returned home.

Nothing further came of a great war against the Spanish Hapsburg power. In the spring of 1611, France despatched an embassy extraordinary to the States to give them friendly assurances and to remind them of their financial obligations. The betrothal of the young King Louis XIII. to the Spanish Princess Anne, defined French sympathies. Mutual help was promised.[1] And, still worse, it was evident that England earnestly desired to enter the same coalition by means of a marriage between the prince of Wales and a French or Spanish princess, provided that the Netherlands could be obtained as a dowry.[2] The States-General, thus deserted by her old ally, was left practically alone in the Jülich affair; the insignificance of any aid from the German princes had long since been recognised.

The ambassador Aerssens continued at Paris, although his position did not improve. He was not willing, however, to relinquish a post where the perquisites were very valuable.[3] The advocate approved of his remaining, although little of the old confidence remained between him and Aerssens. The ambassador resented Oldenbarnevelt's publication of his secret reports on Parisian affairs, which he thought was with the direct purpose of effecting his recall and of substituting the advocate's son-in-law,

---

[1] See Zeller, *La Minorité de Louis XIII.*, ii., p. 44.

[2] See Jeannin, *Négociations*, ii., p. 42 ; Ouvré, *Du Maurier* (Paris, 1853), p. 192.

[3] Compare his later avowals in his *Noodighe Remonstrantie*, 1618.

Van der Myle, in his place at Paris.[1] The despatches were undoubtedly published, but it was not due to the advocate, as it was done when he was ill and without his knowledge.[2] However, Aerssens became more and more indisposed to accept Oldenbarnevelt's instructions. He counted himself as a diplomate, not as an envoy, and the breach between the two widened. Aerssens was embittered, too, by his daily experiences at Paris, and he firmly believed that Oldenbarnevelt was thwarting him purposely.

The situation was further strained by the financial demands made by France. According to a treaty signed at Hampton Court in 1603, it was stipulated that the States should pay one-third of the indebtedness incurred by France towards England in behalf of the United Netherlands. This was finally regulated to the wishes of France in the summer of 1613, after causing many unpleasant discussions.[3] There were further points of difference regarding the subsidies pledged to the States for the time of the Truce, and the payment of the French regiments in the service of the States. Aerssens was firm in maintaining the rights of his government, but was not tactful in his manner, nay often almost offensive towards the queen, boasting loudly of his friendship with the late king, and complaining of the degeneration in the French government, etc.

Such was the state of affairs in 1613, when, after seven years abroad, the ambassador went to the Hague on leave. The French government did not desire his return, and gave him a handsome present, which he accepted without conscientious scruple, although its true

[1] *Noodighe Remonstrantie* and Aerssen's discussion with Van der Myle in the same year (1618).

[2] Van der Myle, *Vertoogh*, 1618, p. 15.

[3] The States claimed that Henry IV. had released them from the obligation.

significance was not at all uncertain. It was a customary courtesy to an ambassador who had represented a friendly nation for many years in the midst of important negotiations, and was now returning home for good.[1] But Aerssens had no intention of considering his mission completed. In the Hague he found a staunch supporter in the person of Maurice, the friend of the influential French Huguenots.

The French ambassador then resident in the Hague was Benjamin Aubéry, Sieur Du Maurier, a Huguenot noble of little distinguished birth and of moderate ability, a good friend of the States, formerly in the service of the duke of Bouillon, and on a very good footing with Oldenbarnevelt. After leaving Bouillon he had served under Sully, and had been intrusted with the administration of the subsidies sent to the States, and was thus already acquainted with Netherland affairs.[2] He was no friend of Aerssens, who, in conjunction with the Huguenot party, had on account of Du Maurier's adherence to the new administration, worked hard against his appointment. He was, however, vigorously backed by Louise de Coligny and Oldenbarnevelt, and soon felt himself at home in the Hague in the midst of a numerous colony of French officers and nobles. In the beginning he tried, conformably with his instructions, *en un cas qui peut estre jusques à présent est sans exemple,*[3] to prevent the return of Aerssens to Paris. Aerssens, although also opposed by Reffuge,[4] who still remained in Holland, did not give up the fight, and attempted with the aid of his friends and his princely patron to obtain a renewal of his mission. Meanwhile Du Maurier lost no opportunity, either in public or in private, of proclaiming that Aerssens was *persona non grata* to the French government and to the queen. Prince

[1] Compare Van der Myle, *Vertoogh*, p. 23.   [2] *Ibid.*, p. 205.
[3] Ouvré, p. 198.   [4] He had been sent thither in 1611.

Maurice became cold towards Aerssens, although the ultra-Calvinists continued to support his pretensions. In February, 1614, Aerssens received his formal dismissal. From that moment he was the deadly foe of Oldenbarnevelt, who he asserted had desired to supplant him by his own son-in-law.   Had the advocate had the appointment of Van der Myle in mind, he did not now venture to make it.   Gideon van Boetzelaer, lord of Langerak, was given the post, which he, too, had long desired.   He was neither able nor distinguished for diplomacy.   He was counted as a tool of Maurice, but as the prince evinced little inclination to take part in politics, the new ambassador obediently followed the advice of the great leader of the foreign policy.

In France matters came to a crisis.   The counsellors of the young king took an open stand against his mother and her government, and were supported by the Huguenots.   A civil war seemed imminent.   Aerssens might have urged an alliance between the States and the Protestant party, but Van der Myle came to Paris as envoy extraordinary to preserve a good understanding between the regent's government and the States.   Thus the weight was thrown in the other balance.   Peace was restored between the two parties in France, but by means of Aerssens the Huguenot nobles remained in close relations with Prince Maurice and the orthodox reformers in Holland, while Oldenbarnevelt had evinced sympathy with the government.

In the meantime affairs in Jülich had entered on a new phase.   According to the treaty of Dortmund, Neuburg and Brandenburg were joint possessors of the contested inheritance, but the former did not cease secret negotiations with Maximilian of Bavaria, leader of the Catholic party, and with Matthias, who had succeeded his brother Rudolph in 1612.   Unpleasantness between the " possessors " and their officers made a joint rule impossible. Their differences soon came to an open breach. After a summer of hostilities in which both Maurice and Spinola took part with troops of the States and of the archdukes, the treaty of Xanten was made (November 12, 1614), wherein it was agreed to divide the duchy into two parts for administration, while its unity was nominally preserved. Brandenburg was to rule the Cleves-Mark portion with Cleves as his capital, Neuburg the Jülich-Berg territory with Dusseldorf as his. Spinola and Maurice both agreed to hold what they had gained during the summer and to abstain from hostilities. Envoys-extraordinary had come from France and England to Xanten and taken part in the negotiations. The armies were then disbanded, but the evacuation of the fortresses, which was stipulated in the treaty, did not take place at once. Nor was Spain nor were the States willing to renounce the advantages gained, notwithstanding attempts made by France and England to bring them to an agreement. The peace of Xanten can, therefore, be called little more than a cessation of hostilities, although possibly thereby the division of the heritage might be easier in the future.

There was little mention of the emperor in the whole affair. Matthias counted for as little as his brother. There was no central power, the empire was almost a phantom, and many North German princes and cities, as the elector palatine in the south, sought friendship from the powerful States-General, who were in a position to defend them against the attacks of foes within and without their territories. The alliance with the palatinate was of great importance. The elector was at the head of the Protestant Union and could be counted the most influential of the Protestant princes.

In East Friesland the old troubles still continued in force. The nobles, Emden and the count, were at swords' points with each other. In the spring of 1611, an embassy of the States-General under Joachimi appeared at the diet of the countship to reconcile the contending parties, and succeeded in helping form the treaty of Osterhusen, wherein the obligations of people to count were regulated.

The Hanse, too, in opposition to Denmark, which tried to retain sovereignty of the Baltic and imposed a sound tax rigorously, found it a necessity to seek an alliance with her old rivals the Netherlanders, who had long since surpassed the towns of the ancient commercial league. Oldenbarnevelt at once grasped the significance of such an alliance for Netherland commerce. As soon, therefore, as the cities showed an inclination thereto, Frederick Henry gathered an army of 7000 men, with which he crossed the boundary in the middle of November, 1615, and approached the city of Brunswick, besieged by Duke Frederick, and King Christian of Denmark. The coming of States' troops decided the duke to conclude a treaty which bound him closely. But the most important result of the affair was the agreement entered into by the six cities first involved and four others,[1] with the States-General in 1616. This insured mutual protection on the North and Baltic seas and the tributary streams. Virtually, the protectorate of the States was greatly extended.

The efforts of the Brussels government to extend her influence in Germany, her garrisons in Soest and Lippestadt, in Wesel and Rijnberk, showed her fear of the expansion of the reputation of the States. But the latter were far more powerful, and had gained a position which would insure weight in the approaching crisis in the empire.

A similar line of policy was pursued by the States in the north. Oldenbarnevelt proposed to support Sweden

[1] Lubeck, Hamburg, Bremen, Brunswick, Lüneburg, Magdeburg, Wismar. Rostock, Greifswald, and Stralsund.

against Denmark. Besides being dangerous to the commerce of the Netherlands, the facts that Denmark had been an ancient ally of Spain, and that the latter power had helped the Catholic Wasas in Poland in their pretensions to the crown of Sweden, naturally induced Sweden to incline towards the States. Charles IX. made several efforts towards negotiation, and received Cornelis Haga, not as official envoy of the States, but as agent to look after the interest of a few Netherland merchants during the war between Poland and Sweden. He finally sent an embassy to persuade the Netherlands to make a formal alliance against Denmark and Poland. This they refused, but despatched an embassy on their part to attempt to effect a reconciliation between the sovereigns. It was too late. War was already declared, and, moreover, the envoys were informed by Christian IV. of Denmark that he knew their king and master, the king of Spain, but recognised no States-General as an independent power. He refused moreover to lighten the Sont-tax, and was indignant at the arrival of a number of Netherland colonists at the newly founded city of Gothenburg, which was to command the Sont. The fact that Denmark held control of this passage made diplomacy necessary to avoid the exclusion of Netherlanders, and in 1618 a new embassy under Floris van Pallandt, lord of Culemborg, was sent by the States to confer with Christian. In addition to the Sont-tax, they were to protest against the formation of a Danish East India Company.

In connection with the policy pursued towards Sweden and Denmark, the first diplomatic relations were opened with Russia. For years the Netherlanders had had important interests to defend both on the White Sea coast and in the interior of the immense empire. In 1614, the first Russian embassy ever sent to the provinces appeared in The Hague under the conduct of the Holland merchant,

Isaac Massa. Russia then tried her diplomacy in the north, and peace was effected, thanks to the States' ambassadors, Veenhuizen, Bas, and Joachimi.[1] Amicable relations with Russia and Sweden were of inestimable value for Netherland commerce, while the advent of the United Netherlands in the region as an European power greatly increased their reputation, to the keen annoyance of the English, who tried to represent the States as mere *protégés* of the English king. Poland, too, made advances towards the States. King Sigismund had fully realised their influence and their political significance in connection with his plans against Sweden and Russia, and offered (1617) an alliance with an assurance of important commercial privileges in his kingdom.

In the south of Europe, too, important international relations were gradually established. Common enmity to Spain led to the first relations with the Turkish empire. At the recommendation of the Netherland merchant, Jacob Gijsbrechtsz., resident in Constantinople, and in consequence of the numerous piracies to which Netherland ships were exposed by the pirates in the Mediterranean, Cornelis Haga went to Turkey in 1612, accompanied by several youths eager to see the world. The skilled diplomate succeeded in overcoming the difficulties raised by the French, English, and Venetian embassies against his reception, and in bringing about a friendly and commercial treaty wherein it was stipulated that Netherland merchants might enter Turkish harbours under their own flag; Netherland slaves were freed, protection was assured against the pirates, and consulates in the chief ports were promised. Haga remained in the East for years to represent the interests of commerce and policy. His presence in Constantinople was especially important as a protection against piracy on the

[1] Vreede, *Nederland en Zweden*, p. 163.

coasts of Barbary, really furthered by the maladminis-
tration of the African provinces under Turkish authority
and through the feeble sea-power of the European commercial peoples.   The well-known Simon de Danser of
Dordrecht and his English contemporary Warde were in
1609 the most notorious leaders of the international piratic
bands who had found footholds among the inaccessible
cliffs of Africa's north-west coast, whence they made onslaughts upon the passing ships.   A commercial treaty
with Morocco (May, 1609) did not check the depredations
of these lawless pirates, who were worse than those of
Dunkirk.

In course of time Savoy and Venice also became
formal allies of the States.   The duke of Savoy, a bitter
opponent of Spain, sent, in 1614, Count John of Nassau,
a grandson of Prince William's brother, who served in
his army, to ask aid from the States in money or soldiers.
Although the petition was not approved, still relations
were maintained with Savoy.

More pains was taken in regard to Venice, which had
always been Spain's foe in Italy.[1]   It was not, however,
until after the Truce that the Venetian government intimated their readiness to receive a confidential envoy
from the Netherlands.   Informed of this by Aerssens,
Maurice proposed to accept the suggestion, and in August, 1609, Van der Myle was charged with the mission.
He was received with distinguished honours, to the sore
annoyance of Spain and the pope, who protested against
forming relations with the Netherland rebels, while, on
the other hand, the French and English ambassadors at
Venice — the latter was Dudley Carleton — supported
him.   The appointment of an emissary of the Venetian
Republic to the States-General in return was the desired
result of this embassy.   In the spring of 1610, Tommaso
Contarini appeared as such.   But prudent Venice was

[1] De Jonge, *Nederland en Venetie*, p. 9.   's Gravenhage, 1852.

quite unwilling to accede to the alliance which the States desired. For the time being this interchange of formal civilities was all. A Netherland consul was not officially recognised in Venice until 1615.

In the following year the republic found itself in straits with its war with the Uscoques on the Dalmatian coast. Lionello was sent to ask aid from the States, and was quickly followed by Suriano to enforce the request. They wished especially to obtain permission to levy 3000 men under Count John Ernest of Nassau, who had offered his services. Permission was granted readily by the States, and also for a second regiment of 1000 men under the Seignior of Wassenhoven. It was not a successful expedition. There was no preparation for the warm climate, and John Ernest was among the many who died. Only a remnant returned in 1620. But owing to Suriano, Venetian ambassador to the States, the tie between the two commonwealths became steadily closer, and there were many thoughts of a close alliance between the " lion with the sword " and the " lion with the book." Oldenbarnevelt and Count Maurice both appreciated to the full the value of such an alliance, considering the possibility of renewing the war with Spain, and the statesman showed his inclination to make it permanent, although for the moment he was unwilling to offend Spain.

Thus very shortly after the conclusion of the Truce, the state of the United Netherlands was honoured as a desirable ally or feared as a dreaded foe throughout Europe. Nay, her name was honoured beyond Europe. Political relations were opened with distant Persia, which might be of great profit in the future. And everywhere it was the clear sight of the advocate that watched opportunities to make the state whose foreign policy he conducted recognised as a sovereign independent power, and to protect her commercial interests by diplomatic ties.

In proportion as the Netherlands gained new friends and as her weight in the European scale was recognised, her difficulties with her oldest friend, England, increased.

Nearly everywhere that Netherland commerce gained a foothold, English competitors were on the ground—in Europe, north and south; in Asia, south and east; in the Polar sea and the Atlantic Ocean. The fisheries were a perennial subject of discussion; the freedom of the sea and the right to trade in the north and in India gave the regular ambassadors, Noël de Caron at London and Winwood in the Hague, plenty of occupation, while from time to time envoys extraordinary were despatched on special missions to settle pressing difficulties.

It was these commercial rivalries which made James I. —in spite of the marriage of his daughter (1613) to the young Protestant Frederick, elector palatine — reluctant to join forces with the United Netherlands and present a strong front for the defence of Protestant interests in Germany, in Europe. He constantly evinced sympathy for Spain. Not until the conclusion of the Truce and on the occasion of Maurice's investiture with the order of the Garter, did James actually recognise the States as a sovereign power.

It was very desirable, therefore, for the States to free themselves from this uncertain friend and redeem the cautionary cities so long held by England. That alone would avert the danger that James might transfer those cities.

The financial difficulties in which James was always involved made him ready to listen to the negotiations, many times half opened, when Caron approached the subject in 1615.[1] The States were already paying £40,-000 annually to England, but nearly three-quarters of this sum went directly to the garrisons maintained by England in Briel, Flushing, and Rammekens, and the English government needed ready money. In the spring

[1] *Carleton Letters*, i., pp. 33, 57.

of 1616 it was finally decided to finish the matter for £100,000 down and three payments of £50,000 at six months' interval, while the garrisons were to pass over to the service of the States.

It could not be denied that this arrangement was hardly advantageous for England, who claimed £600,000, even apart from the interest it had in the possession of the cities. But Oldenbarnevelt was clever enough to push the affair through quickly, to the annoyance of many English government officials; yes, speedily of James himself, who soon repented of what had happened. In June, 1616, the pledged cities were formally returned to the States-General.

The English ambassador,—Sir Dudley Carleton, just transferred from Venice to The Hague—retained his seat in the council of state. Carleton was a man who showed himself adequate for the heavy task of maintaining the good understanding between England and the United Netherlands in spite of the commercial points that were continually presenting themselves and the political complications which were not lacking. His personal relations with Oldenbarnevelt were not cordial, however,—a fact that led to sad results.

In the midst of all other events, the advocate kept his eyes on the action of the " papistical league," which he considered very menacing to the safety of Europe. In his letters to Caron in London, to Aerssens and Langerak at Paris, to Haga at Stockholm, to Sticke at Berlin, to Brederode at Heidelberg, to other agents and emissaries, this note was sounded repeatedly: Keep an eye on the sail, watch the movements of troops in Italy and Austria, in Bavaria and Burgundy, look to the coöperation of our old and new allies, try to solve their difficulties, and to keep their force together.[1] The probable European war constantly occupied his thoughts. He did not know

[1] See Motley, *John of Barneveld*, ii., p. 3 *et seq.*

when the blow would fall or where, but of its coming he was sure. No phenomenon of the slightest weight in the political world escaped his experienced look. He lived long enough to see the beginning of the strife. The choice of Ferdinand of Styria as king of Bohemia in 1617, the beginning of the Bohemian revolt in May, 1618, the death of the Emperor Matthias in March, 1619, —all this happened during the last years of Oldenbarnevelt. But just in those days his power was seriously weakened by civil disturbances in his own state; the thinking head wherein majestic plans of coöperation between the threatened states were conceived was on the point of falling from the sturdy shoulders which had borne the burden of more than forty years' work in the service of the state. And when the elevation of Frederick of the Palatine to the throne of Bohemia, in August, 1619, coincident with the choice of his rival Ferdinand of Styria as new emperor of Germany, brought the long-expected outbreak of war between Protestant and Catholic which gradually extended over almost the whole of Europe, to spread death and desolation for almost thirty bloody years—then Oldenbarnevelt was no more.

In him disappeared the single man who was at the moment able to gauge the significance of these events and— possibly — to defend the threatened interests by a union among all those interested. From The Hague he had predicted the explosion for years, but when it came he was not there to lead the young state in the conflict for those same interests for which it had striven for years practically unaided, and which at length involved not only the one little realm of the Netherlands but all Europe. Others plucked the fruits that he had sowed, and carried on his policy, but with less vigour and less talent. His successors had to acknowledge that to his policy was due the rank attained by the United Netherlands. It hardly ranked as an independent state in the beginning of the Truce; at the end it enjoyed an honour-able place among the European powers. This was primarily the work of Oldenbarnevelt, in this respect the greatest statesman ever produced in the Netherlands.

It was he who in the interest of Netherland commerce, as well as that of statecraft, laid the foundations of the relations which the republic of the seventeenth century maintained brilliantly; it was he who gave her a seat in Europe's council-chamber.

CHAPTER XIII

THE FORM OF GOVERNMENT IN THE UNITED NETHERLANDS

RARELY has any state government been so complicated as was that of the young commonwealth in its early years of acknowledged independence. The countships of Holland and Zealand, the episcopal Sticht and upper Sticht, ducal Gelderland, lordless Friesland and Groningerland now united by Maurice's sword to parts of Flanders and of Brabant, really formed no coherent state. It was a union of unassimilating provinces, in whose midst, moreover, lay a number of separate lordships, besides several portions of conquered territory.

Certain ancient mediæval conditions which had hampered the Burgundian overlords in their efforts to attain unity in their dominions, which, during the revolt, had been patent from the variance in the individual needs of the different provinces, and again patent in later times as new necessities arose,—these same conditions still continued to form the basis of the national and municipal governments. The confusion which had existed when one hand held the sceptre over all was still existent when that sceptre was broken.

The Union of Utrecht dominated the body politic, but the mass of regulations, drawn up in time of war, were not planned for and ill adapted to the peace administration of a regulated state. Such administration had not

377

been the intention of the founders of the union. The resolution taken in 1607 to renew and strengthen the union was accompanied by a proposition for revision.[1] But no revision followed at the time, although it was urged by both Jeannin and Henry IV. as absolutely necessary.

A vigorous central government did not exist. After Leicester's departure the council of state was entirely overpowered by the States-General in civil affairs, and only maintained a moderate power in the realm of military affairs and of finance owing to the circumstance that Maurice and William Louis had seats therein.

In accordance with the instruction of 1588, Holland had three, Guelders, Friesland, and Zealand each two members, while the less important provinces of Utrecht, Overyssel, City and Land[2] (after 1594) had only one member in the council. The English ambassador was still entitled to a seat in consequence of the treaty of 1585.[3] The members were indeed nominated by the provinces, but voted without consultation and per capita. They had to renounce their own provinces " to be for the generality." In the days of the Truce the first duty of the council of state was to insure the contributions from the various provinces for the support of the army and the land defences—marine affairs were never subject to them. The necessary increase was provided for by the *Generale petitie*[4] presented to the States-General in November or December. From this, petitions to the separate provinces were drawn up. The petitions respecting the contributions of the various provinces, the quotas,—a name and a thing dating from Burgundian times,— had to be followed by the " consents " of the provinces in question.[5]

[1] Slingelandt, *Staatkundige geschriften*, ii., p. 58.
[2] Groningen and the neighbouring country.
[3] See p. 207.
[4] Aitzema, *Saken van Staat en Oorlog*, i., p. 781.
[5] See Part II., p. 264.

But consent, often obtained with difficulty, was not synonymous with payment. Holland and Zealand alone were in the habit of fulfilling their obligations regularly. Gelderland and Overyssel were, before the Truce, usually exempt on account of the presence of the foe within their territories; the other provinces were always behind-hand.

Thus in the interest of regular support of the army a so called " repartitie " was introduced, that is, every province was made responsible for the support of troops on its territory. The division of these payments took place according to the " state of war " [1] drawn by the council of state, which was arranged for several years in succession. What exceeded the quotas was to be passed over by the provinces to the receiver-general of the Union.

The fixing of the quotas had many feet in the earth. As the various provinces were freed from the Spanish yoke, Holland and Zealand, who had together after 1586 borne more than 80 per cent. of the costs of the war,[2] made the other provinces of the north gradually assume their share in proportion to their area and to their wealth. But at the time of the Truce many questions arose.[3] Little Zealand complained that she was assessed far too high. Instead of 16, 14, 12, not more than 9 per cent. was considered her share in view of her decreasing prosperity.[4] They haggled over this until 1612 before the council of state and the two stadtholders succeeded in coming to a decision by means of an arbitration conference. It was then decided that Holland should pay 57.1 per cent., Friesland 11.4 per cent., Zealand 11 per cent., Utrecht and Groningen (City and Land) 5.5 per cent., Overyssel

---

[1] Slingelandt, ii., p. 42.

[2] Compare Pieter Paulus, *Verklaring der Unie*, i., p. 239.

[3] Jeannin and Winwood were consulted at this time. Jeannin, *Négocia-tions*, iv., pp. 96, 143–165.   [4] Slingelandt, ii., p. 33.

3.5 per cent. This apportionment remained in existence, although in 1616 Zealand's share was finally reduced to 9 per cent. on account of her decay, while the lacking 2 per cent. was imposed upon the other provinces and Drenthe. In all financial affairs the treasurer-general of the union was the chief councillor of the council, which also took action in regard to the *brandschattings*, to foreign subsidies, to revenues from confiscated property, and to the financial administration of the portions of Flanders and Brabant immediately ruled by the States-General. The treasurer of the union and the secretary of the council of state were accordingly very important state officials.

The instruction of 1588 gave, moreover, the conduct of the war to the council of state. It controlled the engagement and the dismissal of troops, kept the lists of soldiers, looked to the fortifications and magazines of ammunition, etc., and exercised supreme military jurisdiction. Moreover, the council of state, in virtue of its instruction, was empowered to pronounce judgment in all questions between the provinces or members thereof. Naturally friction with the States-General resulted as the larger body gradually absorbed the sovereign functions of the council of state.[1]

Only seven of the provinces which had originally subscribed to the union were now represented in the States-General. The attempts of Drenthe and of the portions of Brabant conquered by Maurice (1608) to obtain admission to that body were frustrated by the influence of Holland. The dominating province was unwilling to increase the number of little provinces having a vote while the Brabant districts and Drenthe[2] could in case of need be counted as conquered territory, although the latter

[1] Compare p. 237.
[2] Lijndrajer, *Drente's recht op sessie ter Generaliteit*, p. 2 et seq. Gron., 1893.

jure postliminii had claims to be reckoned as a part of the union to which it had subscribed in 1580. The college of " My Lords the States-General " was virtually the assembly of the deputies of the " sovereign " provinces to guard the common interests[1] referred to them. Thus, originally, it was in no sense a sovereign body, although counted as such by foreigners and even by Netherland writers, and later it made that impression upon those not closely acquainted with Netherland institutions, as its members were honoured with the title of " High Mightinesses." It based its administrative powers, gradually acquired, upon certain stipulations of the Union of Utrecht which mentioned common deliberations of the provinces.[2] Each province sent an indeterminate number of deputies to The Hague, where the sessions had been permanent since 1593, instead of taking place once or twice a year. The terms, compensation, etc., of the deputies varied in the different provinces. Some members were appointed for life, some for one or more years. The usual pay was four to six florins a day, besides travelling expenses. Owing to the expense and inconvenience of long sojourns in The Hague, the representations of many provinces was restricted to two or three deputies, while Holland had many.

The ranking of the provinces in the assembly was as follows: Gelderland took precedence, as it had ranked as a dukedom in the Burgundian States-General; then came Holland, Zealand, Utrecht, Friesland,[3] Overyssel, and City and Land (Groningen). The chairmanship passed around week by week in the above order. In many cases, as in matters pertaining to peace, war, and finances, either by virtue of custom or as stipulated in the articles

---

[1] De Groot, *Memorie van mijne Intentiën* (*Werken Hist. Gen.*, no. 14), p. 7 *et seq.*

[2] Compare p. 135; Wijnne, *Geschiedenis*, p. 26.

[3] Occasionally precedence was disputed between Friesland and Utrecht.

of union, unanimity was essential; in others a majority of votes was sufficient.   Except in certain matters of a purely formal character, the deputies did not vote according to their conviction, but as they were instructed to, which fact proves that, even though the States-General were empowered to exercise certain sovereign rights,[1] nevertheless they were not a sovereign body, but, on the contrary, this sovereignty was vested in the provinces individually.   Many, many times do instances occur when the deputies return home or write to their constituents for instructions, declaring that they were not " charged." Very rarely do they venture to decide any point on their own authority, and then only with the reservation of approval from their principals.

This tedious method of procedure had serious results in proportion as the States-General assumed greater authority.   After 1588, the council of state was robbed of control of foreign affairs, especially in connection with the articles of the union respecting peace, treaties, etc., and the presence of the English ambassador in the council. Jurisdiction in military affairs, on sea and on land, became vested in the States-General, who gradually limited the functions of the council to the administration proper. Marine affairs were wholly under them; the admiral-general was appointed by the States; the admiralty colleges had to recognise their supremacy, especially after the extinction of a college of superintendence in marine affairs.   The captains-general of the provinces and other officers had to swear fealty to them.   Finances and coinage were under their supervision.   The exercise of sovereign rights, the administration of the conquered lands in Brabant and Flanders,—the " generality lands,"—belonged to them.   General ordinances were issued from them, but could only be proclaimed in the provinces by the provincial Estates.   They had jurisdiction over crimes

[1] See Kluit, *Holl. Staatsr.*, iii., p. 138.

against the Generality perpetrated by officials in the service of the Generality. They alone could arbitrate in the differences between the provinces or people. They appointed ambassadors, field-marshals, consuls, the treasurer-general of the Union, their own clerk (*griffier*), the secretary of the council of state, and several other officials of especial significance.

There was, not unnaturally, frequent friction between the States-General and the provincial Estates, just as there was between the former and the council of state.[1] The circumstances of the revolt against Spain gave to the Estates of Holland and Zealand (1572) and to the Estates of the provinces allied to them after the Pacification of Ghent and the Union of Utrecht, the sovereign power of the north. Succeeding events—Prince William's death, etc.—left the provincial Estates executive *de facto*. But the provincial Estates in their turn were nothing more than a collection of the representatives of cities and nobles. In Holland, after 1585, the deputies had to take an oath " to help decide and resolve in all affairs as they should be charged by their principals."[2] They could only judge for themselves upon " incidental matters," "according to their understanding in good conscience." Moreover, on the one hand their sovereignty was limited by the restrictions set by themselves in their acts conferring certain sovereign rights to central bodies like the States-General and the council of state; on the other by the privileges claimed by the individual members of the provinces,— the component parts of the Estates,— especially now that there was no overlord to dispute them. Thus a door was opened for differences and conflicts respecting authority.

This was the more marked as no one province possessed true unity. As already said, certain little independent lordships refused to accept the union. Vianen

[1] Compare p. 155.   [2] Slingelandt, p. 114.

in Holland, formerly a fief of Utrecht, later a seigniory of the Brederodes; Kuilenburg, the countship of the Pallandts; the Cleves's estates of Ravestein and Zeven-aar; Buren, the countship of the Oranges, formerly of the Egmonts; Ameland, the heritage of the Camming-ghas,—all these were examples of this condition.   Fur-ther, every province was composed of an agglomeration of heterogeneous parts,—cities, estates, lordships,—each a tiny entity possessing individual rights, customs of administration and jurisdiction, partly originating in mediæval Germanic conditions, partly instituted by the Burgundian princes in the fifteenth and sixteenth cent-uries.[1] No city, no village, was wholly like its neigh-bour.

In Zealand, the nobles were little significant, less even than in burgher Holland.   In Utrecht, Guelders, Over-yssel, and Drenthe, on the other hand, they were very influential; in Friesland and in City and Land (Gron-ingen) they were somewhat subordinated, but still they exercised great influence owing to their extensive estates. Thus in the various provinces the gatherings of the States presented a very different picture.   In Holland and Zea-land they were a coherent college.   In Utrecht there was a sharp opposition between the three members.   The Frisian diet was far from being a unity with its four quarters each possessing a vote.   Groningen consisted of two separate and diverse members, while the assembly of Overyssel was composed of the three cities and of the nobles from the three quarters.   In Gelderland the three quarters deliberated in a sort of separate gathering of the Estates, and then later met in a diet.   All these differ-ences were the result of the different historical develop-ment of each province.

And similar differences existed within the provinces

[1] Compare an admirable review by P. L. Muller in his work, *Onze Gouden Eeuw*, i., pp. 91–178 ; ii., pp. 1–314.

themselves. In the Estates of Holland the cities enjoyed eighteen votes to one of the nobles. In Zealand the First Noble had his seat with the six cities. In Utrecht only one city had representation in conjunction with the two other branches of the Estates — the elect and the nobles. In Gelderland in the three quarters still in existence, the petty country towns had to contend with an influential nobility. In Overyssel the cities could barely hold their own in opposition to the nobles. In Friesland they formed, mainly little market-places, one quarter as opposed to three of the country. In the province of City and Land the powerful city of Groningen was continually at swords' points with the country. The advocate of Holland had a counterpart only in Zealand. The Utrecht advocate, formed after his model, was, after the death of the clever Floris Thin (1590), replaced by a secretary of the Estates with functions very similar to those enjoyed by the secretary " of state " which existed in Friesland and elsewhere.

But none of these statesmen and officials had the power of Oldenbarnevelt, the political leader of the important province which had assured its position through him as member of the Holland representation at the States-General and through the weight of his personal authority.

The syndics and advocates of other towns never attained the reputation of the influential pensionaries of the Holland cities. De Groot, the pensionary of Rotterdam, De Haan at Haarlem,—regular attendants at the assemblies of the Estates,—were nominally servants but virtually leaders of their municipal governments as early as in the days of Leicester.[1] In the Holland and Zealand cities, the burgomasters did not, universally, exercise much influence in the municipal government; in Amsterdam they were almost supreme owing to their free election

[1] Fruin, *Tien Jaren*, p. 39.

by the town council; in the majority of the other cities they were more or less dependent upon the stadtholder as well as on the town council, since he possessed the right of appointment from the nominations made by the council.

In the cities of Guelders and Overyssel, colleges of tribunes designed to represent the citizens still exercised some control upon the government of the patricians. In Groningen this body was practically dominant, while it signified little in some of the other provinces, since the magistrates had these colleges almost completely in their power, and had, as a rule, great influence in their composition. In the Frisian communities (*grietenijen*), the Groningen districts (*gouwen*), the Drenthe *dingspels*, land-ownership was of great influence in the government, and many an old Germanic usage was in vogue.

There was wide variance, too, in the ordinary government of the provinces. In Holland and Zealand this was exercised by a deputed council who enjoyed great independence as regards the provincial Estates, from whose midst they were not even deputed, as they were themselves appointed direct by nobles and cities. In Holland there were two colleges: the general college of ten members in The Hague, and one of seven members in Hoorn with local jurisdiction over Holland north of the Y, which last had, since the days of Sonoy, remained in existence at the request of the small cities of north Holland. In Zealand every member of the Estates appointed one to the college of deputies, whose capacity was on a par with that of Holland. In the remaining provinces the colleges of the Deputed Estates had great influence in the regular administration as mayor and aldermen, but far less power over the course of affairs as compared to the Estates.[1]

In general it was true that, in proportion to the growth of the United Netherlands as a state, wherein Holland

[1] Compare p. 158.

took the lead, Holland's example exercised a steadily increasing influence on the forms of government of the other provinces. The increasing power of the cities, and, within them, of the municipal patriciate, resulted in bringing about a greater uniformity throughout the provinces, even though there were some exceptions in this uniformity, especially as regarded the government colleges. The patrician character of the administration was dominant.

The authority of the stadtholder, or governor, also varied in the various provinces, although in a less degree than that of the government. Both title and office of stadtholder were virtually hardly legitimate in such a state as the United Netherlands had become. That both name and office still were in vogue was the result of the particular circumstances which had existed in 1585. The desire of the States-General to oppose someone to Leicester in Holland and Zealand to whom the administration of domestic affairs could be intrusted without fear had led to the restoration of the stadtholderships in favour of Prince Maurice. Villiers and Nuenar in Utrecht, Gelderland, and Overyssel, William Louis in Friesland, were installed by the provinces into the office under about the same circumstances.[1] The tradition of the presence of stadtholders under the Burgundian administration, the need of an official who could exercise local authority in civil matters, had defined the functions of the office. Of old, civil and military authority in the provinces had been in the same hands; it was thus comprehensible that the captain-generalship of the province remained united with the stadtholdership.

At the beginning of the Truce, Maurice exercised this function in not less than five provinces, and William Louis in the two northern provinces with Drenthe. Besides receiving commissions in the name of the provincial

[1] See p. 207; Wijnne, *Geschiedenis*, p. 34.

Estates, the two stadtholders had also received them from the States-General, and had given their oath to this latter body, a result of the circumstances existing when Leicester came to the Netherlands. When the stadtholder function was regulated, the instructions to the old stadt-holders under the Burgundian government had been taken as a basis, a method of procedure which had curious results owing to the non-existence of the sover-eign, personally represented by the Burgundian stadt-holder. The new stadtholders, or governors,[1] although now officers of the States, possessed on that account rights which really were not suitable for their new office, —rights which properly belonged only to the sovereign. Hence it happened that the first official, as he also chanced to be the prince of Orange, influential from his inherit-ance and his possessions, stadtholder of several provin-ces, at the same time that he was, as commander, head of the army, and in general charged with the executive power, was considered chief ruler. In the eyes of those who were not closely acquainted with the government of the States, yes, in the estimation of the majority of the subjects, Maurice obtained the character of what was called in the later republic, with a half-monarchical title, the " eminent head " of the state, although the States supported their sovereignty as opposed to his. He was, according to the Holland instruction for the stadtholder, to maintain the prosperity of the province and the re-formed religion,[2] have supervision of the administration of justice, appoint the municipal magistrates according to the municipal privileges, fill the high offices subject

---

[1] In regard to this difference in title, compare Wijnne. p. 55. In later times this difference was preserved in order to bring out the difference from the Burgundian stadtholders.

[2] This was partially because his Burgundian predecessor had been charged with the maintenance of the Catholic religion as opposed to heresy, and partly because of his alliance with the Reformed, who had been in the minority since Prince William's time and were so in Maurice's.

to the state, grant pardons, and conduct the defence of the country on land and sea as captain-general and admiral.   In the other provinces placed under Maurice, his authority was about the same, but William Louis enjoyed far less power in his provinces than his cousin, again the result of the manner in which he had obtained the stadtholdership of Friesland. Under these circumstances it was evident that stadtholder authority must often come in direct conflict with that of the States. The official who through his influence upon the appointment of magistrates appointed, in a certain sense, his own masters, did not find it easy to consider himself their underling, and they could with difficulty regard him as such.

It was significant that the prince was financially independent of the States. Immediately after the conclusion of the Truce, Jeannin, commissioned by his king and in coöperation with Oldenbarnevelt and William Louis, had attempted to put an end to the disputes between the sons of Prince William respecting their inheritance. As the eldest son, Philip William, was heir to his father's estates in the north and in the Burgundian provinces, and he had come to the Hague in November, 1608, to urge his rights, and was little inclined to renounce his claim, although he was quite ready to resign to Maurice what fell to him in accordance with his mother's settlements. In a convention (June, 1609) Philip William received the Burgundian possessions and those in Brabant and Flanders; Maurice received the right of possession in Vianden and in other Luxemburg estates, besides the marquisate of Veere and Flushing and all other estates on Walcheren, together with the territory of Kuik, the lordships of Niervaart, of Leck and Polanen, and the right to Lingen and Kloppenburg. Frederick Henry received for his share the lordship of Geertruidenberg with the adjacent estates. Moreover, each one of the three brothers received one-third of the sum of 300,000 florins allotted by the archdukes as compensation to the prince's family, while other financial matters were also adjusted.

This arrangement and the doubling of Maurice's political salary and the increase of his military salary to 120,000 florins a year, all as compensation for domains, rights, and ecclesiastical estates originally his and ceded to the state, and, finally, the 25,000 florins, income settled upon him and his heirs, placed him in a position to maintain princely state even in time of peace.

The character of the government in the northern provinces can in general be described as aristocratic tempered by the stadtholder's authority, allied to the municipal, territorial, and provincial privileges of ancient origin, conferred by the overlords. Their maintenance assured the inhabitants a certain measure of freedom and the enjoyment of the laws and statutes formerly bestowed by the municipalities with approval of the overlord. But this aristocratic government, composed of city and country aristocracy, became in the various provinces more and more the privilege of a close caste, whose members, the " regents," retained the authority as much as possible in their own hands. In elections, both in Friesland and elsewhere, the so-called " kuipen " of votes was usual[1] (1600), and mutual agreements about the filling of the offices were in vogue.

It often happened that people of humble station succeeded by means of cleverness, personal consideration, or property, in forcing themselves into the circle of the regents. There was not much opposition to receiving such parvenus into the government of a city, or, as far as Holland was concerned, even into the nobility. The economic conditions prevailing in the beginning of the seventeenth century caused this to happen more than

[1] Compare Slothouwer, *Oligarchische Misbruiken in Friesland*, *Nijhoffs Bijdragen*, new series, i., p. 67.

once. During the Truce the numerous patents of nobility given by the kings of England and of France to members of embassies to their courts were accepted not without pleasure by the burghers, although they rarely used the new knight's title on Netherland soil. There was practically no popular influence in the government. The one way in which the populace could make itself felt was by revolt. The ancient democratic institutions of the cities in Gelderland and Overyssel were nothing more than names; as a matter of fact community rights had all come under the control of the municipal aristocracies; the guilds and archers had long since lost all political influence, and national institutions were dominated by the great landowners.[1] But this was all done with the approval of the population itself, " more obedient than any other nation," who were willing to leave government to those who liked it, and had an " aversion to all ambition in political matters."   The regents were, on their part, held in check by their fear of revolts in case abuses were too many and the taxes too high. The popularity of the stadtholder's authority, too, was a constant reminder that the stadtholder might gain greater influence, yes, even wish monarchical dignities. The influence of the preachers, whose pulpits offered an excellent opportunity to affect the populace, was also something to be considered. A powerful means of exciting agitation was the mass of little blue books scattered among the people, wherein, as of old, the acts of the government were criticised. Thus a certain guaranty was given against encroachments of the regents, although some efforts were made to curb the freedom of the press. The Holland resolution of 1591, providing that the Court and High Council of Holland and Zealand, in case of a complaint against a municipal government by an individual, must furnish documents to the city and ask for information; the right

[1] Fruin, *Tien Jaren*, p. 39 *et seq.*

to banish suspected people from city jurisdiction without giving reasons; the aid given by one city to another in the prosecution of printers or authors of " fameuse libellen," all show that municipal governments had no intention of permitting too much liberty, although they encountered some difficulty in enforcing war regulations in times of peace.[1] Nevertheless much liberty remained deep-rooted in the people's spirit.   In the inns, the barber and book-shops, on public boats and diligences where men came together, burghers and peasants expressed their opinion about the actions of town councils, burgomasters, and States — yes, of the prince himself.   Many a regent thus heard the sharpest criticism upon his contemporaries from the mouth of the people.   Although he was treated with respect, the people retained the right of individual opinion, and often expressed it by word and by pen in the most unequivocal terms.   In spite of vigorous ef-forts of the regents, freedom of speech continued to be a marked characteristic of the Netherland populace,— a means, too, whereby the regents could feel the public pulse.[2]

Such was the condition of the United Netherlands, ill adapted in many particulars for a system of national ad-ministration. During active hostilities many difficulties passed comparatively unobserved, but it was a question whether even Oldenbarnevelt's remarkable powers of persuasion could continue to compensate for a central government incapable of forcing willing and unwilling to coöperate to the behoof of the nation.   It was also quest-ionable whether Maurice's influence would be equally potent in time of peace, when there were no armies to lead or cities to beleaguer.

[1] Kronijk, *Hist. Gen.*, xxvi., p. 97.
[2] See Blok's article, *De Nederlandsche vlugschriften over de vrede-onderhandelingen te Munster*, in *Versl. en Med. Kon. Acad.*, 4th series, i., p. 292.

The existence of these defects was acknowledged universally, and there were various plans mooted for their remedy.[1] There was talk of promoting Maurice to be president of the council, stadtholder, or even prince in name over all the provinces.[2] It was urged that the real liberties of the land would be thus assured, as by the proposed elevation of Prince William in 1584. But Maurice, a man of military authority, who could brook no opposition, did not wish a limited sovereignty, and the other provinces were afraid of any greater centralisation of power in Holland. Oldenbarnevelt himself understood Maurice and the interests of the land too well not to fear great difficulties in case of such a step, and remained firm in his conviction that it was advisable to preserve existing conditions. Jeannin, the French ambassador, whose sovereign had exerted pressure to induce improvement in the Netherland administration,[3] finally conceded that there was little danger in making no change. Thus nothing came of all the schemes mooted.

The contests with Zealand about the quotas (not ended until 1617), however, revealed the clogs in the state machinery. In Utrecht, theological deputies, like those in the time of Leicester, were revived. The Catholics manifested a threatening attitude during the festivities over the Truce,[4] while many democrats were eager for an opportunity to reinstate burgher rights in opposition to the dominant influence of the landed nobles and the regents.

Under leadership of a clever man of distinguished birth, Jonker Dirk Canter, and of the ex-schepen, Hendrik van Helsdingen, soon joined by the old firebrand,

---

[1] See Jeannin, *Négociations*, i., p. 185 ; iv., p. 116.
[2] *Ibid.*, iii., p. 205.
[3] *Ibid.*, iv., p. 132.
[4] Van Meteren, p. 955 ; *Winwood Papers*, iii., pp. 108, 115, 132, 139, 149.

Van Brakel, a serious agitation broke out (January 20, 1610), and the authorities were forced into changing the municipal government which dated from 1588.

The new officers confirmed by Maurice as stadtholder, after consultation with the States-General, immediately attempted to attain their ends in the provincial Estates wherein the nobles were still dominant, and demanded restoration of the first branch, that of the "elect," in the old form, exclusion of certain nobles from the second branch, that of the nobles, besides freedom of religion for the Catholics. Many ancient hangers-on of Deventer, too, again took courage and showed themselves in the city.[1] The Estates of Utrecht, fearing lest thé nobles might lose their hold on provincial affairs, refused to accede to these demands, and were actually attacked in person by the armed populace. They were obliged to call on the States-General and the prince to put an end to the riots. The States sent the prince, his brother, and five distinguished statesmen from various provinces to the city. The result was that arbitrary powers were offered to Maurice, as once before they had been to Leicester. The prince was not averse to accepting the offer, believing that he would find effective support among the people as against the regents. In connection with these plans the city government demanded that the States-General should release Maurice from his ancient oath as stadtholder, so that he might receive more ample instruction. The prince speedily found himself in a false position, while the Utrecht democracy took on a more defined opposition to the States-General, and all attempts to bring about a more amiable attitude failed. It really looked, at Utrecht, as though they were striving to wreck the republic, and many thought the prince's attitude suspicious in connection with the plans of 1609.

Warned by Oldenbarnevelt, the States-General per-

[1] Arend, Van Rees, and Brill, *Geschiedenis des Vaderlands*, iii., 2, p. 446.

ceived the danger, and informed the French and English ambassadors of what measures they were to take further. Then they and the council of state established themselves at Woerden (March 16, 1610), whither the province of Holland, too, sent her deputies.   Thus the first statesmen of the republic were assembled, accompanied by the two envoys.   Hither, too, were invited the Estates and the city government of Utrecht, together with the prince and the other members of the commission still in the city, who had to promise to return at a fixed date.   A statement of the grievances was made by both parties. The city demanded the prince as arbiter with the condition that he should be absolved from his oath to the States-General as stadtholder, which was contrary to the wishes of the Estates, while the States on their part refused their consent to the prince's return to Utrecht. On March 19th, the city deputies left Woerden in high dudgeon, and civil war seemed only too possible.

It did not, however, go so far, but Utrecht's delay in acceding to the demands of the States-General gave rise to a report that the republic was at once to be turned into a monarchy with the prince at the head.[1]   A resolution was taken at The Hague to compel the refractory city to submission by force of arms.   Maurice opposed this measure, and roundly refused to lead the troops in person or to permit Frederick Henry to do so.[2]

Utrecht at first refused to admit the garrison of 2000 men.   But after Canter had tried in vain to obtain aid from Amsterdam, the ringleaders consented to open negotiations with Frederick Henry, the council of state, and, later, with the States-General themselves.   On April 6th, the city submitted, according to the demands of the conquerors, to the decision of the foreign ambassadors, the States-General, the council of state, and Prince Maurice,

[1] *Winwood Papers*, iii., p. 134.
[2] The force in all amounted to 9000 men.

under promises of an universal amnesty,—an issue which displeased many on account of the implication that Canter and his followers were to be left unpunished.

The difficulties were not wholly solved. A few weeks later the States-General found occasion to open negotiations again and meantime to replace the ex-regents in the government—a violation of the treaty of April 6th, but a measure counted as imperative on account of the rebellious attitude of Canter and his accomplices, who had sent an embassy to the cities of Holland, and at length alienated even Maurice by their violent behaviour. New oaths of fidelity were exacted from all officials, an incipient conspiracy was promptly quelled, and serious disturbances were at an end, thanks to the strong hand of the government directed by Oldenbarnevelt.

At Leeuwarden, too, a popular movement gained some strength (1609) for a time. And here, too, it was evident from the part taken by William Louis, as it had been from that played by Maurice at Utrecht, that the people's resistance to the regent aristocracy was not wholly displeasing to the stadtholder, and this made the matter the more serious, as the church disputes, already only too prevalent, began gradually to assume a more definite form and to ferment the discontent of the people against the States' government. It was not unnatural that rumours gained credence of great changes in the government institutions of the provinces through the influence of the democrats or of the monarchical idea. The dangers which had menaced the authority of the States in the time of Leicester were revived. Then the States had emerged from the contest stronger than before. But then the opposition had been led by a foreigner, and foreigners had always been distasteful to native Netherlanders. If the prince were openly to oppose the States, with whom he had come into collision during the past year, then it was difficult to foresee how a strife might

end.   But as long as Oldenbarnevelt kept a firm hold on
the reins, such perils did not appear imminent, and the
party in office in Holland, Utrecht, and the chief cities
of Gelderland, Overyssel, and Friesland looked with confidence to the man — as the very personification, as it
were, of the States' government — who had administered
national affairs so brilliantly since 1588.   So long as an
authority like his, even if it were chiefly through his masterly personality, stood at the head of the government,
the difficulties existing in the early years of the Truce
did not seem overweening, and the hope of Spain that
this too would give rise to broils was far from realisation.

But there were elements in existence which could cause
this peace to disappear and bring Holland to the eve of a
civil war.

CHAPTER XIV

REMONSTRANTS AND CONTRA-REMONSTRANTS

CALVINISM was divided into two schools from the earliest days of its appearance in Holland. In the first synods, the precisians and the liberals, different fundamentally in character, were already ranged into parties.[1] One side accused the other of being still tainted with the leaven of papistry or of being Pelagians, Socinians, and atheists, to which the others answered freely. Men like Coolhaes at Leyden, Duifhuis at Utrecht, Coornhert and his sympathisers, were exposed to fierce attacks, and even to persecution. In the times of Leicester the quarrels about the convention of a national synod again set the factions at open variance. At that time it had been evident that, as a rule, the regents were in sympathy with the liberals rather than with the ultra-orthodox. Many of the so-called " politycque " regents had been educated in their youth under the influence of Erasmian ideas.[2] They believed in reform within the church, but disapproved violent measures, and there had always been opposition between the class to which they belonged and the theologians, who gave too much weight, urged their opponents, to all matters of religion, and who would have liked to follow the example

[1] *Preciesen en rekkelyken.* Compare p. 58.
[2] De Groot, *Verantwoordingh van de wettelicke Regeering van Hollant ende Westfrieslant*, p. 29. Paris, 1622.

of Calvin at Geneva and direct the state according to biblical principles. The " politicals " preferred to speak in general terms of the " Christian " or " evangelical " religion, while the zealous Calvinists were wont to declare that they embraced " reform " principles. The former, with Prince William at the head of the Reformed Church, had favoured its interests in Holland and the other provinces, rather for the sake of state interests than from any conviction of its particular right, while protecting other shades of opinion as much as possible against the claims of the Calvinists, and shielding them from total destruction.[1] Many would have agreed with Prince William in wishing universal religious toleration for all creeds that were not dangerous to society.

The example of Geneva under Calvin was a constant warning, and the bias was plainly shown in the manner in which Oldenbarnevelt and his followers, in parrying church influence in political matters, had attempted to organise the church in the province of Holland in consultation with moderate preachers of both parties. From that time, the orthodox party had justly regarded the advocate as the head of their political foes, or rather as the head of the " libertines," whose motto, *Nil scire tutissima fides*, was equivalent in their eyes to unbelief.

As long as " heresy " remained confined to a few preachers, the orthodox majority in the church had little difficulty in holding the widespread elements of opposition in check by means of classis and synod. The removal of Cornelis Wiggertsz. at Hoorn in 1596 is one proof of this. And the States, both in that case and in that of Coolhaes, finally acted according to the opinion of the " precisians "; although more because they were unwilling to displease the populace than because they disapproved of the preachers; and they were, moreover, more

[1] Compare Naber, *Calvinist of Libertynsch*, chapter i. Utrecht, 1884.

desirous of putting an end to the quarrels than of showing sympathy for the majority.   This was especially plain both in the case of Duifhuis and (1591) in that of Herman Herbertsz. at Gouda, who was retained in spite of orthodox opposition.   The authorities of many another Holland city gave convincing proofs of such trend of opinion although they acted in conformity with the demands of the church.[1]   Moderate theologians like the Leyden professors, Franciscus Junius, Tuningius, and Trelcatius, like Johannes Uyttenbogaert, once preacher at Utrecht, later at the Hague, and chaplain of Prince Maurice, offered, in the removal of troublesome preachers like Wiggertsz., a helping hand to more zealous colleagues like Plancius of Amsterdam, Donteclock of Delft, Acronius of Leeuwarden, and Franciscus Gomarus, professor at Leyden (1594).   But the moderate were not inclined to submit in all cases, or to give in where the principles of church teaching were at stake.   From the beginning, the stringent doctrine of predestination had aroused the opposition of many liberals, while the demand of complete submission to all the theological doctrines in the Netherland confession and the Heidelberg Catechism was used by the orthodox as a powerful method of settling all variance in dogma.

Among the leaders of the moderate thinkers in Holland the chief was Jacob Harmensz., known as Arminius after his call to Amsterdam in 1588.   He was a native of Oudewater, and educated by his studies at Leyden, at Geneva under Beza, and at Basel, by his travels in Italy and Germany, to be a zealous student in dogmatic theology and in philosophy, which he had pursued in the tenor of the famous Huguenot philosopher, Pierre de la Ramée, the antagonist of the dogmatism of Aristotle. These studies had brought him under suspicion of the orthodox, first in Geneva, later in his native land.   Then

[1] Naber, p. 42.

his participation in the composition of the " libertine " church-ritual of 1591 had increased this suspicion, not without reason. His calling as preacher had kept him, as well as others of his tendency, within the bounds desired by the majority under the influence of the supervision of classis and synod. The deaths of Junius and Trelcatius of the pest which raged in Leyden in 1602, afforded an opportunity to the curators of the university to consider this gifted, versatile, and very moderate Amsterdam preacher as eligible for a chair as the colleague of the stricter teacher Gomarus, in spite of the opposition of the latter and his allies. The influence of his friend and congenial spirit, Uyttenbogaert, and of Prince Maurice, effected the nomination of Arminius.[1] The prince and his chaplain thought that Arminius would make as little scandal as professor at Leyden as he had as preacher at Amsterdam, and even Gomarus at first did not appear dissatisfied with the opinions of his new colleague, whom he had examined when the latter received his doctorate.

Shortly after the arrival of Arminius at Leyden, Gomarus' opinions began to change. The eloquent new professor attracted the students, but speedily annoyed his colleague by the lack of Calvin's and Beza's principles and by the introduction of doctrines of the liberal Coornhert; yes, even those of the Catholic Thomas Aquinas, and of the Jesuits, Suarez and Bellarminius. Gomarus, native of Bruges, had emigrated with his family on account of their religion to the Palatinate, was educated at Heidelberg, and had been preacher in Frankfort. There he had grown up in a strictly Calvinist environment. Later he was active in the Netherland churches of the exiles. As soon as he grasped the tendency of the teaching of

---

[1] Baudartius, *Memoryen*, 2nd edition (1624), p. 4 ; Rogge, Uyttenbogaert, i., pp. 107–227. See p. 305, where these points are touched in connection with the truce.

Arminius he was greatly displeased, especially when it .
was evident that the students were more and more impressed by the doctrines, which no longer seemed so
innocent as Gomarus had thought, discussed them among
themselves, and later proclaimed them from their pulpits,
thus spreading the ideas of their master through the
land.   In the summer of 1605, Arminius was admonished by the deputies of the north and south Holland
synods not to publish his objections to the established
doctrine in his lectures, but to discuss them privately
with them.   Arminius rejected this suggestion, and refused an invitation of the Leyden church council to discuss opinions with them.[1] He also declined to appear in
public outside the academic lecture-room.

This attitude of Arminius made bad blood.   Certain
preachers began to attack him in the pulpit and in writing.
In the closed synods and assemblies of the classis in
Holland, bitter attacks were also made.   On the other
hand, some of the older preachers espoused his opinions
in regard to certain points; the disputes of the students
increased, and many young ministers fresh from Leyden
taught his opinions with ardour.   Academical disputes,
which excited more or less scandal from October, 1604,
were continued by the two professors to defend their
points of view, especially in regard to predestination and
free-will, and did much to stoke the fire of contention.[2]

Neither the warnings of Uyttenbogaert not to go too
far, nor the threats of the opposition, served to silence
Arminius, while Gomarus, egged on by his friends, had
equally little desire to consign the dispute to oblivion.
And the utterances of Gomarus caused Arminius to
develop his own opinions still more strongly, so that
the difference became more and more defined.   A resolution adopted by the south Holland synods at this period
in order to force the preachers within their jurisdiction

[1] Baudartius, pp. 5 and 6.   [2] Uyttenbogaert, *Kerk. Hist.*, iii., p. 109.

to subscribe to both Catechism and Confession, roused the supporters of Arminius to violent opposition. Duplessis-Mornay, the old Huguenot, watched the quarrel anxiously from France, and gave earnest and repeated warnings of the danger.

There had long been talk of a national synod. This was now eagerly desired by the more orthodox party in the majority among the preachers throughout the land, though not in Holland, in order to tighten the bands established by Confession and Catechism against the dissenting doctrines. It could not be denied that the history of the origin of the Reformed Church in the Netherlands plainly proved that a national church in the Netherlands was impracticable. The utmost to be expected was provincial churches whose interconnection would be a loose bond. Article 13 and the following in the Union of Utrecht established the provincial character of religious affairs beyond doubt. In the provinces, synodal alliances existed. Still the synodal bond was not itself very strong, and the connection between the congregations was rather by means of the classis than the synod. That was the higher unit in the estimation of the congregations.[1]

While it was evident that a national synod would further the interests of unity and of coöperation in theological matters, fear was entertained by the liberals and the politicals of a reformed state church *in optima forma;* and they were unwilling to risk a synod, while the orthodox urged it vigorously.

At the end of 1605, the synods of north and south Holland petitioned the States-General in the name of " the Netherland churches " to convene such an assembly under their authority. The States were disinclined to accede to this request. In March, 1606, they finally

---

[1] The church council, *kerkeraad*, was equivalent to the consistory of the American Dutch Reformed Church.

consented to a preliminary meeting wherein the topics of discussion should be decided, while it was intimated that a revision of Confession, of Catechism, and of church ordinances was to be expected. The members of the preliminary commission were to be appointed by the States at the first opportunity.¹ Averse as were the ortho-dox to state interference in church affairs, they agreed to the conditions for the sake of obtaining the synod. There was some difficulty about the revision, which Olden-barnevelt claimed did not imply alteration.

Some delays ensued owing to the peace negotiations, so that it was May, 1607, before the commissioners met. Meanwhile the excitement about the doctrines of Ar-minius caused some anxiety. To the annoyance of the ultra-orthodox, the commission of advice *de forma et modo synodi* was not chosen by the churches, but by the provincial Estates. Arminius and Uyttenbogaert and two deputies from Utrecht were opposed to a majority of thirteen more orthodox members.

There was a violent dispute regarding the eight points which they were ordered by the States to consider, but unanimity of opinion could not be obtained, and both parties presented their memorials to the States, while an attempt of the majority to limit the prudent Arminius to a mere discussion of his grievances failed. Such was the position of the States in regard to the decision in the great questions that were discussed between the adherents of Arminius and those of Gomarus, considering that they must define the principles upon which the national synod was to rest.

Already people began to talk of an approaching schism in the Netherland church. Pamphlets wherein predesti-nation was discussed by its friends and antagonists in sharp terms embittered the contest. Personal enmity was manifest in the attacks of the leaders of both sides.

¹ Baudartius, p. 9.

" Considerations " (1608) on the missive of Prosper and
Hilarius to Augustine about Pelagianism opened the
series. Coolhaes took a position between Gomarus and
Arminius, and his " theses," translated in 1609, were
published and widely read.[1] Bitter " answers," " warnings," and discussions followed each other. Among the
most violent defenders of the theories of Gomarus appeared the preacher emeritus Smoutius at Rotterdam,
Sibrandus Lubbertus, professor at Franeker, the preachers Donteclock at Delft, Festus Hommius at Leyden,
Johannes Bogerman at Leeuwarden, Johannes Acronius
at Groningen. On the other side, Arminius was supported by the violent Venator (de Jager) of Alkmaar, by
the Leyden theologians, Bertius and Corvinus, and others;
not the least being Uyttenbogaert, who was at one with
him in the main matter. An anonymous Catechism,
which appeared in 1607 at Gouda, rightly attributed to
the notorious Herbertsz. and approved by Arminius,[2]
gave rise to a fierce war of words as the Heidelberg
terms were changed for biblical phrases. Immediately
after the truce, the Netherland church was in a blaze,
especially in Holland and Utrecht, where Arminius
counted the majority of his followers. In the other
provinces the existing church ordinances gave an opportunity to the Calvinist majority to enforce their doctrines.

Under these circumstances the reluctance of the States
to convene a synod where excited discussion might have
an injurious effect upon the peace negotiations was natural. The Estates of Holland had the same dread, and
had delayed the assemblies of the provincial synods until
the summer of 1608 so as to avoid dangerous disputes.
This was a great annoyance to the ultra-Calvinists.
Political and church differences began to be intermingled.
The Gomarists, sure of a majority in the desired synod,

[1] Rogge, Uyttenbogaert, i., p. 370.
[2] *Acta Synodalia*, ed. Reitsma en Van Veen, iii., p. 301.

declared in favour of its convention, provided it were independent of the States, and at the same time they expressed their disapprobation of the peace with Spain, the ancient foe of their church. The Arminians, somewhat doubtful as to the outcome of the synod, attached themselves in general to their protectors, the States, who, led by Oldenbarnevelt, were rapidly nearing their goal—the truce with Spain.

The Estates of Holland tried to put differences aside and to reconcile the opponents with each other. The two leaders, accompanied by several followers, were given an opportunity, once before the High Council, afterwards before the assembly of the States, to expound their doctrine, but they could not really agree, although some understanding was effected. The " tribune of authority," regarded distrustfully by the stronger party, —yes, unjustly suspected of intruding lay authority into ecclesiastical matters,—thus saw the failure of their attempts to attain unity.[1] On the contrary, Arminius was obliged to expound his opinions in full, and Gomarus was quite ready to oppose his. The points in dispute were more sharply defined. Nor did anything result from a conference summoned, August 20, 1609, by the Estates of Holland at the Hague, wherein each of the two professors with four preachers of his school, defended his standpoint before the assembled Estates. After two days' discussion they separated. Thus the quarrel of the theologians dragged on, to the annoyance of many at home and abroad, until Arminius, long suffering from consumption, died at Leyden (October 19th). The Truce was then half a year old, and the Gomarists perceived with chagrin that the Arminians gained favour with the States, as Coolhaes and his sympathisers had done earlier. Indeed, they made even closer cause with the States, and recognised their authority in church matters.

[1] Baudartius, p. 13.

Even before the death of Arminius, this had been very evident in the church quarrels where the impetuous preachers, Venator (de Jager) and Hillenius (Van Hille), had been in bitter opposition for years. In September, 1608, the Alkmaar classis wished to force their preachers into signing the Confession and Catechism and to suspend the dissenters — like Venator. They were supported in their action by a synod of north Holland, which met at Hoorn with special permission from the Estates. The Estates demanded reversion of the suspension, and the municipal council, whose majority—as was almost universal in Holland — consisted of politicals or liberals, retained Venator for the time being, to the chagrin of the council, classis, and synod, who charged him with adultery as well as heterodoxy. The latter accusation rested on a basis too insufficient to prosecute Venator, and a decision of the High Council to that effect was brought to the knowledge of the council. By the end of 1609, the suspension was not repealed, in spite of the repeated orders of the Estates, before whom Hillenius appeared reluctantly. This serious interference of the Arminian Estates with what appeared to be a purely church matter awakened bitter indignation among the Gomarists, who were in great majority among the population of the city.

A change in the Alkmaar magistracy at the end of 1609 brought about such a marked alteration in the government that the Hillenists, immediately counting on new supporters, renewed their attacks on Venator, an attitude which, on New Year's Eve, encouraged the archers to armed rebellion against the administration, still mainly Arminian.

This threatened uproar induced the Estates to take vigorous measures. A commission was appointed from them to restore order, first by attempting a reconciliation, and then, when this failed, by the appointment (February, 1610) of a new town council in accord with the Estates, which, desirous of breaking the opposition of the rebels effectually, banished Hillenius from the city, took a determined stand against classis and church council, and finally (July) dismissed the preacher as a disturber of the public peace. Venator, too, who was, in truth, not less turbulent than his opponent, was obliged to renounce preaching for a year, but was appointed rector of the Latin school.

The Hillenists refused to accept this decision, unjust to them, and insisted on recognising their leader as preacher. They went to Koedyk to hear him, where he had established himself, and were supported in their action by the classis. The consistory at Alkmaar was then changed at command of the new corporation for another which would submit to the will of the Estates and of the city government.[1] Thus the interference of the Estates was apparently necessary to put an end to the troubles in Alkmaar, and it was to be expected that the same thing might happen elsewhere.

The death of Arminius did not finish the quarrel. '' The fire was too hot and too much burnt into many hearts and minds.'' [2] His adherents and those of Gomarus wrote bitter pamphlets against each other. Coornhert's writings from the days of Leicester and earlier, were again widely disseminated. Gomarus himself, the Delft preacher Donteclock, Acronius of Schiedam, Smoutius of Rotterdam, Baudartius of Zutphen, appeared on one side; Corvinus, Venator, Bertius, Uyttenbogaert, on the other. The famous treatise on the office and authority of a higher Christian government in ecclesiastical affairs, written by the last-named, appeared in February, and called forth bitter responses. That by the Arminians was joyfully greeted as an eloquent plea for the rights of the Estates as opposed to the church, and was received

[1] Bruinvis, *Het Alkmaarsche kerkgeschil op't ergst.* Alkmaar, 1894.
[2] Baudartius, p. 22.

with satisfaction by all upholders of the government. Even an orthodox man like François van Aerssens was in accord with it. The book was composed in consultation with Oldenbarnevelt and other statesmen, and thus it was virtually an official declaration respecting the state's right in the midst of church discord, and the writer was protected against attacks made upon him.

Uyttenbogaert, the friend and protector of the dead theologian, was then the acknowledged head of the Arminians, the learned and influential leader of their party. It was through his influence, after he himself had refused the office, that the moderate theologian, Conradus Vorstius, author of *De Deo*, was called from Steinfurt to Leyden in 1611 to take the vacant chair. This call was bitterly opposed by the opposite party, who had wished to appoint a second orthodox professor as colleague to Gomarus, and a new war of words was excited, waged by Lubbertus and Bogerman, and answered by Arminians like Taurinus of Utrecht, sometimes moderately, but usually with acridity.

In the meantime secret meetings had been held at Gouda by twoscore Arminian preachers and laymen to make a defensive alliance against the majority of their confessional opponents in the Holland church. Under leadership of Uyttenbogaert this convention decided, again after a private consultation with Oldenbarnevelt,[1] to present a *Remonstrantie* to the Estates of Holland (June, 1610).

They wished to explain their point of view both to home opponents and to the learned world in general, and they did this by drawing up five articles formulating their opinions, hitherto somewhat fluctuating.[2] In adopting the declaration of November, 1608, and in order not to arouse suspicion of wishing " changes in religion," the

[1] Verhooren van de Groot, *Werken Hist. Gen.*, No. 14, p. 237.
[2] See Baudartius, p. 26.

preachers summoned before the Estates then urged the convention of a national synod for the revision of Confession and Catechism, as had been desired by the States-General in 1606.

They declared briefly that nothing new was implied therein, and that they themselves did nothing unjust by leaving the direction of the affair, as concerned manner and time of the convention, to the States. They protested against the attempt of the individual synods in Holland and elsewhere to force subscription to Confession and Catechism for the purpose of submitting the signers henceforth to a close "censure" which they deemed as undue pressure, as the introduction of a "papal basis wherein such human decrees or writings were placed beyond bounds and in like grade to God's written word," which they counted as insufferable. This was preliminary to the five points which they held as antagonistic to God's word, as also antagonistic to the spirit of Confession and Catechism. They declared themselves opposed to the following doctrines:

I. Predestination in its defined form, as if God by an eternal and irrevocable decision had condemned men, some to eternal bliss, others to eternal damnation, without any other law than his own pleasure. On the contrary, they thought that God by the same resolution wished to make all believers in Christ who persisted in their belief to the end, blessed in Christ, and for His sake would only condemn the unconverted and unbelieving.

II. To the doctrine of election, according to which the chosen were counted as necessarily and unavoidably blessed and the outcasts necessarily and unavoidably lost. They urged the milder doctrine that Christ had died for all men, and the believers were only chosen in so far as they enjoyed the forgiveness of sins.

III. To the doctrine that Christ died for the elect alone to make them blessed and no one else, ordained as mediator; on the contrary, they urge the possibility of salvation for others not elect.

IV. To the doctrine that the grace of God affects the elect only, while the reprobates cannot participate in this through their conversion but only through their own strength. On the other hand, they, the " Remonstrants,"—a name they received later from this, their " Remonstrance,"— hold that man " has no saving belief in himself, nor out of the force of his free-will " if he lives in sin, but that it is necessary that " he be born again from God in Christ by means of His Holy Spirit, and renewed in understanding, affection, or will and all strength," since without grace man cannot resist sin, although he cannot be counted as irresistible to grace.

V. To the doctrine that he who had once attained true saving grace can never lose it and be wholly debased. They held, on the contrary, that whoever had received Christ's quickening spirit had thereby a strong weapon against Satan, sin, the world, and his own flesh, although they would not decide at the time without further investigation—later they adopted this too—whether he could not lose this power " forsaking the beginning of his being in Christ." They regarded this opinion as fully in accordance with the Word of God and with the spirit of Confession and Catechism which they accepted as the basis of " Harmony and unity with the Reformed Churches in Europe."

They appealed to the authority of the Estates as "having the supreme direction and the highest jurisdiction over ecclesiastical and lay affairs under God and in accordance with His Word in these territories," to hold a national synod, and begged to be allowed to retain their opinions until such synod. Further, they asked the protection of the Estates in case an ecclesiastic censure were proclaimed against them on account of this Remonstrance, declaring that they did not wish a schism, but reconciliation.

On this basis a discussion was once more considered possible by the Estates. Accordingly they summoned both parties to send deputies, six from each side, to attempt to arrive at an agreement.

The Gomarists perceived that it would be desirable for them also to publish a statement. Their six deputies were charged with the task. It was some time (March, 1611) before these gentlemen, who could not at once obtain a copy of the Remonstrance, were ready with their response, or " Contra - remonstrance," in which the opinions of the Arminians were vigorously controverted. Seven articles, preceded by a long general statement, served to expound their opinion. The subscribers were six clergymen of the party of Gomarus, deputed by the classis of Holland to go to the Hague in response to the demand of the Estates. It was drafted by the pugnacious Festus Hommius.

The document began with a sharp contradiction of the introduction of the Remonstrance in which it was demonstrated that there was already reason to accuse their opponents of the introduction of novelties, now that they had refused to broach their opinions in the church assemblies; their desire, too, for revision of the Confession, which was quite unnecessary, proved this, for they themselves desired nothing other than the old without alteration. Confession and Catechism were human, to be sure, but serviceable as formularies of unity in doctrine, naturally not so immutable as God's Word, the only precept; but as they were drawn up with due deliberation they were not to be changed on the assertions of a " testy and curious spirit," on account of the danger of inconsistency and instability, a great disaster for the doctrine of the church and for theology. There was much defection from church doctrine, as appeared plainly. Therefore the Contra-remonstrants held fast to Confession and Catechism as bulwarks against such defection.

What the opponents considered church virtue was evident from the appeal for protection from the Estates against the censure. They also protested against the method of procedure of the opposition party, who had said to the Estates what they had declined to state to the church authorities. They declared the five points, wherein the opinions of the Arminians were comprised, were not clear, ambiguous, and in part conflicting with God's Word. Therefore it was necessary to make a counterstatement and the following articles were presented:

I. God had, after Adam's fall, reserved a certain number of human beings from destruction, and, in His eternal and unchangeable counsel, destined them to salvation through Christ, leaving the others alone in accordance with His righteous judgment.

II. The elect are not only the good Christians who are adult, but also the " children of the covenant as long as they do not prove the contrary by their action."

III. In this election God does not consider belief or conversion, but acts simply according to His pleasure.

IV. God sent His son, Christ, for the salvation of the elect, and of them alone.

V. The Holy Ghost in the Scriptures and in preaching speaks to them alone, to instruct and to convert them.

VI. The elect can never lose the true belief, but they obtain power of resistance through the Holy Ghost active in them.

VII. This would not lead them to follow the dictates of the flesh carelessly, but, on the contrary, they would go God's way, considering that thereby alone could they be saved.

At the end of this statement respecting the points touched by the Arminians, follows a sharp attack on certain false deductions and slanders drawn from these premises by " human intellect and the understanding of the flesh." Further, they refer their opponents to a lawful free synodal gathering in which they would take part even though accused by the Arminians of being quarrelsome, but first they must know precisely wherein and how far alteration is desired, considering that the Remonstrance did not make a sufficiently plain statement. For those who wished to be received later into the service of church and school, and who accepted the Remonstrance, there could be no question, for their discord would never cease.

The Contra-remonstrants were well inclined to closer conference and disputes about the matter, provided that it was on the earlier footing, and provided that the decision should rest with the church—that is, if not with a national, then with a provincial synod, if need be with advice from foreign churches. For the formation of a Holland church wholly of a different doctrine was certainly not intended by the Estates, nor would it have been allowed by the great majority of Netherland preachers and laymen. This violent and sharply defined document ended with a request to the Remonstrants to come out roundly also in regard to the last point not decided in the Remonstrance, and further to put everything into writing in the hope of a good outcome of all this difficulty.

The difference between the two parties is very evident in these two documents. On the one side a very moderate conception, averse to extremes, drawn up with the use of elastic, vague terms; on the other a strict tenacity of the doctrine, sharply formulated statements, violent tone of speech, aversion to any concession to opponents. It was indeed the " precisians " *versus* the liberals of an earlier time. On the one hand, the dogmatists, the zealous Calvinists, the like-minded with Moded and Dathenus, and with them the orthodox majority; on the other, the gentler-minded, those averse to strict formulas, the intellectual kin of Coornhert and Duifhuis, and with them the minority of learned and cultivated people in

the Holland cities, and the regents themselves. Moreover, it is clear from this exposition how, in the estimation of the political regents, the difference between the
doctrines of the two parties might seem very " subtle "
and not so important that an agreement would be difficult, and also how they could at the beginning regard
the quarrel as purely theoretically theological — yes, as
hair-splitting.[1] This was also the belief of some of the
Arminians. The Gomarists, on the other hand, had quite
different views. They regarded the foundations of Protestantism as in danger, and accused their opponents of
socinian, pelagian, and papistical heresies.

The latter accusation made an especially deep impression
on the great mass of the reformed, fearful of the considerable majority of the Catholics, who still formed two-thirds
of the population, " *la plus saine et la plus riche partie.*"[2]
Fierce pamphlets against the mass, the bread-god of the
Romanists, appeared in the early years of the Truce.
Rumours of secret nocturnal meetings, of expected
attacks of the Catholics on churches and stadthouses
crept out now and then. The activity of Catholic powers
then evident in Europe, the secret but not unknown work
of the Jesuits to strengthen Catholicism, the gradual increase of spiritual and religious exercises had much influence on this opinion of the reformed. Also in the north
it was perfectly plain that the religious zeal of the priests
and the activity of the Jesuits had affected the Catholics,
who had been very discouraged about 1580. When the
" archbishop " Vosmeer laid down his weary head in 1614,
and was followed in his apostolic vicarate by Philippus
Rovenius,[3] the outlook for the future was encouraging,
the more as no persecution was to be dreaded from the
uppermost party in Holland.

[1] See Uyttenbogaert's pamphlet, *Clare Justificatie.*
[2] Oldenbarnevelt in Carleton, i., 220.
[3] Knuttel, *De toestand der Nederlandsche ten tyde der Republiek,* i., p. 81.

Before his departure in 1609, Jeannin had earnestly warned the States-General to be more lenient towards the Catholics—yes, to grant them complete freedom of religion. Had they not participated in the opposition to Spain ? Had they not shared the common danger ? Jeannin thought it was now time to repay those services by conceding to them the very point for which the reformed had striven—free exercise of religion.[1] But the States were disinclined to take that step. They refused the ambassador's demand and even kept it secret, but promised, generally, without giving much publicity to the matter, to act in a moderate manner. For the time being, Jeannin and Henry IV. rested content with that. The synods and classes repeatedly urged measures against the papal superstition, and their pressure resulted in the edict of the States-General of 1612 forbidding instruction in foreign Catholic or Jesuit schools, against meetings to celebrate Catholic rites, against the activity of the priests who had flocked across the borders in great numbers since the Truce. But Catholicism remained in existence, the more because the orders were not really enforced, much to the dissatisfaction of the people.

With the deliverance of the Remonstrance and the Contra-remonstrance the conflict really opened, and the two parties, now called to The Hague by the Estates to a conference, each represented by six preachers, were to defend their respective articles. On March 11, 1611, they were convened on the authority of the Estates of Holland and West Friesland. The conference promised as little as the earlier disputes and discussions. Instead of being satisfied, the people became embittered. For two months there was a violent war of words and a flood of pamphlets, both about the appointment of Vorstius and all other important points, and as to whether the five

[1] *Négociations*, iv., p. 217.

articles of the Remonstrants were in accord with the Confession and Catechism. From the advices and explanations presented, it was plain that no accord was possible between the two parties, and the conference ended in May without result.

But the Estates did not relinquish hope of deciding the matter by their authority. An attempt emanating from them to submit the examination of the candidates and calls to ministers to control by establishing *commissarissen politycq*, and to have such deputies regularly appear in the church assemblies, aroused fierce opposition in the stronger party, who were bitterly averse to the States' interference with church matters. Also they thought the commissioners would further the acceptance of Remonstrants as preachers.

In various places the quarrels assumed such proportions that the Estates considered it their duty to step in as mediators.

The appointment of Vorstius at Leyden gave rise to a violent controversy, especially when, in April, this very pugnacious theologian, after some hesitation, accepted the call of the curators.[1] Gomarus, refusing to accept the heretic as colleague, resigned his office and betook himself to Middelburg as preacher and professor in the Athenæum. In Friesland a storm was raised at once against the new Leyden professor. The Estates of the provinces protested about it to the States-General and Prince Maurice, at the instance of Lubbertus and Bogerman, and backed by the chancellor and council of Gelderland and the governments of Dordrecht, Amsterdam, and other cities. The English ambassador, Winwood, himself an earnest orthodox Protestant, and also inspired by the Contra-remonstrant preachers, became a violent partisan. His king, the theologically inclined James I., made repeated complaints about the extravagant

[1] Rogge, *Uyttenbogaert*, ii., p. 88.

and schismatic opinions of Arminius and the appointment of Vorstius,[1] "the blasphemous monster." When
the complaint received no sufficient answer, James wrote
(February, 1612) a second letter, wherein the law was laid
down to the Estates of Holland in a lofty tone. The attacked at first paid little attention to the king's protests.
They said he had been misinformed by Winwood and
others. Then they thought it wiser to be conciliatory,
for the sake of a good understanding with England.
Vorstius was persuaded, through the mediation of Oldenbarnevelt, to go to Gouda for a time, where he busied
himself in the composition of a mass of pamphlets for
the defence of his opinion.[2] His chair and that of
Gomarus were filled by the moderate teacher, Johannes
Polyander, and Simon Episcopius, the latter a Remonstrant, against whom little could be urged at the time.

At Rotterdam there was a violent quarrel between the
preachers Geselius and Grevinchovius, similar to that
between Hillenius and Venator at Alkmaar. Here, too,
the result was to the advantage of the Remonstrants.
Geselius was removed by the municipal government, with
the approval of the Estates, and banished from the city,
together with the violent Smoutius, who had settled
there. At Rotterdam the orthodox remained faithful
to their cause, and on Sundays visited the neighbouring
places of Schieland to hear preachers of their tendency,
and formed, in imitation of what had happened at Alkmaar and elsewhere, a dissenting church council.

In other provinces, too, the situation began to be
strained.

After the victory of the ancient government at Utrecht,
which was mainly due to the powerful support given by
the Estates of Holland, they had become the protector

[1] *Winwood Papers*, iii., pp. 293, 309, 316.
[2] Compare Petit, *Bibliographische lijst der werken van de Leidsche
hoogleeraren*, i., p. 96. Leyden, 1894.

of the Arminian preachers Taurinus and Spanhovius against the opposition of the orthodox. Gilles van Ledenberg, secretary of the Estates, was in Utrecht the leader of the political liberals in office; the influential Adolph, lord of Moersbergen, member of the Utrecht nobility, led the body of the nobles in the same direction; the advocate of Holland was in constant relation with both. The circumstance that Canter and Helsdingen, the leaders of the opposition of 1610, were orthodox Calvinists, shows fully that the Utrecht disturbances of that year found, too, support in the church movement.[1] The enemies of the Arminian States government recognised in them their opponents in theological affairs.

It is also not surprising that we find Uyttenbogaert appearing here in November, 1610, to regulate church conditions in consultation with the victorious regents. He was asked to preach there, and he had serious thoughts of accepting, but refused, although in the following year he allowed himself to be persuaded to go to Utrecht for a time. He succeeded in reconciling the parties, and in abolishing the dissenting church, although the preacher, Van Dongen, remained at Jutphaas. At the request of the Estates of Utrecht he established at the same time, to oppose to the " satanic spirit," a church order for the province which was similar in many respects to the Holland order of 1591, never enforced. This was accepted (August, 1612) by the Utrecht synod, whereby " toleration was asserted by a law of state and church." Three years later, Uyttenbogaert could boast that this " formula of unity " had put an end to the differences here, although " works of former misunderstanding still smouldered and certain firebrands were trying to wake them with the bellows of blind zeal to a flaming fire."[2] Indeed, his last sermon at Utrecht can be taken as a model of unity and religious enthusiasm.

[1] Rogge, *Uyttenbogaert*, ii., p. 133.　　　　[2] *Ibid.*, p. 149.

The same spirit was manifest in the Overyssel capitals. In the north-west of this province, the old jurisdiction of Vollenhoven, the orthodox held the field, as also, since the "Reductie" of 1594, in the ultra-Calvinist provinces City and Land and Drenthe, where, under the leadership of the preachers of the city of Groningen, the Netherland Confession and the Heidelberg Catechism had been adopted in 1613 as fixed precepts of creed. There and in Zealand, where of old the stricter wing of Calvinism had prevailed, there had been little or no talk of Arminianism.

In Friesland some seething discontent prevailed for a longer period, but the Leeuwarden troubles of 1610, as well as those of Utrecht, had some connection with church troubles, and the government had been blamed by the people for favouring Catholics and Arminians against the acknowledged orthodox. Canter and Hels-dingen, Utrecht leaders, had also sought a refuge at Leeuwarden under the protection of the rigid Calvinist, William Louis, who of old had little sympathy with the liberal regents. In Friesland there was no question of any action on the part of the Arminian minority. The manner in which opposition was expressed by Lub-bertus and his followers against Vorstius; the suppres-sion of all utterances of Arminian tendency wherein the Estates of the province and the orthodox stadtholder lent effective aid; the violent discussion waged by Lubbertus against his colleague Drusius, suspected of Arminian heresy; the rapid increase in the number of orthodox preachers in Friesland—all point to the triumph of the stricter party in the north who decidedly opposed the tendency of the Estates of Holland and Utrecht.[1] Franeker, William Louis's foundation where Lubbertus gave the tone, remained a stronghold of orthodoxy, and the university established at Groningen in 1614, where

[1] Reitsma, *Honderd jaren uit de geschiedenis der hervorming in Friesland*, p. 364. Leeuwarden, 1876.

Gomarus himself was called in the following year, mainly owed its foundation to the desire of founding a new orthodox school in the north for the education of preachers in opposition to the apostatised school of Leyden. Ubbo Emmius, the first rector magnificus, belonged to the leaders of the stricter party, and the call of Gomarus showed what was wanted.

In Gelderland, Arminianism held its own in some districts as against the orthodox majority. In 1610, lack of unity did not result in quarrels, although they were alarmed at the increasing bitterness in Holland, and some were wholly at one with Arminius. As a preventive of the threatening schism, the Gelderland synod, where the Arminian preacher was influential, had urged Holland to hold a meeting at Harderwijk, whither all provincial synods should send a couple of representatives to discuss the differences—a national synod in miniature. The plan roused the opposition of the orthodox, who wanted to settle their own differences in order to see the quarrels arranged elsewhere. The preachers in Nimwegen and elsewhere were obnoxious on account of their sympathy with Arminius' doctrines, against which men like Professor Thysius at Harderwijk, the preachers Baudartius at Zutphen and Fontanus at Arnhem, were eager to work. The Harderwijk provincial assembly of 1612 accepted Confession and Catechism as precept, and enforced acceptance of them from the provincial preachers. Still the quarter of Nimwegen remained Remonstrant in sympathy, and a writ of Uyttenbogaert in 1613 strengthened many preachers in this opinion. In Arnhem a certain tendency to Arminianism began to show itself, but the other portions of the province kept true to the orthodox tendency.[1]

Such was the condition of church affairs in the spring of 1613. The reformed population of the republic were

---

[1] Rogge, *Uyttenbogaert*, ii., p. 125.

averse to the Remonstrants by a good majority. Three provinces with Drenthe could be rated as completely orthodox, and in four others there was again no doubt that a large majority of people and preachers were of the same opinion. But the Remonstrants had a majority in the Estates of Holland, of Utrecht, and of Overyssel, and in the quarter of Nimwegen. Moreover, most of the members of the municipal governments of the three provinces, even those in Gelderland, were in sympathy with them. Feeling strong from this support, they were wholly disinclined to strike colours to their opponents and to retreat from the standpoint of toleration towards other opinions. Relying on the sympathy of their friends in office, they refused to submit to the decision of a purely church synod, where they would undoubtedly be outvoted by the orthodox majority. This consideration determined Oldenbarnevelt and his followers to reject the propositions made in the spring of 1613 for a synod.

The advocate had watched the growth of church discords with anxiety. The attitude of the ultra-orthodox preachers made him dread a renewal of the strife of the time of Leicester. All attempts to reconcile the parties had failed. The admonitions to unity given by the honoured Huguenot, Duplessis-Mornay, who pointed out the desirability of mutual toleration, and advised a sober treatment of doctrines, was ineffectual to curb party spirit. A new conference was held at Delft between Uyttenbogaert and Hommius, at the instance of William Louis of Nassau, and lasted two days (February, 1613). Each preacher was accompanied by two colleagues of his party. It was as fruitless as all earlier discussions had been. Oldenbarnevelt thought that civil war could only be averted by asserting the authority of the Estates. As in the time of Leicester, he urged that it was better to be overlorded than to submit to mob rule.[1] The

[1] Oldenbarnevelt, *Verhooren*, pp. 10, 79, 93.

republic could not be ruled by the common folk, uneducated and easy to lead astray, '' the most dangerous, shameful, and ruinous government '' which a state could endure.   The lawful authority was lodged in the Estates, in the town councils which had existed for two centuries. under the government of the counts.   He was as averse to monarchical as to democratic principles, and was very much afraid of church domination in the state.[1] He had little interest in the theological disputes themselves.[2]   Arminian ideas about predestination were not exactly to his taste, but he counted a good government compatible with the doctrine of the Arminians, while he feared confusion and church tyranny from the supremacy of the Contra-remonstrants.   Toleration towards all, even the Catholics, was his cry, but at the same time he proposed to suppress all refractoriness.

King James made some effort to espouse the cause of the Contra-remonstrants, with whose religious views he sympathised.   Through the envoy Caron, the advocate now persuaded the king to write a letter,[3]—really drafted by Uyttenbogaert and Oldenbarnevelt,—urging that the supreme power, the *authorité publicque*, had a right to interpose in theological disputes in order to restore peace. The king added that both opinions were in accord with Christian truth and the nature of the human soul.[4]

Great was the chagrin of the Contra-remonstrants, and not less that of Winwood, at this unexpected action on the part of the king.   The English ambassador saw through the whole game, and warned his prince of the result.   Just then the embassy of 1613, charged with settling the difficulties respecting commerce and fishery, was on the point of departure for England.   Hugo de Groot, one of the members, was instructed by Oldenbarnevelt and Caron in regard to what had happened,

---

[1] De Groot, *Verhooren*, p. 239.   [3] Sent by mistake to the States-General.
[2] *Ibid.*, p. 181.   [4] *Winwood Papers*, iii., p. 451.

and succeeded in keeping the king, for the time, on the line he had adopted. James remained firm in his approval of government intervention in theological matters for the purpose of ending the dissensions. On his return, De Groot made a detailed report to Oldenbarnevelt, and also said that the opinion of the chief English theologians agreed in the main with the king's. Winwood's departure from the Hague in August was efficacious, too, in aiding the opposition. Still it was January, 1614, before the advocate succeeded in obtaining the resolution he desired from the Estates of Holland. The opposition of various cities had to be overcome, but finally the resolution was accepted by a majority of votes, though Amsterdam, Edam, and Purmerend, ruled mainly by the Contra-remonstrants, refused their adherence. The resolution decreed on the part of the Estates as "legal high supremacy," that the exposition of points of difference, universally known from the conference in 1611, should be handled with modesty and moderation, that the preachers must acknowledge God's mercy as the source of salvation and belief, and not represent God as the cause of sin or as the destroyer of those elected for salvation. It was also forbidden to discuss the contested points in the pulpits. Sermons must be according to God's Word, and respect must be paid to the resolution.[1] De Groot, pensionary of Rotterdam from 1613, and thus admitted to the assemblies of the States, had moved the resolution and added to it for publication a commentary with references from the Bible and the works of famous theologians.

Although this resolution did not exactly represent the views of either of the two parties, James approved it, and the more tolerant Remonstrants accepted it, but the Contra-remonstrants, very uneasy at this state interference in church matters, refused to consider it. It really went much farther in the realm of doctrine than James

[1] *Groot Placaatboek*, iii., p. 46.

wished or deemed desirable for political authority. It certainly laid down an instruction for the church, and one incapable of satisfying either party. The Amsterdam preacher, Trigland, wrote a sharp pamphlet expressing the discontent of himself and his followers. And the Remonstrant Taurinus and others óf his party also expressed a bitter dissatisfaction. Thus the reconciliation resolution proved a new bone of contention. There was an overwhelming storm of controversial pamphlets. Uyttenbogaert's *Defence of the Resolution for the Peace of the Church* was semi-official, being approved by the States and dedicated to Prince Maurice, but was ineffectual in restoring peace. On the contrary, it only evoked a bitter reply from Trigland.

Violent disturbances broke out at Amsterdam and elsewhere. Many of the classes would not submit to the resolution. Some of the municipalities took a stand against both parties. At Leyden the Arminian regent, Petrus Bertius, of the States' college for the training of preachers, was removed. At the Hague the Contra-remonstrant Rosaeus had to abandon the field. He preached at Rijswick, whither his congregation followed him—'' mud-beggars,'' jeered the Remonstrants. Amsterdam, the seat of the Contra-remonstrants, where they had gradually gained control of the whole college of burgomasters, besides a small majority in the town council,[1] encouraged the Gomarists against the resolution and supported such schismatic churches as had freed themselves from church ties in various localities where the Remonstrants were in the majority. It was, unfortunately, now open rebellion with which the politicians had to combat. Many classes offered sturdy opposition. The same scenes were enacted in 1614 and 1616 in Gelderland and Overyssel.

The Estates of Holland prevented the call of Contra-

[1] Hooft, *Memoriën en Adviezen*, p. 70.

remonstrants, suspended and fined unruly preachers, forbade the holding of secret religious services of the schismatic churches, favoured, on the other hand, the moderate in opinion who submitted to their orders, and urged the municipal governments to preserve the peace rigorously.   At the end of 1615, a plan was made to enforce the church ordinance of 1591, whereby the right of the government to regulate church affairs was acknowledged.   This attempt roused the most violent opposition of the Contra-remonstrants; they complained about the inquisition, the tyranny of the liberals, and warned the people from the pulpit against Oldenbarnevelt and his adherents, whom they now regarded as their bitterest foes.   In their attacks they made no distinction between the Arminian heresies and the " libertine " tendencies of the regents.   They called on faithful Israel to take arms against the children of Belial.

Before the political leaders took further steps, they wished to make sure of the still dissenting voices in the assembly of the Estates.   An embassy (April, 1616) of the Estates to Amsterdam for the purpose of inducing the city to withdraw all opposition, had De Groot as its mouthpiece.   He had discussed with Uyttenbogaert and Oldenbarnevelt the attitude to be taken.   Among the members of the Amsterdam town council, there were, in point of fact, several who were at one with Oldenbarnevelt, and who objected to the tendency of the churches.   Cornelis Pieterszoon Hooft, the hoary ex-burgomaster, who had once coöperated with Prince William, and in the days of Leicester had fought for freedom, but now was regularly excluded from office, was their leader.   Attached to the aristocratic government and averse to the immoderation of the preachers, he delivered solemn warnings against a repetition of the discord which had been the ruin of Flanders and Brabant, and had brought the nation to the brink of destruction in Leicester's days.   He pointed out how

·many preachers had assumed the right to express themselves in lay matters, and cited famous ancient and
modern writers to show the evil of so doing, and at the
same time to prove the right of the supreme authority to
regulate church matters. But neither the warnings of
the old man nor the eloquence of De Groot, the "light
of the world," could convince the majority of Contra-
remonstrants, led by the burgomaster Reinier Pauw, of
the desirability of the measures laid down by the state.
A small majority dismissed the embassy without giving an
answer. In the assembly of the Estates Amsterdam
voted against the resolution to maintain the already
passed resolution in so far as the municipal governments
considered it desirable, and declared its determination
not to submit to this " unchristian and godless affair."
It was asserted that the Amsterdam government had
threatened to reimburse the fines imposed on the Contra-
remonstrants from their national contribution and to
receive the preachers banished from the other cities,
within their walls.[1]

Remonstrant Rotterdam, on the other hand, published
a stringent statute in the bailiwick Schieland, under the
jurisdiction of the Rotterdam burgomasters, against the
Contra-remonstrant conventicle held at Zevenhuizen.
This statute, drawn up by Hugo de Groot as pensionary
of the city, imposed heavy fines on such meetings, and
declared the houses and other places where they were
held, confiscated. Although this was never enacted
it aroused great indignation among the Contra-remonstrants, and was declared a " blood placard of the new
inquisition." In spite of Amsterdam's opposition, the
matter was pushed through. The resolution was passed,
and the Estates, citing the opinion of Prince William and
the usage in other lands, ordered cities and villages to
adopt the church ordinance of 1591. But it was evident

[1] Arend, Van Rees, *Alg. Gesch. des Vaderlands*, iii., 2, pp. 680, 688.

that this could not be done without opposition.   Since the summer of 1615, meetings of the preachers had been held at Amsterdam by the Contra-remonstrants, where like-minded of other provinces appeared.   The orthodox decided herein to urge the States-General to convene a general synod, to support the churches which had been established in most of the Holland cities and villages, and to leave no means untried to frustrate the politicals and the Arminians.   On the other hand, Oldenbarnevelt, in whose immediate neighbourhood in the Hague the litigious Rosaeus was conducting his schismatic church, tried to ascertain how far the Estates could reckon on the help of the armed force to suppress similar schisms and to maintain the resolutions of the Estates.

It was at once evident that a great difficulty would spring into life, not only because the militia were composed of the people, and hence untrustworthy on this point, but also because Maurice could not be relied upon. And the prince's coöperation was necessary, for the army could not stretch out its hand against the will of the captain-general.   Before 1616, the prince had troubled himself little about theology.   Although it was known that he held, in the main, with the Contra-remonstrants, the indolent prince was in no sense a zealous Contra-remonstrant like his cousin, William Louis.[1]   As late as the summer of 1616, he said to a Zealand embassy: "Gentlemen, I am a warrior.   I neither understand nor trouble myself about matters of theology."[2]   Again he showed plainly that he did not grasp the difference between the two parties[3]; he is also said to have declared that he did not know whether predestination were green or blue.[4]   In spite of all that had happened Uyttenbogaert

[1] Motley, *United Netherlands*, iv., p. 250, Groen van Prinsterer, *Maurice et Barnevelt*, p. xiii.–p. 11.

[2] Brandt, *Hist. der Reformatie*, p. 558.

[3] Brandt, *Historie der rechtspleging*, p. 196.

[4] Motley, *John of Barnevelt*, i., p. 45.

continued in his service as court chaplain. Moreover, in 1614, he expressed himself not unfavourably in regard to the advocate, against whom he had nursed serious grievances, recognising the man's talent which made him indispensable for the state. In the spring of 1616, Maurice's opinion was still little evident, although in his train certain persons were very busy in their efforts to arouse his interest. He was very susceptible to influence from without when it was craftily employed and the intention was not too evident. In church matters it was especially his cousin, William Louis, who tried to compel him to take a more decided stand, pointing to what had happened at Leeuwarden, where the magistracy, in January, 1616, had declared a Contra-remonstrant platform notwithstanding the attempts of Oldenbarnevelt and his followers to support their sympathisers there. In the political realm, François van Aerssens was the man, next to the Frisian stadtholder, who egged on Maurice to oppose the all-powerful advocate. On the other hand, old Louise de Coligny, who was, as well as Frederick Henry, perhaps not absolutely Arminian, but still inclined to the milder wing of the church, could be reckoned as the protector of the Remonstrants, in any case as an advocate of the toleration espoused by her great husband; and her influence over her step-son was not slight. William Louis had taken keen interest in the conflict against Vorstius and the " strange opinions and doctrines " of Arminius and his disciples. In the preceding winter he had, in connection with the disturbances at Leeuwarden, warned the prince against a " dangerous change in our state," of which the former must be on his guard; in profound secrecy he urged Maurice to abandon his neutral position and to throw himself into the breach against the plans to attack the Reformed Church — whose earlier relation to Prince William he represented as much closer than it was in reality. He did not cease to warn Maurice of the probable results of the defeat of the reformed religion, the danger of ferment of political freedom. The congregations must be fully free in the choice of their preachers and in the use of the church buildings. If a magistrate were opposed to this, then the prince must replace him by another. If Maurice did not do this, then he must bear the blame of the destruction of the whole state. The Frisian stadtholder did not name the advocate, but it was plain enough whom he counted as the head of the Arminian faction.[1] Sir Dudley Carleton, who came from England in March, 1616, as ambassador to the republic, showed himself a fell foe of the Arminians, and through his protests to the States renewed at once the strife of his predecessor against Vorstius, who still remained at Gouda to the deep annoyance of King James. But the most dangerous of all was the man whom Oldenbarnevelt had made his foe—his former friend and protégé, François van Aerssens. Partly at the instigation, first of Winwood, then of Aerssens, and of Count William Louis, partly, too, on account of his own earlier difference with the statesman, Maurice began to oppose Oldenbarnevelt in regard to church details. At the very beginning of the Truce a certain sympathy between the prince and the Gomarists had been evident.[2] In the affair of Vorstius he had expressed himself in general unfavourably about Oldenbarnevelt's " libertine " disregard of religious interests, equally dangerous, in his estimation, for the state as for the general cause of European Protestantism, considering the threatening attitude of the Catholics in all lands and the rumours of a great Catholic league.[3] But he then said to Winwood that the weight of the other provinces as opposed to Holland, and the help of

[1] *Archives*, 2nd series, pp. 461, 463, 475, 477 ; compare Groen, *Maurice et Barnevelt*, p. 79.

[2] Naber, *Calvinist of Libertijnsch*, p. 52.

[3] Motley, i., p. 319.

certain well-intentioned Holland cities, would be able to break the wrong influence of the advocate, powerful as it was. Moreover, it could not be denied that Oldenbarnevelt and his followers went further than was consistent with " toleration." The prohibition to the Contra-remonstrants to hold meetings, the difficulties that were in general put in their path, began to take the character of persecution, and the Contra-remonstrants complained justly that the Romists and Baptists were better off than they. And that was unjust, indeed.[1]

Suspicious[2] of nature, Maurice suspected Oldenbarnevelt, moreover, of secret intercourse with the French statesmen with whom he had been in close relations for years. He even suspected the advocate, whose avariciousness was not unknown to him, of underhanded, yes, of financial dealings with Spain and the archdukes, in whose interest he was said to have effected the Truce, which he intended to change to a ruinous peace. From this point of view he watched for an opportunity to deprive Oldenbarnevelt of his great influence in the state. As early as 1612, he had thought of an attempt to ruin the policy of the advocate. He had hoped for the coöperation of William Louis and of the English ambassador and the English troops in service of the Estates. His position in the Alkmaar and Utrecht troubles showed that he would gladly have made use of the burghers to curb the power of the Estates.[3]

Without definitely desiring a monarchy, Maurice now began to cater to the will of the States. The difficulties about the Jülich succession, which threatened to renew the war with Spain at any minute from 1609–15, had brought the two men nearer, but the evident desire of the advocate to keep the peace had again exasperated Maurice, who considered the war unavoidable and desirable.

[1] Naber, p. 90. [2] Groen, *Maurice et Barnevelt*, p. 11. [3] Naber, *Ibid.*

And Carleton, whom James I. had recommended on his arrival in the republic—evidently at the instance of Winwood, then secretary of state—to protect the true followers of the Evangel against the errors of the Arminians, fixed the prince in his unfavourable opinions about the plan of the advocate. "Orange," said Maurice, with his customary bluntness, "is as well able to resist Spain as of yore."

But the prudent prince hesitated, too, to unchain the demon of civil war. A moderate neutral position therefore seemed to him especially desirable,[1] although he expressed himself violently, as was his custom, about the inquisition of the Estates towards the Contra-remonstrants. It is plain under these circumstances that he had no intention of backing Oldenbarnevelt's policy with his sword.

Up to now the advocate had avoided discussing church questions with the prince, whose opinion he surmised. On February 23rd, however, he applied to him for support, and was met by a refusal. Maurice declared that he should remain neutral, although he added at the same time that he could not share Uyttenbogaert's opinion regarding God's relation to evil. A second attempt of Uyttenbogaert to make the prince more favourable to the measures taken by the Estates failed entirely. The prince maintained his opinion that these inquisitorial steps taken in the name of toleration were dangerous, and urged anew religious discussions which would effect a reconciliation or separate the two parties into two portions of a general church,[2] like the Walloon congregations. He demanded, moreover, the convention of a completely free national synod.

Maurice began, too, to be more and more alienated from Uyttenbogaert, especially, as it was said, after an admonition directed against him by the chaplain officially

[1] Carleton, *Lettres*, i., p. 219.   [2] Uyttenbogaert, *Leven*, p. 108.

in regard to his manner of life, which was far from irre-
proachable, in regard to which Uyttenbogaert had learned
various details from the prince's chamberlain, whom he
had attended in his last moments.   In the course of 1616,
the prince, under the influence of his Frisian cousin,
who was urging him to declare boldly in favour of the
Contra-remonstrants, promised the Hague "mud beggars," who complained to him about their persecution,
that they should have a church within the city, the chief
church if need were, and declared that he would protect
them, "his father's allies."   Still he hesitated to dismiss
Uyttenbogaert, and clung to the opinion which he had
expounded to the chaplain.

Thus the prince hesitated in accordance with his slow
and irresolute character.   Oldenbarnevelt's party made
no advances.[1]   The resolutions of the States were maintained where it was possible, and in December, 1616, the
adopted resolutions were confirmed, but they still seemed
to hope for an amicable decision, although party spirit
ran steadily higher, pamphlets were bitterer on both
sides, the number of schismatic churches grew, and the
opposition of the Contra-remonstrants increased in the
States' assemblies too.   The advocate made various efforts to persuade his friends to win over the prince by
offering him a monarchical dignity, the countship itself,
if he would support them against their foes and further
their church policy.   But the States party, counting the
remedy worse than the disease, refused to follow their
leader on this path, and thereby lost their last chance.
From that moment the advocate saw that the question
must be settled by arms, and in December proposed to
the Estates of Holland to take four thousand men into
the service of the province.

The die was cast.   The Estates still hesitated to adopt
this course, doubting on the good outcome, shuddering

[1] Naber. p. 85.

at civil war, but the position was taken, and Oldenbarnevelt himself, obstinate as he was, had resolved to yield
nothing further as long as the Estates supported him,
but to combat the attempts of the opposite party which
he regarded as boding disaster for the republic.

At the end of 1616, Maurice, despairing of an accommodation, said to his step-mother, Louise de Coligny,[1]
that the differences could only be decided by arms.   At
the same time it was clear that the conflict would be a
strife between Maurice and Oldenbarnevelt, between the
stadtholder and the Holland Estates' government.   In
this imminent struggle Maurice could reckon on the support of most of the other provinces, on the majority in
the States-General, on a popular majority, too, in Holland and Utrecht, on the army above all, which wor-
shipped him, the renowned commander.   But in a short
time more was involved than a conflict between two
theological opinions in the Reformed Church, — between
two persons.   The question was at stake whether the
union should follow the direction in which Oldenbarnevelt and his friends wished to drive it, and which, in the
opinions of its opponents, would result either in the supremacy of Holland, or in the principle of state unity
as personified in the supremacy of the States-General.
The opposition was not wholly in the spirit of Oldenbarnevelt.   He, too, wanted a strong central power to
keep the provinces to their duty towards the state, but
the manner in which the politico-theological strife developed caused the origin of this conflict.   Oldenbarnevelt is unjustly represented as the advocate of a strongly
federative republic against a centralised government, yes,
the monarchical principles of Maurice and his followers—
a clear misconception of the two aims.[2]

We know, too, that that question was not new in the
young state of the United Netherlands.   The question

[1] Uyttenbogaert, *Leven*, p. 12.   [2] Naber, p. 76.

of the legitimate relations of the central government towards the provincial Estates, was born from circumstance, from the very history of the former independent states from which the new state had sprung. The Burgundian monarchy had been well aware of the difficulty. In such a crisis as the present, which touched the hearts of all citizens, it naturally came to the fore. This was the more so as in Holland the personal influence of the advocate and his adherents, in the union that of his opponents, triumphed. In the province of Holland, Oldenbarnevelt had the majority of statesmen in his hand: in the union, Holland and Utrecht were undoubtedly in the minority. What wonder that the inferior party in Holland staked their hopes on the union and brought the old political question on the tapis! Thus all the conditions of civil war were at hand—political, ecclesiastical, personal opposition, so sharply defined that the parties became factions, persecuting each other with bitter hatred, and not inclined to submit to mediatory measures. And in that satanic medley of political, ecclesiastical, and personal elements, the latter was not of the least weight, now as in the days of Leicester. Then civil war had been prevented, and the fear of the armed foe in the heart of the land had undoubtedly weighed, in addition to Leicester's lack of military leadership, to secure the victory to the powerful States' party. Now a condition of temporary peace was prevailing, and the conqueror, still bitterly hated by the conquered of those days, had indeed a difficult task, for the leader of the opposition party was no longer a stranger, but the Orange prince himself, whose name was brilliant with the glitter of his heritage and from his military reputation.

The events of the two following years were to give the answer to these questions, but not without Maurice's sword being laid in the balance, and not without violent disturbances which shook the state to its foundations.

CHAPTER XV

THE CRISIS OF 1617–1619

BY the end of 1616, a determined action in regard to the theological disputes seemed necessary to support the tottering authority of the Estates of Holland. The advocate's proposition to employ mercenaries was not without precedent. The number of hirelings [1] used for home guard during the absence of the army in the various campaigns had sometimes amounted to two or three thousand men.[2] But then the foe to be combated had been foreign ; now they might be Hollanders, and there was a natural hesitation to employ force of arms against them : The Estates discussed the question during the whole spring. Meanwhile the Contra-remonstrants were greatly encouraged by the prince's sympathy. The congregations held their service in the home of his bookkeeper at The Hague, evidently not without Maurice's knowledge. Then the prince went further ; demanding a church and further privileges for the orthodox party. The Estates showed an inclination to yield to his request.[3] A consistory was granted to the Contra-remonstrants, and there were rumours that the great church was to be cleared for their exclusive use. High words passed between Mau-

[1] The name applied to them, *waardgelders*, was derived from the German *wartgeld*, pay given to troops hired for a definite purpose in distinction from the regular army. See Wijnne, *Geschiedenis*, p. 38.

[2] Lists of earlier *waardgelders* among the papers of Oldenbarnevelt in the *Royal Archives*. Compare *Verhooren van Oldenbarnevelt*, p. 8 ; Wijnne, p. 41.   [3] Uyttenbogaert. *Brieven*, i., p. 244.

rice and Oldenbarnevelt,[1] but the former gained ground. On February 19th, the house of Bisshop, a worthy Remonstrant merchant, was plundered in Amsterdam, and the municipal government — Contra-remonstrant by a large majority — made no effort to defend his property. Elsewhere in the province revolts occurred against Remonstrant town corporations.   And the court of Holland and the high council, sympathising with the Contra-remonstrants, decided, after consulting Maurice, certain cases against the party of the Estates.   The Estates objected, and claimed jurisdiction for themselves, or, in their absence, for the deputed council.   At the same time they evinced some conciliatory spirit by giving the cloister church in the Voorhout to the orthodox party.   The advocate was little pleased with this give and take, which weakened the position of the Estates.   On April 14th, he introduced a resolution defining the obedience owed by the troops to the Estates,[2] as it was clear that the officers had occasionally received secret orders from the prince not to lend their coöperation in church matters. But he did not carry his point.   The Estates avoided issues as far as possible.

The next important question was the opinion of the States-General upon the situation.   Maurice and William Louis could count upon the support of Zealand, Friesland, and Utrecht.   The attendance of their deputies was well looked to.   Overyssel showed an inclination to support the Estates of Holland; Gelderland was persuaded to side with the prince.   In May, accordingly, the four provinces controlled by the princes gave Holland a formal admonition to restore peace and to agree to the convention of a national synod.   In March, James sent the same advice to the States-General.[3]

---

[1] See *Archives*, ii., p. 488 ; *Res. Holl.*, January 13, 14, 1617.
[2] Compare the passages cited by Naber, p. 229, note 115.
[3] Carleton, *Lettres*, i., p. 272.

A majority of the Estates of Holland rejected the motion, while a minority, consisting of Amsterdam and some little towns, urged the synod. As this minority knew that they were in accord not only with a majority of the States-General, but also the people at large, they henceforth opposed every antagonistic resolution of the Holland Estates. Amsterdam, led by Reinier Pauw, was at the head of this opposition.

But the advocate did not yield his own convictions. There were projects of all kinds afoot. Oldenbarnevelt was somewhat inclined to permit two separate churches.[1] The Estates of Holland were convened nearly every day until the end of June, 1617,—almost four months,— but nothing was accomplished.

Pamphlets sprang into existence like weeds after a rain. Hendrik Slatius, a Remonstrant preacher at Bleiswijk, poured out his venom at the schism preachers and their doctrine. Venator raised a storm by his *Theologia vera et mera*, forbidden by the Estates as too radical. The *Calendier*, by the Contra-remonstrant Van Drielenburch, pictured the " apocalypse beast " and " the Babylonian whore seated thereon." The Remonstrant ex-rector of Zierikzee, Reinier Telle, wrote his *Nieuw jaer liedekens* and *Der Contra Remonstrant Kerfstock*. Uyttenbogaert and his allies wrote a *Vertoogh* as a second remonstrance to the Estates to defend themselves from the accusation of seeking novelties. This aroused Trigland's *Klaer en grondich tegenvertoogh*, that, an *Antwoordt*, etc.[2] In the pulpits and the taverns, on the streets and in the shooting-galleries, in high places and low, were heard violent discussions in which no bitter term was spared. The quarrel threatened the existence of the young nation. The academic discussion of Gomarus and Arminius had become a bone of contention which divided

[1] Uyttenbogaert, *Kerk. Hist.*
[2] See Rogge, *Uyttenbogaert*, ii., pp. 386–417.

Holland into two hostile camps. It was evident who would win. The great orthodox popular party, who knew exactly what they wanted, animated by powerful centralised leadership, and steered unswervingly in the direction of its goal, ready to venture everything for religion, and already resolved to drive the Remonstrants from the church,[1] was much stronger than the less numerous opposition, half reluctantly obeying their energetic leader. This party was composed for the most part of moderate elements, who were ready to retreat if it could be done without too much noise.

Such was the state of public opinion when the Estates of Holland adjourned (June 24th) for three weeks. The deputed councillors were charged with the interests of the province during the interim.

On July 9th, the face of affairs was changed by the Contra-remonstrants taking sudden and forcible possession of the cloister church, which had never been actually accorded to them. The deputed councillors were greatly vexed at this action. On the 23rd, the prince showed his approval of the measure by attending the services in the newly acquired church, accompanied by a brilliant retinue of nobles and officers. It was a meagre consolation to the Remonstrants that he had been one of Uyttenbogaert's congregation on the previous Sunday, and that his stepmother and Frederick Henry remained true to the chaplain. Henceforth the Contra-remonstrants counted Maurice one of themselves. William Louis, who had spurred his cousin on to action, wrote that the prince would deserve " the crown of the saviour of his religion and of his land "[2] now that the libertine regents could be removed from office or prosecuted as criminals.[3]

Oldenbarnevelt and his party were goaded to measures

[1] Rutgers, *Het Kerkverband*, pp. 48–52.
[2] *Archives*, 2nd series, ii., p. 530.
[3] *Ibid.*, p. 510.

of defence. The States were again in session, and although votes were equally divided—dangerous omen for the party—in regard to propositions to justify the advocate's authority and to send a written defence of him to the other provinces, he ventured to take these propositions as passed. This excited Amsterdam's just indignation, in which she was supported by Dordrecht and the three little North Holland cities.[1] On August 4th, a resolution was introduced in the Estates, declaring that that body was empowered to exercise authority in church matters, and providing for further discussion of the propositions in question. The above-mentioned cities and Dordrecht opposed this too, but were outvoted by the seven others,[2] with Briel and the less zealous Gorkum, Schiedam, Monnikendam, and Medemblik. The resolution introduced on August 4th was to be decided on the 5th, and not until the prince, the princess dowager, and Count Frederick Henry had been officially informed of the provisions of the resolution. Oldenbarnevelt and his stepson, Veenhuizen, were members of the commission sent to the prince for this purpose. He hoped to be able to convince him of the justice thereof, an expectation that was soon put to flight.

Oldenbarnevelt later confessed without subterfuge that he had drafted this dangerous resolution, notorious later as the *Scherpe Resolutie*, and that he thus formulated the platform of the majority.[3] It was expressly affirmed that, after all the disputes, the Estates of Holland could not approve any synod, provincial or national, which might infringe upon sovereign rights; that the declaration regarding the supremacy of the Estates in church

[1] Edam, Enkhuizen, and Purmerend.
[2] Haarlem, Delft, Leyden, Gouda, Rotterdam, Alkmaar, and Hoorn.
[3] *Verhooren*, p. 266. Among his minutes was found a draft of the points upon which was based the *Resolutie*, August 4, 1617 (*Rijksarchief*, ms. Old., AA., 61, No. 3).

matters should be printed and disseminated, with the answer of Zealand on the subject.[1] The city officials were authorised to employ all ordinary methods to keep the peace, and, if necessary, to increase their force of men-at-arms. Any question about the legality of this was not to be settled by the ordinary "colleges of justice," but referred to the Estates. All regents and officials, all members of the army, were called upon to take an oath of obedience to the Estates and the deputed councillors and to the magistrates of the cities where they were in garrison, "on pain of dismissal."

This resolution could well be called *sharp*. The enraged Maurice characterised it as an "extravagant resolution."[2] It ended the prolonged uncertainty, but it might easily bring about civil war. The advocate, already ill and hardly in a condition to go up- and downstairs, had not hesitated to urge the measure with a deep feeling of the importance of the crisis. "My hope," he says,[3] "is staked upon God the Almighty and upon that which shall shame those who wish other than His honour and the prosperity of the country with maintenance of freedom and justice," etc. Whoever can speak so is evidently convinced of the right of his cause, but it is also clear from Oldenbarnevelt's words that the leader was not sure of his followers.

The resolution was adopted by a majority, although the prince, as he had declared his intention of doing to the commission, attended the meeting of the Estates on August 5th in order to encourage the minority in their opposition. The protest was violent, especially from Reinier Pauw, the Amsterdam leader of the Contra-remonstrants. He assured the prince that the motion

[1] Compare Baudartius, i., p. 37.
[2] *Archives*, ii., p. 532.
[3] Minutes, letter to Caron, July 31, *Hand. Maatsch. Letterk.*, 1895–96, p. 180.

expressed only the individual opinion of the advocate and of his immediate party.

The question came to issue almost immediately in Briel, where the Contra-remonstrants were excluded from a church by troops who had given their oaths to the Estates. Maurice was greatly enraged, and succeeded in carrying a motion in the States-General whereby Holland was forbidden to impose such an oath. The province thereupon agreed to renounce the imposition, a concession which showed a readiness to be prudent. The Estates adjourned; their deputies refrained from attending the States-General, so as to give no occasion for disputes; Oldenbarnevelt himself left The Hague after a visit to the prince, whom he urged to compliance. He went first to Vianen, later to Utrecht, partially for his health and partially to urge his Utrecht allies to steadfastness. During his absence Holland affairs were administered by De Groot and the deputed councillors, who tried to further the interests of the Estates' party. There were frequent meetings of the leaders [1] at the home of Oldenbarnevelt's son-in-law, Van der Myle, "Barnevelt's hind wheel."

Meanwhile Leyden, Haarlem, Rotterdam, Gouda, and other towns took several hundred hirelings into service under command of provincial nobles. The oath imposed bound the troops to obedience to the Estates and to each city alone. Naturally this did not happen without cognisance of Oldenbarnevelt,[2] who continued his conference with his Holland and Utrecht allies. He showed no immediate intention of returning to The Hague. He was, indeed, suspected of planning the formation of a new union.

The prince, dissatisfied at all this, persuaded the majority in the States-General to oppose a levy at Utrecht and to send a messenger to warn both city and

[1] De Groot, *Verhooren*, p. 246.   [2] Wijnne, *Geschiedenis*, p. 133.

provincial Estates of the dangerous character of these events. But the Estates of Utrecht, strengthened by the deputed council and emboldened by the presence of Oldenbarnevelt, refused to stop the levy, declaring that they were afraid of a disturbance such as that of 1616, and that the ordinary garrison was too weak for a crisis, etc.   The levy continued, to Maurice's great annoyance.

Again Zealand urged a national synod, and the deputed council of Holland took a firm stand against it. When the four provinces, supported by Carleton in his king's name, again proposed it in the States-General, Holland came forward with a counter-proposition for a provincial synod.   Her leaders had been in correspondence with the advocate.   It was soon clear that they could only count on Utrecht, for Overyssel was soon influenced by the warnings from the prince and Carleton. Thus the two provinces—where Carleton's warnings had effected little [1]— stood practically alone, and it was questionable whether they could push through the levy of mercenaries to assure their position.   Nor was Holland herself a unit.   Delft, Gorkum, and the little places did not venture to accept the mercenaries, so that only eighteen hundred men were collected.   But in Holland all hope had not been abandoned of help from the regular army, and it was still hoped that Frederick Henry might be the leader of the united forces of the two provinces [2]— an expectation without basis.   In Briel the presence of Maurice himself caused a revulsion of sentiment.   The hirelings were abandoned, to the great joy of the Contra-remonstrants, who also gained ground elsewhere.   A clash between the Leyden populace and the Arminian guard protecting the town council showed how much danger there was of civil war.   Maurice, although openly partisan, still evinced some moderation and avoided extreme

---

[1] *Lettres*, ii., p. 61.   [2] De Groot, *Verhooren*, p. 43.

measures, following William Louis's advice,[1] to proceed with rigour and with prudence against the Arminians, and to see that nothing was begun that could not be carried through.   He hoped, with the Frisian count, that the Remonstrants would finally yield churches to their opponents until this " difference might be decided."

For, that the national synod should be convened was the fixed intention of the prince and a majority of the provinces.   A day before the prince went to Briel a resolution of the majority regarding this was adopted.   In October, a commission from the majority of the States-General drafted the chief preliminaries, providing, among other things, that the synod should meet in May, 1618, and be composed of representatives from the Netherland provincial churches, while King James, the Huguenots, the elector palatine, the landgrave of Hesse, the reformed of Switzerland and of East Friesland, should be invited to send deputies.   The States-General was to exercise supervision over the assembly by empowering two members from each province to lead it and by requiring a submission of the acts to the approval of their college. Holland, Utrecht, and Overyssel persisted in withholding their consent, however, and Oldenbarnevelt declared that he was unwilling to advise his masters to a measure which he deemed adverse to national sovereignty and to justice. Discussion continued for a month, Hugo de Groot being at the head of the deputed councillors, and showing no inclination to compliance.   Not until November 6th did Oldenbarnevelt return to The Hague, physically dependent upon a cane, but pugnacious and obstinate as ever. December 8th was the date of the convention of the Estates of Holland.   Before then, Maurice and William Louis visited or wrote to the cities to persuade them to adopt their views.   De Groot and Oldenbarnevelt were forced into similar canvassing to hold their own.   When

---

[1] *Archives*, 2nd series, p. 538.

the assembly took place it was doubtful whether Holland could longer maintain her position. A conference between Maurice and Oldenbarnevelt seemed to point to her possible yielding. Du Maurier and Carleton watched events closely in behalf of their respective governments, and kept them informed. Oldenbarnevelt would have resigned, but his adherents violently opposed the suggestion, although Delft, the little towns,[1] and the nobility were ready to yield something if any concessions were offered on the other side. Du Maurier even appeared before the Estates in a formal audience to urge some mutual concession. This interference caused some scandal, as it was not the custom for foreign ambassadors to appeal to the provincial Estates.[2] Meanwhile a middle party sprang up in the Estates, which had six votes, and, combined with the five Contra-remonstrants, was able to hold the eight Remonstrants in check if they wished. The eight remained solid and had frequent discussions at this time, but their minority was no longer concealed, and they were less self-confident. The "factious league" of these eight cities, as it was called by their opponents, was not so powerful as they imagined.[3] Indeed reconciliation seemed almost possible, when a quarrel between Carleton and the Remonstrants widened the breach. Du Maurier meanwhile remained on good terms with Oldenbarnevelt, but was unwilling to alienate Maurice, and tried to take a middle course, so that French sympathies were less pronounced than English. Carleton openly urged a national synod, and finally persuaded King James to write a letter to the States-General approving that measure as the only means of maintaining the true religion. This was greatly to Oldenbarnevelt's annoyance, as he saw his own weapons turned upon him. At the

---

[1] Schiedam, Medemblik, and Monnikendam did not attend the assembly on August 4th.
[2] Carleton, *Lettres*, ii., p. 138.   [3] Wijnne, *Geschiedenis*, p. 206, etc.

request of the Contra-remonstrants, Carleton appeared in person before the States-General in the beginning of October and expressed himself clearly on theological questions in an oration which was printed and widely disseminated—something desired by neither the States-General nor by Holland.   It called forth a bitter pamphlet entitled *The Balance to Weigh in all Justice the Oration of Carleton*.[1]   This was evidently written on the Remonstrant side and possibly by the preacher Taurinus. It was widely read, repeatedly reprinted, and aroused the indignation of Carleton and King James, who were not spared, while the cause of the Remonstrants was fiercely defended.   Carleton appeared in the States-General, accused De Groot and Uyttenbogaert of being the writers, and Oldenbarnevelt as their accomplice, and demanded satisfaction.   The satisfaction they thought they could give, with the coöperation of the Estates of Holland and Utrecht, by suppressing the pamphlet.   But Carleton demanded more,—condemnation of printer and authors by an official placard of the States-General and public burning of the book.   The four provinces consented, but Holland, Utrecht, and Overyssel refused to go so far. Carleton urged and threatened; the four provinces pushed the matter through by their majority, but Holland was then unwilling to permit the official printer of the generality to print the placard, so that the president of the States-General sent it to the individual provinces, under protest from the three, to have it locally printed and published.   Not until this had been done, at the end of January, did Carleton let the matter drop, although he soon lifted his voice again when a French translation of the objectionable pamphlet, with a very sharp preface, renewed the quarrel.

By the beginning of 1618, the affair seemed practically

[1] Knuttel, Catalogue No., 2366: *Wegschaal om in alle billickheijdt recht to overweghen de Oratie van Dudley Carleton.*

ended. James conceded that a provincial synod might suffice under the circumstances, and Du Maurier hoped that all would pass well. Similar rumours came from all sides. The very letters of Maurice and William Louis breathed a spirit of conciliation. But many knew better than to hope for plain sailing. Among them was the experienced Louise de Coligny, who expressed her anxiety about the future in a remarkable letter, of December 28th, to her old friend, Duplessis-Mornay. "It is not only the question of religion; the whole state is involved, and it will go to destruction if they do not beware." She urged him, "who aided my late husband to establish the state," to come "to help his children to save it from ruin." And she adds: "If the dead know what passes here below, I am sure he would conjure you to do this in his name and by his ashes." [1]

The prince's intention was soon made evident by the events in Nimwegen. On its conquest he had been empowered [2] to change the magistracy at the annual terms, —"provisionally and during the war." In January, 1618, he used this power to replace the Remonstrant officials by Contra-remonstrants. In the little cities of Holland there were frequent violent disturbances at the magistrates' election during the spring.

After the Christmas vacation the Estates of Holland were again convened. A proposition made by Remonstrant Haarlem seemed to confirm the hesitating majority in their position. The question of contributions to war expenses was to come before the assembly, and Haarlem declared through the pensionary De Haan that she would only contribute her share if all privileges and rights were preserved, including those

[1] De Jonge, *Louise de Coligny*, p. 55.
[2] This was changed later to the privilege of confirming the election as made by the municipal government.

respecting the election of magistrates, and provided that provincial rights were duly recognised in church matters. An appeal was added to all for protection against every infringement, if necessary with the help of troops, who should be obliged to swear a separate oath to the city and province wherein the garrison lay.[1] Seven cities[2] declared that they accepted Haarlem's lead. This proposition formulated the plan cherished by the " Barneveldists," and it came out later that the proposition was drafted by the leaders of the party, shown to Oldenbarnevelt, and approved by the eight cities before it was offered. The three pensionaries of Haarlem, Leyden, and Rotterdam—De Haan, Hogerbeets, and De Groot— were credited with being the authors. It was thus regarded as a manifesto of the Estates' party, and the facts that six hundred archers were dismissed at Leyden for refusing the new oath, and that there was an expressed intention of paying the mercenaries from the public treasury, showed that the situation was serious. But it was also evident that the former majority no longer existed.

Du Maurier again appeared before the Estates in the name of his king,[3] and urged that a provincial synod should be held first and all conciliatory measures taken to avoid an outbreak of civil dissension. His warnings had the result that the contributions were finally given, while the eight cities were satisfied with a weak declaration,— a mere shadow of Haarlem's proposition. This was a worse sign because the deputies were all pledged generally to support the sovereignty of Holland, and were guaranteed by their town councils against any ill resulting therefrom ;[4] this and defeat presaged the sequence.

[1] De Groot, *Verantwoordinghe*, p. 235 ; Wijnne, *Geschiedenis*, p. 211.
[2] Leyden, Gouda, Rotterdam, Schoonhoven, Briel, Alkmaar, and Hoorn.
[3] *Res. Holl.*, March 13, 1618.
[4] De Groot, *Verhooren*, p. 283.

Meanwhile the Contra-remonstrants were not idle. There was active canvassing on both sides to win support. The prince himself went to Overyssel and gained their vote for the national synod, although the Estates had been before him in their efforts. Five provinces were now allied against Holland and Zealand, while these two were weakened by internal dissension and weighted with the heavy burden of the mercenaries.

A bitter series of pamphlets appeared during this time, attacking the man who was regarded as the soul of the Estates' party—Oldenbarnevelt. During the entire year 1617 the presses in Holland were barely able to turn off the controversial pamphlets of both parties. Trigland and Uyttenbogaert, Smout and Grevinchoven, Taurinus, Teelinck, Telle, Van Drielenburch, Slatius, and others expressed their sentiments in bitter language nearly always anonymous. The point of view was sometimes theological, sometimes political, and again personal. The " sharp " resolution called forth a mass of writings for and against. " Defences," " refutations," " explanations," etc., followed each other with extraordinary rapidity, until 150 pamphlets in prose and verse were in circulation in Holland. Another crop ripened in the spring of 1618. Caricatures and lampoons held up to view the failings of both parties.[1]

There were bitter personal attacks upon Oldenbarnevelt. " A necessary and living discourse " (*Noodtwendigh ende levendig discours*) was ascribed, probably unjustly, to François van Aerssens[2] and Reinier Pauw, the advocate's bitterest foes. Another pamphlet, entitled *Oprechte tonge van de Weeghschael proeft den Reuckappel met den Vraegch-al*, reached many editions, and was

[1] Compare Tiele, *Bibl. van pamfletten;* Knuttel, Catalogue of the years 1617 and 1618.

[2] Publications over Aerssens's own name were very different in style and language; compare his *Noodighe Remonstrantie*, p. 5.

bound in with the equally bitter *Practijcke van den Spaen-schen Raedt*. The contents were venomous, and accused the advocate of the most shameful actions, especially of treason with Spain. He was charged with having sold himself, with avarice, with unbounded ambition and arrogance. There was discussion of his origin, his marriage, the behaviour of his sons, etc. There were, indeed, certain points which were difficult to explain away. The advocate was fond of money — it was his greatest fault; his insistence upon the authority of the Estates did result in extending his own authority; he laid claim to noble descent without being able to prove it; his father and grandfather, his brothers, sisters, and sons were far from blameless in their lives; a stain rested on the birth of his otherwise worthy wife; in his marriage with her, her wealth had been a great inducement; his political transactions were not always upright. But all this did not justify the outrageous manner in which he and his were attacked. All attempts to discover and punish the actual authors of this and similar libels at Amsterdam[1] failed. After many verbal complaints to the States, the advocate sent to the Estates of Holland and West Friesland a *Remonstrantie*,[2] in which he defended himself courageously and with dignity under his own name. This document, wherein the old statesman reviewed his whole life and defended his successive actions, was sent to Maurice with a long, serious letter.[3] Oldenbarnevelt tried to show that, in just and pure intent, he had never opposed the prince, but had always supported his interests and those of his house. He begged him, remembering the events in Leicester's time, not to give heed to his arch-foes and to the foes of the

[1] Under the eye of Pauw, the all-powerful burgomaster !
[2] Printed as pamphlet and incorporated into *Waaragtige Historie van J van Oldenbarnevelt*. Rotterdam, Naeranus, 1670, p. 146.
[3] *Ibid.*, p. 132.

state, who sowed distrust through seditious and libellous pamphlets. A bitter attack on Aerssens, probably by Van der Myle, appeared at the same time. These defences failed to accomplish their end. In behalf of Aerssens an answer was published by an anonymous writer in the bitter *Provisionele openinghe*, while he himself entered on a quarrel with Van der Myle through the publication of a *Noodighe Remonstrantie* directed to the States-General and the Estates of the provinces, which Aerssens wrote, claiming that he did not know the author of the attack on himself. Oldenbarnevelt replied in a brief explanation [1]; Van der Myle in a sharp *vertoogh* that excited again a *corte antwort* from Aerssens, followed by a bitter *naeder vertoogh* from Van der Myle, replied by another short *antwort* from Aerssens. All are full of personalities and odious abuse, evincing dire personal enmity between Aerssens and the advocate's family, an enmity which was to bear still more bitter fruit. The pamphlet strife between Van der Myle and Aerssens ceased in the beginning of August, 1618, when the latter was one of the chief persons to crush the rebellious leaders of the opposition party. The concluding pamphlets are little more than *résumés* of the preceding wherein the two gentlemen made mutual charges of slander and demanded the production of original documents to support the charges made.

In this excited state of feeling the apparent reconciliation between the majority and minority of the Holland cities could accomplish little. There were various attempts at friendly measures. Du Maurier did his best, and even Oldenbarnevelt agreed to accept a national synod whose purpose should be conciliatory and which should condemn no one. Meanwhile the ultra-orthodox party had grown steadily stronger. Before Carleton's departure on June 6th, he received private assurance

---

[1] *Kron. Hist. Gen.*, vi., p. 41.

from the States-General that the synod would be convened, and on June 25th, in spite of the opposition of
Holland and Utrecht, it was actually appointed for the
following November.   The prince and his cousin, who
had come from Friesland to be present at the close of
the discussion, signed the notification sent to the various
provinces.   Maurice was counted as the protector of
God's church by the Contra-remonstrants.   Relying upon
his aid they refrained, in general, from violence, although
the excitement grew among the people, and there were
some outbreaks in Oudewater, Leyden, and elsewhere.
But the Contra-remonstrant leaders, sure of the weight of
five provinces in the States-General, thought they would
be able to suppress the Arminians by legal measures, and
were now anxious to avoid popular disturbances.

The conflict between Holland and Utrecht and the
States-General was to be decided in the latter body.
Holland accepted the contest.   At the advice of Oldenbarnevelt and under his leadership, the eight cities made
a close alliance.   On May 14th they gave their deputies
a *procuratie*,[1] as had been done in Leicester's time,
whereby the deputies were empowered to advise with the
nobles and representatives of the cities, and were guaranteed from any ill results to their persons or property from
their decisions.   It was further decided by a majority in
the provincial Estates to urge the " generality " to relinquish the synod and to take measures to suppress the
objectionable pamphlets, especially those attacking the
advocate.   In the same session it was resolved that all
soldiers were bound by oath to their paymasters, *i. e.*, to
the provincial Estates, and were pledged to obey and protect those who composed these Estates, *i. e.*, the municipal magistrates in whose jurisdiction the garrisons were.
But the generality refused to accede to the requests, and
answered in regard to the pamphlets that it would be

[1] De Groot, *Verhooren*, p. 283.

better to remedy the evil against which the pamphlets were directed.

Thus Holland was forced to depend entirely upon herself. In spite of the protest of the six cities, measures were taken to stop the dissemination of the pamphlets, especially those attacking the advocate. Moreover, he was offered the protection of the Estates, and was begged to continue his public services.[1] An effort was also made to gain ground by asserting Holland's financial dominance in the union.

On June 28th, one more protest was made to the States-General, in the presence of Maurice and of William Louis. The deputation from Holland was headed by Oldenbarnevelt, who made a long speech[2] pointing out the violation of provincial rights in convening a national synod against Holland's vote. He proposed a provincial synod to which learned theologians should be invited at the expense of the Estates. If they failed to agree, then foreign theologians should be asked to assist them. Further, Holland was unwilling to grant further contributions to the general fund until the other provinces had fulfilled their part,—some having been behindhand since 1609; they demanded payment of moneys advanced for the French regiments, and protested against the despatch of an extraordinary embassy to France. Owing to the lack of unity among the cities, Holland was not, however, really in a position to fulfil her threat of refusing her contribution, for Amsterdam was strong enough to prevent it. They contented themselves by paying the provincial share in the military expenses monthly.[3]

It was evident that Holland and Utrecht would yield to the generality only if forced. Utrecht was taken in hand first, as the weaker province. On July 9th, the majority in the States-General brought up the matter of

[1] *Res. Holl.*, 22 Juni, 1618.   [2] *Ibid.*, 3 Juli, 1618.
[3] Naber, p. 142.

the mercenaries. Holland protested that it was a purely provincial question, but finally resolved to withdraw her opposition, as Utrecht was lukewarm in her support. It was further decided in the States (July 23rd) to send a commission to Utrecht to enforce the dismissal of the *waardgelders*. As stadtholder of the province, Maurice was the head of this commission. Eight members of the States-General accompanied him.

Having vainly demanded a postponement of this step, Holland decided to send emissaries of her own " to help conduct the matter to the best accommodation," to persuade the province which had been allied to her for so long to maintain her rights, and to remind the garrisons of their duty towards their paymaster, Holland. There was some hesitation at going so far. Moreover, it was an ominous fact that when the important resolution was taken, only the nobles were present and three of the cities. The quota of the latter was filled, according to usage, by calling on the substitutes of the deputies, who sat in the college of the deputed councillors, and were entitled to represent their cities in the absence of the ordinary deputies. Oldenbarnevelt was evidently the ruling spirit in every move.[1] On July 24th, the appointed commissioners, Hogerbeets, De Groot, Torenvliet, and Schoonhoven,—the last two from Gouda and Leyden,—set out for Utrecht, where they arrived on the following day. On the evening of the 25th, the deputation of the States-General appeared with the prince, accompanied by a large escort of officers from The Hague and the adjacent cities.

Great uneasiness had been felt at Utrecht at the news of the commission of the States-General.[2] And the anxiety was fully justified by the events. Sharp words

[1] Naber, p. 148; Wijnne, *Geschiedenis*, p. 147.
[2] *De Verhooren* of De Groot and his *verantwoording* are the best sources for the events at Utrecht.

passed between the prince and the Holland commission, but Maurice succeeded in carrying all before him in spite of opposition backed by Holland. An attempt to influence the troops by reminding them that Holland was their paymaster, failed. Discussions with the prince were equally fruitless. The difficulties of the Holland deputation increased when, at the instance of William Louis, who had remained in The Hague, the six Holland cities of the Contra-remonstrant minority also resolved to send a deputation to Utrecht to thwart the plan of the majority.

On the evening of July 30th, the Holland deputies invited Colonel Ogle, governor of the city, Ernest Casimir of Nassau, Sir Horatio Vere, and other commanders of the mercenary troops, to see them, and warned them of the possibility that Holland would not pay them if they were not obedient to her. But Ogle and his officers were already informed of the new Holland deputation, and hesitated to take a stand in opposition to the prince and the States-General. New troops under Maurice's command entered the city in the night of the 31st. All were agreed that it was necessary to yield to force and unwise to risk battle.

At the break of day Maurice guarded the gates of the city and collected a considerable force on the plain of Neude, where a company of mercenaries kept watch. At the prince's command, they laid down their arms, the other companies followed suit, and before day Utrecht was delivered, disarmed, to the prince. The municipal government fled. The Holland deputation, too, hastened their departure, fearing arrest. The Estates of Utrecht, among whom a small minority had opposed the other members, submitted. Without further ceremony, the municipal council was at once changed by the prince, " at the request of the Contra-remonstrant citizens," into a council chosen for life, from which the defeated party was naturally excluded. Vacancies were henceforth to be filled, not by choice of the Estates, but by the prince out of a double list furnished by the council. The appointment of burgomasters and aldermen was left wholly to him. In general, the rules established in 1584 were followed. After some demur, the provincial Estates approved these changes at the instance of the prince and the deputies of the States-General. In both branches of the Estates, too, there were changes. Various members were removed. Seven new members of the nobility destroyed the existing majority.[1] All this was accomplished before August, and therewith Utrecht was gained for the Contra-remonstrants. The two chief churches (*Buurkerk* and *Domkerk*) were given up for their service. Ernest Casimir of Nassau replaced Ogle as governor, and remained in the city to keep watch. These events at Utrecht had been directed by Maurice in spite of the efforts of Oldenbarnevelt and De Groot. And for those vain efforts they were to pay dearly.

Holland now stood alone in opposition to the other six provinces. It was not to be expected, however, that more vigorous resistance would be offered there than in Utrecht if the prince determined to push his measures through. A conciliatory attitude began to be manifest, although protests were still made in the States-General against Maurice's action in Utrecht. France sent an envoy extraordinary, Thuméry, Seignior de Boissize, to coöperate with Du Maurier. Aerssens tried to arouse public opinion against this foreign intervention, but the new envoy immediately established close relations with the prince and William Louis, and his presence was a weight in the balance against reconciliation between the parties.

In the Estates of Holland the succeeding events showed

[1] See, for these changes, *Bijdr. en Med., Hist. Gen.*, xvii., p. 71 ; ii., p. 90.

that reconciliation was far distant.   The eight cities declared their intention of retaining the *waardgelders* as
protection against the prince; the incidents at Utrecht
led to mutual recrimination, and the six cities showed no
willingness to yield.   On August 18th, another deputation, headed by Oldenbarnevelt, waited on Maurice to
beg him to use no measures of force until the convention
of the Estates.   The prince gave almost no answer to
the advocate, but remained surly and silent.   That very
day it was resolved in the States to call for the dismissal
of the mercenaries in Holland within twenty-four hours.
In spite of vehement protests, the placard was published
on the 20th.   Holland yielded.   The troops were dismissed at once, so that, when the Estates of Holland
convened on the following day, the proclamation of the
placard was needless.   An attempt to persuade the advocate to return to Rotterdam, put himself at the head
of his adherents, and, if necessary, await a siege, failed
on his firm refusal.[1]

After this events moved quickly.   Holland had bowed
her head, and it seemed as though the advocate was
weary of the strife.   What happened ?   The dismissal of
the mercenaries was one point gained, and on the 25th
the resolution on the synod was introduced.   Three days
later Oldenbarnevelt was warned that his personal safety
was menaced.   The old statesman expressed his gratitude
for the warning, but would not flee.   In the early morning of the following day he sat at his desk, anxiously
awaiting what was to happen, when Uyttenbogaert came
to discuss the synod, and spoke consolingly of the examples of great men who had been equally ill rewarded
for their great services to the common weal.   A couple
of hours later [2] the advocate drove, according to his cus-

[1] De Groot, *Verhooren*, p. 29.
[2] *Verhaal der gevangenschap van Oldenbarnevelt*, written by his servant,
Jan Francken, published by Fruin, *Kroniek Hist. Gen.*, p. 134, 1874.

tom, to the assembly of Estates, where the question of the national synod was to be finally decided. He alighted in the Binnenhof and met the prince's chamberlain, who begged him to go to Maurice. In the prince's antechamber Oldenbarnevelt was arrested by a lieutenant of the prince's guard. A similar fate met De Groot and Hogerbeets. Ledenberg, who had been the chief leader of the opposition at Utrecht, returned thither only to be arrested and brought back to The Hague. The prince met the natural protest of the indignant majority of the Estates of Holland with an appeal to the charge given him by the States-General, and refused to discuss the right and jurisdiction of Holland, with the idea that the States-General would be able to avert a possible quarrel.[1] A charge had, indeed, been given to the prince and his fellow commissioners by the States on August 28th. It was so framed as to avoid exciting the suspicions of the Holland deputies, and empowered him generally to take measures necessary for the welfare of the land. Then, without cognisance of the Holland deputation, it was secretly agreed in a conference between certain commissioners of the other provinces to the States-General, the eight members of the commission[2] appointed on July 23rd, the prince, and William Louis, that the three statesmen and Ledenberg should be arrested on the following day. Not until this had been accomplished was the resolution which had been proposed earlier adopted in the secret proceedings of the States-General ; this provided that the three gentlemen should be taken into custody because, in the course of the investigation of the troubles at Utrecht and elsewhere, matters had been discovered which were dangerous to the state ; the States-General therefore regarded

[1] *Res. Holl.*, 29 Aug., 1618.
[2] De Groot, *Verhooren*, p. 367; compare Kluit, *Holl. Staatsreg.*, iii., p. 490; *Broeders Gevangnisse*, edited by Vollenhoven, p. 36; Brandt *Hist. der Reformatie*, ii., p. 840.

the arrests as necessary for the maintenance of security, unity, and friendship in the land.[1] At the same time thanks were offered to the prince and his fellow deputies for the measures taken on the " resolution and authority " of the States.

These unexpected arrests caused a panic among the advocate's adherents. Uyttenbogaert, Van der Myle, and others left The Hague, some taking refuge in France, some in the southern provinces. The announcement of the event in the newly convened Estates of Holland was received in dead silence, broken by the seigneur of Mathenesse, who said that the stillness was not surprising, for the Estates had lost " head, tongue, and hand."[2] So it was in very truth. No protests, no requests even, that the prisoners should be guarded in their own dwellings, availed. The States-General refused official and family appeals alike. On August 30th the Estates adjourned to September 12th, in order that the deputies might consult their constituents.

The prince saw that he must prevent the reassembly of the Estates as they were then composed. On September 6th he went to Schoonhoven with a large retinue and a bodyguard and later proceeded to the little cities, Briel, Schiedam, Oudewater, Woerden, Monnikendam, and Delft, where he arbitrarily replaced the municipal officials suspected of sympathy for the advocate by Contra-remonstrant persons, assuring the burghers that this was done without prejudice to their privileges and without danger of ill-consequences. In some places there was resistance, which was easily overcome. In others, as Enkhuizen, Purmerend, and Edam, no change was necessary. In the branch of the nobles a majority was obtained by the appointment of five new Contra-remonstrant members.

---

[1] Compare Van der Kamp, iv., 280.   [2] Carleton, ii., p. 290.

On October 12th the prince announced these changes to the Estates. The majority being changed, no protest was made against his action. Then the prince proceeded to use the same methods in Leyden, Haarlem, and Rotterdam, the bulwarks of the advocate's party. In Amsterdam, Hooft, the hoary partisan of freedom, was the only one who ventured to protest. The prince answered his remonstrance in a dry but not unfriendly manner: " My good father, this time it must be so. The needs of the land require it." [1] And the government was altered, though with moderation. A similar change in The Hague (November 8th) completed the round. In certain places, as Dordrecht, change was impossible, but the desired majority was gained without it.

On November 17th the Estates passed a vote of approbation wherein the new order was applauded, and the prince was heartily thanked for " his upright affection, care, and fidelity," while he was empowered, if need were, to take further measures.[2] The nomination of three new curators at Leyden in addition to the two already in function assured the Contra-remonstrants of the predominance in the college charged with the oversight of the University of Holland, whence the quarrel had emanated — an important office at this time.

Thus the opposition of the Estates of Holland was completely broken, and unity was restored in the national administration. It did not all take place legally, but still with sufficient care to avoid bloodshed and civil strife.[3] The prince, evidently under the advice of William Louis, who was still staying in The Hague,[4] hesitated to give

[1] Brandt, p. 877 ; Hooft, *Memoriën en Adviezen*, p. 327.
[2] *Archives*, ii., p. 544.
[3] *Res. Holl.*, 17 Nov., 1618.
[4] *Archives*, ii., p. 557, " *Selon la résolution prinse à nostre partement* "; Carleton, ii., pp. 292, 309.

ear to the vengeful demands of the bitter Contra-remonstrants, among whom was Reinier Pauw from Amsterdam.
Nor was he ready to accept the suggestion of his adherents, and declare himself sovereign.[1] He had also stopped
all popular demonstrations in the cities, to the disappointment of the ultra-partisans.

The attempt of the councillors of the high council and
those of the court of Holland to assail the sovereign
rights of the Estates by allowing their colleges to rank
above the latter was refused by the new assembly, and
in this respect, at least, the claim to sovereignty by the
Estates was maintained, although the prince was willing
enough to approve the demands of the councillors.   The
Contra-remonstrants, too, urged the regents, now that
they had driven their opponents from power, to yield no
thumb breadth of the privileges of the Estates either to
prince, States-General, or to any States' college whatsoever.   Like their predecessors, they were fully convinced that the Estates-provincial were sovereign.   The
revolution of 1618 brought no change in the provincial
administration, but only in the persons who exercised
the authority.   The people were for them merely an instrument to overcome their opponents.   The Estates
remained what they were. If, for the moment, the authority of the States-General and the prince in relation to the
provinces seemed increased, the Estates of Holland did
not acknowledge that they were by any means subordinated to his Excellency and to their High Mightinesses.
According to their theory the prince was their servant,
although there were evidences of his being their master.
Actually, too, the States-General remained the college
of the deputies of the sovereign provinces, although for
the moment authority was conceded to them as the head
of the nation.   The prince could undoubtedly have had

[1] Compare Hooft, *Memoriën en Adviezen*, pp. 19, 134; De Groot, *Verhooren*, p. 10; Oldenbarnevelt, *Verhooren*, p. 218.

himself acknowledged as sovereign under a royal monarchical title.   This he did not desire,[1] being contented
with the great power which he actually enjoyed under his
old title, and little inclined to risk more limited authority with a higher title.[2]   Lacking lawful descendants, he
had no strong dynastic leanings.   Perhaps he was fearful
of the opposition of the regents, who had grown accustomed to power, and also of his own party, among whom
republican elements too were strongly represented.[3]   He
was too little of a statesman to have comprehensive plans
now that he had attained his point.   Thus no real improvement in the government was introduced — which
was to be regretted, as appeared later.

The disposition of the prisoners was the first immediate
question to be settled.   They protested continually
against the proceedings, against the detention of their
letters, etc., asserting that the States-General had no
jurisdiction over them—servants of the Estates of Holland and of the cities.   They could be tried only by the
College of the Estates or by the municipal courts.

Two days after their arrest the three prisoners were
transferred from the prince's apartments to rooms made
ready for them in the Binnenhof.   Where the admiral of
Aragon had been imprisoned the advocate of Holland
was placed, while De Groot was confined in an adjacent
room, the former register chamber of Holland, and
Hogerbeets opposite.   At the end of September, Ledenberg was brought to The Hague and put in an adjacent
chamber.   A numerous watch was entrusted with the
guard.   All attempts to ameliorate their situation, or
even that of Oldenbarnevelt on account of his ill-health,

[1] Fruin, *Hugo de Groot en Maria van Reigersbergh*, De Gids, 1858, ii.,
p. 310 ; Groen, *Maurice et Barnevelt*, p. 11.

[2] De Groot, *Verhooren :* Oldenbarnevelt, *ibid.*   The prince said that he
had rather fling himself from The Hague tower than take the countship on
such conditions as it had been offered to his father.

[3] Compare Hooft, *Memoriën en Adviezen*, p. 154.

failed.   The condition of the rooms was such as to induce illness.   Some correspondence was allowed, but it
was closely supervised.   A dignified letter from Oldenbarnevelt to the prince and William Louis [1] had as little
effect as the proofs of patriotism and good intentions
towards the prince and his house which he and his
fellow prisoners did not fail to give.   De Groot went
further in his letter to the prince,[2] and threw the blame
of everything upon Oldenbarnevelt.   How much finer is
the letter of his noble wife![3]   The accused had need of
courage, for all public protests, even of Leyden and Rotterdam, in behalf of these pensionaries ceased after the
changes in the municipal governments, and the prisoners
were left to themselves.

By means of stratagems and ingenious devices the
prisoners' families managed to convey to them some
news of the world.   Letters in fruit, or laid between
linen, packages in the form of charcoal, new lines introduced into the proof-sheets of newly published
poems, words written in so-called sympathetic ink between the lines of books that were permitted,[4] gave
them slight knowledge of the changes in the government,
etc.   In similar ways they acquired paper, pens, ink, and
certain books secretly.

A commission, appointed by the States-General, began
its work of preliminary investigation at the end of September.   This proceeding was questionable in itself, as
the three Hollanders were thus placed under the jurisdiction of aliens.   Moreover, one of the commissioners,
Pieter van Leeuwen, from the court of Utrecht, was
known to be a personal enemy of Ledenberg.   Hendrik

[1] *Archives*, ii., 2, p. 553.

[2] Fruin, *Verhooren van De Groot*, p. 87 ; also Brandt, *Historie van de
rechtspleging*, p. 10.

[3] *Brieven van Maria van Reigersbergh*, Vollenhoven ed., p. 2.

[4] This was conceived by Peter Scriverius at Leyden, who corresponded in
this fashion with Hogerbeets and De Groot.

Pots was made clerk of the commission. Despairing of receiving justice, Ledenberg took his own life by cutting his throat with a bread-knife.   His body was embalmed, however, to await the result of his trial, and his property inventoried as preliminary to confiscation.   The suicide was deemed a proof of guilt.

De Groot's examination was pushed through promptly, as his first evidence of cowardice excited hope that he might be led to incriminate Oldenbarnevelt, or even Count Frederick Henry and his mother.   But, thanks to the efforts of his more spirited wife, the ex-pensionary of Rotterdam recovered his self-confidence, and did not allow himself to be wheedled into confession.[1]   After the first examination Oldenbarnevelt and Hogerbeets were remanded to confinement, and detained, in spite of their protests, for weeks before the trial proper began. The rigour with which they were treated was increased after the discovery of the methods by which their friends communicated with them.[2]   It was thus mid-November before the real examination began.   By that time the change of the magistracies in Holland had been effected, and four members from that province were added to the commission.   Until then the States-General had conducted the case in virtue of the order of August 28th.[3] The Holland members were all personal foes of the advocate, but their presence was an answer to the complaint of the prisoners that their judges were alien.   Holland thus safeguarded her rights over her burghers for future time, but no unbiased decision could be expected for the present prisoners from a court composed as this was.

The examinations were protracted.   Oldenbarnevelt appeared before the judges sixty times, and was quest-

[1] Brandt, *Historie van de rechtspleging*, p. 9.
[2] Compare the *Verhaal van Jan Francken*, p. 760.
[3] Compare for the irregularity of all this, Fruin, in *Versl. en Meded. Kon. Acad. Afd. Letterk.*, 2nd series, v., p. 230.

ioned in detail about the events of the preceding years, especially those connected with the *waardgelders*, his relation to the Estates of Utrecht, his action in Utrecht, —which finally, as *crimen perduellionis*, turned the scale of the trial,[1]—his relations to Uyttenbogaert, to De Groot, to Hogerbeets, and to Ledenberg; further, his opinion regarding theological and political differences, about the East and West Indian Companies, foreign policy before and at the time of the Truce, the sovereignty in Holland, his sentiment towards the prince, his alleged understanding with the enemy; in brief, about his whole life and his whole versatile activity. He had to draw on his memory for every item until a copy of Van Meteren's history was finally, after repeated requests, put at his disposal to enable him to recall the facts of his long life. Van Meteren, a Bible, and a French psalm-book, and, later, copies of the Union of Utrecht and of the Pacification of Ghent, besides the pamphlet, *Practijcke van den Spaenschen Raedt*, were the only books he was allowed to see. He was not even permitted to put his defence into writing, and was thus exposed to the danger of contradicting himself in details. De Groot and Hogerbeets were treated with the same methods, while they were urged in all kinds of ways to incriminate Oldenbarnevelt.[2] In the same autumn public sentiment was excited against the advocate by a bitter and malicious pamphlet accusing the imprisoned statesman of alliance with Spain and secret leanings towards Catholicism — two accusations which had great effect upon popular feeling.

The court proper appointed by the States-General to try the accused in form, proceeded with as much rigour as the examining commission. In order to overcome the scruples of Holland in regard to the privileges of her "subjects," twelve members were chosen from the native

[1] Compare Wijnne, *Geschiedenis*, p. 130.
[2] Compare, for all this, Brandt, *Historie van de rechtspleging.*

province of the prisoners, to two from every other province. The Estates of Holland proceeded to appoint twelve commissioners. The four members of the preliminary committee were reappointed, in addition to four deputies of the Estates and four members of the Court of Holland. The appointees from the other provinces were by preference the examiners who had already taken part in the investigation. On February 20th, these twenty-four judges received a commission from the States-General. The composition of this court was not above criticism, both as regards the individuals and their station in life.[1] Several were without legal training, and nearly all were personal enemies of the advocate. They and their descendants were guaranteed against ill-consequences from any action taken. The proceedings were secret. The commissioners were also charged with the trial of the lord of Moersbergen, who had been implicated in the troubles at Utrecht. Having fled to Münster, he had been arrested there and brought to The Hague. Further, the court was empowered to take cognisance of what concerned the matter either " directly or incidentally." This gave them practically unlimited power towards anyone who had the slightest connection with the events. The prosecuting officers or fiscals who had officiated in the examination were reappointed for the trial. They were Anthony Duyck of Holland, Sylla of Gelderland, and Leeuwen of Utrecht. All requests of Oldenbarnevelt's family to obtain the addition of other jurists were refused.

At his first hearing before the court, Oldenbarnevelt again appealed to the privileges of the sovereign state, Holland, whose servant he was, and who had guaranteed him against all extraordinary procedures and alien judges. His appeal was made in an elaborate, bold, but imprudently sharp speech which lasted for three days—March

[1] De Groot, *Verantwoordinghe*, p. 145.

7–9, 1619 [1]—and wherein he gave a clear exposition of his policy, ending with the declaration that he was fully prepared to answer any questions.

It was remarkable to hear this old statesman declare to the judges appointed by the States-General that Philip II. had forfeited his undoubtedly legal claims to the sovereignty by just such " unheard-of proceedings," and that the States-General absolutely possessed no sovereign rights, but was simply a gathering of sovereign allies who bore the same interrelation as the German circles or the Swiss cantons, or even as France, England, and the United Netherlands might in case of the conclusion of a general union between them. He asserted the right of the provinces and cities to take paid troops into their service and the right to regulate church matters on the part of each province. He gave an historic sketch of the doctrine of predestination, and declared that the Estates of Holland had only desired to give individual freedom of opinion in that regard, and to permit all laymen to judge independently upon theological points. He maintained the sovereign jurisdiction of Holland in all cases, defended the mission to Utrecht on the ground of the close alliance between the two provinces since 1534. Finally he protested again against the extraordinary court and the presence therein of his deadly foes, and declared the allegation of an understanding between him and the enemy false, an assertion he would be ready to maintain to the defence of truth and his honour.

The questions then put to him and his fellow prisoners were of the same nature as before; their answers, although often showing some natural bitterness, differed little from what had been said earlier.   De Groot's trial was finished in mid-April, that of Hogerbeets in March, that of Oldenbarnevelt on May 1st.   The sentence yet remained

[1] *Verhooren*, pp. 183–210.

to be pronounced, but it was decided to wait for that until the conclusion of the synod.[1]

Since the changes in the municipal councils the position of the Contra-remonstrants was quite different from what it had been. Now they were in the majority. By November, they were permitted to use the city churches, and the defeated Arminians seldom ventured to oppose them even in regions where they controlled the troops. The election of delegates by the provincial synods to the proposed assembly at Dordrecht resulted in a Contra-remonstrant majority from five provinces. In Utrecht, the Remonstrants were allowed half the quota of delegates.[2] In Holland the matter remained in doubt for some time. But finally—after many of the preachers had been removed by the provincial synod— the twelve delegates were selected. The majority were Contra-remonstrant, among whom were Lydius, Festus Hommius, Voetius, and Trigland. A little later (February, 1619) the Remonstrant preachers in the city of Utrecht were all removed by the new council.

On November 13, 1618, the assembly was opened at Dordrecht, and consisted of more than one hundred members.[3] Thirty-seven preachers and nineteen elders represented the Netherland churches. There were thirty foreign divines, five professors, Polyander from Leyden, Gomarus from Groningen, Lubbertus from Franeker, Thysius from Harderwijk, Walaeus from Middelburg, while eighteen political commissioners represented the States. The sessions of the synod lasted more than six months, and cost the provinces—which bore the expense

---

[1] Carleton, *Lettres*, iii., p. 46.

[2] Compare *Acta Synodalia*, published by Reitsma and Van Veen. The assembly is known as the synod of Dort, the shorter term for Dordrecht.

[3] There were delegates from Geneva, Berne, and other Swiss places, from Bremen, East Friesland, Hesse, and the Palatinate. Owing to the disapproval of the treatment of Oldenbarnevelt no envoy was sent from France. From England came the Bishop of Llandaff with several clergymen.

—at least three tons of money! This included travelling and lodging expenses, printing, witnesses, festivities, and presents in coin and medals. The meetings were public, and were attended by many curious and interested. Latin was used when foreigners were present. The president was Bogerman, with Rolandus from Amsterdam and Faukelius from Middelburg as assessors, Hommius from Leyden, Damman from Zutphen, as secretaries. The theological disputes were taken into consideration at once. In the fourth session it was decided to invite Episcopius and twelve Remonstrants to make a statement of their views. This was, in a way, citing them to appear before a tribunal, not giving them an opportunity to present their opinions in an open discussion. The Remonstrants had a preliminary meeting at Rotterdam to consider the best course, and decided to present their defence to the synod. On December 6th they entered the assembly, and took their seats at a table placed in the middle.[1]

Then followed a long contest, opened by Episcopius in a Latin harangue — lasting nine sessions — wherein he argued that the synod was not capable of acting as tribunal. The opposite party did not really discuss, but contented themselves with demanding defence. No advance was made. On January 1st, the wearied synod obtained a resolution from the States-General wherein the assembly was duly recognised as a court in relation to the accused. The Remonstrants refused to accept this. Violent scenes ensued. Bogerman, the president of the assembly, delivered a speech full of contumely, attacking the Arminians as liars and traitors. " With a lie did you begin, and you end with a lie," he said to them in Latin. " You are not worthy to be treated further by the synod. You are dismissed. Go hence." And they went, calling down God's judgment between them and their opponents.[2]

[1] Compare Glassius, *Geschiedenis der Nationale Synode.*   [2] *Ibid.*, p. 298.

It was plain what would be the lot of these exiles from the synod. Not that they accepted their exclusion quietly. Remonstrances, addresses, protests, and pamphlets of all kinds were addressed to prince, to synod, to States-General, and to the public at large. The exiles waited together at Rotterdam to watch the coercion of their opponents.[1] Grevinchoven became the leader in the proceedings of half a score of preachers and elders composing this anti-synod, which drew up the platform of the later church society of the Remonstrants. The Bible was taken as the sole foundation. No further confession or catechism was accepted.

In the absence of the Remonstrants, the synod proceeded to an examination of the five articles of the Remonstrance. Months passed, and finally, on April 23rd, the canons pronouncing judgment upon them were read aloud and signed; the opinion of the Reformed Church was defined respecting predestination; and the doctrines of the Contra-remonstrants were embodied in a logical, connected document. On the following day sentence was passed upon the offending persons in so far as they differed from the newly formulated dogmas. They were declared introducers of novelties, disturbers of the church,[2] obstinate leaders of party quarrels, teachers of false doctrine, guilty of falsification of religion, of disturbing unity, etc., in spite of the opposition of some foreign members. Martinius of Bremen especially urged moderation. Further, the Netherland Confession was unanimously acknowledged as conforming to the Holy Scriptures and the Heidelberg Catechism. This last was done on May 1st. Finally, after long discussions, Vorstius, who had remained at Gouda, was condemned by the synod, and it was declared that he was

[1] See *Acten van het gebesoigneerde*, Brandt, iii., p. 481.
[2] The words " of the fatherland and of the republic " were also introduced first, and then omitted as beyond the capacity of the synod.

unworthy to bear the name of an orthodox professor and doctor of the Reformed Church, that he was an impostor and sophist, a blasphemer and godless heretic, whose writings should be suppressed by the States-General. At the end of June he was dismissed by the Estates of Holland as professor and banished from the United Netherlands. He gave no heed to the summons to come to Steinfurt, but remained for a time secretly at Utrecht, and afterwards took refuge in Holstein.

Thus the synod dissolved. In the course of deciding the Remonstrant difficulty other doctrinal points had been settled. On May 6th, the articles and decisions were solemnly proclaimed in the great church before a large concourse of people after a prayer by Bogerman. Three days later, in the 154th session, in the shooting-gallery, the delegates took formal leave, and the synod closed with a banquet, amid congratulations on the good work accomplished. The " Netherland moon had risen from the obscurity of misery, having received new lustre from her sun," as Bogerman said. A gold medal was struck in commemoration of the event, and presented to the foreign theologians. The theological battle was finished, with complete defeat to the Remonstrants.

But bitterness remained. The Arminian resistance to the synod, the mass of pamphlets, the caricatures, and lampoons all had sown seed which bore fruit of party hatred.

This party spirit was evident, too, in the sentence pronounced two days later at The Hague against the three prisoners. Many attempts were made by the friends of the accused to persuade the prince and the States to be lenient. From the very beginning the French envoys, Boissize and Du Maurier, had exerted themselves to the utmost in their favour. Their king had written to the States urging unity, peace, and the maintenance of the existing form of government. A special envoy,

Châtillon, came from the French court, and effected as little as his official compatriots. The States resented their interference, but finally consented to defend their action in discreet terms, while giving reassuring declarations about maintaining their old alliance with France. New difficulties arose in France owing to the escape of the queen dowager from the half imprisonment in which she had been held. Boissize, discouraged, finally took his leave at the end of March, not without again urging the release of the prisoners, whose guilt, he said, was unproven. His remonstrance was again without effect.

Nevertheless the assertions of the French ambassadors that the charges of treason made against Oldenbarnevelt were unsustained by evidence were true. All that his accusers had obtained was a general statement from two Utrecht gentlemen, who in August, 1618, had heard one of the advocate's dependents say in a certain inn that he had understood from the most prominent persons in Holland that the Estates must force the prince to compliance by enlisting troops, and, if he did not yield, by making a treaty with the archdukes.[1] In addition to this there was the evidence of the former burgomaster of Utrecht, Berck, to the effect that, just at the time of the first secret overtures to the Truce, Oldenbarnevelt had said that the best means of stopping the war would be submission to the house of Burgundy, which had ruled the provinces not ill, and rewarded her servants fairly, while the difference of religion was less than appeared. Both the advocate and Uyttenbogaert, also incriminated by Berck, indignantly repudiated this charge, and proved Berck's personal hatred. Finally, the old clerk, Aerssens, the father of Oldenbarnevelt's deadly enemy, said that at the time of the negotiations with Father Neyen and Cruwel, he had discussed the presents offered to him and other gentlemen, which he evidently would have liked to accept,

[1] Wagenaar, x., p. 261.

while it was also believed that he had paid out for his son 14,000 guilders in Spanish pistoles. The advocate denied this accusation with indignation. When his papers were examined later—this was not done before the trial — nothing was found which suggested the pistoles or treason, a fact which cannot be impressed too plainly.[1]

Still the advocate was bound to be condemned. A letter [2] from William Louis to Maurice, begging him to show mercy to the old statesman and not to use torture, shows that there was some idea of more rigorous efforts to extort evidence. The prince asked again and again if Oldenbarnevelt begged for pardon. But neither he nor his children would imply his guilt by such a step. The latter excited the anger of Maurice and the judges by their show of confidence. They went so far as to erect a maypole before the prisoner's house and to celebrate the festival to evince their freedom of anxiety. As early as March, Louise de Coligny had made efforts to soften her stepson, but in vain. He might pardon his adversary, but he would not acknowledge his innocence. Rumours of Remonstrant risings, of attempts on the prince's life, further embittered him.[3] The judges hesitated to pronounce the sentence of death and sought for some middle way, though at the beginning the majority had been for extreme measures. The confident attitude of the advocate's family finally decided the hesitating members of the court. In the afternoon session, Sunday, May 12th, the advocate was condemned to capital punishment. This was communicated to him in the evening by the two fiscals and the provost-general, Nijs, who informed

---

[1] Compare Fruin, in *Versl. en Med. Kon. Acad.* Carleton's (iii., p. 83) reference to a packet, "which leads to the conjecture that there was a project of submission to Spain," shows the lack of proof. Compare Groen, *Maurice et Barnevelt*, p. 44.

[2] *Archives*, ii., p. 564 ; compare Carleton, iii., p. 84.

[3] *Archives*, ii., p. 568.

him in an unsympathising manner that the judgment would be executed on the following day after a solemn public reading of the sentence. The hoary statesman was more surprised and indignant than despondent. Leaving to the judges the responsibility before God, he asked for pen and ink to write a farewell letter to his people. This was allowed, while the fiscals stayed with him until Anthony Walaeus, summoned by the States from the synod of Dort, should arrive to offer him the last consolation. Walaeus came soon, waiting until the advocate had written his last letter, a touching and sad reminder of his activity, even to the last years, an earnest word of consolation to his people, a warm testimony of his innocence towards the fatherland, his fidelity to his masters, the Estates of Holland, evident in word and deed.

Until late at night he talked with Walaeus [1] at length, and often violently, about the course of the synod, and about his unjust trial, and then more calmly about religion. The preacher noticed to his surprise that, in his opinion about predestination, Oldenbarnevelt was really more Contra-remonstrant than Remonstrant, and only averse to the so-called absolute predestination, to damnation without consideration of belief or unbelief. At the request of the prisoner, Walaeus went in his name to the prince to testify his willingness to ask forgiveness if he had done him any injury, and to recommend his children to him. The advocate, however, said expressly, in answer to Walaeus's question, that he asked no mercy. The rough prince was evidently touched at this visit. He answered pleasantly that the admiral had always been dear to him, and he was sorry for his misfortune; that he had been obliged to oppose him because he had wished to introduce a new form of government; that he gladly forgave Oldenbarnevelt for what he had done against him, even

[1] Compare *Vita Walæi*, published by his son.

though the advocate had wished to alienate his soldiers from him, had accused him of seeking the sovereignty, and endangered his safety in Utrecht; that he had asked the judges not to take into account the attacks on his own person; that he would care for the children as long as they did well. As Walaeus was leaving, the prince called him back to ask whether the advocate had said nothing of pardon, and when the preacher said " No," Maurice hardened his face.

Oldenbarnevelt remained absolutely firm in his assertions that he was innocent and that he had been unjustly condemned by unqualified judges. He passed his last night in conversation and in reading in a French psalm-book, and accepting the usual ministrations of his faithful servant, Jan Francken.

His family asked and obtained permission to see him, but when the advocate was asked if he desired their presence, without being told that the matter was already arranged, he refused for fear of new complications. Thus deception was practised against him and his to the very end.

During the night the scaffold was erected. At the very break of day Louise de Coligny made a last effort to see Maurice, but was not admitted to his room. Du Maurier, too, appealed to the States-General in his sovereign's name, urging a stay of proceedings. He was told that the judges had full power. The prince, still believing that pardon would be asked, remained firm in his conviction that the sentence was just, and took no step to save the statesman. The hard, unfeeling tone of the letter in which he informed his cousin, William Louis, of the execution, shows his utter alienation from the old friend of his house.

At eight o'clock troops had assembled, and the advocate was summoned to the hall of the judges. They were not ready, and he returned to his room to be again

summoned in half an hour.   Only a few lookers-on, members of the States, were present.   Then the sentence was
read to the prisoner by the clerk, Pots.   The tedious
document [1] set forth how it was plain from his confession
—without torture—that the prisoner had tried to excite
a " blood-bath " in Utrecht, and risked the prince's life;
that he had tried to establish states within states, governments within governments, and new alliances within and
against the union; that he had tried to excite general
perturbation both in church and political affairs; that he
had exhausted the finances; further, had caused general
dissension among the allies; that he had broken up the
union, unfitted the nation for self-defence, and exposed
it to danger; that he must be punished as an example to
others, and was therefore condemned to be taken to the
Binnenhof on the place already prepared, and to be beheaded with the sword so that death would ensue.   All
his property was confiscated.   Well might the advocate,
after he had heard, restlessly but silently, these points
through, declare his innocence, turn, and say, " The
judges put much in my sentence that they could never
find in my confession."   He protested against the confiscation, and asked whether that was the reward for
serving his country forty-three years.   In response, one
of the judges, Vooght, shouted at him, " Your sentence
is read.   Forth, forth!"

It was about nine o'clock on Monday, May 13th.   The
old statesman, clad in a black suit covered by a brown
cloak, and leaning on a stick, passed out of the room
through the great hall, where a crowd stood, some of his
friends included, whom he did not heed, preserving his
ordinary air of hauteur [2] as he made his way to the scaffold, assisted by his faithful servant.   A large crowd was
gathered in the Binnenhof.   The windows of the prince's

[1] Brandt, *Historie der Reformatie*, iii., pp. 198–210.
[2] Carleton, iii., p. 77.

room opposite the scaffold were all closed. No court of-
cial appeared. The prince had withdrawn into an inner room.[1] Having pushed aside his cloak with the help
of his servant, and after a moment of silence during his
last prayer, shared by the bystanders, the prisoner said
to the crowd: "Men, do not believe that I am a traitor:
I have acted uprightly like a good patriot, and as such I
die. Jesus Christ is my leader." Adding, "Lord God,
Father in Heaven, receive my spirit," he drew his cap
over his eyes, turned first south where the sun was in his
face, then north, with his countenance towards the old
court chapel. Trembling somewhat, he begged the ex-
ecutioner to make his work short. The sword flickered
in the sun and the head of the greatest Netherland
statesman, who had "carried Holland in the heart,"
rolled down in the sand. He died as he had lived, firm
to his opinions, obstinate and authoritative to the end.
There lay his body to show what personal hatred and
bitter partisanship could do. On the same day Ledenberg's dead body was condemned to be placed on the
gallows, and his property was declared confiscated.
There was some delay in pronouncing sentence upon the
other prisoners, as it was expected they would sue for
pardon. But even De Groot had recovered from his
weakness, and all persisted in declaring their innocence.
On May 18th the jurist was condemned to perpetual imprisonment with loss of property. "I know of no eternal
punishment but hell," he said. Nor was it eternal, as he
succeeded, owing to the ingenuity of his wife, in escaping
in a box of books from Lovestein, where he was confined.
The other prisoners and suspected persons met various
fates, but all finally escaped with their lives.

Thus the national tragedy of 1617–19 ran to an end.
The black curtain could fall on the scene, but the death
of the great statesman remained a bloody stain on the

[1] Compare the account of Rivet, *Opera* iii., p. 1165.

historical pages of the famous republic,—a stain, too, on
the reputation of the mighty marshal who, acting in all
good faith, was still prejudiced and vengeful towards the
man of whom the dry records of the Estates of Holland,
under the heading *Outhoudt de Memorie*, recount the
execution and the years of service, with the comment
that he was a man of great industry, energy, memory,
and direction, yes, singular in everything, and thereon
follows [1]: " He that stands let him see that he does not
fall, and may God be merciful to his soul! "   Amen!

In the same spirit Winwood says, in one of his last
letters [2]: " I know Barenveld well, and know that he has
great powers and abilities, and malice itself must confess
that never man has done more faithful and powerful service to his country than he."   This testimony of one of
his arch-enemies is a judgment on their action towards
him and his followers, even if it be true that in times of
party spirit the voice of heart and conscience is less plainly
heard, that " reasons of state," the " *respublica poscit*,"
seem to urge to greater strictness than in other circumstances, that, finally, Oldenbarnevelt and his adherents
also sinned on their side through obstinacy and wilful-
ness, through intolerance towards the opinions of others,
through measures of force, through violation of right
and fairness.

The last word about the troubles of the Truce must be [3]
that both parties were culpable in their actions, but that
the dominant party committed the greater sin by the judicial murder of their great opponent—a judicial murder,
as Macaulay, Motley, and Fruin rightly termed the atrocious execution of May 13, 1619.   Oldenbarnevelt was
not condemned according to the demands of justice, but

---

[1] *Res. Holl.* (1619), p. 102.
[2] Carleton, *Lettres*, ii., p. 92.
[3] Compare Fruin, in *Konst. en Letterbode* (1861), pp. 401 *et seq.*

according to those of policy conflicting with principles which he himself had earnestly espoused.   And the unfortunate statesman grasped the true reason of his misfortune with his customary clear-sightedness in the last night of his life when he said [1] that his judges had not decided in accordance with accepted laws of past time, but of the present.   The maxims of 1588—his maxims —were not those of 1618, and he fell as a sacrifice to the change.

[1] *Vita walæi*, p. 24 ; compare Carleton, iii., p. 74.

CHAPTER XVI

THE LAST YEARS OF THE TRUCE

THE defeat of Oldenbarnevelt and his party, accomplished in such a tragic manner, made little apparent difference in the condition of the United Provinces. Individuals exercising authority were replaced by others. There was at first no suggestion of more radical changes in home affairs or foreign relations. But, as a matter of fact, the prince had become virtual ruler. He saw to it that in both provincial Estates and States-General only those came to the fore upon whom he could rely personally. He was an untitled monarch. Nay, more, the people were spoken of as his subjects.[1]

The death of Philip William of Nassau (February, 1618) made Maurice head of his house and sovereign prince. His own military reputation as first general of his time, the circle of officers who surrounded him, which, in spite of his personal simplicity, gave an effect of pomp, made the impression of his being a reigning prince. There was, moreover, talk of a Brandenburg marriage, of the restoration of the duchy of Gelderland and of the countship of Holland in his behalf. But he showed little ambition in that direction.

One factor in the expansion of the prince's power was the loyal support given him by other members of his house. The unexpected death from apoplexy of the

---

[1] Van der Capellen, *Gedenkschriften*, i., pp. 15, 84, 347.

sixty-year-old William Louis of Nassau (June, 1620), at Leeuwarden, was a great loss to Maurice. The experience of his forty years of faithful military and political service in the Netherlands would have been very valuable in the difficulties ensuing from the Arminian disputes and the end of the Truce. His last letter gave evidence of his devotion to the country and to his religion.[1] Maurice was chosen as his successor in Groningen and Drenthe, but Friesland's fear of Holland's ascendency prevented his elevation to the vacant stadtholdership in that province, and Count Ernest Casimir of Nassau succeeded his brother.

Another loss suffered by the house of Nassau was the death of Louise de Coligny at Fontainebleau (March, 1620). She had never recovered from the shock of the execution of her old friend, Oldenbarnevelt. Moreover, she had herself been hooted at in Delft where her husband had laid down his life, and so had left her adopted country for France. On her way thither, escorted by her son, she had received Uyttenbogaert at Antwerp with great friendliness. She only survived her return to the land of her birth a short time. Her body was taken back to Delft, where it was buried beside that of her husband.

Her son, Frederick Henry, had a difficult rôle to fill at this epoch. He did not hide his sympathy for the fallen party, and was keenly interested in the fate of the exiles. So there was, indeed, some talk of refusing him his brother's dignities in case of Maurice's death, from fear of a reaction. But the " *safte* " prince was no ardent partisan. He kept aloof from political and state matters, and busied himself with military affairs. As general in the open field he even surpassed his brother, whose faithful pupil he had been. He was much more cultivated and polished than Maurice, whose only diversions were chess and tactical studies and the society of his officers,

[1] *Archives*, ii., p. 570.

accustomed to camp life, while the younger brother had introduced French customs into his household. He, too, had little inclination for marriage. To his brother he was devoted heart and soul.

Owing to Maurice's personal aversion to political details, the conduct of affairs, although nominally in his control, fell virtually to his friends,—Aerssens and his party. Reforms were postponed owing to the approaching end of the Truce, although in 1620 Haarlem made an effort to discuss a revision of the union in the provincial Estates.[1]

Andries de Witt, pensionary of the oldest Holland city, Dordrecht, held the advocate's post during his imprisonment. No one ever inherited Oldenbarnevelt's position. There was some talk of dividing the office into several,[2] and the title was changed to that of *Raadpensionaris*, council pensionary; the term was made for five years instead of for life, and the appointment was made by the Estates and stadtholder from a nomination of three persons. The functions remained about the same as those of the former advocate, but were more closely supervised. In short, the council pensionary was reduced to the position of provincial official of Holland, while the advocate had exercised a general authority. Upon these conditions, with a few more, as, for instance, that no gifts could be received and no influence exercised on the appointment to office, the councillor Anthony Duyck accepted the office, January 21, 1621. The conduct of foreign relations remained nominally in the hands of the States-General, actually in those of any persons whom the then dominant prince might appoint. The persons were Aerssens, commonly called Sommelsdijk, Marquette, Pauw, and Noordwijk of Holland; Joachimi, Man-

[1] *Res. Holl.*, 20th March, 1620.
[2] Vreede, *Gesch. der Diplomatie*, ii., p. 23; *Archives*, ii., pp. 575, 577, 579.

maker, and Vosbergen of Zealand; and some others, who performed their duty with zeal and prudence. Maurice was rather their tool than their master, and did nothing without them.[1]

Their first act was to remove from office all adherents and kinsfolk of Oldenbarnevelt. The examination of the advocate's papers, about which the Estates of Holland and the States-General had a long contention, brought many of his friends into difficulties. No trace of treason with Spain was discovered, but it was thought that there was plain evidence of close alliance with France,[2]—something that Oldenbarnevelt undoubtedly approved without any idea of making the provinces subject, as his enemies asserted. Sommelsdijk and Marquette made the most of this. Having obtained a commission from the Estates to investigate the character of all officials, they used the power to the utmost in order to wipe every trace of Arminianism from city and village.[3]

The preachers and influential members of all Remonstrant congregations also were called to account. The States-General warned all Remonstrant members of the synod that they were no longer preachers, and imposed an " act of cessation " upon them, which they had to sign on pain of banishment. This forced them to abstain from all preaching, and to live simply as private individuals.[4] Only one of them yielded. The remaining fourteen were escorted (July 6, 1619) to the borders in the name of the States-General. Some took refuge in Cleves or Bentheim, and others in Waalwijk in Spanish Brabant.

Assemblies of the Remonstrants were forbidden by act (July) of the States-General, but in the larger places, as Amsterdam, Rotterdam, and Gouda, this was not enforced, and their meetings in or near the cities were

---

[1] Ouvré, p. 308.
[2] Ibid., p. 273.
[3] Carleton, iii., p. 233.
[4] Brandt, iii., p. 687.

overlooked, much to the annoyance of the zealots.   Sixty South Holland preachers were removed and went into exile after refusing to sign the act of abstention.   Nearly all their brethren in North Holland and Utrecht consented to sign.

Out of the whole number of two hundred Remonstrant preachers removed from office, about seventy signed the act and lived quietly in retirement.   About forty bought their restoration to their profession by accepting the Dordrecht articles, while at least eighty preferred exile. Exiles who went to Brabant, where the Brussels government rejoiced at the dissent in the north, were left untroubled in the hope that their services might be useful. Uyttenbogaert, who continued his residence at Antwerp, was repeatedly urged to aid in bringing about a reconciliation with the archdukes, but steadfastly refused Spinola's overtures.   Episcopius and Grevinchoven, too, were quiet.   The press at Antwerp,— the headquarters of the Remonstrants,— however, showed the mental activity of others of the exiles.   Masses of pamphlets and lampoons were issued, attacking the triumphant party in the republic, termed " little monsters of the new Holland inquisition," etc.   A very few, among whom was the Leyden professor, Bertius, adopted the Catholic faith, and became involved in risky negotiations with some of their Netherland friends.   Persecution was not lacking against the banished preachers found within the boundaries.   In 1620, Grevius van Heusden was, thanks to the price of five hundred guilders placed on the preachers' heads, arrested and placed in the house of correction at Amsterdam, among ordinary criminals.   Church councillors, schoolmasters, etc., of suspected doctrine were also removed from all their posts.

Naturally this disposition on the part of the government to repress the opposition party excited much bitterness.   Sommelsdijk's violent attitude did great harm, and the state of public opinion in 1620 made the prince very uneasy.[1]   There were strong garrisons wherever the presence of Arminian opinions made disturbances dreaded. Tumultuous scenes were enacted at Gouda, Rotterdam, Hoorn, Schoonhoven, and Woerden, where Arminian street sermons were forbidden.

Sommelsdijk, Pauw, Marquette, Duivenvoorde, etc., determined to remove their political foes from every office in city and country.   The States-General yielded to their arguments that this must be done for public safety, but the deputed councillors hesitated to undertake such a disagreeable duty.   The States therefore assumed it themselves, and on the advice of a commission not less than twenty-eight sheriffs and secretaries were removed (January 15, 1621) from office in cities and villages, while others were severely reprimanded.[2]   The local governments were empowered for this once to fill vacancies without nomination by Estates and stadtholder, provided the candidates were " lovers and upholders of religion and government."

Many Remonstrants in private life thought emigration the wisest step.   So many went to Holstein that the duke granted a charter (September, 1619) to William van den Hove, seigneur of Wedde and Westerwold, De Groot's cousin, to found a new city of Remonstrants on the river Eider.   This was the only Holland colony of importance formed at that time in Europe.   The citizens were empowered to retain their religion, which alone should give political rights, their Holland privileges, and institutions.[3] Two years later the first settlers founded the city of Frederiksstad, named after the duke, who appointed Adolph van Moersberg as his stadtholder.   Van den

[1] *Archives*, ii., p. 578 ; Carleton, iii., pp. 283, 297.
[2] Arend, Van Rees, and Brill, *Algemeene Geschiedenis des Vaderlands*, iii., pp. 3, 456.
[3] Brandt, *Historie der Reformatie*, iv., pp. 134, 655.

Hove, the Haarlem pensionary De Haan, and many others took up their abode there, but the colony did not flourish owing to floods and then to the war. It was so near Holland, too, that return was easy when the persecutions ceased and liberty of conscience could be enjoyed there. Only about sixty families seem to have remained permanently at Frederiksstad, mainly well-to-do people whose descendants were less prosperous.[1]

The changes in the various municipal governments were made cautiously, so as to avoid exciting enmity among the chief families. Many an individual libertine remained in office when more was to be feared from his dismissal than retention. In Gouda alone, and, out of Holland, at Bommel and Kampen, a constitutional change seemed urgent, and Count Ernest Casimir effected it in the prince's name in those localities. But even in Amsterdam, the stronghold of opposition to Oldenbarnevelt, there was a certain aversion to the continuance of severity. As early as 1622, the Arminian spirit was again in evidence.

There was a proposition to introduce an article into the Union of Utrecht restricting official positions throughout the provinces to members of the Reformed Church. But it was never adopted, though various limitations in the individual provinces dated from that time. In 1616, Catholics were excluded from certain elective capacities, though not legally from office-holding. In Overyssel and Gelderland no restriction was made until after the Truce. In Holland, where many non-reformed had seats in the regent's colleges, it was thirty years before similar laws were made, although in certain cities like Gouda, preference was given to those committed to " the true Christian religion." But in the majority of cities no one was constitutionally ineligible for the exercise of political rights

---

[1] Mensinga, *De Hollandsche familien in Frederiksstad aan de Eider*, *Nijh. Bijdr.*, new series, ix., p. 331.

or for nomination to office upon theological or religious grounds. Catholics and Dissenters could be legally sent as deputies to the States-General, and were sent, at least up to the period in question.[1] But the victory of the stricter party resulted, practically, in a gradual change and furthered the supremacy of the Reformed Church, although it was not actually made a state church. Indeed, the Dordrecht articles in regard to church regulations had to be modified by various restrictions, except in Utrecht and Gelderland. The synodal church discipline, based on The Hague ritual of 1586, which had never been adopted in Holland, would have withdrawn the church too much from state influence, something which the new government wished to guard against. In Holland the modifications were so radical that they were abandoned by the two provincial synods, and on the refusal of the States to renounce the restrictions, the conditions previous to 1618 remained unchanged. In Friesland and the other provinces the Estates refused to yield their authority to the Dort regulations on church organisation. There was universal opposition, too, to ceding the academies to the supervision of the church. The utmost that the dominant party could obtain was that subscription to the formula of unity should be demanded from the professors of theology at Groningen. At Leyden and elsewhere greater diversity of opinion was allowed.

But, as concerns doctrine, the articles adopted at Dordrecht were completely accepted, and this had a great influence on the people's life. In 1619, Carleton complained that Sunday was no day of rest.[2] Long before the synod of Dort, the States had, at the instance of the preachers, published edicts against Sabbath-breaking,[3]

---

[1] Naber, "Dissenters op't kussen," in *De Tijdspiegel*, 1884, p. 45.

[2] *Lettres*, iii., p. 114.

[3] Van Veen, *Zondagsrust en sondagsheiliging in de 17de eeuw.* (Nijkerk, no date.)

but these affected the people little.   There were occasional afternoon sermons, but that was all.   During the.
entire seventeenth century, there was a continual struggle
between the church authorities and the people, unwilling
to abandon their ancient customs and averse to afternoon
service.   But the church kept on insisting, and, by the
middle of the century, obtained her desire, and Sunday
was more generally observed.

The influence of the synod was apparent in its effect
upon the stage, upon letters, and upon art in general.
Preachers of the stricter school — always opposed to the
rhetoricians—condemned the " sinful vanity and unfruit-
ful works of darkness " of the theatre.   The devil was
the father of the theatre, in the eyes of some, of lay
poetry in general.[1]   Consequently there was a new burst
of opposition to the stage, a revulsion against secular
poetry.   This was in part due to the fact that in the disputes between " Gommer " and " Armijn " the poets had
never sided with the former.

Amsterdam was the chief scene of a fierce contest between theology and art, between theatre and consistory,
because the drama was flourishing there just at that time.
In Coster's *Iphigenia and Polyxena*, the prevailing orthodoxy was scourged with an unsparing hand, while the
academy,[2] founded 1617, was the object of the most violent attacks from the Amsterdam preachers.   The Amsterdam consistory repeatedly appealed to the government
to suppress the poets.   The government was not inclined
to proceed severely against Coster and his followers, and
contented themselves by giving the poets an occasional
reprimand to satisfy the popular preachers.   The reaction
against the pagan renascence emanated from the church,
and the biblical element became more and more prominent in products of literature.   Thus the struggle between

---

[1] Kalff, *Literature en toneel te Amsterdam*, p. 155.   Amsterdam, 1896.
[2] Compare Gallée, *Academie en Kerkeraad.*   Utrecht, 1878.

the two theological parties militated towards making the United Netherlands into a state wherein there was not the slightest idea of legal equality for all creeds, and where the reformed element steadily gained the upper hand. The numbers of church members, too, increased. Many inclined to Arminian opinions and to the ancient faith found it easier and safer to join the dominant communion. The way was thus opened to official positions, and they were safeguarded from the extortions of sheriffs and sheriffs' servants charged with the maintenance of the placards, but who were open to bribes. By the middle of the seventeenth century the Catholics no longer had the numerical advantage in the provinces.

But it must be remembered that the very fact of the presence of so many in the Reformed Church who were by no means zealots was at the same time a guarantee for moderate observance of the articles adopted at Dordrecht. Practically many of the most stringent observances fell into the background.

The fact, too, that the States were not inclined to give complete freedom to the church, but asserted their own authority and repudiated the influence of the consistories and church dignitaries, was a keen disappointment to the ultra-orthodox. They had hoped for a complete victory and for power beyond the realm of theology, even if they did not attain a state church. But after the first manifestation of rigour the States pursued the path of moderation on which their predecessors before 1618 had sought the weal of the young state. In no country of Europe was there as much freedom of conscience as was finally enjoyed under the domination of the victors of 1618 and 1619.

The course of the above events was of great significance for the foreign relations of the state.

Aerssens and his party deviated very slightly from

Oldenbarnevelt's policy. Carleton writes: " To tell the truth, they have not yet found means to settle affairs." [1] The one evident result of Oldenbarnevelt's fall was a certain approach to England and alienation from France.

The French government was not upon fast and stable foundations. The disastrous quarrels between the king and queen-mother were patched up by a reconciliation in the spring of 1619, but all the acts of the government were weak, irresolute, and ineffective.

Du Maurier, deeply grieved at Oldenbarnevelt's fall, kept in the background for a time, and only reappeared in the assembly of the States at the end of the year to complain of the injury inflicted upon French merchants by Holland sailors in India and elsewhere. The attitude of the States towards him was careless and not conciliatory. At the same time the approach of the end of the Truce rendered alienation from France very unwise, and there were suggestions of sending an embassy to France to renew the ancient alliance. But there was difficulty in achieving that because the French government refused to receive Sommelsdijk, who would necessarily have appeared as leader of foreign affairs. Thus it was 1621 before an embassy went to France with assurances of the States' friendship, to solve commercial difficulties, to allay the grievances against Sommelsdijk and others, and to promise that the States would furnish no aid to the Huguenots against the government,—a promise that showed that the States had no intention of pursuing a strictly religious policy, and were anxious for a renewal of their ancient alliance. Jeannin, charged with the negotiations, met the overtures rather coldly, and the embassy returned in April without having obtained anything more than friendly words and assurances of inability of France to aid the republic with money or troops.

The relations with England had, on the other hand,

---

[1] *Lettres*, iii., p. 147.

greatly improved, owing to the support given by James, Carleton, and the English theologians, to the dominant party, while commercial difficulties were somewhat alleviated. This was very desirable in view of the danger that James might throw himself into the arms of Spain and be the declared enemy of the States.

In the East, however, international relations were neither smooth nor friendly. There hostilities against the Spanish and Portuguese had been pursued by Coen as though no truce existed. Only Malacca and the Philippines remained in the power of the foe. But the Netherlanders had no notion of sharing their conquest with their English rivals. The English East India Company, established 1609, had built one of their many factories at Macassar in order to press their way into the Moluccas. The friction between the two nations was unceasing, and sometimes the English made alliances with the natives against the Netherlanders.

The Netherland factory at Bantam had to be protected from English onslaughts by a considerable force. The director-general, Coen, urged the company to proclaim war. The English had sworn his death, and he was their fell enemy.[1] He urged them, too, to strengthen their position in Jacatra on Java's northern coast. "God is with us. . . . Great things can be accomplished in India," he wrote, September 29, 1619.

From the time of Coen's appointment as director-general (June, 1618) dates the energetic opposition to English competition in India. At the end of 1618, fifteen English ships arrived before Bantam to further English interests. The first encounter (January 4th) showed the superiority of the English. It was decided that Coen should seek reinforcements at Molucca wherewith to drive the English from India. It was a very

---

[1] See De Jonge, *Opkomst van het Nederl. gezag*, iv., pp. 72, 207.

critical moment, and Coen complained bitterly of the
negligence of the directors, who precipitated the disaster
by failing to heed his warnings or to respond to his appeals for money and ships. " I swear by the Almighty
that the General Company has no more injurious foes
than the ignorance and thoughtlessness which prevail
(though I do my best) among your Honours and deaden
the intelligence." So rang his reproach.

During his absence at Ambon, his deputy at Jacatra,
Van den Broeck, was lured to the court of the regent of
Jacatra, together with a number of his men, and treacherously taken prisoner. The others held out for a time,
but finally found themselves forced to yield. On January 31st, the Netherlanders were, accordingly, preparing
to vacate the fort when a quarrel broke out between the
two allies, and the Bantam government laid claim to
Jacatra. The English prepared to come to Bantam to
defend the interests of the Javanese, while the Netherlanders took a new resolve to hold out. This state of
half siege lasted until the middle of May, when suddenly
Coen returned with sixteen ships and 1200 men. All
danger was passed. On May 30, 1619, Coen razed Jacatra to the ground, sword in hand. " In this manner,"
he wrote, August 5th, " we have become foot and master
in the territory of Java. The foundation of the long-
wished-for rendezvous is laid." He proceeded to attack
what English ships he could, determined to drive " the
unendurable nation " out of India for ever. His next
aim was to turn Jacatra into the " staple of Indian commerce." In the course of 1619–20, a new city was
founded on the ruins of Jacatra, which was officially
named Batavia in 1621, and destined to become the queen
of the archipelago.

All this was accomplished by one man at the head of a
weak naval force of scarcely thirty bottoms, great and
small, scattered over India and the Philippines, and as

far as China and Japan,[1] supported in the forts by a little army of 1500 to 1600 soldiers of every nationality—" all the force of the Indies." Well might he exclaim, " We lack nothing except everything "; but he never lacked courage, while, ill supported as he was by the directors, he pushed through his great work — the establishment of the commercial sovereignty of the Netherlanders in India.

The policy of universal peace, conceived in Europe, did not suit Coen. The plan was to stop competition by a union of the English and Netherland companies. In 1618 an embassy went to England to thank James for his assistance in the theological disputes and to make some negotiations in this regard. The English company was ready to join her more flourishing rival, and the Netherland company saw that it might be advantageous not to be obliged to maintain a large military force in the East against the English, who would be useful allies against the Spanish. The States were quite ready to put an end to hostilities in India, especially as they had the company more or less in their power owing to the approaching expiration of their limited charter. Many points came up in regard to this. Other provinces, like Friesland and Groningen, were anxious to gain some share in the profitable Indian commerce, and the advocates of the West Indian Company began to urge their claims to recognition now that their opponent, Oldenbarnevelt, was out of the way.

In the spring of 1618, Oldenbarnevelt and De Groot had been the chief persons in the negotiations with England. In the autumn, when they were in prison, Carleton began to be more arrogant and threatened reprisals in Europe for the injuries inflicted by Coen in the East, and for the hostile attitude of the northern company in the whaling ground.

[1] See De Jonge, *Opkomst van het Nederl. gezag*, iv., p. 184.

In December, an embassy set out for England.[1]   It
consisted of five directors and the company's advocate,
Boreel, accompanied by three deputies of the States-
General, to aid the ordinary ambassador, Caron, and to
further the negotiations with the English company.   The
discussions were mainly limited to Indian affairs, and resulted (July 17, 1619) in a treaty of union between the
English and Dutch companies.   This was to last twenty
years, during which period the two governments were to
assure a monopoly to the companies.

This union naturally displaced Coen, who was triumph-
ing over the English in the East without the necessity of
concessions.   He declared that the company had taken a
" serpent into its bosom " with this act, and complained
that the Indian commercial interests were sacrificed to
European politics.   Though forced to make some outward show of yielding, he was resolute in his determination not to allow other authority than his own in Java or
elsewhere in that region, a determination which augured
ill for the desired coöperation.[2]

For the time being, however, this agreement removed
one difficulty from the political relations of the Netherlands with England.   The envoys were not equally successful in arranging the whale fishery in the north,
although England agreed to leave the Netherlanders untouched for three years.

It seemed possible that this better relation to England
might be of great importance in the general European
policy in which the United Netherlands were deeply
involved.

The long-expected outbreak of hostilities in Germany
had come.   In their revolt against the Catholic Ferdinand of Styria (in 1618), the Protestant Bohemians

---

[1] *Kron. Hist. Gen.*, vol. xxii., p. 385 ; vol. xxvi., p. 254 ; Arend, Van
Rees, and Brill, iii., p. 254.

[2] De Jonge, iii., p. 204.

appealed to the States-General for aid. They were not contented with the assurance of friendship given by the States, afraid to do more from dread of Spain's enmity, and demanded a loan of 600,000 guilders. The States finally gave a promise of three months' aid at 50,000 guilders a month, and, when, Frederick, elector palatine, was chosen king of Bohemia, were inclined to continue the subsidy, reckoning on the help which King James would give his son-in-law. But this the English monarch refused to do, in spite of many petitions from Frederick and other Protestants. The States therefore restricted their aid to subsidies.

Then, too, the small German princes began to beg for money and troops from the States, whom they regarded as their most powerful friends. In 1619 and 1620 their envoys appeared frequently in The Hague, and more than once obtained large sums. Maurice gave advice to them and to the Bohemians upon the defence of their lands. Finally, in the spring of 1620, the actions of the archdukes gave the prince excuse to collect his troops on the eastern border to the number of 12,000 men.

The archdukes had watched events in Germany closely, and were prepared to aid the Catholic party. Spinola's operations made it evident that he intended an attack on the palatinate during Frederick's absence in Bohemia. This aroused great anxiety both in the provinces and in England, and James consented to enlisting troops for Bohemia. In a short time, Sir Horace Vere appeared in the Netherlands with a force which was divided for a time among the garrisons on the eastern borders. Spinola set off southwards in August with about 2000 men, took possession of Dietz in Nassau on his way, and overpowered a great part of the palatinate. Maurice went so far into Germany as to lay siege to Wezel, which Spinola passed by. He was unwilling to go farther afield under the circumstances existing at home, but sent his brother with the States' cavalry and 2000 musketry to escort the English troops to the palatinate, unheeding imperial rights. He himself took possession of an island in the Rhine between Bonn and Cologne, where he erected the stronghold Papenmuts. At the end of the year, Frederick's army returned through Cologne and Westphalia, harrying the land as they came, exciting protests, but fighting no pitched battles.

The young king of Bohemia met only defeat in his new realm. Great was the interest in the Netherlands in the fate of the defender of the Protestant cause, and the pamphlets describing the course of events were read eagerly. The battle of Prague, in November, made an end to the brief sovereignty of the winter king, as he was called. Nor could he regain his hereditary lands from Spinola's troops. In April, 1621, the unfortunate prince established himself and his family in The Hague under the protection of his cousin Maurice.

In the spring of 1621, the cause of the German Protestants was in sorry case, mainly owing to James's refusal to back his son-in-law and to the hesitation of the States to involve themselves in a great war without England and France. Their attitude, vacillating between sympathy for the Bohemians and fear of Spain, showed the lack of Oldenbarnevelt's strong hand at the helm. Still, at the end of 1620, the States' army was considerably reinforced and 4000 mercenaries were enlisted to protect the cities. Military expenses amounted to more than eight million guilders a year, which necessitated the imposition of heavy taxes, especially in Holland. All attempts made to rouse James to the necessity of vigorous action in favour of Protestantism failed.

It was evident that the Netherlands must seek effective allies elsewhere than in France or England or Germany, whose princes were only a drain upon the purses of their friends. Even before Oldenbarnevelt's fall, closer connections had been made with Denmark owing to their common interests in North Germany. After a series of negotiations, which Maurice left entirely in the hands of the States, a friendly alliance with Denmark was concluded in The Hague (May, 1621), which was of great importance to the Baltic trade. Sweden and the Hanse towns were ill-pleased with this, as the latter saw that they could not hope for any aid from the States against their old Danish foe.

In the south, too, an ally was gained. In 1620, Sommelsdijk conducted a brilliant embassy to Venice, and made a formal alliance with the republic, but was unable to obtain a promise that they would take arms against the emperor or the duke of Savoy, or that they would prevent the transport of Spanish troops to Germany through neighbouring territory.

There was a general feeling that Spain would not prolong the Truce. Preparations were therefore made for a renewal of hostilities in the spring of 1621 with better will because the dominant party, always opposed to the Truce, were still more averse to its extension or to peace.

Reinforcements were therefore made until one hundred ships were added to the navy, and the whole army consisted of 50,000 foot with 4000 cavalry, the united cost of which was nine and a half millions.[1] New taxes were imposed, and the necessary sums were found with the greatest difficulty. Some people talked gravely of an unavoidable state bankruptcy. The council of state tried to abolish the innumerable abuses in the levying of taxes by a rigorous investigation, under direction of Sommelsdijk, of the accounts of the admiralty and other colleges. The necessary millions were actually raised, however, in spite of complaints of cities and individuals. The rates of exchange rose in an alarming manner, and

---

[1] *Kron. Hist. Gen.*, xxvi., p. 507; compare the state of war for 1621 in *Kron. Hist. Gen.*, xxx., p. 74.

special laws had to be made against the coinage of false money.

There were many advocates for peace, especially in the exposed territories. The Brussels government was not anxious for a renewal of hostilities, and an attempt was made (1621) to persuade Maurice to peace. A prominent Brabant lady, Juffer Tserclaes, living in The Hague, acted as mediator in this effort. While Maurice did not reject the overtures at once,—indeed, he even wrote to the king of Spain on the subject,[1]—he soon showed little inclination to be tempted even by the offer of virtual sovereignty over the revolted provinces.

At the end of March, just before the expiration of the Truce, the chancellor of Brabant, Pecquius, appeared in The Hague with credentials empowering him to express to the States-General the archdukes' wishes for a definite restoration of peace. The opportunity was given him, although it had been evident from the discussions preliminary to his arrival that little was expected. When he announced that the archdukes still considered as possible the union of all provinces under one head and the recognition of themselves by the States as their " natural princes,"— nay, more, that they counted such recognition as necessary, it was soon evident that the north could not even discuss it, even if the archdukes were liberal in their interpretation of " acknowledgment " of " the natural princes." Before the end of the month, Pecquius left The Hague. Many deemed that his coming had no other purpose than to show the population of the south, eager for peace, that the breach was irremediable in spite of all the attempts of the Brussels government.

Thus the great war might be renewed within a short time, but now more or less as a part of the general European war, which Protestants and Catholics were about to wage. It was no more to be hoped that the States-

[1] Gachet, *Lettres inédites de Rubens*, p. xx.

General would come forward in this war energetically with the clear-sighted statesmanship of their great leader, who had foreseen for more than twenty-five years the conflagration which was to involve Europe.   Those responsible for the United Netherlands at this epoch lacked his skill, his ability, and the results were evident as soon as the torch of war was lighted.

APPENDIX

SOURCES OF NETHERLAND HISTORY, 1559–1621

THE publications issued at the expense of the Belgian government by the *Commission Royale d' Histoire de Belgique* during the life-times of the archivist G. P. Gachard and of his successor in the Belgian Royal Archives, Charles Piot ; the minor publications in the reports of the same commission and the collection of *Mémoires sur l'histoire de Belgique et des Pays-Bas ;* the long series of the works of the historical society at Utrecht supplemented by the numerous briefer articles in the chronicle (*Kronijk*), the reports (*Berigten*), the articles (*Bijdragen*), and contributions (*Mededeelingen*) of the society; the voluminous collection of unedited documents pertaining to the history of Spain (*Coleccion de documentos ineditos para la historia de España*); the numerous publications of provincial and municipal societies in Holland and Belgium; the publication of the sources by smaller societies, by families and individuals, among which the most important was the publication of the archives of the House of Orange-Nassau (*Archives de la Maison d'Orange-Nassau*), under the charge of Groen van Prinsterer; the information about material still to be found in German, French, and English archives, comprised in Blok's *Archivalia*, and the publications of Brugmans, Huet, and others—all these form a library in itself. If one considers the studies by Groen van Prinsterer, Bakhuizen van den Brink, Gachard and Fruin, Kervijn de Lettenhove and Piot, P. L. Muller and A. Nuyens, besides many others who have tried to work out the historical details of a period or epoch from unpublished material, then it becomes plain that a complete bibliography, either of the published sources proper, or of writings based immediately upon the sources, or even of literature upon the period in general, is beyond the capacity of these pages. It must be confined to a summary of the most important, arranged according to some system. The best system for our purpose is one based on the attitude of the authors towards the events of a period which gave rise to so many varying opinions and towards the political parties. As much as possible, the chronological order of the events treated must be preserved.

Three divisions can be made: the writings which explain the dynastic and political point of view of the Spanish government or are written in sympathy with Spain; those which take the point of view of the majority of the South Netherlanders loyal to the Catholic religion and to the royal authority, but unwilling to see Netherland interests sacrificed to the demands of a dynastic or general European policy; finally, those which defend the revolt and can serve for explanation of events which happened on that side. In many cases it is impossible to keep these headings separate, but in general this division seems rational.[1]

A

WRITINGS ON THE SPANISH SIDE

The ideas of Philip II. and of his chief statesmen can best be learned from the secret correspondence gathered by Gachard in the various archives, chiefly of Brussels, Simancas, and Madrid. The most noteworthy of these collections is *La Correspondance de Philippe II. sur les affaires des Pays-Bas* (ed. Gachard, 5 vols., Brux., 1848–62). This comes to 1577, and must be supplemented by other series, as *La Correspondance de Marguérite d'Autriche avec Philippe II.* (ed. Gachard, Brux., 1867–87). Margaret's correspondence with Alexander Farnese

[1] The bibliographical references are to the most important editions simply as an introduction to the study of the sources without making claim to completeness. The name of the editor is given. Compare Pirenne, *Bibliographie de l'histoire de Belgique*, Gand, 1893.

is also published (Brux., 1853), besides the *Lettres écrites par les souverains des Pays-Bas aux États de ces provinces* (Brux., 1851), and the letters the industrious king exchanged with his regents, governors, and agents about Netherland affairs.[1] Very important is Granvelle's voluminous correspondence, comprised in two collections, one of his *Papiers d'État*,[2] to 1565, and one of his later letters.[3] A great number of such letters are also printed in the collection of Kervijn de Lettenhove (*Relations politiques des Pays-Bas et de l'Angleterre sous le règne de Philippe II.*[4]), wherein, indeed, many sources coming under the second and third divisions are to be found. For the opinions of Philip's first two successors and their statesmen there is less material, although many letters are to be found in the above-mentioned *Coleccion* for the first half of the seventeenth century.[5]

All these letters give us an insight into the ideas of the leaders of Spanish policy and into their secret plans and deliberations, into the genesis of political and military measures for the suppression of the revolt; the information sent from the Netherlands enlightens us concerning events and opinions as they were reflected in the minds of the foe. To this same division belong the minutes of the Brussels council of state drawn up by Berty and explaining the early period of the troubles.[6]

The work of the Jesuit, Famianus Strada (b. at Bonn, 1572, professor at Rome), *De Bello Belgico*,[7] was drawn from sources of similar nature. This covers the period 1555–90. With impartiality, inasmuch as he criticised the action of the Spanish

---

[1] *Coleccion de documentos ineditos.* Compare the complete list of those relating to Netherland history in this series of more than one hundred volumes, Bussemaker, in *Nijh. Bijdragen*, 3rd series, ix., p. 352.

[2] Ed. Weiss, 9 vols. Paris, 1841–52.

[3] Ed. Poullet and Piot, 12 vols. Brux., 1878–97.

[4] Ten vols. Brux., 1882–92.

[5] For example, those of the governor, Castel Rodrigo (1644–45), and of the Spanish envoys at Münster,—Fajardo and Peñaranda (1643–50).

[6] Appendices in the *Cor. de Phil. II.*, iv., p. 475.

[7] Two vols., folio, Romæ, 1640–47 ; 8vo, Antv., 1640–48 ; in 12mo, Lugd. Bat., et Romæ, 1643–50. Various other Latin and translated editions.

government at Madrid from the point of view of Margaret and Alexander of Parma, he sketches, in good Latin, the events in the Netherlands. He made use of everything which earlier writers and the *arcana tabularia* of the Farneses could give him. His models were Tacitus and Sallust and other great historians of antiquity. Even towards Prince William, whom he had to regard as *belli incentor*, as an ambitious rebel against his lawful sovereign, he was moderate. Half a century, too, had softened the inimical opinion of the prince. Gallucci's work, coming down to 1609, is virtually a continuation of Strada's. Gallucci was also a Jesuit and professor at Rome in the middle of the seventeenth century, and had access to the letters of Spinola, Neyen, etc. At the same time, and in the same spirit, Guido Bentivoglio wrote his book, *Delle guerre di Fiandra*,[1] and his *Relationi*.[2] He was nuncio at Brussels, 1607–17, and both works were rather from the Romish than the Spanish point of view. They are mainly valuable for what he relates of the general condition of the Netherland provinces at the time of his residence there.

Remarkable, too, on this side are the military accounts of the Spanish and Italian generals and soldiers from the armies of Alva, Requesens, Parma, and Spinola, among which, after mentioning *La Correspondance du Duc d'Albe sur l'invasion du comte Louis de Nassau en Frise* (ed. Gachard, Brux. et Leipzig, 1850), one of the most important is the *Comentarios*[3] of Don Bernardino de Mendoça, general under Alva and Requesens, 1567–77, later ambassador at London and Paris. He played a great rôle in the Netherland troubles and the politics connected therewith. His work covers the war, in which he took part, and is partly composed from his own notes and memoranda. In connection with this are the remarkable *Comentario* of Don Sancho de Londoño, on the campaign of 1568,[4] the

---

[1] Three vols., Col., 1633–39. Many later editions and translations.
[2] Venetia, 1633.
[3] Published in Spanish and French, Paris, 1591. Reprinted in modern translation, Brux., 1860. Compare Fruin in *Konst- en Letterb.*, 1860, p. 231.
[4] Published by Fruin in *Bijdr. en Meded. Hist. Gen.*, xiii., pp. 1–97.

Mémoires of the Antwerper M. A. Del Rio on the times of Don John [1] (1576–78), and his *Commentarius brevis* [2] on the Netherlands after Parma's death, when he was there (1592–96). This was published with the description of the deeds of Spinola by Gamurino. Of the same nature are the writings of Carnero: *Historia de las guerras civiles* (1559–1609); of Campana: *Della guerra fatta per difesa de religione* (1559–1600); of Conestaggio: *Delle guerre della Germania inferiore* (1555–1600); of Cornejo: *Sumario de las guerras civiles ;* of Lanario: *Le guerre di Fiandra* (1559–1609); of Giustiniano: *Delle guerre di Fiandra* (1601–09); of the very reliable and well-informed Coloma: *Las guerras de los Estados Baxos* (1588–99) [3]; of the Brusseller, J. B. de Taxis: *Commentarii,* [4] covering 1559–98, and giving many data about the times of Requesens, of Don John, and of the League wars in France, which took place during his embassy at Paris; of F. de Verdugo: *Commentario,* important for the war in the north [5] ; the letters of Francisco de Mendoza, [6] etc. In the majority of these works much political and military information from eye-witnesses and other sources is introduced. For the period of Ernest and Albert of Austria there are the voluminous *Annales Ferdinandei* of the Austrian historian Khevenhiller, [7] which run with the sequel to 1637, often very important, since they are drawn in great part from the imperial archives at Vienna, and thus from the archives of Matthias and Rudolph II.; also for the later war for which the writings of Vincart [8] worthily close the series of these works.

Not until the nineteenth century, with its scientific treatment

---

[1] Published in Spanish, Madrid, 1601 ; in French, by Delvigne, 3 vols., Brux., 1869–71.   Compare Fruin in *Ned. Spect.*, 1869, p. 289.

[2] Col., 1611.

[3] Amb., 1625.   Compare Fruin in *Tien Jaren*, 5th edition, p. 6.

[4] Hoynck van Papendrecht, *Analecta*, ii., 2, p. 123.

[5] Published by Lonchay, Brux., 1899.   Compare, too, *Nuevos datos biograficos*, ed. Villa, Madrid, 1890.

[6] *Docum. ineditos*, xli. and xlii.

[7] Ratisb., Viennæ, Lips., 1640–46.

[8] Ed. Henrard, Bruxelles, 1869 ; *Docum. ined., passim*, ed. Villa, Madrid, 1884.

of history by publication of sources, was interest for the period awakened in Spain. The issue of the *Documentos ineditos* after 1843, as a result of Gachard's investigations, incited many similar publications of material for the history of Philip II. and his successors in works like those of Forneron (1880–82), which cannot indeed stand the test of scientific criticism, although they rank somewhat higher than the famous work of Cabrera de Cordova: *Felipe Segundo, Rey de España*, that was published in 1619 at Madrid, and reprinted in 1876–77, with the addition of the second volume. In 1605 Coloma also published an Italian biography of Philip II.; in 1822, Dumesnil one in French.

B

WRITINGS ON THE ROYALIST SIDE MAINLY EMANATING FROM THE CATHOLIC NETHERLANDS

From the beginning of the troubles there was a large party both in the south and in the north, which at first agreed with Viglius and Hopperus, keeping the interests of the Netherlands more or less in view, but opposed the revolt. Later this party —at the time of the Pacification of Ghent—entered into negotiations with the rebels and expressed a Catholic and royalist, but strongly Netherland policy. The chief writings of this faction, usually condemning the prince of Orange very severely, and sharply opposed to Calvinism, are the following :

First of all, Florentius van der Haer's excellent little work, *De initiis tumultuum Belgicorum*,[1] dedicated to Alexander of Parma, and acknowledged by writers of both parties in earlier and later time — although he was a zealous Catholic and fervent admirer of Parma—as one of the most unbiased authorities on the events. The author was a priest, professor in divinity at Louvain, later canon at Lille, where he died in ripe old age in 1634. His work, written in very good Latin, runs to Alva's arrival in the Netherlands and is based on contemporaneous information and his own experiences. Further,

[1] Duaci, 1587. Compare De Wind, *Bibl. der Ned. Geschiedschrijvers*, i., p. 210.

Hopperus' *Recueil et mémorial des troubles des Pays-Bas*,[1] together with the later discovered continuation,[2] besides his letters to Viglius[3] and Viglius' own letters and drafts to him,[4] is well fitted to show the standpoint of these two friends, moderate, clever, and well-informed statesmen, at the outbreak of the troubles.

Less trustworthy on account of his fanaticism, and full of bitterness against the prince, are the works of Assonleville's son-in-law, Renon de France, *Histoire des causes de la désunion, révoltes et altérations des Pays-Bas*[5] (1555–92), a dissertation sometimes degenerating to gossip and rumour, but important for the events in the Walloon provinces, and for the information taken from Assonleville's papers, who played a great part under Margaret of Parma. Little better in this regard are the *Mémoires* (1559–78) of the president of the Council of Artois, Pontus Payen,[6] also a bitter anti-Protestant and foe to Orange. Less violent, but somewhat of the same general character, are the *Mémoires* of Champagney,[7] of Emanuel de Lalaing, baron de Montigny,[8] the *Mémoires anonymes sur les troubles des Pays-Bas* (1565–80),[9] the letters of various Walloon nobles of those days,[10] the *Documents inédits concernant les troubles des Pays-Bas* (1577–84),[11] especially valuable for a knowledge of the agitation among the Walloon nobles at the time of the Pacification, of the administration of Don John, and of the first appearance of Parma. Living first in the north and emigrating south after the conquest of Deventer by Maurice in 1592, the learned Pontus de Huyter or Heuterus, of Delft, who

[1] Published by Hoynck van Papendrecht, *Analecta*, ii., 2, p. 17.
[2] Given by Fruin in *Bijdr. en Med. Hist. Gen.*, xiii., pp. 115, 343 ; compare xvi., p. 373.
[3] Traj. ad Rh., 1802.
[4] Ed. Hoynck van Papendrecht, *Anal.*, i., p. 287.
[5] Ed. Piot, 3 vols. Brux., 1886–91.
[6] Ed. Henne, 2 vols. Brux., 1860.
[7] Ed. Robaulx de Soumoy. Brux., 1860.
[8] Ed. Blaes. Brux., 1862.
[9] Ed. Blaes and Henne, 5 vols. Brux., 1859.
[10] *Bull. de la Comm. royale d'histoire, passim.*
[11] Ed. Kervijn de Volkaersbeke and Diegerick, 2 vols. Gand, 1847–49.

narrowly escaped death in Gorkum at the time of Lumey's raid, examined in the course of his later travels many books and consulted many contemporaries in relation to his historical studies, the results of which he used in his *Rerum Burgundicarum libri sex*, dedicated to Philip II., and his *Rerum Belgicarum libri quindecim*, dedicated to the Archduke Albert. The latter comes down to 1565, and was continued in the forbidden and almost extinct work *Historia Secessionis Belgicæ*, which came to 1575,[1] but the part we have stops with 1569.

The priest Michael ab Isselt of Amersfoort, probably a native of Dokkum, wrote the *Historia belli civilis Coloniensis* on the hostilities between Gebhard and his opponent, and a *Historia sui temporis*. The latter comes down to 1586, in the form of annals treating of twenty years of the war. After the fall of Nimwegen in 1592, he lived five years at Cologne.[2] From his pen,[3] too, come the first parts of the remarkable annals known under the name of *Mercurius Gallo-Belgicus*,[4] beginning with 1588. After his death, this was continued by other compilers down to 1625. One of these continuations, the *Mercurius Gallo-Belgicus succenturiatus* of the learned Dantzig compiler, Gotthard Arthus, really rather a sequel to Sleidanus' famous work on Charles V., is differentiated from earlier writings of this name by its strong Lutheran, anti-Catholic tendency, and on that account is also favourable to the party of the opposition, to the Netherlanders in general. The last work, continued by various persons, comes to the middle of the seventeenth century.

These writings, descending to the smallest details, relating the remarkable political and military events of the time, are really products of journalism as it then existed. The founder of this journalism was the Austrian Michael von Aitzing or Aitzinger, who from 1583 replaced the earlier " time correspondence " in loose reports which had, from the first half of the

---

[1] Compare De Wind, i., p. 193.
[2] See De Wind, i., p. 213, 549.
[3] De Jonge in *Nijh. Bijdr.*, 3rd series, viii., p. 71.
[4] First part published at Cologne, 1592.

century, been occasionally disseminated in print, for the use
of the merchant, by more coherent works of the kind appearing twice a year in connection with the great commercial fairs.
In 1581 he published the unpartisan book, *De Leone Belgico*,[1]
a historical-geographical description of the condition of the
Netherlands from 1559 to his own time.   He had lived there
more than twenty-three years and watched *rerum, personarum,
ac temporum vicissitudines*.   Later he lived at Cologne and
issued his periodical *Relationes Historicæ*, 1580–99, besides the
later editions of his *Leo Belgicus*, enriched with a great number
of excellent illustrations by Frans Hogenberg.

These works show how closely Netherland affairs were observed at Cologne in the interests of the Catholic policy.   The
Cologne Jesuits appear to have exerted an influence upon this
historical activity.

To the same category of writings belong the *Commentarius
brevis rerum in orbe gestarum*,[2] of the Cologne Carthusian
Surius, running from the beginning of the sixteenth century to the taking of Middelburg in 1574; the *Commentarii*
of the Antwerp jurist Johannes Carolus, procureur-general at
the court of Friesland, later councillor and vice-president of
the high council at Mechlin : *De Rebus Casparis a Robles
Billæi in Frisia gestis* (Leovardiæ, 1731), running through the
year 1573 and glorifying the deeds of Robles; the *Onparty-
dighe Verklaringhe der oorsaken des Nederlantsche oorloghs*
(1566–1608) (Antv., 1612), the *Annales Ducum seu Principum
Brabantiæ*, coming to 1609 (Antv., 1623), by the learned
Utrecht priest, Franciscus van der Haer or Haraeus, a clever
compiler who greatly improved the latter portion of his work
later; the *Veridicus Belgicus* (Antv., 1624), by the Brussels
Jesuit, Carolus Scribanius, who lived in Antwerp for many
years, where he had great influence in commercial affairs, knowing the most important statesmen and learned men of his time,
his history of the war to the Truce being written, naturally,
in anti-Reformed spirit; the Catholic *Annales* (1566–1616),

[1] Coloniæ, 1581, and later.   Compare Stieve, *Ueber die ältesten halbjähr-
igen Zeitungen oder Messrelationen*, p. 25.   München, 1881.
[2] Col., 1574.

by the Leyden advocate, Frans van Düsseldorf,[1] living in the Hague, later at Cologne, where he died 1630; the *Opkomste der Nederlantsche beroerten*, by the Haarlem Jesuit, Augustinus van Teylingen (Münster, 1642, often reprinted), etc. Out of all these the best, next to the volume of Florentius van der Haer, is the remarkable book of Nicolaus Burgundius, professor at Ingolstadt and historian of Duke Maximilian of Bavaria, later member of the council of Brabant until his death shortly before the peace of Münster. His *Historia Belgica, ab anno 1558* (Ingolst., 1629), written in excellent Latin, was based on the papers of Viglius and Tisnacq and the correspondence between Philip II. and Margaret of Parma, to which he had access. Although writing "*sine amore, sine odio partium, quibus hactenus vitiis maxime laboratum est*"—he is not as unpartisan as van der Haer. Remarkable, too, is the great *Chronycke* (Antw., 1620) of Adriaan van Meerbeeck, rector at Aalst, who tried to write from a Catholic standpoint as opposed to the reformed historians, van Meteren, etc. His *Nederlantsche Mercurius* belongs to the series of contemporaneous chronicles from the Catholic side.

From the nature of the case, little can be said of official state papers coming under this head; the ideas of the Spanish sympathising Netherlanders and Germans are expressed, however, in certain documents. In this connection one can refer to the remonstrances of the States-General and of the provincial Estates of the south, of the governors and officers of lesser rank, addressed to the governments at Madrid and Brussels, to the king and his regents in the Netherlands and printed in many collections already mentioned. Attention must be drawn to the *Actes des États Généraux*, issued by Gachard for this period in three collections, 1576–1585 (2 vols., Brux., 1861–66); 1600 (*ibid.*, 1849); 1632 (2 vols., *ibid.*, 1853–66). These give a good picture of the opinions of the loyalists who yet wished to prevent the sacrifice of Netherland interests.

With the peace of Münster this kind of history ceased for a

---

[1] Published in extracts by Fruin in *Werken Hist. Gen.*, 3rd series, No. 1. Den Haag, 1894.

time.   In the middle of the eighteenth century, however, at the time of Maria Theresa, a member of the council of Flanders, L. J. J. van der Vynckt, again undertook to treat the *Troubles des Pays-Bas* from a Catholic South-Netherland point of view, making use of state documents from the South-Netherland archives placed at his disposal by the Austrian representative, Count Cobenzl.   The book was written in French and at first only known in manuscript.   In 1793 it was published in German and later repeatedly in the original French.   In 1823 it was translated into Dutch under the title, *Nederlandsche beroerten onder Philips II.* (3 vols., Amst., 1823).   Later Leo and Holzwarth laid the basis in their works: *Zwölf Bücher Niederländischer Geschichten* (2 vols., Halle, 1832-35) and *Abfall der Niederlande* (4 vols., Schaffhausen, 1865-72), for a further consideration from this standpoint.

Under the influence of the revival of knowledge among the Catholics of Holland and Belgium at the middle of the century, Nuyens, in his *Geschiedenis der Nederlandsche beroerten der 16de eeuw* (4 vols., Amst., 1865-70), from a Catholic point of view, and Kervijn de Lettenhove, in his interesting and well-written book, *Les Huguenots et les Gueux* (6 vols., Bruges, 1883-85), have given, in opposition to the Protestant historians, their opinions upon the revolt, its causes, its course, and its results.   These are the best, but both in Holland and in Belgium many brief studies by Catholic authors have been published since then.   The majority were written simply to support the above-mentioned authors.   The early years of the revolt, the character of the prince of Orange and his friends were zealously studied and criticised usually very severely. Many of these were as violently partisan as writings of the period.   The celebration in Holland of events of the time of the revolt, from that of the battle of Heiligerlee, in 1868, to that of Mook, in 1891, gave occasion to the publication of polemical writings wherein Catholic and non-Catholic historians tried to defend their opinions in relation to their celebrations, and attention was fixed anew upon the nature and defects of the tradition in regard to the events.   The polemics bore some fruit, both in the juster valuation of certain sources and for the knowledge of facts of the time and for the exercise of historical criticism in general.[1]

C

WRITINGS ON THE SIDE OF THE REBELS

The greatest number of published sources for the epoch, as well as the best descriptions of the events, emanated from the rebels, who wrote many vivid narratives for the sake of giving publicity to their cause.

On the side of the States, too, there was an active correspondence between the leaders. Attention must first be given to the admirable collection, *Archives ou Correspondance inédite de la Maison d'Orange-Nassau*,[2] edited by Groen van Prinsterer and printed by that excellent critic of the period under discussion in a text which is available, though not always diplomatically exact, and embellished with valuable notes. The work is divided into two series, the first covering the period of Prince William I. and ending with his death in 1584; the second, an immediate sequel, but less comprehensive, less complete, with notes less accurately compiled, ending with the expedition of Prince William III. to England in 1688. Most of the documents incorporated or touched on in these volumes are taken from the royal archives at the Hague; many others from the archives at Besançon, Paris, Brussels, Cassel, Wiesbaden, etc.

Gachard furnished a very necessary complement to this work for the period of Prince William in the *Correspondance de Guillaume le Taciturne* (6 vols., Brux., 1847–66). These letters were collected by Gachard from the archives at Brussels, Paris, London, Simancas, Madrid, etc., and published with notes as insignificant as his usually are, but with extensive introductions. Important contributions of the same nature are also given in Bondam's collection of unpublished

[1] Compare, too, a mass of brochures and articles of this kind from the pens of Brouwers, Alberdingk Thijm, Klönne, Allard, Meulleners, etc., besides other anonymous publications, on the one side; Bakhuizen van den Brink, Groen van Prinsterer, Fruin, Blok, etc., on the other.

[2] First series, 8 vols. and suppl., Leyden, 1835–47; 2nd series, 5 vols., Utrecht, 1857–60.

documents for the elucidation of Netherland history (1576–78), (5 vols., Utr., 1779–81), and in the richly annotated and valuable publication of P. L. Muller and A. Diegerick, *Documents concernant les relations entre le duc d'Anjou et les Pays-Bas* (1576–84), (5 vols., Utr. and 's Gravenhage, 1889–99). Minor supplements to these collections of letters are given by Van Someren in his *Correspondance du Prince Guillaume d'Orange avec Jacques de Wesembeke* (1567–73), (Utr., 1896), gathered from the private papers of the latter, with whom Orange was in close relations; by Marchegay in his *Lettres de Louise de Coligny* (1872), and those of Charlotte de Bourbon [1]; by Blok and, under his supervision, by Brugmans and Busken Huet at London and Paris. Further *Archivalia* bearing on Netherland history found in German and Austrian archives have added many unknown or little-known documents to our knowledge, notwithstanding the long extracts from these same archives already given by Motley in *The Rise of the Dutch Republic* and *The United Netherlands*.

Marnix's extensive correspondence and writings on religious and theological topics were collected by Van Toorenenbergen (3 vols., 's Grav., 1871–91); a number of his letters are published by Lacroix in his *Correspondance et mélanges* (Brux., 1860). Van der Schueren cared for the publication of the *Brieven en onuitgegeven gedenkstukken van Arend van Dorp* (2 vols., Utr., 1887–88). Bussemaker worked into his excellent book, *De Afscheiding der Waalsche gewesten van de Generale Unie* (2 vols., Haarlem, 1895–96), a large number of documents extracted from the Belgian archives, publishing separate articles on the period 1576–79. Trosée based his book, *Het Verraad van George de Lalaing, Graaf van Rennenberg* ('s Hertogenbosch, 1894), upon documents taken from all kinds of archives. Scattered letters of the prince and his chief helpers serve to supplement the above-named more coherent publications. There is no period of our history for which we can avail ourselves of such a number of writings from the pen of the chief actors touching passing events.

[1] Compare Delaborde, *Louise de Coligny* (2 vols., Paris, 1890) ; *Henri de Coligny* and *Charlotte de Bourbon* (Paris, 1887).

The number of printed letters and memorials written by the prince himself amounts certainly to more than one thousand, and those of his friends and allies surpass his many times in number if not in significance.

For the periods of Oldenbarnevelt, of Maurice, and of Frederick Henry, we possess a mass of similar data besides those in the *Archives* of Groen van Prinsterer and those mentioned in the *Archivalia*, both of which cover the later periods. The *Gedenkstukken van Johan van Oldenbarneveldt en zijn tijd*, coming, alas ! only down to 1609, published with introduction and notes by M. L. van Deventer (3 vols., 's Gravenhage, 1860–1865), give an insight into the advocate's opinions and policy before the Truce. For the later period we have in print, besides the extensive extracts from his letters in Motley's *John of Barneveld*, chiefly the documents from his trial (pub. by *Hist. Gen.* in *Kronijk*, 1850), and the *Intendit* against him (pub. by v. d. Bergh, 's Gravenhage, 1875), with the proofs, the *Verhaal* of his servant, Jan Francken, respecting his imprisonment (pub. Fruin, *Kron. Hist. Gen.*, 1874), the information in the *Waerachtige Historie*, and the *Historie van het leven en sterven*,[1] etc. Remarkable, too, is the advocate's memoir on the Jülich affairs (pub. by Jansen in *Bijdr. en Med. Hist. Gen.*, 1898). A good adjunct to these for the earlier period is the *Correspondence of Leycester during his Government in the Low Countries* (pub. by Bruce, London, 1844), and C. P. Hooft's *Memoriën en Adviezen* (Utr., 1871), so important for the knowledge of governmental theories about 1600. For later times we have the letters and other writings of Hugo de Groot, of Uyttenbogaert, P. C. Hooft, Van Baerle, the fragmentary memoranda of the treasurer-general, Joris de Bye, etc. De Groot's letters were partly gathered into the great collection (Amst., 1687, *cf. Epistolæ ineditæ*, Haarlem, 1806), later enriched with many more (see Rogge, *Bibliotheca Grotiana*, i., 's Grav., 1883). Uyttenbogaert's are gathered into a comprehensive publication,[2] important for the political and theological history of the

---

[1] Compare Fruin in *Nijh. Bijdr.*, new series, ix., pp. 119, 354.

[2] Ed. Rogge, Utr., 1868–75 ; compare Rogge, *Johannes Utenbogaert en sijn tijd*, 3 vols., Amst., 1874–75.

time. In regard to the latter, too, the *Werken der Marnix-vereeniging* (Utr., 1870–89), and the *Acta Synodalia* help to illuminate the period 1572–1620. In regard to de Groot's trial we have, besides his famous *Verantwoordingh*, his *Ver-hooren* and other information respecting his persecution (ed. Fruin, Utr., 1871). Hooft's letters, with those of Van Baerle, Constantijn Huygens, and others, are a treasure-house of in-formation upon the literary history of those days upon which much light has been thrown in our time, thanks to the studies of Jonckbloet, Penon, Kalff, Worp, and others.

Military affairs are less well treated by sympathisers with the revolt than by the Spaniards. The Spanish officers were more educated and cultivated than the prince's captains. The Englishman, Roger Williams, who wrote his memoirs — later translated into Dutch [1]—at the beginning of the war, has a counterpart in the States' soldier, later Captain Splinter Helmich, who described his military adventures, 1572–87 (Fruin, *Kron. Hist. Gen.*, 1875, p. 159). As sequels to this, Francis Vere's *Commentaries*, 1589–1600 (ed. Dillingham, Cam-bridge, 1657), Fleming's *Oostende* ('s Gravenh., 1621), Ver-vou's *Eenige gedenckwaardige geschiedenissen* (Leeuw., 1841), are all important for the military operations of William Louis in the north; Orlers's *Nassausche Laurencrans* (Leyden, 1610), for those of Maurice; and so is the excellent *Journaal van Anthonis Duyck* (Mulder, 3 vols., 's Grav., 1862–66). The author of this last accompanied Maurice (as fiscal) on his campaigns, 1591–1602.

In certain collections of letters, especially the *Archives* and *Documents* respecting Anjou, are included all kinds of state papers — treaties, remonstrances, etc. Of a wholly official nature are the important *Resolutiën der Staten van Holland en West-Friesland*, from 1524, given in part in the *Register* of Aert van der Goes, but after 1560 preserved in an almost un-broken series and published from about 1670 with indexes and with the secret resolutions of a time later than 1653. For the later period it is complete; for the earlier less so. In all there are 269 volumes. As the resolutions of the States-General

---

[1] Ed. Nijenhuis, Utr., 1864.

from 1577[1] are only to be had in manuscript, these printed proceedings of the most important provinces are of great weight, as herein are contained more or less extensive observations on the discussions and deliberations leading up to the resolutions. Formerly reports of certain sessions for the period immediately after 1568 and the resolutions from September 1, 1577, to August 24, 1578, were lacking, but now these last at least have been recovered from the papers of Hugo de Groot and published (by Unger in *Bijdr. en Med. Hist. Gen.*, 1893, p. 1). Minutes proper of the Estates of Holland were not kept, but certain municipal pensionaries and other municipal representatives in the Estates kept for their own use or for their cities more or less complete notes of the transactions, so that in the town council resolutions, etc., there is a chance of finding further information respecting the States' assemblies.[2]

Especially remarkable is the edition of the *Notulen der hollandsche Statenvergadering van 19 Juli - 27 Juli*, 1572,[3] so important for the beginning of the revolt in Holland. Of the resolutions of the other provincial Estates only a few fragments are printed in various collections. In Zealand there is more to be had, but only one complete copy of the *Notulen van de Staten* can apparently be found there (compare Nijhoff's *Bibl. Hist. Neerl.*, La Haye, 1878, p. 79, No. 1055). Also there are no printed minutes of the council of state, nor, indeed, notes of any kind. Important extracts of the petitions of this council and of the *Staten van Oorlog* are given by Aitzema.

The ordinances and placards of the Estates of the various provinces are contained for the most part in the provincial placard and charter books. For Holland we possess the *Groot Placcaatboek*, 1576–1785, edited by Cau, Van Leeuwen,

---

[1] Some works, among others Van der Kemp's *Maurits van Nassau*, contain copious extracts. Dodt van Flensburg also gives extracts for the early years of the seventeenth century. Compare Vervou, *Aanteekeningen ter St. Gen.*, 1616–1620.

[2] Compare Bakhuizen van den Brink in *Het Nederlandsch Rijksarchief*, i., p. 11. 's Grav., 1857.

[3] *Ibid.*, p. 32.

Scheltus, and Van der Linden (10 vols., 's Grav., 1658–1801); for Utrecht there is that of Van de Water (3 vols., Utr., 1729, supplemented by 2 vols., Utr., 1856); for Gelderland there is that of Van Loon and Cannegieter for the years 1577–1740 (3 vols., Nijm. and Arnh., 1701–1740, 2 vols. supplement to 1769); for Friesland to 1686 there is the *Groot Placcaat- en Charterboek*, ed. by Schwartzenberg (5 vols., Leeuw., 1768–93). Important, too, are the official reports of the ambassadors to foreign powers, many of which are printed in various works on the time, as in the *Gedenkstukken* of Oldenbarnevelt, while documents, translations, or long extracts are given in works like those of Motley, of Arend, of Van Rees, and Brill, in S. Muller's *Mare Clausum*, and Waddington's *République des Provinces Unies*. A complete edition of instructions to envoys would be of inestimable value for a knowledge of the States' diplomacy in the agitated period.[1]

To this division of diplomatic documents belongs the series of foreign ambassadors' reports and agents' correspondences, many of which are now printed, the rest being available in manuscript. As a rule, these reports bear rather upon the side of the rebels than of Spain, as the foreign powers, with full knowledge of the difficulties with which Spain had to battle in the provinces, furnished secret or open aid to the rebels. Besides the documents of this kind quoted from manuscript matter by Motley, Froude, Waddington, Kervijn de Lettenhove, etc., in their historical works, the following are also worthy of notice.

For France we have the *Lettres et Négociations* of Claude de Mondoucet (2 vols., Paris and Rheims, 1891–92), who represented the French government at the court of Brussels (1571–74); the reports of the French agents of Anjou's time in the *Documents* of Muller and Diegerick; the important *Lettres et Négociations* of the first French envoy to the States, Paul

[1] Compare here Vreede, *Inleiding tot de Geschiedenis der Nederlandsche diplomatie* (Utr., 1856, etc.), ii., 1st and 2d documents; Vreede, *Nederland en Zweden* (Utr., 1844); Van der Burgh, *Gezantschappen door Zweden en Nederland wederzijds afgevaardigd* ('s Grav., 1886); Kernkamp, *De sleutels van de Sont*, etc.

Choart, seignior de Buzanval (ed. Vreede, Leyden, 1846; further in *Cod. Dipl. Hist. Gen.*, ii., 1, 2, p. 164); and the papers of his successors, Pierre Jeannin (4 vols., Amst., 1695) and of Aubéry du Maurier (La Haye, 1748; compare Ouvré, *Aubéry du Maurier*, Paris, 1853). There is also the extensive memoir literature like the works of Michel de la Huguerye (ed. De Ruble, 3 vols., Paris, 1887–90), secretary of Count Louis of Nassau, and those of Duplessis Mornay (ed. La Fontenelle and Auguis, 12 vols., Paris, 1824–25), and the works of Turenne, wherein many details about events in the Netherlands are recorded by eye-witnesses.

For England there is a less important series. Kervijn de Lettenhove gave some of the English agents' correspondence of the earlier period (*Relations politiques, passim*). The above-mentioned *Leycester Correspondence* follows, while in Burgon's *Life and Times of Sir Thomas Gresham* (2 vols., London, 1839) many interesting references to the early period of the revolt occur. For the later time there are the *Winwood Papers* (3 vols., London, 1725), covering the last years of Oldenbarnevelt, and Carleton's *Lettres* (French edition, 3 vols., La Haye, 1759; London, 1780), of great weight, but far from complete. They can indeed make even less claim to completeness than the old editions of Jeannin's, of Du Maurier's, and of d' Estrades's letters. The great English publications, *Calendars of State Papers*, for this period, furnish many interesting contributions.

From the German side, we have the *Annales Ferdinandei* of Khevenhiller, for the later period; for the earlier, Bezold's edition of the *Briefe des Pfalzgrafen Johann Casimir* (2 vols., München, 1882–84), besides Ritter's *Briefe und Acten zur Geschichte des dreissigjährigen Krieges* (3 vols., München, 1870–77), especially for the period of the Truce and just before, while the *Urkunden und Actenstücke zur Geschichte des Kurfürsten Friedrich Wilhelm von Brandenburg*, are important for the last part of this period.

Very interesting for Netherland history of this epoch is the great collection of the *Relationi degli ambasciatori veneti al senato* (Alberi, 15 vols., Firenze, 1839–62). In this special attention should be given to the letters of the ambassadors Lionello and Suriano (1616–18), and the report of Trevisano (Utr., 1883), 1620. The purpose of the missions of all three was to make closer ties between Venice and the Netherlands.

In general, the diplomatic correspondence of the time is very rich when the United Netherlands began to play a part in European politics, especially after the beginning of the Truce. Both here and in the kindred memoir literature, it must be remembered that all is more or less coloured by personal and political conceptions, or taken from unsound sources. Often, however, they throw a clear light on events and negotiations the significance of which we could only guess at otherwise. Often the skilled diplomat saw causes and results better than his unskilled contemporaries, or than posterity, and observed facts whose knowledge is now of great service to us.

Finally, there is an extraordinarily long series of historians who have devoted works of greater or less compass to the conflict against Spain.

In the early period these writings are purely of a compilatory nature, and usually made by the hand of a foreigner, as that of the Rostock professor, David Chytraeus, who played a part in the attempts to pacify the theological quarrels in Germany in the second half of the sixteenth century, and later compiled his great *Chronicon Saxoniæ et vicinarum gentium* and a *Continuatio historica* — 1595–98 (Lipsiæ, 1599); that of the Basel jurist, Adam Henrici Petri, whose German work (Basel, 1576), embellished with many original documents and received, according to the author, " in writing from a councillor at Brussels," was translated into Dutch by Theophilus (Noortwitz, 1579 and 1581; compare De Wind, *op. cit.*, pp. 270 and 562), and in 1582 published in French by the same person anonymously; that of the Huguenot, Richard Dinothus, who issued a book *De bello civili Belgico libri sex* (Basiliæ, 1586). These are all forerunners of Aitzinger's and Van Isselt's histories. According to Van Reyd, who calls them his own predecessors, the authors knew as much of " our history " as the blind do of colour. Although he praises their zeal, he thinks that they themselves would have to acknowledge that they touched their work with unwashed hands.

Less even than these books can we rank as historical works proper, polemical and political writings, even such political manifestoes as the printed writings of Wesembeke and Marnix, or the apologies of the prince and his followers, issued in 1568 and the succeeding years, among which the prince's own famous apology of 1581 is the chief. Also the numerous pamphlets which accompanied every important event, and were scattered over Europe in French, German, and English translations, do not absolve the historian from the task of a discriminating, careful investigation before forming a just opinion of the events. Some of these pamphlets, however, issued in book form,—Fruytiers's *Corte Beschryvinghe* of the Leyden siege,[1] the books and booklets on the prince's death,[2] on the siege of Ostend, the death of Oldenbarnevelt, and the peace of Münster,—all belong to the best sources for the knowledge of the events, but their testimony must be weighed very carefully.

The first North Netherland historian of the revolt in general was Peter Bor, b. 1559, at Utrecht, where later he was notary. At an early age he collected material for the composition of his famous work *Oorsprongk, begin ende aenvang der Nederlantscher oorlogen*, three books of which he published in 1595 and three six years later. This publication attracted the notice of the Estates of Utrecht, who permitted him to use their archives, and voted him a pension. In 1615 Holland followed their example, at the same time appointing Bor steward of North Holland. He then established himself at Haarlem, where he died in 1635. Here many revised and improved editions of his book were published which finally covered the years 1555–1600 (4 vols., Amst., 1679). He used not only original documents and pamphlets, many of which, under the supervision of the Estates, he incorporated into his compilation, but also Italian, Spanish, and French historians of the time, as Coloma, Thuanus, etc. He also made evident use of the unpublished

---

[1] Delft, 1574. Compare Fruin, Hooft, and Elsevier, *De oude verhalen van het beleg en ontzet van Leiden.* 's Grav., 1874.

[2] Compare Frederiks, *De Moord van 1584.* 's Grav., 1884.

papers of contemporaries. His work is one of the most important sources for the knowledge of the epoch, but is rather a series of data and documents than a consecutive narrative.

Above him in knowledge of the times and of men ranks Emanuel van Meteren.[1] Born at Antwerp in 1535, a cousin and friend of the geographer Ortelius, his business made him spend many years in London as merchant, and there he became (1583) the consul of the Netherland merchants. He died in 1612. He, too, was a devoted collector throughout his life and first compiled (1583), with the help of the documents he had gathered from north and south at the advice of Ortelius, a simple chronological narrative of the revolt. At first he had no idea of publication, and his book was only issued in 1590, after his manuscript had appeared in German and Latin with his consent.[2] His book, *Belgische of Nederlantsche Historie* (Delft, 1599), later called *Historie der Nederlandscher ende haerder nabueren oorlogen*, was the first really connected narrative of the war so far waged, written in moderate tone, and " with the least passion," borrowing here and there from Bor, Heuterus, and others. He brought out much which the authorities deemed unfitting, or which annoyed living persons, not because his matter was false, but because they objected to his presentation. The book was accordingly forbidden at first,—afterwards, however, allowed to pass. The Estates, influenced by preachers and other influential persons, would not give permission to the issue of a new regular authorised edition, so that there was none until 1609, and then that was privately published at Amsterdam in a revised form.[3] The author revised the book continually, but did not see any edition later than that of 1611 improved under his supervision. In 1614, after his death, a new edition appeared, revised with the heirs' approval, by a commission from the States. Several important alterations were made, and the work was thus published as the official edition, and repeatedly reprinted. Prominent members of the States' party, Ledenbergh and Tresel, possibly De

---

[1] Compare Fruin in *Nijh. Bijdr.*, new series, iv., p. 86.
[2] Fruin in *Nijh. Bijdr.*, 3rd series, iv., p. 425.
[3] Compare Fruin, *Nijh. Bijdr.*, new series, iv., p. 91.

Groot himself, were charged with this revision. These circumstances, and the valuable data used by the author, his un-
common knowledge of commercial and marine affairs, render
his book an exceedingly valuable historical source. The edition of 1614 is much improved in style, but, being official, is less
trustworthy than the earlier issues wherein the opponents could
find very few actual errors. Van Meteren never acknowledged
the translations as authoritative.

The third of the older contemporaneous historians was
Everard van Reyd, native of Deventer and adherent to the
Reformed faith. As an exile he entered the service of Count
John of Nassau, returned with him to the Netherlands in 1578;
after 1584 he was councillor and confidential friend of William
Louis, and often went to the States-General as deputy from
Gelderland. He died at Leeuwarden in 1602. His life from
1583 gave him good opportunities of observation in Gelderland, Friesland, and the Hague. He was behind the scenes
in many things and had the opportunity of collecting information from reliable persons. For the two first-mentioned provinces his elaborated narrative is of especial value. In his
preface he expresses the hope that others would follow his
example for other provinces until perhaps the States-General
would allow someone to investigate all the secret state papers
both in their archives and in those of provinces and cities.
He did not seek, he said, "the glory of non-partisanship,"
not believing that the "pen can be so controlled that conviction can be concealed," but he tried to use the pen truly,
"concealing neither the virtues of his foes nor the failings of
his friends." For the years previous to 1583 (his narrative
runs to 1601) he gives only a brief summary, based on his own
experience, and the information of "excellent" statesmen.
His narrative, entitled *Historie der Nederlantschen oorlogen
begin ende voortganck* (Arnh., 1626) is also valuable. It was
translated into Latin by Dionysius Vossius (Lugd. Bat., 1633),
and continued by Van Reyd's nephew, the distinguished jurist,
Johan van den Sande, one of Oldenbarnevelt's judges, as *Ne-
derlandtsche Historie* (Leeuw., 1650), which work was after the
author's death (1638) brought down to 1641. The last book

passed through various editions, of which some bore the title of *De waeckende leeuw der Nederlanden* (Amst., 1663), and is an independent book for the period after 1601; the earlier portion is nothing less than an abbreviated form of Van Reyd's writing. The work of Van Reyd is undeniably better written than that of Van Meteren and others, too, which are more read, but it is not so exact in the description of the noteworthy things, as, in the first place, it only discusses those details at large which the author knows from his own experience. The sequels of Van den Sande and others are much more condensed and of less significance.

About parallel with the work of Van Reyd is that of J. F. Le Petit, in 1577 keeper of the records at Béthune in Artois, later in Prince William's service, and at the end of the century notary at Middelburg, where he devoted himself to historical studies. He began with translating into French the old Dutch *Divisiekroniek*, which, at the cost of the various provincial Estates, he enlarged with the other chronicles, at the same time revising and continuing it to 1600. The first portion of his *Grande chronique ancienne et moderne* (2 vols., Dordrecht, 1601) is of little worth. The second part, beginning with 1566, is more valuable on account of the use of original documents and of the adaptation of the information of others and of his own experience. The chronicle is especially good for Zealand, and on account of his personal recollections of Prince William. His geographical-historical work, *Nederlandts Gheschiedenebeste* (Arnhem, 1615), is a very worthy imitation of Guicciardini.

The really best works on the side of the revolt, both from a historical and literary point of view, are the two of Hugo de Groot and P. C. Hooft. The desire of many that a worthy author should undertake at the charge of the States the history "of the disturbances in these lands," a desire shared by Oldenbarnevelt and the States of Holland, induced the youthful De Groot to undertake the task in 1601. He was aided by a subsidy and afforded access to all kinds of information and documents. In 1612 he completed his *Annales et historiæ de rebus Belgicis* (Amst., 1657), and submitted it to the States for approval. Delays ensued, and De Groot continued to work at it and revise it until the day of his death. It was not published by his family until 1657, and has been often reprinted, besides being translated into French, and has excited continued admiration for style and matter. Indeed, it was regarded as taking the first rank in historical literature, surpassing Tacitus and Thuanus, his models, in the style and the exactness and the impartiality with which he treated the *Annales*, 1559–88, the *Historiæ*, 1588–1609. His *Obsidio Grollæ* (Ams., 1629), and his *Parallelon Rerum Publicarum* (4 vols., Haarlem, 1801–1803), a comparison between the ancient states of Greece and Rome, and the new Netherland republic, belong to the best historical literature of the time.

Hooft's *Nederlandsche Historien* (2 vols., Amst., 1642–54) cannot be ranked so high in every respect. It surpasses De Groot as regards the scope and accuracy of his own investigation of published works and stray papers, wherefrom he expected to strike a harmonious melody. He received the last from statesmen and commanders and common citizens, and he tested them to the smallest details by availing himself of the recollections of his father and other contemporaries.[1] He worked for ten years (1628–38) upon his story, and then delayed several more before he published the first twenty books, which came down to the death of the prince. The sequel, on which he was busy during the last years of his life, runs to the end of Leicester's administration. In impartial judgment Hooft is equal to De Groot. Both espouse no one political or theological party, although their sympathy for the middle course does not always enable them to give a fair judgment on the extremes of both sides. But undoubtedly Hooft's book, as regards form, must yield the palm to De Groot's historical work in classic simplicity. His pronounced artificiality, the strained choice of words and expressions, the continued attempt to equal Tacitus' terseness in Dutch, make it impossible — with all respect for Hooft's extraordinary mastery over the language — to consider his book a work of art. In spite of defects, his work must be put with that of De Groot

[1] Compare Breen, *P. Cz. Hooft als schrijver der Nederlandsche Historien*. Ams., 1894.

and Fruin's *Tien Jaren* as the best historical works written in the Netherlands up to now.

For the northern provinces in particular, the *Memorien* of Rienk Fresinga,[1] burgomaster of Franeker, are valuable. The matter covers the years 1576-82, and is based on his own experiences, on original documents, and recollections of trustworthy persons. Again we have the *Chronique ofte Historische Geschiedenissen van Friesland* (Franeker, 1622), by the Franeker professor, Pier van Winsem, or Petrus Winsemius, running to 1622, and his *Historiarum per Frisiam gestarum libri quatuor* (2 vols., Leovard., 1629), from 1555 to 1581, and rated very highly by his contemporaries as impartial and veracious. In many particulars he gives unpublished details of Frisian history. Then we have the Latin chronicle of the States' sympathising Groninger, Eggerik Phebens, 1565-94 (ed. Feith, Utr., 1867), which describes the condition of his province at his time; the chronicle of Abel Eppens—soon to be published by Brugmans —of the same nature as the above, and written in his native dialect, especially important for the relation to East Friesland; the *Historia nostri temporis* of Ubbo Emmius, the excellent Groningen historian, who describes in this book the complications in East Friesland, and in his *Guilielmus Lodovicus Comes Nassovius* (Gron., 1732) the events in which this prince took part. He writes in fair Latin, and is full of enthusiasm.

Among the various histories on brief periods, the genial but thoughtless jurist, later professor in history at Leyden, Dominicus Baudius, writes in admirable style, *De induciis belli Belgici libri III.* (Lugd. Bat., 1613; in Dutch, Amst., 1616), a worthy record of the negotiations for the Truce. His colleague, the learned classical and historical scholar, Johannes Meursius, treated the period of Alva and the last years before the Truce, in his work, *Rerum Belgicarum libri IV.*, to which his *Induciarum historia* forms a fifth book; he also published a remarkable book on the prince, *Guilielmus Auriacus*, covering the years to the death of Requesens. Meursius was tutor to Oldenbarnevelt's sons, and after the advocate's death went to Denmark, where he became professor at Sora. The books of

[1] Deventer, 1584; Dumbar, *Analecta*, iii., p. 1.

Baudius and Meursius about the Truce, which the States-General commissioned them to write, were both approved and printed by the States, while Meursius was also commissioned (Baudius died in 1613) to pursue his work as state historian with the aid of the archives. Owing to the circumstances of Oldenbarnevelt's death, this was never done.

The most important book on the Truce is that of Willem Baudart, born at Bruges, preacher first at Sneek, later at Zutphen, a zealous Contra-remonstrant and one of the great champions of the principles of the synod of Dort. It is entitled *Memorien ofte cort verhael der gedenckwaerdigste 30 kercklicke als wereltlicke geschiedenissen van den jaere 1603 tot in het jaer 1624* (2 vols., Arnh., 1624), and is the expansion of a brief continuation to Van Meteren, which he had published earlier. His animus against the Remonstrants is very strong. This is rather a collection of contemporary documents, pamphlets, journals, etc., strung together, but, though lacking in style, dry and partisan, it is invaluable as a source and an expression of the opinions of the dominant party. Of the same nature is Trigland's *Kerkelijke Geschiedenissen* (Leyden, 1650).

Whoever wishes to view this controversy from the Remonstrant point of view should read Uyttenbogaert's *Kerkelicke Historie* (1646), to controvert which Trigland wrote his book, and which is full of original documents. Gerard Brandt's great *Historie der Reformatie* (4 vols., Amst., 1660–1704), written entirely from the Remonstrant side and indeed at the request of the Remonstrant Brotherhood, is to some extent a protest against Baudart's representation of the events and thus bears a polemical character. It describes, with great partiality for such men as Coolhaes, the predecessor of Arminius, and "libertines" like Coornhert, the origin of the religious movement of the sixteenth century and its course to about 1600, and then treats especially of the contest between "Gommer" and "Armijn."

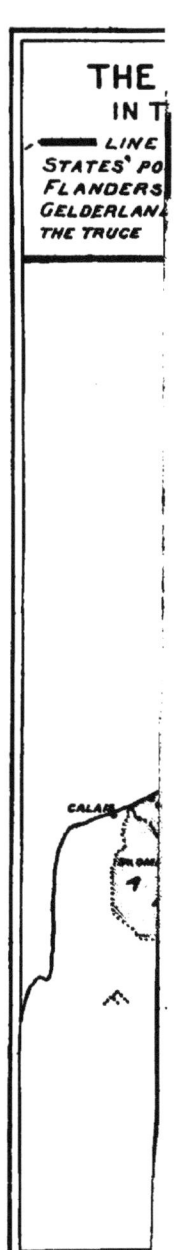

THE

IN T

━━━ LINE

STATES' PO

FLANDERS

GELDERLAN

THE TRUCE

CALAI

ST. OME

INDEX

Chief names (appendix not included).

A

Aachen (Aix), 54, 275

Aalst, 97, 103, 137

Acronius, Johannes, of Schiedam, 400, 408

Aerschot, duke of, 7, 15, 26, 87, 96 *et seq.*, 113, 115 *ff.*, 142, 204, 256, 281

Aerssens, Cornelis (d'Aerssen, van Aerssen), 201, 301, 358

—— François, 296, 306, 358, 363, 371, etc., 429, 449, 451, 456, 472 ; called Sommelsdijk, 482–485, 497

Alençon, Francis, duke of, 98 ; *see* Anjou

Alexandria, 268

Alkmaar, 67, 69, 73, 201, 324, 408, etc.

Alteras, vice-admiral, 300

Alting, Menso, 349

Alva, duke of, 4, 9, 38 *et seq.*, 50 *ff.*, 70–76, 105, 127, 187, 221, 308

Ambon, 294, 297, 492

Ameland, 341, 384

Amersfoort, 145, 235

Amsterdam, 34, 67, 112, 175, 184, 231 *et passim*, 323, 335 *et passim*, 424, 437, 460, etc.

Anastro, Gaspar d', 162

Anhalt, Christian of, 305, 360, 361

Anjou, duke of, 110, 130, 143 *ff.*, 148 *ff.*, 155, 160–167, 170 *ff.*; death of, 173, 177 ; 193

Antwerp, 24, 68, 75, 95, etc. ; Spanish Fury in, 103 *ff.*; 112, 118 *ff.*, 138, 151 ; attempt of Anjou to seize, 166 ; 182, 193 ; siege of, 203–206 ; 245, 310 *et passim*

Aquinas, Thomas, 401

Aremberg, count of, 26, 31, 35, 204, 256, 281

Arend, 69

Armada, the Spanish, 222, 230, 244–248

Armenteros, secretary, 9

Arminius, Jacobus (Harmensz., Jacob), 241, 306, 400–406

Arnemuiden, 67, 325

Arnhem, 68, 183, 276, etc.

—— John, 135

Arras, 29, 137

—— Anthony Perrenot, bishop of, 1, 133, 256, etc.

Arteveldes, the, 124

Artois, 133, 141

—— Estates of, 105, 137

Assche, lord of, 100

Assonleville, 87, 96, 99, 256

Atjeh, 293, 294

Aubéry, Benjamin, Sieur Du Maurier, 365 ; *see* Du Maurier

Auchin, Jean d', archbishop of Mechlin, 189

Austria, Albert of, 258, 264, 265, 275, 281, 284, 286, 322, 360, etc.

—— Andrew of, 265

—— Anne of, 363

—— Archduke Ernest of, 255, 256, 258

—— Archduke Matthias of, *see* Matthias

—— Don John of, 97, 102, 105, 113, 117, 129, 131, 141, 193, 222

—— Isabella of, 222, 258, 264, 265, 281, 284, 322, 360, etc.

—— Margaret of, 319

—— Mary of, 319

Avalos, 39

527

34

AUTHOR'S CORRECTIONS

(IN ADDITION TO THOSE INCORPORATED IN THE TEXT)

Page v., *line* 25, *change* crystallised *to* brought.

p. vi., *l.* 3, ¶ This period.

p. vii., *l.* 23, *for* property *read* properties.

p. 187, *l.* 10, *for* Scandinavian *read* Danish.

pp. 206, 212, *etc., for* Deventer *read* van Deventer.

p. 217, *l.* 21, *for* archers *read* militia.

p. 221, *l.* 15, *insert* again *after* they.

p. 227, *l.* 6, *after* Francken *read* pensionary of Gouda.

p. 250, *l.* 23, *after* Treaty of Reduction *read* of Groningen.

p. 264, *l.* 30, *after* buried alive *read* in Brussels.

p. 285, *l.* 21, Noël de Caron was the Netherland ambassador in England, not the envoy extraordinary.

p. 296, *l.* 16, *for* Baptist *read* Mennonite.

p. 300, *l.* 21, *for* protection *read* cannon.

p. 301, *note, after* Van Rees *read* Staathuiskunde, ii.

p. 332, *l.* 4, *add* after the season *to end of sentence.*

p. 366, *l.* 15, *read* The counsellors of the young king.

p. 379, *l.* 14, *read* which was sometimes arranged.

p. 380, *l.* 1, *after* apportionment *read* generally speaking.

p. 401, *l.* 22, *read* Gomarus' relation to his colleagues began to change.

p. 403, *l.* 19, *read* in Holland itself two of these synodal alliances existed, etc.

p. 408, *l.* 25, *omit* Acronius of Schiedam, Smoutius of Rotterdam.

p. 412, *l.* 16, *omit* probably.

p. 415, *note* 3, *insert* Katholicken *after* Nederlandsche.

p. 423, *l.* 19, *after* sympathised *insert* but he was also convinced of the necessity of upholding civil authority.

p. 425, *l.* 23, *after* him *read* even on stormy and rainy Sundays
to that village in the neighbourhood.

p. 430, *l.* 22, *new* ¶ ; *note* 1, *after* archives *read* de la maison
d'Orange Nassau.

p. 432, *l.* 23, *after* share *read* his chaplain's.

p. 479, *l.* 6, *for* laws *read* maxims.

p. 481, *l.* 11, *insert* Field Marshal *before* Count.

Dutch History

A History of the People of the Netherlands

By Petrus Johannes Blok, Ph.D., Professor of Dutch History in the University of Leyden. Translated by Oscar A. Bierstadt and Ruth Putnam. To be completed in five parts.

Part I : From the Earliest Times to the Beginning of the Fifteenth Century. 8°. $2.50

Part II : The Gradual Centralization of Power, and the Burgundian Period. 8° $2.50

Part III : The War with Spain. 1568–1621. 8° . 2.50

William the Silent, Prince of Orange

The Moderate Man of the XVI. Century. The Story of his Life, as told in his own Letters, in those of his Friends and of his Enemies, and from Official Documents. By Ruth Putnam. Fully illustrated. 2 vols., 8°, gilt tops, $3.75

Half calf extra, gilt tops 7.50

"It is doubtful if any previous works on this interesting character are more readable and accurate than this of Ruth Putnam. Her book shows a vast amount of intelligent research among original documents, and an un-biassed, thoughtful, discriminating study of the histories of her subject."— *N. Y. Times.*

"It is certain that the author's book will be read with pleasure, for it throws new light upon the struggle for religious and civil liberty in the Netherlands, and renders it easier for us to detect in the most conspicuous figure of its earlier stages the real lineaments of the man."—*N. Y. Sun.*

Holland and its People

New revised edition. With 77 illustrations. 8°. . $2.00

Vandyke Edition. Printed from new pica type. With 84 illustrations from designs by Gifford, Platt, Pennell, Colman, and others. Full gilt, cloth extra, gilt top . . $2.25

"The beauty of De Amicis' travels is that they are more than travels. They are not merely the record of so many passages a day ; they are travellings, plus seeings, listenings, feelings, thinkings, talkings, love-makings, and about all that a warm-hearted, imaginative, educated young tourist would engage in ; yet they are told without displeasing egotism or tedious detail."

The Story of Holland

By James E. Thorold Rogers, Professor of Political Economy, University of Oxford. No. 22 in the Story of the Nations Series. Fully illustrated. 12° . . $1.50

"He has brought to his task a complete understanding of his subject, and in his limited space has condensed a wonderful amount of information, which is conveyed in a straightforward manner that is steadily impressive." —*Boston Gazette.*

G. P. Putnam's Sons, New York and London

Records of an Earlier Time.

Knickerbocker's History of New York.

By WASHINGTON IRVING. *Van Twiller Edition.* From new plates. With 225 original illustrations by E. W. KEMBLE. Each page surrounded by an appropriate artistic border. 2 vols. 8°, gilt tops, with slip covers, $6.00. Three-quarters levant . $12.00 Other editions from 75 cts. upwards.

"A work honourable to English literature, manly, bold, and so *altogether original*, without being extravagant, as to stand alone among the labours of men."— *Blackwood's Magazine.*

Last Days of Knickerbocker Life in New York.

By ABRAM C. DAYTON. With an introduction by RICHARD B. KIMBALL. New edition, reset with selected full-page illustrations, specially produced for this volume. 8°, gilt top $2.50

"This interesting work, written in 1871 and originally published in 1880, is now for the first time put before the public in a shape befitting its merits as a historic record of an interesting period in the life of this city. The volume is illustrated with a number of portraits and curious old drawings."—*N. Y. Sun.*

The Ayrshire Homes and Haunts of Burns.

By HENRY C. SHELLEY. With 26 full-page illustrations from photographs by the author, and with portrait in photogravure. Second edition. 16°, gilt top $1.25

A book of interest to all lovers of Robert Burns and of Scotland. The value of this little work is enchanced by the views of the homes and scenes which are placed by the side of the verses with which Burns has made them immortal.

Historic New York.

Half Moon Series of Papers on Historic New York. First Series (1897). Edited by MAUD WILDER GOODWIN, ALICE CARRINGTON ROYCE, and RUTH PUTNAM. With 29 illustrations and maps. 8°, gilt top $2.50 Second Series, (1898). Illustrated. 8°, gilt top $2.50

"A delightfully attractive volume possessing much historic value, and illustrating a careful, conscientious scholarship worthy of high praise. The papers describe old New York in a simple, vivid, picturesque, and truthful fashion."— *The Congregationalist.*

G. P. PUTNAM'S SONS, New York and London.

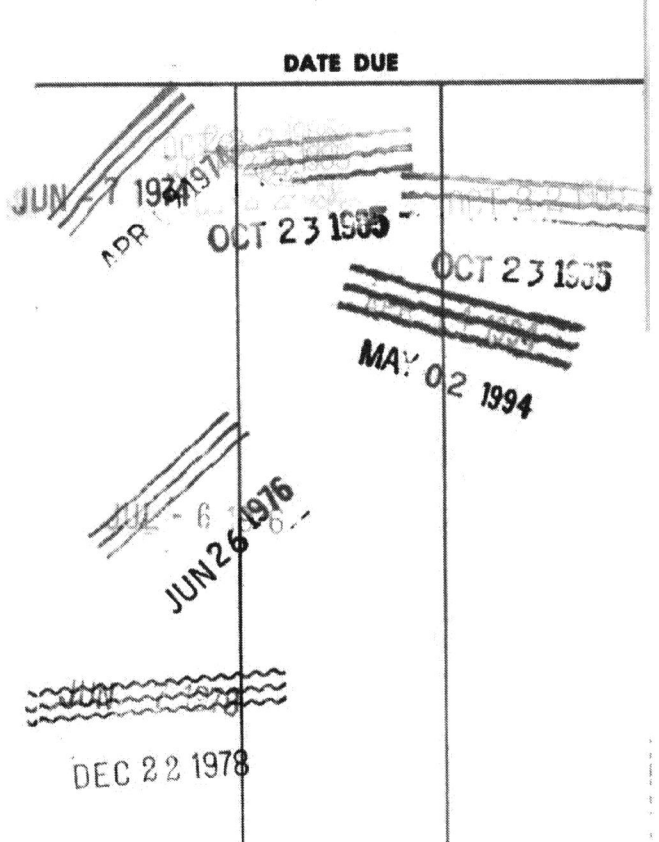

DO NOT REMOVE
OR
MUTILATE CARD

Lightning Source UK Ltd.
Milton Keynes UK
UKHW022223240520
363742UK00015B/584